Africa-China-Taiwan Relations, 1949-2020

African Governance, Development, and Leadership

Series Editor: Sabella O. Abidde, Alabama State University

Advisory Board: Getachew Metaferia, Georges Nzongola-Ntalaja, Adebayo Oyebade, Gloria Chuku, Gorden Moyo, and Olubukola Stella Adesina

The African Governance, Development, and Leadership series identifies and elaborates on the strategic place of governance, development, and leadership within African studies. Reflecting the fact that life in Africa continues to change; particularly in political, development, and socio-economic arenas; this series explores issues focusing on the ongoing mobilization for good governance, viable and impartial institutions, and the search for sustainable and economic development. Addressing gaps and larger needs in the developing scholarship on Africa and the African diaspora, this series publishes scholarly monographs and edited collections in the humanities, social science, and social scientific traditions.

Recent Titles

Africa-China-Taiwan Relations, 1949-2020, by Sabella Ogbobode Abidde

Kwame Nkrumah's Political Kingdom and Pan-Africanism Reinterpreted, 1909-1972 by A. B. Assensoh and Yvette M. Alex-Assensoh

Africa in the Twenty-First Century: The Promise of Development and Democratization edited by Gashawbeza Bekele and Adebayo Oyebade

Nigeria-United States Relations 1960-2016 by Olayiwola Abegunrin

The Illusion of the Post-Colonial State: Governance and Security Challenges in Africa by W. Alade Fawole

Africans and the Exiled Life: Migration, Culture, and Globalization edited by Sabella Ogbobode Abidde and Brenda I. Gill

Africa-China-Taiwan Relations, 1949-2020

Edited by
Sabella Ogbobode Abidde

LEXINGTON BOOKS
Lanham • Boulder • New York • London

Published by Lexington Books
An imprint of The Rowman & Littlefield Publishing Group, Inc.
4501 Forbes Boulevard, Suite 200, Lanham, Maryland 20706
www.rowman.com

86-90 Paul Street, London EC2A 4NE

British Library Cataloguing in Publication Information Available

Library of Congress Cataloging-in-Publication Data

Names: Abidde, Sabella Ogbobode, 1962- editor.
Title: Africa-China-Taiwan relations, 1949-2020 / edited by Sabella Ogbobode Abidde.
Description: Lanham : Lexington Books, [2022] | Series: African governance, development, and leadership | Includes bibliographical references and index. | Summary: "This book provides an insightful analysis from complementary perspectives of the seven-decades-long contest and contestation between the People's Republic of China and the Republic of China for diplomatic recognition on the Africa continent. It examines China and Taiwan's presence and active involvement in African affairs"—Provided by publisher.
Identifiers: LCCN 2022017313 (print) | LCCN 2022017314 (ebook) | ISBN 9781793649669 (cloth) | ISBN 9781793649683 (paperback) | ISBN 9781793649676 (epub)
Subjects: LCSH: China—Foreign relations—Africa. | Taiwan—Foreign relations—Africa. | Africa—Foreign relations—China. | Africa—Foreign relations—Taiwan. | China—Foreign relations—Taiwan. | Taiwan—Foreign relations—China.
Classification: LCC DS740.5.A34 A35 2022 (print) | LCC DS740.5.A34 (ebook) | DDC 327.5106—dc23/eng/20220504
LC record available at https://lccn.loc.gov/2022017313
LC ebook record available at https://lccn.loc.gov/2022017314

To
Professor Yawsoon Sim
for his profound understanding of
and brilliant, clever, and illuminating writings
and commentaries about Africa-China-Taiwan relations.
He was indeed one of the major lighthouses for
scholars who desired a deep understanding of
"Chinese power rivalry" in Africa.

Contents

List of Figures and Tables

FIGURES

TABLES

List of Abbreviations

AAPSO	Afro-Asian Peoples' Solidarity Organization
ATEF	Africa Taiwan Economic Forum
AU	African Union
BRI	Belt and Road Initiative
BRICS	Brazil, Russia, Indonesia, China, and South Africa
CCP	Chinese Communist Party
CAR	Central African Republic
CCECC	China Civil Engineering Construction Corporation
CCP	Chinese Communist Party
CETRA	China External Trade Development Council
CI	Confucius Institutes
CMT	Chinese Medical Team
COVID-19	Coronavirus SARS-CoV
CPA	Communities of Practice Approach
CPC	Communist Party of China
CPSU	Communist Party of the Soviet Union
CYCU	Chung Yuan Christian University
DPP	Democratic Progressive Party
DRC	Democratic Republic of the Congo
EU	European Union
EximBank	Export-Import Bank
FDI	Foreign Direct Investment
FOCAC	Forum on China-Africa Cooperation
GDP	Gross Domestic Product

HAINA	Huawei Authorized Information and Network Academy
ICDF	International Cooperation and Development Fund
IPOB	Indigenous Peoples of Biafra
IR	International Relations
IRL	Institute for Research and Learning
KMT	Kuomintang
MOFA	Ministry of Foreign Affairs
MoU	Memorandum of Understanding
NAM	Non-Aligned Movement
NGOs	Non-governmental organizations
NIIA	Nigerian Institute of International Affairs
NTU	National Taiwan University
PLA	People's Liberation Army
PLAN	People's Liberation Army Navy
PRC	People's Republic of China
ROC	Republic of China
ROC-RSA MCETC	Economic and Technical Cooperation
ROCSA	ROC/RSA Economic Council
RSA	South Africa
SAFTO	South African Foreign Trade Organization
SAJOREC	Sino-Africa Joint Research Center
SAROC	RSA/ROC Chamber of Economic Relations
SMEs	Small and Medium Scale Enterprises
SOEs	State-Owned Enterprises
SSC	South-South Cooperation
SWADEPA	Swazi Democratic Party
TABA	Taiwan-Africa Business Association
TABA	Taiwan-Africa Business Association
TAITRA	Taiwan External Trade Development Council
TANZAM	Tanzania-Zambia Railway
TATPO	Taiwan-Africa Trade Promotion Office
TAZARA	Tanzania-Zambia Railway
TeChA	Teaching of China in Africa
TECRO	Taipei Economic and Cultural Representative Offices
TRC	Teaching, Research, and Community Service
UDI	Unilateral Declaration of Independence
UN	United Nations
UNESCO	United Nations Educational, Scientific and Cultural Organization

UNGA	United Nations General Assembly
UNPKO	United Nations Peacekeeping Operations
UNSC	United Nations Security Council
USA	United States of America
USD	United States dollar ($)
USSR	Union of Soviet Socialist Republics
WHO	World Health Organization

Preface

The ongoing power rivalry between China and Taiwan in Africa and indeed elsewhere in the world is, first and foremost, a continuation of the Chinese Civil War. It is also a competition between the two governments in terms of legitimacy even if the question of legitimacy is moot as China is now the dominant and only recognized *China* in the world. In their quest to win over Africa, both Beijing and Taipei employed wide-ranging tactics that encompass overt and covert threats and actions, diplomatic maneuvers, economic inducements, and promises of support in Africa's quest for growth and development.

The People's Republic of China (PRC/China) and the Republic of China (ROC/Taiwan) are, for the most part, culturally and natively indistinguishable. Geographically, however, they are separated by a 180-kilometer-wide strait. They are also separated by their very distinct political, legal, economic, and social systems and are also differentiated by their worldview and attitude toward the international system.

Although a very small island, Taiwan is everything China is not: a Western-style democracy with a capitalist economic system. It is an open society with a government that is non-expansionist and non-territorial and unaggressive in the pursuit of its national agenda and foreign policy. Taiwan is loved and admired in much of the world and is perhaps the most Western and most welcoming of Westerners of all Asian countries.

China, on the other hand, is this massive landmass with the world's largest population and a massive economy and massive military to match. Unlike Taiwan, China is seen as a rigid and closed society—even if it seems to be gradually opening and accepting of outside influence. It is also a communist country with perhaps the largest political party in the world, the Communist

Party of China. China, from all indications, seems to have a polarizing government that is viewed with suspicion around the world.

Other than culture and genetics, both countries are connected by their seven decades of power rivalry. My interest in the rivalry between China and Taiwan dates to several decades. However, it was rekindled in 2017 when the Nigerian government ordered Taiwan to move its trade office from Abuja, its current capital, to Lagos, its former capital. It was a move many were not happy with—especially the Taiwanese government which saw it as a power play by Beijing. This and similar moves are common across the African continent where, for more than five decades, Beijing has been at work and very successful in getting governments to sever diplomatic ties with Taiwan.

The power rivalry between the two Chinas was never on my research and publication agenda. At least it was not in the same way I was interested in the Israeli-Palestinian conflict or Fidel Castro and Cuba's internationalism. However, in the fall of 2018, I began to think of expanding my research and publication agenda which was christened "Africa and the World." Essentially, I was thinking about Africa's relationship with the rest of the world. I wanted a detour because many scholars of African origin write primarily on topics such as ethnic and religious conflicts; governance, institutions, and leadership; democracy and political liberalization; globalization; wars; violence and terrorism; colonialism and decolonization; corruption; and Pan-Africanism.

Those are important topics, but I wanted to branch out and not devote too much time to the obvious. At the very least, I didn't want to stay in the vicinity of those topics for too long. As someone who entered the academy late in life, I wanted to traverse a distinct path. The areas that interested me include the connection between Africa, Latin America, and the Caribbean in terms of bilateral and multilateral relationships and comparative study of social issues in the three regions. I am also interested in Africa's engagement with countries in East Asia. But for now, we look specifically at the contest and contestations between the two Chinas in Africa.

By putting together this edited volume, I adhered to three simple rules: no propaganda, no falsehoods, and no taking of sides. It was important to me that I remain neutral and objective. I also endeavored to have an equal number of Chinese and Taiwanese scholars as contributors. In this regard, I was more successful with the Taiwanese contributors as virtually all the Chinese scholars I invited did not respond to my invite or outrightly refused to participate. The irony is that some of the Taiwanese scholars whose abstracts were accepted did not, in the end, submit their chapters even though they were allotted more than six months.

In 2019, I was awarded the Taiwan Fellowship by the country's Ministry of Foreign Affairs to enable me to conduct archival research at the Center for Chinese Studies which is located at the National Central Library, Taipei, from May to December 2020. The National Taiwan University, located in Taipei City, Taiwan, kindly agreed to host me. However, I did not take up the fellowship because of the COVID-19 pandemic which necessitated travel bans and border closures. Also, my Fulbright US Scholar Program—which would have enabled me to go to Peking University in Beijing, China—was not approved. I look forward to both countries.

My intention, after the archival research (in Taipei and Beijing), was to produce two monographs and a series of journal articles and book chapters. This edited volume is therefore a consolation endeavor. A balanced view of the contest and contestation between both countries is important to this and future generations of scholars.

Furthermore, the Africa-China-Taiwan relationship is a very important topic and an important component of the history of modern Africa. But for whatever reason, there remains a huge gap in the scholarship—be it in academic journals or books. The focus, as far as I can tell, has been on *China in Africa*. They cannot—we cannot and should not ignore Taiwan's role and place on the continent. Long before China became a powerhouse, Taiwan was one of the most important, most consequential, and most benevolent of all the states that engaged with states and societies on the African continent.

Sabella Ogbobode Abidde, PhD Alabama State
University Montgomery, Alabama

Acknowledgments

The project is useful in many ways and at different levels but primarily in the areas of international relations, international security, area and conflict studies, diplomacy, the history of modern Africa, and geopolitical reasons—but largely because it fills the gap in our knowledge and understanding of Africa-China relations beginning in 1949 until the present.

In editing a book of this nature, many debts and gratitude are owed, especially in terms of those who provided tangible resources, intellectual contributions, and wise counsels, or for just being there to banter ideas with. Dr. Yao-Yuan Yeh (associate professor and chair of International Studies and Modern Languages at the Saint Thomas University, Houston, Texas) provided a list containing the names and contact information of a dozen or so Taiwanese scholars to contribute chapters. Ms. I-wei Jennifer Chang (research fellow at the Global Taiwan Institute, Washington, DC) also made suggestions. Thank you!

I would also like to thank Dr. James Lin (a historian of Taiwan and its interactions with the world in the twentieth century) who is based at the University of Washington, Seattle. He was an invaluable guide. He responded to all my inquiries and helped to distribute the Call for Papers. I would also like to thank all the chapter contributors for expending time and other resources toward this volume. Finally, I would like to express my sincere and profound gratitude to Ms. Shelby Russell—the talented acquisition editor at Lexington Books. She was gracious, patient, and professional. It is to her great credit that this edited volume was brought to fruition. And finally, to Ms. Sydney Wedbush who took over from Ms Shelby (for her patience and benevolence).

Thank you, thank you, and thank you to every one of you. Stay safe and stay well.

—Sabella Ogbobode Abidde

CHAPTER 6

Abdul-Gafar Tobi Oshodi would like to acknowledge and thank the Social Science Research Council's NextGen Fellowship program for their generous financial support.

****

CHAPTER 8: KRISTINA KIRONSKA
AND THIOMBIANO DRAMANE

Funding Statement: This work was generously supported by the European Regional Development Fund—Project "Sinophone Borderlands—Interaction at the Edges" CZ.02.1.01/0.0/0.0/16_019/0000791.

Introduction

Power Rivalry and the Quest for International Recognition by the Two Chinas *in Africa*

Sabella Ogbobode Abidde

The African continent was one of the earliest battlegrounds for power rivalry and competition for diplomatic recognition between the People's Republic of China (PRC), hereafter referred to as China, and the Republic of China (ROC), henceforth referred to as Taiwan. Yet, the China-Africa-Taiwan relations remain under-researched. In earlier times, Taiwan—as opposed to China—was the more influential of the two countries. But today, save for one country, Eswatini (Swaziland), Taiwan has lost all its allies and is diplomatically isolated on the continent. China, on the other hand, looms large on the continent. What we have here, then, is a reversal of fortune and misfortune.

Not long after the Kuomintang (sometimes referred to as KMT or the nationalists) were expelled from China and berthed in Taiwan in 1949, they laid the foundation for what that country has become. Along the way, they developed diplomatic relations with Apartheid South Africa which, at that time, was staunchly anticommunist and opposed the PRC's admission to the United Nations (UN). South Africa, at that time, recognized Taiwan as the seat of China's legitimate government. However, as African countries gained independence and with a shift in the international structure, the *balance of recognition* began to change as both China and Taiwan contested for African votes at the UN. Beijing's strategic support for national liberation movements and radical regimes on the African continent, for instance, helped tilt the balance of recognition in favor of the PRC.

The current Sino-Africa relations began in the 1950s when Zhou Enlai, the first premier of the PRC, visited Africa and signed bilateral agreements, further elevating Beijing's standing among African countries. Beginning with the initial foray of Chinese leaders into Africa, the principal aim of China—without disguising its intention—was to isolate Taiwan both on the continent

1

and elsewhere in the world in furtherance of its "One China" agenda. In Africa and elsewhere around the world, China has used various tactics—persuasions and threats and or an admixture of both—to get countries to adhere strictly to the "One China" policy and, wherever possible, to expel Taiwan.

But instead of outright expulsion, countries like South Africa and Nigeria have simply downgraded Taiwan's embassies from full-fledged diplomatic posts to Economic and Cultural Centers. Essentially, Taiwan is seen as a trading partner and not an independent nation-state deserving of all the rights, responsibility, and respect it once enjoyed on the continent. China, a country that was once struggling economically and politically and searching for respect and recognition, is today posing a challenge not only to the United States but also to all the European powers that once colonized Africa.

How China got to where it is, is one of the marvels of the twentieth and twenty-first centuries. Beginning in 1949 and for the next seventy years, the PRC didn't seem hasty, desperate, or irrational in its foreign policy insofar as the ROC was concerned. Behind the curtains, the PRC was steady and firm: it threatened countries that needed to be threatened, offered carrots to those that needed carrots, and partnered with countries that needed its money and expertise. In public and on the global stage, it played nice and acted reasonably even to countries whose leaders were monsters and terrorized their people. Such leaders and countries were won over when China—smarting from one of the preconditions of Western governments—publicly stated it was not going to interfere in their domestic politics and foreign policy.

The ROC, on the other hand, took a different approach—believing that, perhaps, all they needed to do was to partner with African countries to bring about home-grown growth and development. Hence, it embarked on a lot of agricultural and training programs across the continent. Many African civil servants and technicians were also brought to Taiwan for technical skills and other forms of training. For decades, Taiwan was courteous and nonaggressive and with a foreign policy that was not expansive or territorial; however, it was reactionary in that it was mostly reacting to China's moves and pronouncements as opposed to setting a firm agenda.

In the end, the ROC simply could not match or outmatch the PRC in terms of spending and other resources numerous governments on the continent needed. And so it is that seven decades later, all but one African country has diplomatic relations with Taiwan. Well, two—that's counting Somaliland. The Taiwan-Somaliland alliance is a move that has angered Somalia and perplexed the rest of the continent. How this move will play out is still unknown. It is an unknown factor in Africa-China-Taiwan relations. However, it is possible that—as was the case with other African countries—China's threats and inducements will be too much for Somaliland to bear, causing it to switch sides as was the case in Burkina Faso, the Gambia, Senegal, and others.

The case of Eswatini (Swaziland) is easy to predict simply because its ongoing relationship with Taipei is predicated mostly on a personal relationship as opposed to an institutional or ideological relationship. It is, therefore, possible that when Mswati III (the king and paramount ruler of the kingdom) dies, becomes incapacitated, or is overthrown, the next leader or leadership will switch sides. But what if these scenarios, these hypotheses don't materialize? This is also another unknown factor in the tripartite relationship. Beijing is very patient. It can afford to wait. The contest and contestation between China and Taiwan have been an interesting and intriguing one and are likely to be so several decades into the twenty-first century.

Even so, the future is not guaranteed. Even for China. This is so because things do happen and can happen on the African continent. Economically and politically, it is a young and fluid continent with a demographic that is increasingly rejecting the ideas, ideologies, and vision of the old brigade. They may reject China; or more likely, embrace both China and Taiwan. In other words, the day may come when the *new Africans* entertain and embrace separate but equal China—having full diplomatic relations with the PRC and ROC is good for states and societies on the continent. But what if China annexes Taiwan in this or the next decade? What if China is weakened politically and economically or implodes because of endogenous and or exogenous undercurrents? The questions are almost inexhaustible.

This book is divided into three parts. Part I, "Foreign Policy and Their Implications," has five chapters; part II, "Issues and Strategies," has four chapters; and part III, "Beijing and Taipei: At Home and Abroad," has four chapters.

In chapter 1, "China's Foreign Policy toward Africa, 1949–2020," Yen-Hsin Chen writes that the relationships with African countries have become one of the most visible examples of China's growing confidence in establishing its diplomatic relations with other developing countries. During the Cold War, China saw itself as the potential leader of the developing world, so China offered military support, medical aid, and loan assistance to African countries even though China's economic capacity was limited during this period. Post-Mao Chinese leaders began to base the legitimacy of their rule on improving the living conditions of the Chinese people, so China was less interested in spending money overseas. As the overall state capacity of China increases, the African continent again has attracted the attention of Beijing. Having natural resources has made Africa valuable and critical to continue powering China's economic growth. Besides, the issue of excess capacity will be redressed if China plays the role of the leading goose in the industrialization of the African continent. The Chinese model of development promises economic development while securing the political privilege of African dictators. Last, but not the least, China-Africa solidity is essential for promoting China's multipolar worldview against US global dominance.

In chapter 2, "China's Foreign Policy toward Africa, 1949–1971: Africa-China-Taiwan Relations," Saidat Ilo posits that the Chinese Revolution of 1949 brought about the creation of the PRC, a communist government, and the ROC that embraced democracy. With the spread of communism, the PRC, an ally of the former USSR, and the ROC began to think about becoming global players to advance their respective interests. The competition between the PRC, ROC, and the USSR played out on the battlefield of Africa during this period. Each region sought supremacy in Africa and fought to prevent the other from establishing or maintaining bilateral relationships with these newly independent states in Africa. The decade of the 1950s, however, altered the PRC and the ROC's view of Africa. In the 1950s and 1960s, developing nations (which the former Soviet Union was not) believed the issues that affected them could be solved by working together. Nations were beginning to coalesce under the umbrella of the Non-Aligned Movement and South-South Cooperation. Both movements helped foster the relationship between the PRC and ROC and some African nations.

And in chapter 3, "China's Foreign Policy toward Africa, 1949–1970," Andrew Michael Mashingaidze asserts that although contact between China and Africa pre-1949 was negligible, China's passive interest in Africa changed after 1949 when the Chinese Communist Party (CCP) gained control of a unified China (PRC). The CCP's rise to power ignited an active and thriving Africa foreign policy that has gained momentous traction to this day. What compelled China to direct its diplomatic focus on Africa? What strategies did it put in place to accomplish this goal and to what end? To address these questions, Andrew states that the period 1949–1970 constitutes a crucial period in China's Africa policy. It is crucial in that it is the foundational stage of China's Africa foreign policy and a perfect opportunity to discern and gain insight into China's short- and long-term foreign policy aspirations. China's Africa policy from 1949 to 1970 was premised on China's grand political strategy to reform world politics and that all policies and policy strategies adopted and implemented by China during this era had one common goal, the reemergence of a strong China and the survival of a legitimate CCP. Thus, without a revisit of the first two decades of China's approach toward Africa, one cannot conduct a meaningful in-depth analysis of the current state of China's expansion on the continent.

Emmanuel Obuah and Charles Ijuye-Dagogo's chapter, "Building Community of Practices: China's Relations with Africa, 1971 to Date," divides the post-1971 China-Africa relations into three eras: the post read-mission era (1971–1990), an era of reinvigorated engagement (1990–2000), and an era of vigorous engagement signaled by the creation of the Forum on China-Africa Cooperation (FOCAC) (2000 to date). The FOCAC is one multilateral mechanism that has increased China's engagement with Africa. China's diplomatic practices with Africa included the use of high-profile visits to African countries, the use of public diplomacy, and provincial diplomacy. Trade between China and Africa has the same imbalanced exchange that characterizes Africa's trade with developed countries. However, China tries to level the playing field by granting tariff exemptions to the least developed African countries. China also provides infrastructures to facilitate trade with Africa under its Belt and Road Initiative (BRI). China's investments in Africa tend to focus on areas that were previously overlooked by developed countries. China's aid to Africa is provided based on mutual benefit. China gains access to natural resources and investment opportunities while Africa gets the infrastructure it desperately needs. The conditions attached to China's aid do not include institutional reforms for Africa but demand that Africa do not relate with Taiwan. In terms of peace and security, this chapter looks at the development-security nexus as the guiding principle to peace and security in Africa. The chapter also looks at how China uses scholarships and the Confucius Institute (CI) to promote the Chinese culture in Africa. The chapter concludes that the benefits from China's practices in Africa be emulated in future engagements with the continent.

Priye Torulagha, in chapter 5, "African Relations with China and Taiwan: A Web of Anticolonialism, Cold War, Recognition Politics, and Debt Trap," examines African relations with China and Taiwan in a tense global system that requires the recognition of either China or Taiwan and not both, based on a One-China Policy. The task is accomplished by (1) exploring the factors which contributed to the emergence of the two Chinas; (2) identifying the factors which motivated African states to derecognize Taiwan and support China; (3) determining whether African states are beholden to China due to massive indebtedness that threatens their sovereign right to do business with Taiwan; and (4) determining whether China's assertive effort in isolating Taiwan could backfire as its actions are increasingly being viewed as exploitative, hegemonic, and racist in Africa.

Priye Torulagha's chapter concludes by making the following extrapolations. First, the civil war between China and Taiwan has not ended. Second, the conflict between China and Taiwan is still predicated on the Cold War between the Western and Eastern worlds. Third, China is driven to achieve three principal goals, including integrating Taiwan with the mainland, spreading its influence globally through its BRI, and ensuring a steady supply of raw materials to feed its industrial machines as well as create markets for its products in Africa. Fourth, African states are compelled by historical experience and massive China's investment in the continent to break diplomatic ties with Taiwan. Fifth, China's proactive involvement in engaging in the infrastructural development of Africa could transform the continent into a major economic and industrial power center of the world. Sixth, however, the massive debt incurred by African countries could dampen the enthusiasm for doing business with China due to the concern that the continent could be colonized by China if African states are unable to pay back the debt. Seventh, some African states could be tempted to reestablish relations with Taiwan if the perception that China is increasingly an exploitative, hegemonic, and racist power continues to persist. Therefore, the relationship between Africa, China, and Taiwan depends greatly on China's ability to maneuver in a manner that does not threaten the sovereignty of African states due to the debt issue.

In chapter 6—"China, Taiwan, and the African University"—Abdul-Gafar Oshodi and his coauthors contend that beyond serving as an arena for academic conversation, the university is a platform for international struggles. In the latter sense, the African University offers a lens to deepen existing knowledge of Taiwan's decline and China's rise in Africa. Adopting a thick conceptualization of the university that locates its functionality, they address two questions: (i) What are manifestations of China and Taiwan on the African University campus? (ii) What are the implications of these manifestations for China, Taiwan, and the African University? Their chapter demonstrates that recognition of China by most countries in Africa and the decline of Taiwan are also reflected in the African University. The manifestations of China on campus (in terms of CIs and interuniversity collaborations, construction projects, scholarships, Chinese companies, and the discursive element) surpass Taiwan's limited presence. While this places China in a stronger position vis-à-vis Taiwan on the continent, the dominance of China in the struggle offers the African University an alternative to the hitherto dominance of Western governments, agencies, and philanthropists in the African University landscape. They conclude by highlighting some unanswered questions for scholars of Taiwan and Chinese struggles.

Isaac Frimpong, in chapter 7—"China's Emerging Security Diplomacy and Its Implications for Taiwan in Africa," situates China's rising security focus as part of its overall foreign policy strategy toward Africa contra the dwindling influence of Taiwan in what the author refers to as China's emerging "security diplomacy" in Africa. Although Taiwan is not the main target, he argues that this security diplomacy has the potential to eliminate the dwindled influence/presence of Taiwan on the continent. The chapter also presents a historical narrative on the diplomatic and military competition between the PRC and ROC, which is followed by a discussion of China's evolving security practices in Africa. The chapter attempts to conceptualize/define China's emerging "security diplomacy" and distinguishes it from military diplomacy. Isaac submits that this security diplomacy will influence security discussions in Africa in Beijing's favor, build an alliance for China's superpower ambitions, as well as deter and defend its interests on the continent. He employs arguments from neoclassical realists to explain how systemic factors and domestic constraints/concerns have shaped China's emerging foreign policy in its engagement with Africa, especially around security, and how this has impacted Taipei's presence on the continent. There is an evaluation of the implications of such a move for China-Taiwan engagement in Africa.

Kristina Kironska and Thiombiano Dramane, in chapter 8, "How Taiwan Lost Africa, and What the Future Holds for Its Last Remaining Alliance with Eswatini," state that several decades after the Chinese Civil War in 1949, the ROC in Taiwan enjoyed the status of sole representative of China to the detriment of communist China. In the 1960s, after many African countries had gained independence and become members of the UN, they also established diplomatic ties with the ROC. The cooperation between Taiwan and African countries was mostly based on Taiwanese agricultural and technical aid. At the same time, the PRC began competing for recognition through infrastructure projects and ideological campaigns to support the independence of countries still under colonial rule. This led many countries to vote in its favor to enter the UN and replace the ROC as the representative of China. Since then, Taiwanese influence on the continent has gradually diminished. Nowadays, only one country in Africa has diplomatic ties with Taiwan—Eswatini (formerly Swaziland). They have been allies for almost half a century, although Eswatini is only Taiwan's 156th largest trading partner. In all, the chapter provides a historical account of how Taiwan lost its African allies, but managed to maintain an unlikely alliance with Eswatini.

In chapter 9, "The Future of Taiwan: A Brief Commentary," Sabella Abidde contends that no one knows for certain what the future portends for Taiwan. However, one of five scenarios is likely: (1) the invasion and forceful takeover of the island nation; (2) the continuation of the status quo—in other words, Taiwan remains a contested state just as it has been since 1949; (3) succumbing to threats and the political reality of the region, the people and government of Taiwan *agree* to be part of China; (4) the UN member states—led by the United States or other Western nations—agree to grant Taiwan statehood and international recognition; or (5) the unilateral declaration of independence by the people and government of Taiwan. The first and last options are fraught with the gravest danger. The second option would have been possible decades ago, but with a changing demographic and a changing political, social, and economic culture, surrender is out of the question, while international recognition at the UN is not a possibility primarily because of the structure of the UN which gives China a veto power. Even so, he insists that because military and political partners do not always show up in times of crisis, the people and government of Taiwan must chart their course and determine their future.

Guanie Lim and Ding Fei, in chapter 10, "China and Taiwan in Africa: Foreign Direct Investment, Institutions, and Regional Development," unpack the differentiated manners in which Chinese and Taiwanese investment has taken shape in Africa. The chapter compares the institutions and mechanisms utilized by the Chinese and Taiwanese in the propagation of their investment into the continent. They also examine the geographical distribution of their investment in Africa. The overarching argument is that Africa's large, affordable labor pool and rich natural resources complement the investment strategies of Chinese and Taiwanese firms eager to explore market opportunities outside their home economies. Relatedly, the vast size and heterogeneity of the African economy imply that there is ample room for Chinese and Taiwanese investors to not only coexist but also establish mutually beneficial cooperation between themselves and with the relevant host economies. Adding depth to the understudied topic of China-Africa-Taiwan relations, the chapter contributes to detailing the prominent features of Chinese and Taiwanese investment in the African continent.

Chapter 11, "Communist China's Medical Assistance versus Nationalist China's Agricultural Aid to Africa and the Politics of Recognition, 1961–1971," is authored by Andrea Andrea Kifyasi. He examines how Cold War politics stirred the struggle for political recognition and why conflicting power blocs employed different techniques, including aid to gain allies using the nationalist and communist Chinas' agricultural and medical assistance to Africa as a case study. It shows that the competition between the two Chinas over international recognition determined their aid policy toward Africa. Thus, both communist and nationalist Chinas lobbied African states through distinctive assistance to gain their political recognition. The chapter unpacks the contexts which made agricultural and medical aid a necessity to most independent African states. It shows that the two Chinas provided desperately needed assistance to Africa. Indeed, agriculture was the backbone of most independent African countries' economies. But inadequacies in the health sectors jeopardized the well-being of their populations. Nationalist China used its knowledge and experience in agriculture as a bargaining chip, while the communists employed their medical knowledge and experience to dispatch medical assistance to the continent. So, both medical and agricultural assistance was of importance to African countries, and the political elites strived to get either or both. As a result, African countries became the focus of the two Chinas' overall search for global political hegemony. The chapter argues that the two Chinas used aid as a weapon to win international recognition and political leverage to serve their national interests.

Chapter 12, "Rereading Nigeria-Taiwan Affairs: Alternatives to Sino-Centric Narratives," is a collective effort by Abdul-Gafar Oshodi, Jeremiah Anakor, and Oluwasola Obisesan. They posit that the deepening Africa-China relations over the past fifty years have coincided with a decline in Africa-Taiwan relations. However, academic literature and popular media often reduce this complex dialectical shift to a troubling but simplistic binary. In simplistic terms, the dominant (Sino-centric) narratives suggest that Africa's shift in favor of China and against Taiwan is in the latter's inability to match up with what we highlight as "China's development diplomacy" characterized by Chinese funding of large projects, loans, investments, and so on in Africa. Adopting a critical theoretical approach and using the example of Nigeria, their chapter draws attention to five alternative explanations—(i) those linked to the Biafran Civil War and Nigeria's first shift, (ii) legacies of military rule, (iii) persistence and dictates of Nigeria's national question, (iv) Pan-African ideals, and (v) extended pragmatism—for the shift and continuous recognition of China. By drawing attention to these alternative arguments, the authors not only challenge the Sino-centric argument but also contribute to an emerging discourse about Africa's agency in its relations with China.

Bhaso Ndzendze and Nomzamo Gondwe in chapter 13—"Eswatini-Taiwan Relations: Absolute Monarchy, Domestic Audience Absence, and China's Irrelevance"—examine the role of authoritarian survival within the Kingdom of Eswatini's foreign and economic policy. Findings show that the government of Eswatini is fundamentally unresponsive to the economic imperatives which have made other African countries switch to China. The economic comparative advantage offered by China has no mechanism of filtering to the population and generating a change in direction as has been seen in other African countries since 2000. Based on these findings, their chapter argues that relations with Taipei are likely to continue insofar as its system continues to be headed by an authoritarian, absolute monarchy that has an asymmetrical social contract with its population and thus has no pressure to switch to potentially more lucrative economic relations with Beijing. In this sense, relations with Taiwan are likely to be relinquished only if there is a change in governance or, at the very least, meaningful reforms that render the monarchy more responsive to domestic audience costs. A small but noticeable drift is taking place between parliament, which is elected, and the monarch over the One-China policy of the country.

The struggle for supremacy and diplomatic recognition between China and Taiwan was fought, not just in Africa, but around the globe. There is ample literature that bears out this assertion. However, their struggle for diplomatic recognition in the continent of Africa is under-researched. With this project, we intend to show and/or examine the "how, why, and the implications" of

China and Taiwan exerting considerable time and resources into winning the hearts and minds of states and societies in Africa. And because we cannot approach the Africa-China-Africa-Taiwan relations in isolation, we have decided to take an all-inclusive approach. It is an approach that looks at issues relating to (a) the modern history of both countries; (b) issues relating to self-determination, international recognition; (c) the foreign policy of both countries toward Africa; (d) the overt and covert action of both countries and their countermeasures; (e) political rivalries; and (f) the politics of the Cold War and post–Cold War era.

Furthermore, the contentious relationship between China and Taiwan is a timely issue to address because it intersects with the ongoing debate about China's rising power and the isolation of Taiwan. Second, while there are untold numbers of books dealing with "China in Africa," there is a gap in the literature regarding Taiwan's role and place in Africa even though it has had a noticeable presence since 1949. While China's role and place in Africa have garnered a lot of scholarly attention—be it praise or condemnation—not much has been written about Taiwan. But more telling is the fact that there is a dearth of books on the "contest and contestation" between the two Chinas. Within and outside of the academy, Taiwan seems to be an afterthought— with many forgetting that between 1960 and 1971, more countries on the continent had a diplomatic relationship with Taiwan than with mainland China. Taipei, not Beijing, therefore, was the preferred capital. The reverse is true for mainland China where it is seen—not just as regional power—but as an emerging global hegemon ranked second only to the United States.

There are several reasons why the contest and contestation between China and Taiwan on African soil deserve our attention. It, for instance, offers us a view of power rivalry on the continent. It is also an indication of how powerful and significant the continent is on the global stage. But, unfortunately, Africans and their governments are oblivious to these facts. Instead, the actions and pronouncements of a succession of African leaders and elites have caused the continent to suffer in terms of growth and development.

Part I

FOREIGN POLICY AND THEIR IMPLICATIONS

Chapter 1

China's Foreign Policy toward Africa, 1949–2020

Yen-Hsin Chen

INTRODUCTION

The relationship between China, the largest developing country in the world, and Africa, the largest developing continent in the world, has been the subject of interest of many scholars. China's foreign policy toward Africa can be divided into several historical periods with different objectives and concerns. The Bandung Conference in 1955 offered an opportunity to the new Chinese regime to build diplomatic relations with African countries. During the Cold War, China developed its Three Worlds Theory to distinguish itself from the two superpowers. Meanwhile, this ideological justification was used to define and regulate Sino-African relations. During this period, however, China's engagement in the African continent was economically costly.

After the death of Mao Zedong, post-Mao Chinese leaders largely focused on improving economic conditions at home, so China was less interested in spending money overseas. Under such circumstances, China's aid to African countries significantly decreased. Meanwhile, because China needed foreign aid and investments to develop its economy, the relations between China and the Western modern countries improved substantially, while China was in direct competition with African countries seeking aid from developed rich countries.

Sino-African relations improved after the Tiananmen Square Event in 1989. Because of the event, China was again being isolated by Western countries. To repair its international reputation and compete with Taiwan for international recognition, China resumed relations with African countries. As China continued its economic development, the African continent has become critical to China for two reasons. First, China needed natural resources from overseas to support its consumption, so it could maintain the scale and pace of economic growth. The African continent served that need, so it became a critical area for China's energy security. Second, beginning with labor-intensive production in the late 1970s, today China's economic development has reached a stage to upgrade its industry into a more innovation-driven economy. The newly developing African countries appear to be an ideal destination for China's excess capacity.

China's Belt and Road Initiative (BRI) aims to build a new international trade network, and Africa plays a crucial role in this project. China's engagement in Africa has solidly changed the continent, but different segments of African people have different opinions about China's presence in Africa. On the one hand, the Chinese model of development has been welcomed by African authoritarian leaders. On the other hand, concerns about human rights and environmental issues have made many observers and citizens in Africa question the intention of China.

The purpose of this chapter is to introduce China's presence in Africa from 1949 to 2020. This chapter is organized in the following order. I first introduce the meaning of the Bandung Conference to China's diplomacy, then I analyze the differences in China's Africa policy during and after the Cold War. The return of a wealthy China will be discussed in the following section, and I present a brief conclusion at the end of this chapter.

THE BANDUNG CONFERENCE

At the end of World War II, the Chinese people did not get peace but brutal civil war between Kuomintang, the ruling party, and Chinese Communist Party, the challenger, from 1945 to 1949. Mao Zedong and the Chinese Communist Party (CCP) established the People's Republic of China (hereafter China) in 1949. Meanwhile, Chiang Kai-shek and the central government of the Republic of China (hereafter Taiwan) retreated to Taiwan and continued to fight for the reunification of China. After its establishment, the main task of this new Chinese regime was to conquer Taiwan to unify Chinese territories by force. However, the outbreak of the Korean War in 1950 and the presence of the United Nations military forces made China miss the opportunities to cross the Taiwan Strait, so Chinese authorities decided to send Chinese troops to fight the United States in Korea. Although there were still occasional fights between the two sides of the Chinese Civil War at the coastlines in the following years, China finally got its first war-free year in 1954.[1]

The year 1955 was a remarkable year for the diplomatic relations of the new Chinese regime. There were twenty-nine Asian and African countries that met in Bandung, Indonesia, in 1955. Among the twenty-nine attendances, six of them were African countries: Egypt, Ethiopia, the Gold Coast, Liberia, Libya, and Sudan.[2] This conference not only introduced a newly formed Asian-African force to the post–World War II international community, but it also marked as the first Chinese diplomatic contact with African countries.[3] This conference provided then China's premier Zhou Enlai and Chinese delegation opportunities to address the common experience of China and Africa regarding their efforts against colonialism and China's support to African people's independence movements. In the conference, the then premier Zhou spoke about the "Five Principles of Peaceful Coexistence" theory to define the Sino-African relations in the new era: mutual respect for sovereignty and territorial integrity, mutual nonaggression, noninterference in each other's internal affairs, equality, and mutual benefits and peaceful coexistence.[4] As a result, China successfully expressed its willingness to build a comprehensive partnership with African countries to support African people's anticolonialism campaign.[5] Egypt, for example, began trading steel and cotton with China in 1955.[6] One year later, Egypt became the first African country to establish formal diplomatic relations with Beijing in 1956.[7]

THE COLD WAR AND CHINA'S
THREE WORLDS THEORY

During the Cold War, the interaction between China and Africa was under the guidance of China's Three Worlds Theory.[8] This theory categorized all countries into one of the following three worlds: the First World, the Second World, and the Third World. The United States of America and the Soviet Union, the two superpowers during the Cold War, constituted the First World. The industrialized allies of the two superpowers, such as Japan and Canada, made up the Second World. The Third World countries were the remaining countries that were generally less developed and nonaligned.

There were two applications of this theory. First, China saw itself as belonging to the Third World instead of a natural ally of the Soviet Union; the Three Worlds Theory was used to form the united front to counter the threat of the Soviets.[9] Second, the Three Worlds Theory emphasized the growing importance of the developing world in international affairs, and China saw itself as the potential leader of the Third World bloc.

The Chinese revolutionary model was also introduced and promoted to the continent of Africa during the Cold War. Different from the classic argument of Marxism that emphasized the class struggle between the capitalists and industrial workers, Mao and his theory focused on the struggle between the capitalists and rural peasantry, which better represented the societal condition of many developing countries. Due to the similarity between the societies of

China and Africa, respectively, China asserted the usefulness of its experience for the revolutionary movements in the African continent.[10] In practice, the Chinese officials compared Africa's suffering under the European colonialists with China's so-called hundred years of humiliation since the First Opium War in 1842 and argued that the Sino-African relationships should center on the ideas of opposition to colonialism and imperialism. From the perspective of Beijing, the continent of Africa at that time was underdeveloped in general, and in developed regions, income distribution was highly uneven. This situation was similar to Chinese society in the 1920s, the time before China's socialist revolution occurred. Therefore, China and Africa shared a very similar experience, so the African countries should adopt China's strategy, while China and Africa should form a comprehensive partnership. More specifically, in one speech in 1959, the paramount leader of China, Mao Zedong, described Africa as an important player in the struggle against imperialism, therefore China and Africa should unite to promote a more peaceful and just international order.[11]

Under this circumstance, China's relationships with Africa were considered financially costly while politically narrowly focused.[12] During this time, the goal of Beijing was to position China as a friend of the African people and to align itself closer to African countries. In practice, although the domestic economy of China in the 1960s and 1970s was almost completely isolated from the international economic system, China offered military support, medical aid, and loan assistance to thirty African countries given that China's financial resources were relatively limited during this period.[13] As a result, in addition to the two superpowers, the effort of China made it became a key backer of several revolutionary movements in the Third World as well as an important supplier of many newly emerged governments in Africa during the Cold War.[14]

The most famous project China made in Africa during this period was the TANZAM railway project that linked the interiors of Tanzania and Zambia to the coast.[15] The requests for assistance were rejected by both the West and Soviet Union, while China decided to support this over 1,000-mile-long project. The railway was constructed between 1970 and 1975 with financing and technical support from China amounting to over $400 million. At the time China was still considered a poor country and was experiencing the Cultural Revolution at home. This Chinese-sponsored project was not only China's largest foreign development project at that time, it was also known as the "Free Railway," a symbol of anticolonialism and anti-imperialism, and the effort to combat the hegemonism of the two superpowers.[16] By sponsoring this project, China sent a message to the world that it was willing to invest where the Western powers were unwilling to support the development of its African friends.[17] In return, the newly emerged African countries supported

China's effort to gain international recognition and to replace Taiwan in the international community.[18] The most remarkable case was that African votes played a key role in unseating Taiwan from the United Nations and the UN Security Council in 1971.[19]

The preceding discussion shows that during the Cold War, China's involvement in Africa was guided by its political ideology with little concern for the economy of China. African countries were seen as natural allies of China, so China provided aid to support revolutionary movements as well as newly independent African countries in Africa. As a result, China's engagement in Africa during this period was considered narrowly focused and economically costly.

CHINA AFTER MAO: AN ESTRANGED FRIEND

Regime survival has always been the primary concern of the CCP regime since 1949. Under the leadership of Mao Zedong, the CCP government largely emphasized the importance of ideology to create a society with perfect equality, which gave legitimacy to the rule of the CCP. Internationally, the Beijing government aimed to show the world that the new China was the genuine friend and true supporter of all oppressed people: not only in mainland China but also in the world. In practice, although China's financial capacity was limited, China spent a huge amount of money overseas to support liberation movements in the Third World.[20]

After the death of Mao Zedong, however, Chinese leaders began to base the legitimacy of their rule on improving the living conditions of the Chinese people. When Deng Xiaoping came to power, the priority of post-Mao Chinese leaders was to improve domestic economic conditions, so they shifted their focus from ideological struggles to economic reforms. In other words, moving from ideology to pragmatism made post-Mao Chinese leaders concentrate on improving economic growth domestically rather than spending money overseas based on ideological justifications. Moreover, China's economic reforms made it seek aid from Western economies, so not only did China's criticism of Western powers decline, but the relations with the Western advanced countries were also largely improved and normalized. Nevertheless, China's modernization in the late 1970s left the country short of capital and unable to provide Africa the same level of economic assistance. As a result, from the late 1970s to the 1990s China's interests in adding African countries significantly decreased.[21] Scholars also point out that not only Chinese aid dropped in the late 1970s, the number of medical teams sent to Africa also dropped; the Chinese assistance increasingly took the form of training or joint financing plans instead of pure financial aid.[22]

Another impact of China's economic reforms on the Sino-African relationships was that economic reforms placed China in direct competition with African states over economic aid from international institutions, such as the World Bank and International Monetary Fund, and investment from Western developed countries.[23] Largely focused on building economic ties with modern East Asia and western countries, the importance of China's ties with the African continent was deemphasized. More specifically, as the priority of Beijing was to build trade ties with capital-rich Western economies instead of capital-poor Africa, the ideological justification for African engagement, which was financially costly, faded.[24] The then premier of China, Zhao Ziyang, announced the Four Principles on Sino-African Economic and Technical cooperation, which emphasized "mutual benefits and no political conditions, practical results, diversity in form, and common development," to guide Sino-African relations. These four principles could be interpreted as China paying more attention to its economic development at home, so its Africa policy moved from simply offering financial aid to pursue cooperation for mutual benefit. In short, China's economic reforms made China's Africa policy shift from political ideology centered to economic oriented.[25]

During this period, China largely focused on rebuilding its economy and improving the living conditions of Chinese people. The priority of post-Mao Chinese leaders was to participate in international trade networks to develop its economy, so it was crucial to rebuilding its overall relationships with East Asian and Western modern countries. As a result, after decades of support, the relationships with African countries were no longer the primary concern of Chinese leaders after its economic reforms.

THE RETURN OF THE OLD FRIEND

China's incentives to improve relations with Africa increased after the Tiananmen Square incident of 1989.[26] Shootings at Tiananmen Square made China again feel isolated by the West, so the desire to repair its international reputation made Beijing focus on resuming relations with its old African friends.[27] In addition, Beijing reassessed its aid policy in order to compete with Taiwan for international recognition in the African continent.[28]

Along with its development, China in early 1990 has become a manufacturing powerhouse and transitioned from an oil exporter to an oil importer.[29] The growing interest in joint development of African commodities and energy resources has made China renew the emphasis on strengthening economic ties with African countries.[30] For example, the trade between China and Africa grew up from 1.4 billion in 1990 to almost 10 billion in 2000.[31] Eventually, the ideological dimension of Sino-African relations was largely replaced by expanded economic considerations. In 2000, China proposed a new strategic partnership with five principles of cooperation: equality and mutual benefit, diversity in form and content, emphasis on practical results, the pursuit of common progress, and an amicable settlement of differences. These principles illustrated that this new aid policy aimed to promote local industries and to create local employment instead of simply offering economic aid to African countries.[32]

China's economic growth has made China heavily dependent on imported natural resources, and China's major oil companies have moved their operations to sources overseas.[33] Further, China's deeper involvement with some of the main oil-rich and resource-producing African countries reflects its ever-growing need to secure energy security. During this period, the trade between China and Africa reflected a unique pattern. That is, on the one hand, the products China exported to Africa are diversified with various categories. On the other hand, Africa's exports to China were largely concentrated in raw materials, such as mineral products and crude oil.[34] Trade with Africa benefited China as it secured long-term access to raw materials and resources needed for its economic development.[35] This pattern presents the increasing demand for natural resources to continue its economic development. In 2009, China had overtaken the United States to become Africa's largest trade partner.[36] In addition to economic exchanges, China and African also engage in educational, cultural, and professional exchanges to facilitate a higher degree of mutual understanding. Beijing pledges to continue a sincere, equal, and friendly relationship between China and Africa.[37]

China's economic presence and its reengagement in Africa have two major concerns. First, China positions itself as an alternative trade and assistance partner for African countries, and China is less interested in interfering in local governance or attaching conditions to its economic deals. Second, China's economic development is presenting a new model of economic growth for developing African countries.[38] These two concerns will be further elaborated in the following sections.

THE PLAN OF THE RED DRAGON

As mentioned in the previous sections, the CCP regime has based its legitimacy on improving the living conditions of Chinese people since the late 1970s. As its accomplishment is impressive, Beijing needs to continue the current scale and pace of its economic development in order to maintain its legitimacy. The rise of China is attributed to its efforts to integrate its economy into the international community. Starting from its neighboring economies in the region of East Asia, the Chinese economy was manifested by the growth in the economic interchange between China and foreign countries throughout the world. In the early 2000s, China joined the World Trade Organization and now has become the second-largest economic body in the world since 2011.

China has been the world's fastest-growing major economy, while its economic success has reshaped its foreign behavior, too. First, being the second-largest economy in the world, China has successfully converted its economic capacity into international influences. Different from the first several decades of its post–Civil War history, its current economic success has given Beijing confidence to actively engage in international affairs, and confident China requests to be recognized as a global power that cannot be ignored by anyone anymore. Second, largely benefited by its integration into the world economy, a wealthy China realizes the importance of regional and global stability to its domestic economic growth. Thereby, China asserts that China's interests need to be considered whenever the international community makes decisions, which makes Beijing conclude that the best strategy to defend China's national interests is to actively participate in the decision-making process of important international affairs.[39]

The biggest concern of the CCP regime is US supremacy. In order to counter US global hegemony, Beijing proposes and promotes the structure of multipolarity, which allows China as well as other international actors, especially the vast array of developing countries, flexibility to pursue a more favorable international and economic order.[40] More importantly, China believes that it can play a pole within the multipolar system, which serves the interests of China.[41] Further, Beijing also claimed that rising China will not bring any threat to anyone but bring more opportunities to the development of the world.[42]

Chinese-African solidity is essential for promoting China's multipolar worldview and standing firm against US global dominance.[43] In order to differentiate itself from Western powers, China portrays itself as a developing country to promote the idea that China is the largest developing country in the world while Africa is the largest developing continent in the world.[44] In practice, there were more than hundred high-level meetings between Chinese and African envoys that took place between 2003 and 2005 to build a stronger connection between the two.[45] China continues to show its support to African efforts to determine their own political and economic system without outside interference, including not taking positions that would be seen to be interfering in the controversial internal affairs of African countries.[46] By doing so, Beijing aims to position itself as an alternative trade and assistance partner for Africa, and one less interested in inferring local governance or attaching conditions to its economic deals.[47] The fast economic and diplomatic ties between China and Africa suggest that China's influence in

Africa is rising without question.[48] For African countries, China is presenting a new model of economic growth for developing states. For Beijing, the African continent is filled with natural resources, which benefits China's search for energy security.[49] Further, although individual African countries might not pose substantial leverage in international politics, the number of African countries together makes up a force that is crucial to make decisions in international organizations. Thus, from the perspectives of Beijing and that of African leaders, Sino-African solidarity is constructive and is a win-win scenario for both.

China's rise occurs within the current international system. More specifically, China has been raised within the international structure that is built, supported, and maintained by the West. To continue its development, the president of China, Xi Jinping, proposed the BRI in 2013. The objectives of this project are to connect China's underdeveloped hinterland, such as Xinjiang, to central Asia and Europe, while China's developed southeast provinces will be connected to the fast-developing Southeast Asian economies. By doing so, China will be able to establish a whole new international trade network. Criticisms from the West to this project mainly claim that this China-centered geopolitical network reveals China's ambition of becoming a global hegemony. On the other hand, Beijing argues the aforementioned interpretation is Western biased; the BRI is a purely economic project that connects and benefits all Asian, European, and African participants.[50] While the intention, progress, and accomplishment of the BRI have been widely discussed and under scrutiny since it was proposed, there is no doubt that this project will redress some of the concerns of China regarding its economic development. Among all, the BRI will benefit China's effort of upgrading Chinese industry and dealing with excess capacity.[51] This statement is related to the topic of the following section: the flying geese model.

THE FLYING GEESE MODEL IN AFRICA

The flying geese model is a well-known economic development pattern that explains the rapid economic development of East Asia, "the East Asian Economic Miracle," after the end of World War II.[52] The flying geese model describes the pattern of a regional transmission of industrialization. In this framework, a country starts with labor-intensive industries. When its development reaches a certain stage, this country will look for more advanced industries to upgrade its economy, while its experience, technology, and production line will be learned and passed to neighboring newly industrializing societies. In other words, the first developed country plays the role of innovator and the leader in the region, while the neighboring economies follow and catch up.

In the case of East Asia, Japan started to reconstruct its economy after the end of World War II. When Japan's industrialization reached a level that resulted in rising costs, the labor-intensive production was transmitted to the neighboring newly industrializing societies in the region, such as Hong Kong, South Korea, Taiwan, and Singapore (the Four Asian Tigers). Meanwhile, the economy of Japan switched toward capital-intensive production. When the economies of the following countries also reached the time to upgrade, they started to do what Japan did before: passed the labor-intensive production to the newer developing societies in the region. As a result, the industry of East Asia economics formed a hierarchy that looked like a group of ranked wild geese flying orderly in an inverted V formation: the leading goose was Japan, the second tiers were the Four Asian Tigers, the third tiers were the members of Association of Southeast Asian Nations such as Thailand and Malaysia, and then followed by China and Vietnam.

China imported secondhand production lines in the 1980s from its neighbors to build its cheap mass manufacturing model of development. Starting from labor-intensive production, China has now reached the time for upgrading its industries, and one of its focuses is to transmit its old production lines to newer industrializing economies. Using the flying geese model, scholars have focused on the presence of China in the industrialization of less developed countries.[53] The African continent, a much less developed area, shapes up to be a key area to China's plan. For example, Bräutigam investigated the Chinese investments in Mauritius and Nigeria and finds the trading networks transmit information and resources efficiently for entrepreneurs to learn how to industrialize with greater ease.[54] Xiaoyang Tang studied the Chinese investments in Ghana and finds that industrial upgrading and attraction of African markets' long-term potential are the two main driving forces for the arrival of Chinese investors.[55] In sum, by supporting the industrialization of African countries, China plays the role of leading goose to guide the industrialization of developing African countries.

THE CONSEQUENCES OF CHINA'S RETURN TO AFRICA

China's engagement in Africa is a combination of economic development, politics, and the global balance of power.[56] The so-called Beijing Consensus, the Chinese model that represents state capitalism under an authoritarian government, appears to be preferred by the African authoritarians.[57] Literature on the current relations between China and Africa also points out the mixed concerns about China's presence in the developing African continent. For example, Alden argues that compared to other powerful countries, the Chinese government's Africa policy has conformed to the interests and needs of African countries to a greater degree than any other foreign power.[58] In addition to the geostrategic concerns and the competition with Taiwan, Beijing indeed adopts an approach that largely reflects the shared interests of China and Africa. He also believes that China's flying geese model in Africa is facilitating the economic development of the African continent. Zhao also argues that for African countries that are unwilling or could not meet the requirement to get aid from the Western countries, aid from China is not only an alternative but also serves as an economic lifeline for them.[59] From the perspective of optimists, China is a sincere partner of African people, and closer ties with China present external opportunities for African development.[60]

Another group of scholars expresses very different concerns. They argue that like the major donor states, China's aid and engagement in Africa was primarily an important foreign policy tool to the pursuit of China's national interests, including exploiting resources and building a new international order that favors China.[61] Meanwhile, unlike Western donors, China's aid does not attach any political conditions, with the exception that a country maintaining diplomatic relations with Taiwan cannot expect aid from China. More specifically, the "Beijing Consensus" does not link aid to issues such as good governance, human rights practices, and any political or economic reforms that are generally the concerns of Western donors, so African authoritarians are pleased with Chinese assistance that comes without political conditionality. The presences and aid from China allow them to maintain their political power while developing their economies. As a result, the Chinese model of development is embraced by African authoritarian leaders.[62]

The preceding discussion indicates that the close ties between China and Africa are generally considered mutually beneficial by authoritarian leaders. Chinese assistance, however, can also be problematic to African leaders. First, thus far there are plenty of examples of very large promises followed by little implementation for a variety of reasons on the Chinese side.[63] Further, Chinese aid has been criticized because it comes in the form of loans that must be repaid; Chinese aid is also usually tied to the purchase of Chinese goods and services. Nevertheless, the Chinese-financed projects usually require the use of Chinese labor in African countries to carry out Chinese-supported projects. Nathan and Scobell argue that the African continent is a good place for Chinese companies to gain experience in doing business internationally.[64] They can test their technologies and abilities, and this experience can be used elsewhere against Western competitors and rivals. These studies reveal that China's engagement in Africa still mainly serves the interests of China. Meanwhile, ordinary African people also express their concerns regarding China in Africa. For example, Mlambo et al.[65] point out that China's presence in Africa has caused anti-Chinese protests in several African states: African people expressed their concerns of economic, environmental, and labor rights regarding Chinese investment in Africa. In addition to the fact that civil society groups and labor unions are more critical of Chinese aid to authoritarian governments in Africa, they also point out that Chinese-sponsored projects are less attentive to international labor standards when employing Africans. It results in a growing number of African complaints against Chinese activities in African, which serve the interests of China. As a result, it is not surprising to see active civil society groups in African countries mobilize protest of Chinese practices.[66]

In sum, Beijing has made extensive efforts to build a comprehensive tie with African countries in the hope to build win-win scenarios. On the one hand, the Chinese model of development is appealing to African leaders as it facilitates economic development while allowing authoritarians to stay in power. On the other hand, Chinese activities in Africa, especially its efforts to resource extractions, remind African people of Western colonialism. As a result, the return of China to Africa presents a negative consequence that does not contribute to long-term peace, stability, and democracy on the African continent.[67]

CONCLUSION

China's foreign policy toward Africa in different periods reveals different priorities and concerns. The Three Worlds Theory gave China ideological justification to support African revolutionary movements during the Cold War. Although newly independent African countries offered their support to China in competition with Taiwan for international recognition in return, China's presence in Africa was still considered narrowly focused and economically costly. After its economic reforms in the late 1970s, China switched its attention from ideological struggles to rebuild its domestic economy to improve the living conditions of the Chinese people, which was believed to be essential to the legitimacy of CCP rule. Therefore, to attract foreign capital, the priority of Beijing was to build friendly relations with East Asian and Western economies, not poor developing African countries. Therefore, the reasons for continuing to provide financial aid to African countries faded.

As the overall state capacity of China increases, the African continent again has attracted the attention of Beijing. Having natural resources has made Africa valuable and critical to continue powering China's economic growth. Besides, the issue of excess capacity will be redressed if China plays the role of the leading goose in the industrialization of the African continent. The Chinese model of development, the Beijing Consensus, is also appealing to African authoritarian leaders as this model promises economic development while securing the political privilege of African dictators. Last, but not the least, China-Africa solidity is essential for promoting China's multipolar worldview against US global dominance.

Although China's presence in Africa receives mixed reviews, it is fair to argue that the logic behind China's Africa policy is still driven by its self-interest. Like all previous powers in Africa, China engages in Africa mainly because Africa can provide what China wants during different times: ideological justification, international recognition, and natural resources. China's Africa policy might be best concluded by the comment from one of Emeka Umejei's interviews:

> I view China's engagement with Nigeria as providing opportunity as well as taking advantage of Nigeria. But that is what other nations attempt to do everywhere else.[68]

NOTES

1. Larkin, Bruce D. *China and Africa 1949–1970: The Foreign Policy of the People's Republic of China.* 5. University of California Press, 1973.

2. Shimazu, Naoko. "Diplomacy as Theatre: Staging the Bandung Conference of 1955." *Modern Asian Studies* (2014): 225–252.

3. Ayodele, Thompson, and Olusegun Sotola. "China in Africa: An Evaluation of Chinese Investment." *Initiative for Public Policy Analysis* (2014): 1–20. See also Acharya, Amitav. "Studying the Bandung Conference from a Global IR Perspective." *Australian Journal of International Affairs* 70, no. 4 (2016): 342–357; "Who Are the Norm Makers? The Asian-African Conference in Bandung and the Evolution of Norms." *Global Governance: A Review of Multilateralism and International Organizations* 20, no. 3 (2014): 405–417; Appadorai, A. "The Bandung Conference." *India Quarterly* 11, no. 3 (1955): 207–235; and Muekalia, Domingos Jardo. "Africa and China's Strategic Partnership." *African Security Studies* 13, no. 1 (2004): 5–11.

4. Shinn, David H., and Joshua Eisenman. *China and Africa: A Century of Engagement.* University of Pennsylvania Press, 2012. See also Lanteigne, Marc. *Chinese Foreign Policy: An Introduction.* Routledge, 2019; and He, Wenping. "China's Perspective on Contemporary China–Africa Relations." *China Returns to Africa: A Rising Power and a Continent Embrace.* London: Hurst (2008): 143–165.

5. Shinn and Eisenman. *China and Africa: A Century of Engagement.* See also Shimazu, "Diplomacy as Theatre," 225–252.

6. Larkin, *China and Africa 1949–1970.*

7. Lanteigne, *Chinese Foreign Policy*. See also Shinn and Eisenman. *China and Africa: A Century of Engagement*.

8. Yee, Herbert S. "The Three World Theory and Post-Mao China's Global Strategy." *International Affairs (Royal Institute of International Affairs 1944–)* 59, no. 2 (1983): 239–249. See also Alden, Chris, and Cristina Alves. "History & Identity in the Construction of China's Africa Policy." *Review of African Political Economy* 35, no. 115 (2008): 43–58; and Lanteigne, *Chinese Foreign Policy*.

9. Yee, "The Three World Theory and Post-Mao China's Global Strategy," 239–249. See also Ayodele and Sotola. "China in Africa: An Evaluation of Chinese Investment," 1–20.

10. Larkin, *China and Africa 1949–1970*.

11. Lanteigne, *Chinese Foreign Policy*.

12. Mlambo, Courage, Audrey Kushamba, and More Simawu. "China-Africa Relations: What Lies Beneath?" *The Chinese Economy* 49 (2016): 257–276; Wang, Fei-Ling, and Esi A. Elliot. "China in Africa: Presence, Perceptions and Prospects." *Journal of Contemporary China* 23, no. 90 (2014): 1012–1032.

13. Nathan, Andrew J., and Andrew Scobell. *China's Search for Security*. Columbia University Press, 2015.

14. Larkin, *China and Africa 1949–1970*. See also Alden, Chris. "China in Africa." Palgrave Macmillan, 2007; and Alden, Chris, Daniel Large, and Ricardo Soares de Oliveira. "China Returns to Africa: A Rising Power and a Continent Embrace," 2008.

15. Bailey, Martin. "Chinese Aid in Action: Building the Tanzania–Zambia Railway." In *China's Road to Development*, 289–297. Elsevier, 1979. See also Graham, James D. "The Tanzam Railway: Consolidating the People's Development and Building the Internal Economy." *Africa Today* 21, no. 3 (1974): 27–42.

16. Monson, Jamie. *Africa's Freedom Railway: How a Chinese Development Project Changed Lives and Livelihoods in Tanzania*. Bloomington: Indiana University Press, 2009.

17. Ayodele and Sotola, "China in Africa: An Evaluation of Chinese Investment," 1–20.

18. Mlambo et al., "China-Africa Relations," 257–276. See also Sutter, Robert G. *Chinese Foreign Relations: Power and Policy since the Cold War*. Rowman & Littlefield, 2012; and Tull, Denis M. "The Political Consequences of China's Return to Africa." *China Returns to Africa: A Rising Power and a Continent Embrace*. London: Hurst and Company (2008): 27–50.

19. Nathan and Scobell, *China's Search for Security*. See also Wang and Elliot. "China in Africa: Presence, Perceptions and Prospects," 1012–1032.

20. Lanteigne, *Chinese Foreign Policy*. See also Shinn and Eisenman. *China and Africa: A Century of Engagement*.

21. Ayodele and Sotola, "China in Africa: An Evaluation of Chinese Investment," 1–20; Mlambo et al., "China-Africa Relations," 257–276.

22. Shinn and Eisenman. *China and Africa: A Century of Engagement*; Sutter, *Chinese Foreign Relations*.

23. Lanteigne, *Chinese Foreign Policy*; Sutter, *Chinese Foreign Relations*.

24. Lanteigne, *Chinese Foreign Policy.*

25. Shinn and Eisenman. *China and Africa: A Century of Engagement.*

26. Mlambo et al., "China-Africa Relations," 257–276; Sutter, *Chinese Foreign Relations.*

27. Tull, "The Political Consequences of China's Return to Africa," 27–50.

28. Gaye, Adama. "China in Africa: After the Gun and the Bible: A West African Perspective." *China Returns to Africa – A Rising Power and a Continent Embrace.* London: Hurst and Company (2008): 129–142; He, "China's Perspective on Contemporary China–Africa Relations," 143–165.

29. Alden, Chris. "China in Africa." Palgrave Macmillan, 2007.

30. Large, Daniel. "From Non-Interference to Constructive Engagement? China's Evolving Relations with Sudan." *China Returns to Africa: A Rising Power and a Continent Embrace* (2008): 275–294. See also Bräutigam, Deborah. *The Dragon's Gift: The Real Story of China in Africa.* OUP Oxford, 2011; Van de Looy, Judith, and Leo de Haan. "Africa and China: A Strategic Partnership?" *Institute for Defence Studies and Analysis. Strategic Analysis* 30, no. 3 (2006): 562–575; and Zhao, Suisheng. "China's Global Search for Energy Security: Cooperation and Competition in Asia–Pacific." *Journal of Contemporary China* 17, no. 55 (2008): 207–227.

31. Shinn and Eisenman. *China and Africa: A Century of Engagement.*

32. Shinn and Eisenman. *China and Africa: A Century of Engagement.*

33. Zhao, "China's Global Search for Energy Security," 207–227.

34. Goldstein, Andrea, Nicolas Pinaud, and Helmut Reisen. "China's Boom: What's in It for Africa? A Trade Perspective." *China Returns to Africa: A Rising Power and a Continent Embrace.* London: Hurst and Company (2008): 27–50.

35. Gaye, Adama. "China in Africa: After the Gun and the Bible," 129–142; Shinn and Eisenman. *China and Africa: A Century of Engagement.*

36. Lanteigne, *Chinese Foreign Policy.*

37. He, "China's Perspective on Contemporary China–Africa Relations," 143–165.

38. Gaye, Adama. "China in Africa: After the Gun and the Bible," 129–142; Hodzi, Obert. "China and Africa: Economic Growth and a Non-Transformative Political Elite." *Journal of Contemporary African Studies* 36, no. 2 (2018): 191–206; and Adisu, Kinfu, Thomas Sharkey, and Sam Okoroafo. "The Impact of Chinese Investment in Africa." *International Journal of Business and Management* 5 (August 19, 2010).

39. Sutter, *Chinese Foreign Relations.*

40. He, "China's Perspective on Contemporary China–Africa Relations," 143–165.

41. Tull, "The Political Consequences of China's Return to Africa," 27–50.

42. Brautigam, Deborah. "'Flying Geese' or 'Hidden Dragon' Chinese Business and African Industrial Development." *China Returns to Africa: A Rising Power and a Continent Embrace.* London: Hurst and Company (2008): 51–68.

43. Sutter, *Chinese Foreign Relations.* See also Campbell, Horace. "China in Africa: Challenging US Global Hegemony." *Third World Quarterly* 29, no. 1 (2008): 89–105.

44. Sutter, *Chinese Foreign Relations.*

45. Tull, "The Political Consequences of China's Return to Africa," 27–50.

46. Sutter, *Chinese Foreign Relations*.

47. Nathan and Scobell, *China's Search for Security*; Hodzi, "China and Africa: Economic Growth and a Non-Transformative Political Elite," 191–206; and Sautman, Barry, and Hairong Yan. "Friends and Interests: China's Distinctive Links with Africa." *African Studies Review* (2007): 75–114.

48. Mlambo et al., "China-Africa Relations," 257–276; Wang and Elliot, "China in Africa: Presence, Perceptions and Prospects," 1012–1032.

49. Zhao, "China's Global Search for Energy Security," 207–227.

50. Swaine, Michael D. "Chinese Views and Commentary on the 'One Belt, One Road' Initiative." *China Leadership Monitor* 47, no. 2 (2015): 3–24; Huang, Yiping. "Understanding China's Belt & Road Initiative: Motivation, Framework and Assessment." *China Economic Review* 40 (2016): 314–321; Herrero, Alicia Garcia, and Jianwei Xu. "China's Belt and Road Initiative: Can Europe Expect Trade Gains?" *China & World Economy* 25, no. 6 (2017): 84–99.

51. Cai, Peter. "Understanding China's Belt and Road Initiative" Report. Sydney: The Lowy Institute for International Policy, 2017.

52. Blomqvist, Hans C. "The 'Flying Geese' Model of Regional Development: A Constructive Interpretation." *Journal of the Asia Pacific Economy* 1, no. 2 (1996): 215–231; Kojima, Kiyoshi. "The 'Flying Geese' Model of Asian Economic Development: Origin, Theoretical Extensions, and Regional Policy Implications." *Journal of Asian Economics* 11, no. 4 (2000): 375–401; and Edgington, David W., and Roger Hayter. "Foreign Direct Investment and the Flying Geese Model: Japanese Electronics Firms in Asia-Pacific." *Environment and Planning A* 32, no. 2 (2000): 281–304.

53. Ang, Yuen. "Domestic Flying Geese: Industrial Transfer and Delayed Policy Diffusion in China." *The China Quarterly* 234 (2018): 420–443; Chen, Lurong, Philippe De Lombaerde, and Nishalini Nair. "The Changing Roles of Japan and China towards ASEAN's Economy: Beyond the Flying-Geese Model?" *Studia Diplomatica* 64, no. 3 (2011): 79–94; and Xu, Jian, and Yongrong Cao. "Innovation, the Flying Geese Model, IPR Protection, and Sustainable Economic Development in China." *Sustainability* 11, no. 20 (2019): 5707–5084.

54. Bräutigam, Deborah. "Close Encounters: Chinese Business Networks as Industrial Catalysts in Sub-Saharan Africa." *African Affairs* 102, no. 408 (2003): 447–467.

55. Tang, Xiaoyang. "8 Geese Flying to Ghana? A Case Study of the Impact of Chinese Investments on Africa's Manufacturing Sector." *Journal of Contemporary China* 27, no. 114 (2018): 924–941.

56. Tull, "The Political Consequences of China's Return to Africa," 27–50; Mlambo et al., "China-Africa Relations," 257–276; and Wang and Elliot, "China in Africa: Presence, Perceptions and Prospects," 1012–1032.

57. Yao, Yang. "Beijing Consensus." *The Wiley Blackwell Encyclopedia of Race, Ethnicity, and Nationalism* (2015): 1–4; Sautman and Yan, "Friends and Interests," 75–114.

58. Alden, Chris. "China in Africa." Palgrave Macmillan, 2007.

59. Zhao, "China's Global Search for Energy Security," 207–227.

60. Klaver, Mark, and Michael Trebilcock. "Chinese Investment in Africa." *The Law and Development Review* 4, no. 1 (2011): 168–217; and Ayodele and Sotola, "China in Africa: An Evaluation of Chinese Investment," 1–20.

61. Kolstad, Ivar, and Arne Wiig. "Better the Devil You Know? Chinese Foreign Direct Investment in Africa." *Journal of African Business* 12, no. 1 (March 28, 2011): 31–50; Bräutigam, "Close Encounters," 447–467; Brautigam, *The Dragon's Gift*; and Davies, Martyn. "China's Developmental Model Comes to Africa." *Review of African Political Economy* 35, no. 115 (2008): 134–137.

62. Hodzi, "China and Africa: Economic Growth and a Non-Transformative Political Elite," 191–206; Brookes, Peter, and Ji Hye Shin. "China's Influence in Africa: Implications for the United States." *Backgrounder* 1916 (2006): 1–9.

63. Lanteigne, *Chinese Foreign Policy*; Sutter, *Chinese Foreign Relations*.

64. Nathan and Scobell, *China's Search for Security*; Sutter, *Chinese Foreign Relations*.

65. Mlambo et al., "China-Africa Relations," 257–276.

66. Sutter, *Chinese Foreign Relations*; Wang and Elliot, "China in Africa: Presence, Perceptions and Prospects," 1012–1032.

67. Tull, "The Political Consequences of China's Return to Africa," 27–50.

68. Umejei, Emeka. "China's Engagement with Nigeria: Opportunity or Opportunist?" *African East-Asian Affairs*, no. 3–4 (2015): 54–78.

BIBLIOGRAPHY

Acharya, Amitav. "Studying the Bandung Conference from a Global IR Perspective." *Australian Journal of International Affairs* 70, no. 4 (2016): 342–357.

———. "Who Are the Norm Makers? The Asian-African Conference in Bandung and the Evolution of Norms." *Global Governance: A Review of Multilateralism and International Organizations* 20, no. 3 (2014): 405–417.

Adisu, Kinfu, Thomas Sharkey, and Sam Okoroafo. "The Impact of Chinese Investment in Africa." *International Journal of Business and Management* 5 (August 19, 2010): 9.

Alden, Chris. *China in Africa*. New York: Palgrave Macmillan, 2007.

Alden, Chris, and Cristina Alves. "History & Identity in the Construction of China's Africa Policy." *Review of African Political Economy* 35, no. 115 (2008): 43–58.

Alden, Chris, Daniel Large, and Ricardo Soares de Oliveira. *China Returns to Africa: A Rising Power and a Continent Embrace*. New York: Columbia University Press, 2008.

Ang, Yuen. "Domestic Flying Geese: Industrial Transfer and Delayed Policy Diffusion in China." *The China Quarterly* 234 (2018): 420–443.

Appadorai, A. "The Bandung Conference." *India Quarterly* 11, no. 3 (1955): 207–235.

Ayodele, Thompson, and Olusegun Sotola. "China in Africa: An Evaluation of Chinese Investment." *Initiative for Public Policy Analysis* 2014: 1–20.

Bailey, Martin. "Chinese Aid in Action: Building the Tanzania–Zambia Railway." In *China's Road to Development*, 289–297. Amsterdam: Elsevier, 1979.

Blomqvist, Hans C. "The 'Flying Geese' Model of Regional Development: A Constructive Interpretation." *Journal of the Asia Pacific Economy* 1, no. 2 (1996): 215–231.

Bräutigam, Deborah. "Close Encounters: Chinese Business Networks as Industrial Catalysts in Sub-Saharan Africa." *African Affairs* 102, no. 408 (2003): 447–467.

———. "Flying Geese or 'Hidden Dragon' Chinese Business and African Industrial Development." In *China Returns to Africa: A Rising Power and a Continent Embrace*. London: Hurst and Company, 51–68, 2008.

———. *The Dragon's Gift: The Real Story of China in Africa*. Oxford: Oxford University Press, 2011.

Brautigam, Deborah, Tang Xiaoyang, and Ying Xia. "What Kinds of Chinese 'Geese' Are Flying to Africa? Evidence from Chinese Manufacturing Firms." *Journal of African Economies* 27, no. suppl_1 (2018): 29–51.

Brookes, Peter, and Ji Hye Shin. "China's Influence in Africa: Implications for the United States." *Backgrounder* 1916 (2006): 1–9.

Cai, Peter. "Understanding China's Belt and Road Initiative." Report. Sydney: The Lowy Institute for International Policy, 2017.

Campbell, Horace. "China in Africa: Challenging US Global Hegemony." *Third World Quarterly* 29, no. 1 (2008): 89–105.

Chen, Lurong, Philippe De Lombaerde, and Nishalini Nair. "The Changing Roles of Japan and China towards ASEAN's Economy: Beyond the Flying-Geese Model?" *Studia Diplomatica* 64, no. 3 (2011): 79–94.

Cheng, Leonard K. "Three Questions on China's 'Belt and Road Initiative.'" *China Economic Review* 40 (2016): 309–313.

Davies, Martyn. "China's Developmental Model Comes to Africa." *Review of African Political Economy* 35, no. 115 (2008): 134–137.

Dowling, Malcolm, and Chia Tien Cheang. "Shifting Comparative Advantage in Asia: New Test of the 'Flying Geese' Model." *Journal of Asian Economics* 11, no. 4 (2000): 443–463.

Edgington, David W., and Roger Hayter. "Foreign Direct Investment and the Flying Geese Model: Japanese Electronics Firms in Asia-Pacific." *Environment and Planning A* 32, no. 2 (2000): 281–304.

Gaye, Adama. "China in Africa: After the Gun and the Bible: A West African Perspective." In *China Returns to Africa – A Rising Power and a Continent Embrace*, 129–142. London: Hurst and Company, 2008.

Ginzburg, Andrea, and Annamaria Simonazzi. "Patterns of Industrialization and the Flying Geese Model: The Case of Electronics in East Asia." *Journal of Asian Economics* 15, no. 6 (2005): 1051–1078.

Goldstein, Andrea, Nicolas Pinaud, and Helmut Reisen. "China's Boom: What's in It for Africa? A Trade Perspective." In *China Returns to Africa: A Rising Power and a Continent Embrace*, 27–50. London: Hurst and Company, 2008.

Gong, Xue. "The Belt & Road Initiative and China's Influence in Southeast Asia." *The Pacific Review* 32, no. 4 (2019): 635–665.

Graham, James D. "The Tanzam Railway: Consolidating the People's Development and Building the Internal Economy." *Africa Today* 21, no. 3 (1974): 27–42.

He, Wenping. "China's Perspective on Contemporary China–Africa Relations." In *China Returns to Africa: A Rising Power and a Continent Embrace*, 143–165. London: Hurst, 2008.

Herrero, Alicia Garcia, and Jianwei Xu. "China's Belt and Road Initiative: Can Europe Expect Trade Gains?" *China & World Economy* 25, no. 6 (2017): 84–99.

Hodzi, Obert. "China and Africa: Economic Growth and a Non-Transformative Political Elite." *Journal of Contemporary African Studies* 36, no. 2 (2018): 191–206.

Huang, Yiping. "Understanding China's Belt & Road Initiative: Motivation, Framework and Assessment." *China Economic Review* 40 (2016): 314–321.

Johnston, Lauren A. "The Belt and Road Initiative: What Is in It for China?" *Asia & the Pacific Policy Studies* 6, no. 1 (2019): 40–58.

Klaver, Mark, and Michael Trebilcock. "Chinese Investment in Africa." *The Law and Development Review* 4, no. 1 (2011): 168–217.

Kojima, Kiyoshi. "The 'Flying Geese' Model of Asian Economic Development: Origin, Theoretical Extensions, and Regional Policy Implications." *Journal of Asian Economics* 11, no. 4 (2000): 375–401.

Kolstad, Ivar, and Arne Wiig. "Better the Devil You Know? Chinese Foreign Direct Investment in Africa." *Journal of African Business* 12, no. 1 (March 28, 2011): 31–50.

Lanteigne, Marc. *Chinese Foreign Policy: An Introduction*. London: Routledge, 2019.

Large, Daniel. "From Non-Interference to Constructive Engagement? China's Evolving Relations with Sudan." In *China Returns to Africa: A Rising Power and a Continent Embrace*, 275–294. New York: Columbia University Press, 2008.

Larkin, Bruce D. *China and Africa 1949–1970: The Foreign Policy of the People's Republic of China* (Vol. 5). Berkeley, CA: University of California Press, 1973.

Mlambo, Courage, Audrey Kushamba, and More Simawu. "China-Africa Relations: What Lies Beneath?" *The Chinese Economy* 49 (July 3, 2016): 257–276.

Monson, Jamie. *Africa's Freedom Railway: How a Chinese Development Project Changed Lives and Livelihoods in Tanzania*. Bloomington, IN: Indiana University Press, 2009.

———. "Remembering Work on the Tazara Railway in Africa and China, 1965–2011: When 'New Men' Grow Old." *African Studies Review* 56, no. 1 (2013): 45–64.

Muekalia, Domingos Jardo. "Africa and China's Strategic Partnership." *African Security Studies* 13, no. 1 (2004): 5–11.

Nathan, Andrew J., and Andrew Scobell. *China's Search for Security*. New York: Columbia University Press, 2015.

Negara, Siwage Dharma, and Leo Suryadinata. "The Flying Geese and China's BRI in Indonesia." *The Singapore Economic Review* 66, no. 1 (2021): 269–292.

Ozawa, Terutomo, and Christian Bellak. "Will China Relocate Its Labor-Intensive Factories to Africa, Flying-Geese Style?" *Transnational Corporations Review* 2, no. 3 (2010): 6–9.

Sautman, Barry, and Hairong Yan. "Friends and Interests: China's Distinctive Links with Africa." *African Studies Review* 2007: 75–114.

Schröppel, Christian, and Nakajima Mariko. "The Changing Interpretation of the Flying Geese Model of Economic Development." *Japanstudien* 14, no. 1 (2003): 203–236.

Shimazu, Naoko. "Diplomacy as Theatre: Staging the Bandung Conference of 1955." *Modern Asian Studies* 2014: 225–252.

Shinn, David H., and Joshua Eisenman. *China and Africa: A Century of Engagement.* Philadelphia: University of Pennsylvania Press, 2012.

Sutter, Robert G. *Chinese Foreign Relations: Power and Policy since the Cold War.* Lanham, MD: Rowman & Littlefield, 2012.

Swaine, Michael D. "Chinese Views and Commentary on the 'One Belt, One Road' Initiative." *China Leadership Monitor* 47, no. 2 (2015): 3–24.

Tang, Xiaoyang. "8 Geese Flying to Ghana? A Case Study of the Impact of Chinese Investments on Africa's Manufacturing Sector." *Journal of Contemporary China* 27, no. 114 (2018): 924–941.

Tull, Denis M. "The Political Consequences of China's Return to Africa." In *China Returns to Africa: A Rising Power and a Continent Embrace*, 27–50. London: Hurst and Company, 2008.

Umejei, Emeka. "China's Engagement with Nigeria: Opportunity or Opportunist?" *African East-Asian Affairs*, nos. 3–4 (2015): 54–78.

Van de Looy, Judith, and Leo de Haan. "Africa and China: A Strategic Partnership?" *Institute for Defence Studies and Analysis: Strategic Analysis* 30, no. 3 (2006): 562–575.

Wang, Fei-Ling, and Esi A. Elliot. "China in Africa: Presence, Perceptions and Prospects." *Journal of Contemporary China* 23, no. 90 (2014): 1012–1032.

Xu, Jiajun, and Paul Hubbard. "A Flying Goose Chase: China's Overseas Direct Investment in Manufacturing (2011–2013)." *China Economic Journal* 11, no. 2 (2018): 91–107.

Xu, Jian, and Yongrong Cao. "Innovation, the Flying Geese Model, IPR Protection, and Sustainable Economic Development in China." *Sustainability* 11, no. 20 (2019): 5707–5084.

Yao, Yang. "Beijing Consensus." In *The Wiley Blackwell Encyclopedia of Race, Ethnicity, and Nationalism*, 1–4. New Jersey: John Wiley & Sons, 2015.

Yee, Herbert S. "The Three World Theory and Post-Mao China's Global Strategy." *International Affairs (Royal Institute of International Affairs 1944–)* 59, no. 2 (1983): 239–249.

Zhao, Suisheng. "China's Global Search for Energy Security: Cooperation and Competition in Asia–Pacific." *Journal of Contemporary China* 17, no. 55 (2008): 207–227.

Chapter 2

China's Foreign Policy toward Africa, 1949–1971

Africa-China-Taiwan Relations

Saidat Ilo

INTRODUCTION

China's foreign policy toward Africa between 1949 and 1971 was inspired by several factors. As a country that had recently ended its colonial rule and out of solidarity, China developed relationships with several African nations and supported their independence movements. Additionally, intense international conflicts with both the USSR and Taiwan incentivized China to take a larger role on the international stage to counteract the influence of its rivals. To explore these complicated motives and evaluate their impacts on relations, this chapter will analyze the trilateral relationship China had with Taiwan and the Soviet Union and explore how it impacted Sino-African affairs between 1949 and 1971.

Before 1950, neither the People's Republic of China (PRC), a communist government on China's mainland, nor the Republic of China (ROC), democracy supporting government that fled to the island of Taiwan, had established ties with many African countries, partially due to the domestic situations within their respective regions: African nations were under European colonial rule; modern-day Taiwan was governed by Japan; and China was engulfed in a civil war that led to a separation from its communist counterpart, the former Soviet Union.

Saidat Ilo

THE PRC AND THE ROC

It is difficult to classify whether Taiwan is a sovereign state, a territory of China, or some combination of both. Before World War II, Japan had sovereignty over the island, as established by the 1895 Treaty of Shimonoseki but this was stripped following the country's defeat through the 1943 Cairo Declaration and the 1945 Potsdam Declaration, both of which expressed the intention of turning control of the islands over to the ROC, the sole government of China at the time.[1] These treaties and declarations, however, neither had legal standing nor addressed Taiwanese sovereignty directly. Consequently, Japanese forces on the island of Taiwan were forced to surrender to the ROC military.[2]

The issue arose again in 1949, following the conclusion of a civil war in China where the ROC that supported democracy was defeated by the communists of the PRC. Members of the ROC fled to Taiwan while the communists established the PRC, led by Mao Zedong, on the Chinese mainland.[3] Chiang Kai-shek, head of the ROC National Party, "insisted his government continued to represent all Chinese people both on the island and the mainland"[4] and ruled with the understanding that Taiwan would be reunited with the mainland. However, in 1951, when a series of treaties formalized Japan's renouncement of Taiwan and other territories failed to specify a successor state or government,[5] it was unclear which country would have control over the island. This issue has yet to be resolved and remains at the crux of tensions between the PRC and ROC, as both entities believe they are sovereign countries.

SINO-RUSSO-AFRICAN RELATIONS

China and the former Soviet Union have a much longer relationship, dating back to the seventeenth century when initial contact was first established between China and Russia. China and the former Soviet Union both embraced communism as a form of government, which helped cement their alliance, and at least for the PRC initially, influenced its foreign policy with Africa until the end of the 1950s. However, by 1949, Russia was governed by the USSR and an isolated China was dependent on its support and assistance. "In 1950, they established a formal Treaty of Friendship, Alliance, and Mutual Assistance . . . during the early stages of the Cold War, as the Soviets, and some Chinese, referred to the relationship as one between 'elder brother and younger brother.' Soviet aid brought technological and economic benefits for China throughout most of the 1950s."[6] However, the relationship between the two communist regions soured as competition grew, and "the

USSR withdrew precipitously its economic aid and refused to assist China's ambitions to become a nuclear weapons state, reflecting and exacerbating mutual anger and mistrust."[7] Both China and the USSR sought communistic international dominance in the developing world.

China's Africa policy, at the time, was dictated by the former Soviet Union. China engaged with the continent only when leaders of the former USSR told it to do so. Although, as early as the 1940s, China supported African nations' bid for independence, neither the PRC nor the ROC had substantial relationships with any African nation. In the 1950s, however, as China's developmental capabilities increased, its view of Africa and the USSR began to change. China's desire to directly engage with the continent resulted from many factors, both domestic and international. China needed to formulate new relationships around the globe to combat American dominance and to begin distancing itself from the USSR. China saw the United States and the USSR as two powers battling for supremacy. For protection, China needed allies that could counter both the United States and the former Soviet Union. So, the country began to develop relationships in Africa and other parts of the world. Initial contacts between China and African countries began in northern Africa with the United Arab Republic (now known as Egypt) in 1956.[8] Additionally, a small number of prominent African leaders—including Walter Sisulu, an antiapartheid activist and member of the African National Congress, and Funmilayo Ransome-Kuti, mother of Fela Kuti, a musician and political activist—visited China in the 1950s. By 1960, the long historical tie between China and the USSR had unraveled. Sino-Soviet relations ended over what China considered to be "unfulfilled expectations and demands on both sides, including the course of China's domestic development, the Soviet Union's relations with the United States, and the question concerning the best strategy for revolution, especially in the Third World."[9]

PRC AND THE ONE-CHINA POLICY IN AFRICA

As China worked to counter Soviet influence in Africa by developing diplomatic connections, the rivalry between the mainland and Taiwan extended beyond their "domestic" implications, to their relationship with African nations. This concern was not felt by the African countries themselves. "Although Taiwan has deployed aid since the 1960s . . . it is probably true that most Africans do not care much who is the 'real' China or with who official diplomatic ties should be established. Most countries would probably opt for relations with both if this was possible."[10]

African leaders, however, began to leverage the competition between the PRC and the ROC for their economic or political benefit. They would agree to recognize one state and not the other in an exchange for goods and services. This exchange of resources for legitimacy angle soon frustrated the PRC, and, unfortunately for the African nations, the PRC created a strict "One-China" policy, whereby nations could only have diplomatic relationships with Beijing and not Taipei. Since then, "Beijing has been known to react violently to any gestures of support—official or otherwise—to Taiwan."[11]

PRC AND SOUTH-SOUTH COOPERATION (SSC)

The 1950s and 1960s ushered in two decades of African resistance, nationalism, and ultimately independence. As a result of African soldiers fighting in World War II, these veterans returned to their respective countries with a new sense of enlightenment and began organizing and implementing strategies to win their independence. Coupled with the creation of the United Nations, an organization that highlighted the importance of human rights, self-determination, and equality, Africans felt it was time to put these things into practice and make them their reality. The African nations including the Gold Coast (modern-day Ghana) in 1951 demanded independence from their colonial powers. Ghana created a national organization to speed up independence. Ghana was ultimately granted independence from Great Britain sparking inspiration in Africa South of the Sahara that independence can be a reality. Asian nations, including China and Taiwan, supported their fight and sought to offer assistance in these decolonization efforts. In 1955, the Bandung Conference where African and Asian leaders convened to discuss new relationships took place. Taiwan was not in attendance at the Bandung Conference as it was undergoing major domestic challenges. As noted by Larkin, "the Asian-African Conference met in Bandung, Indonesia, 18–24 April 1955. Six of the twenty-nine states represented were African: Egypt, Ethiopia, Gold Coast (later Ghana), Liberia, Libya, and Sudan."[12] The Chinese delegation was led by Chou Enlai and Ch'en I and two other men, Ch'en Chia-k'ang and Huang Hua, served as advisers to the delegates; this group would later become key Chinese ambassadors in Africa. Egypt's Gamal Abdel Nasser and Chou Enlai began discussing the early framework of Egypt-China relations. Larkin notes:

> The Bandung Conference was a meeting of governmental representatives in which China, while maintaining an anticolonialist position, sought to reassure her Asian neighbors and establish a reputation for reasonableness. . . . Acknowledging but not stressing anticolonial and antiapartheid issues in Africa was consistent with China's general demeanor at Bandung. Bandung became a symbol of Afro-Asia as a viable political concept. China could more plausibly

and readily concern herself with African affairs if Chinese and Africans were joined by political ties.[13]

The leaders of the conference believed issues faced by both Africa and Asia could be better addressed as a coalition than by individual countries. The Bandung Conference failed to create any meaningful change in the relationship between China and Africa. Although China had good intentions, the desired Afro-Asia relationship failed to materialize. The conference did, however, encourage China to begin discussing the possibility of substantial relationships with African nations because the first Chinese diplomatic contacts with African nations had taken place.

During this time, however, there was also a growing international sentiment that nations in the developing world should support one another. SSC, as it would soon be called, advocated for the formulation of new bi- or trilateral relationships. Stahl describes this phenomenon, "Originally, South-South cooperation reflected the growing interaction between developing countries during the 1950s and 1960s. More broadly speaking, it describes an exchange of resources, technology, and knowledge between developing countries."[14] From a historical perspective, SSC began during the waning of colonialism. Stahl adds:

> South-South cooperation also became a development philosophy, challenging traditional North-South cooperation. Some leading developing countries like China stress that their financial support to other developing countries is based on mutual benefits and partnership, rather than on what is considered an asymmetric donor-recipient relationship.[15]

In 1957, as noted, Ghana became the first sub-Saharan nation to win its independence from Great Britain. Following Ghana's liberation, the desire and reality of independence spread to other African countries. One year later, independence movements emerged in all parts of Africa from West to East to South, ending decades of colonial rule. Chairman Mao, the founding father of the PRC, offered his support for the liberation movements. His encouragement to look to the developing world aligned with the growing SSC movement. In a speech given to the Union of the Populations of Cameroon where young people from Guinea, Kenya, and Madagascar were in attendance, he spoke of the struggle against imperialism. In his remarks Chairman Mao stated:

> The nature of the revolution there is a bourgeois democratic revolution, not a proletarian socialist revolution. On the whole, the struggle of all of Africa is a protracted one. First, please do not think of immediate victory or an over-night triumph; be prepared for a prolonged struggle. If one is not ideologically prepared for prolonged struggle when imperialism is so powerful, one may be

disappointed. Second, please rely mainly on your own efforts, seeking foreign assistance only as a subsidiary.[16]

Remarkably, he went on to note:

> The present revolution in Africa is a struggle against imperialism and a national liberation movement. It is a question of national liberation rather than communism; on that we all agree. . . . Is Africa to be liberated by relying on foreign countries or by relying on the African people themselves? To liberate Africa, it is essential to rely on the African people. African affairs should be run by the Africans themselves by relying on the forces of African people; in the meantime, they should make friends throughout the world, including China. China certainly supports you. . . . Support is therefore a mutual matter. Your anti-imperialist movement is a support to us. It is a support to you when the Soviet Union and China have done well. You may think of China as your friend. We are checking imperialism to divert its forces, so it will not be able to concentrate its forces on oppressing Africa.[17]

Mao's remarks further encouraged these newly independent countries and those seeking to become independent to look to the developing world for support and guidance. His expression of support would lead to new relationships not just between nations in the Global South but between African and Asian nations specifically.

PRC AND THE NON-ALIGNED MOVEMENT (NAM)

In addition to the SSC movement, developing nations in the 1960s began to coalesce under the umbrella of the NAM, an ideology of independence representing a collective response to decolonization, which facilitated the relationship between China and some African nations. It was founded in 1961 at the Belgrade Conference by Kwame Nkrumah of Ghana, Jawaharlal Nehru of India, Josip Broz Tito of Yugoslavia, Gamal Abdel Nasser of Egypt, and Ahmed Sukarno of Indonesia, and its goal was to form foreign policy based on interests and not pressure from the West. The founders stressed that the NAM was not the same as neutralism in that its nations would not be impartial in international affairs, nor would they always disagree with policies put forth by the West.

The NAM views on independence consisted of five main policies: (1) abstinence from any military alliance (in the context of the Cold War), (2) non-adherence to military pacts, (3) support for liberation movements, (4) pursuit of an independent foreign policy and support peaceful coexistence, and (5) opposition to apartheid.[18] China was an observer of the NAM rather than a formal member, but the movement fostered relationships with African states by supporting their efforts toward liberation.

TAIWAN AND AFRICA

As a result of the decolonization movements that were occurring on the continent, the ROC saw these newly independent countries as an opportunity to formulate new and vital relationships. The ROC needed support, most notably in the United Nations, to maintain its seat as the primary government of China, both on the island of Taiwan and the mainland. These new independent nations in Africa and beyond began to coalesce around the notion that they needed to form alliances to counter the power of the countries in the West. The Third World community believed by joining forces they could improve the conditions in their respective nations without seeking the assistance of the very countries that colonized them. While the leader of the PRC was extending a hand to these nations, Taiwan was also engaging in diplomatic affairs. The ROC from 1949 to 1971 engaged in international relations with African nations in an attempt to stop the spread of communism, form relations with other democratic countries, and garner support to maintain its UN seat as the true government of all of China. Taiwan wanted to convince countries not to allow the PRC into the United Nations and maintain the alliances it was forming with African countries. The rivalry between the ROC and the PRC for representation at the UN, which both sides needed for legitimacy on the world stage, dictated Taiwan's relationship with African nations. "Since 1950, the issue of China's representation had been brought to the General Assembly for debate annually."[19] Africa became a battlefield where both the PRC and the ROC wanted to woo these countries since they were now the most significant voting bloc in the UN. Thirteen African states recognized Taiwan as an independent country between 1960 and 1963 whereas only five nations afforded China the same recognition.[20]

The ROC not only wanted to preserve the bilateral relationships it enjoyed with these African nations, but it also needed to garner more support. The ROC created a strategy to accomplish this goal. "Whenever there were independence celebrations, special envoys were dispatched to attend the celebrations and visit the neighboring nations. In 1960 the ROC's special envoy participated in the independence celebration of Cameroon and then visited nine other African countries."[21] That same year, the ROC sent roughly eight representatives every year to twenty-six African countries to engage in bilateral talks, from discussing much-needed aid packages to infrastructure projects in an exchange for their sole political support. "The ROC's inroads into the African continent at the time were made in the more moderate states, particularly those former French colonies with no left-wing opposition groups or liberation movements, such as Congo (Brazzaville), Chad, Gabon, Ivory Coast, Malagasy, Senegal, Togo, and the Upper Volta."[22] The ROC also created Operation Vanguard to provide technical assistance in the area of agriculture development which many African nations needed.

However, not all countries participated in recognizing or engaging in bilateral relationships with China or Taiwan. The Central African Republic, Ethiopia, Niger nor Sierra Leone stayed out of this rivalry.[23] Even with all its efforts, Taiwan could not compete with a growing China. China was able to form relationships not just with African nations but with countries in Latin America and beyond. China spread its economic wings and fostered new economic ties. The final blow came when the United States changed its China policy. In 1971, President Richard Nixon decided to recognize the PRC and phase out its bilateral relationship with the ROC.[24] "The change of the USA policy towards the PRC and the China initiative were construed by many smaller countries in the world community as the imminent dumping of the ROC and the diminishing of the ROC's importance."[25] The leaders of the ROC reacted bitterly to this change and maintain that they were the true government that represented all of China. What the leaders of the ROC refused to acknowledge was the changing tide and they were losing the cache they once had. "The shift of the USA's policy towards the PRC together with the rigid stance of the ROC leadership eventually led to the latter's loss of international recognition at the UN."[26] This new reality was too much for Taiwan to overcome. With the PRC's population and military might, its admission to the UN was inevitable and countries around the world decided to support the PRC's admission into the UN which became official in 1971. The ROC was essentially isolated and shunned by the international community, making way for the PRC to develop more bilateral relations with nations in Africa unfettered.

CHINA-AFRICA RELATIONS

To reduce the Soviet stronghold in Africa, China first had to convince African leaders that the country understood their plight. The PRC could relate to their fights for independence, struggles with development, and disdain for imperialism. To reinforce its message, "Chou's basic argument was a simple one: whatever our ideological and cultural differences, we have two vital goals in common . . . the establishment of our full independence . . . fight against imperialism, colonialism, and neo-colonialism. Furthermore, we are all involved in the common struggle against backwardness and for economic development."[27] China used all of its resources to turn the tide.

"An example of the Sino-Soviet battle was manifested in China's campaign to win African support to exclude Russian participation at the abortive Afro-Asia conference of 1965."[28] China also appealed to those African nations that were still fighting for independence and vocalized the country's support for decolonization from northern to southern Africa.

Its appeal to northern Africa, however, was a difficult one. Egypt and Algerian presidents (Nasser and Ben Bella, respectively) wanted to be leaders in the region and assist other African nations in their liberation efforts. They did not want China to assume that role. "In Morocco . . . Communists were coming to trial on charges of subversion . . . Nasser's Communists are in jail, exile or in retirement . . . Even Ben Bella . . . made it clear that the Communists will not play a leading role in the Algerian revolution."[29]

China also faced difficulties in East Africa. The Chinese approach was to woo individuals it thought were major players, including journalists, politicians, and student-intellects.[30] In addition to trips, funds, and programs, "the Chinese . . . established one of the world's most powerful transmitters so as to beam Swahili, Arabic and English language programs into eastern Africa."[31]

The PRC also provided significant aid to revolutions and both its moral and financial support to Rwandan exiles wanting to return home and seize power and to leaders in Zimbabwe who desired for southern Africa to be controlled by Africans. It also promised full backing to Angola and Mozambique. Additionally, "on April 13, 1964, a typical Peking 'rally' on behalf of South African 'freedom fighters' was held, with various African speakers being featured."[32] The rationale behind these actions was that by influencing revolutionary groups and offering them trips to China, funds, and training programs they could convince them to consider China as a friend and partner.

In East Africa, the results of these strategies were mixed. The nations in the region did recognize the PRC and began formal relations, but the policy prescription was not a durable solution because "a program of 'buying' individuals is not very costly, but its long-run effectiveness may be questioned. . . . Either they are independent-minded men who will take funds but not orders, or they are opportunists whose 'convictions' last only as long as the subsidies."[33] And this proved to be true for East Africa. Although China's presence and assistance in the region were appreciated by national leaders, they still maintained Africans should depend on other Africans to help in their decolonization efforts.

The PRC produced different results in West Africa. In 1960, China began reaching out to West African countries in the form of credits and aid programs. The Chinese also operated tea and rice plantations and wanted to construct cigarette and match factories that would provide jobs to those in the region. China found success in West Africa, in part, because of the political stability that existed. In addition, China's aid programs were much smaller in scale compared to what was extended to other regions in Africa, a lesson the Chinese learned, which released them from having to be involved in the implementation process.[34]

Like the other regions, however, China's West African efforts were met with some challenges. With Nigeria, for example, in the 1960s, some actions taken by the PRC strained relations between the two countries. In 1963, although the Chinese premier Zhou Enlai made a ten-country trip to Africa, Nigeria was not one of the nations he visited.[35] Then, in the late 1960s, China sided with the secessionist region of Biafra during the Nigerian Civil War. Ndubisi Obiaga states that during the conflict, the USSR gave the Lagos military support by backing the "One Nigeria" concept[36] and as a result, China threw its support behind Biafra and indicated its strong dislike for Lagos' pro-Western policies. Once the Nigerian Civil War ended, the PRC's missteps by supporting the secessionist movement left a negative legacy with the new government of Nigeria. Taiwan remained Nigeria's chosen government and favored trading partner.[37]

Through these experiences, the PRC realized it needed to focus on the best approach for wanting to win the hearts and minds of Africans and their leaders to advance relations. China had gone through its own liberation movement, referred to as the People's War, and moved from a strictly agrarian nation to a modernized one with growing international influence. So, it hoped it could serve as an example and symbol of hope to other countries. China contended that because it was once in the same position as the African nations, it could help them progress similarly.

African nations had grown impatient with their development struggles. Many of them used the Western blueprint for modernization but were not advancing as quickly as they would have liked. Growing frustrations afforded China a prime opportunity to step in and offer its own modernization model. "The West has long held sway over much of Africa with its technological and scientific advances. China, beginning as an underdeveloped society, technologically, scientifically, and otherwise . . . had within a relatively short period achieved a meaningful level of development."[38]

The PRC knew it had to financially assist in these fights for independence but what truly turned the tide for African nations in seriously considering the Chinese model was the country itself. "It mattered not whether the formula could be duplicated and executed; in the eyes of the beholder, the People's War formula represented the symbol of liberation. China stood as an example of what was possible for all who sought liberation."[39]

China's liberation support and calls for a more balanced economic world order worked well. Using Tanzania as an early example for sub-Saharan Africa, after the signing of the Sino-Tanzanian Treaty of Friendship in 1965, the bilateral relationship was official. China financed and built the Tanzania-Zambia railway in 1967 and Tanzania's president Nyerere visited China the following year.[40] Tanzania benefited economically and socially because of its connection with China. The success of this bilateral relationship allowed China to capitalize on it with other nations when making the appeal that it was a Third World brethren. By 1970, China's vision of a new balance of power, with the support of African states and with an evolving Third World structure that would benefit nations in the developing world, had come to fruition. The PRC's standing on the international stage formally changed on October 25, 1971. A draft resolution was introduced at the twenty-sixth meeting of the UN General Assembly where most nations voted to oust the ROC and admit the PRC as the only Chinese representative and granting the PRC as one of the five permanent members of the Security Council.[41]

CONCLUSION

If not for the Cold War, the PRC's African foreign policy may not have materialized as early as it did. However, China would still have focused on Africa because the country wanted to create a new international strategy. The creation of Third World alliances and a new world order would not be easy for the PRC. First, it had to reduce the presence of Taiwan and convince African nations a relationship with the PRC and not the ROC would be a better proposition. The PRC also had to reduce the former Soviet Union's footprint in the continent, which it did by convincing African leaders that the USSR was a European nation, which did not understand the history and struggles of Third World countries. The USSR was engulfed in a war with the United States, and it would serve better the nations of the developing world if it stayed out of the conflict and embraced the NAM. As for the ROC, it ultimately lost the battle with the PRC and, as a result, its relationships with African nations were essentially nonexistent by 1971. Although mainland China's foreign policy toward Africa between 1949 and 1971 faced many obstacles, it met these challenges and was able to solidly bond with these newly independent countries for years to come.

NOTES

1. Charney, Jonathan I. and John R.V. Prescott, "Resolving Cross Strait Relationships between China and Taiwan," *The American Journal of International Law* 94 (2000): 457.

2. Eleanor Albert, "China-Taiwan Relations," *Council of Foreign Relations*, December 7, 2016.

3. Scott L. Kastner, "Is the Taiwan Strait Still a Flash Point? Rethinking the Prospects for Armed Conflict between China and Taiwan," *International Security* 40 (2016): 54–92.

4. Albert, "China-Taiwan," 2.

5. Charney and Prescott, "Cross Strait Relationships," 458.

6. Nishta Kaushiki, "Post 9 11 Sino Russo Entente Reshaping the Asian Security Dynamics and Challenges for India," Thesis (Central University of Punjab, 2019). Retrieved from http://hdl.handle.net/10603/254872.

7. Ibid

8. Yu, "Role in Africa," 97.

9. George T. Yu, "China's Role in Africa," *The Annals of the American Academy of Political and Social* Science 432 (1977): 103.

10. Ian Taylor, "Taiwan's Foreign Policy and Africa: The Limitations of Dollar Diplomacy," *Journal of Contemporary* China 11 (2002): 129.

11. Taylor, "Dollar Diplomacy," 128.

12. Bruce Larkin, *China and Africa 1949–1970: The Foreign Policy of the People's Republic of China* (California: University of California Press, 1971), 16.

13. Larkin, *China and Africa 1949–1970: The Foreign Policy of the People's Republic of China*, 18.

14. Anna K. Stahl, "Trilateral development cooperation between the European Union, China and Africa: What prospects for South Africa?," 2012: 11.

15. Stahl, "Trilateral development," 11.

16. Mao Zedong, "Africa's Task Is to Struggle against Imperialism" (speech, Beijing, China, February 21, 1959), https://digitalarchive.wilsoncenter.org/document /118423

17. Ibid.

18. Guy Martin, *African in World Politics: A Pan-African Perspective* (Trenton, NJ: Africa World Press, Inc., 2002).

19. Song-Huann (Gary) Lin, "The Relations between the Republic of China and the Republic of South Africa, 1948–1998," PhD. Thesis (University of Pretoria, 2001), 47.

20. Timothy S. Rich and Bajerjee Vasabjit, "Running Out of Time? The Evolution of Taiwan's Relations in Africa," *Journal of Current Chinese Affairs* 44 (2015): 146.

21. Lin, "The Relations between the Republic of China and the Republic of South Africa, 1948–1998," 48.

22. Ibid.

23. Rich and Banerjee, "Out of Time," 146.

24. Lin, "The Relations between the Republic of China and the Republic of South Africa, 1948–1998," 69.

25. Ibid.

26. Lin, "The Relations between the Republic of China and the Republic of South Africa, 1948–1998," 70.

27. Scalapino, "Sino-Soviet Competition," 641.

28. Yu, "Role in Africa," 98.

29. Scalapino, "Sino-Soviet Competition," 646.

30. Ibid., 646.
31. Ibid., 646.
32. Ibid., 649.
33. Ibid., 647.
34. Ibid., 648.
35. Pat Utomi, *China in Nigeria Center for Strategic & International Studies.* Retrieved from http://csis.org/files/media/csis/pubs/080603_utomi_nigeriachina.pdf
36. Ndubisi Obiaga, *The Politics of Humanitarian Organizations Intervention* (New York: University Press of America, 2004).
37. Utomi, *China in Nigeria Center for Strategic & International Studies.*
38. Yu, "Role in Africa," 100.
39. Ibid., 102.
40. Ibid., 107.
41. Lin, "The Relations between the Republic of China and the Republic of South Africa, 1948–1998," 69.

BIBLIOGRAPHY

Albert, Eleanor. "China-Taiwan Relations." *Council of Foreign Relations*, December 7, 2016.

Charney, Jonathan I., and John R. V. Prescott. "Resolving Cross-Strait Relationships between China and Taiwan." *The American Journal of International Law* 94 (2000): 457.

Kastner, Scott L. "Is the Taiwan Strait Still a Flash Point? Rethinking the Prospects for Armed Conflict between China and Taiwan." *International Security* 40 (2016): 54–92.

Kaushiki, Nishta. "Post 9 11 Sino Russo Entente Reshaping the Asian Security Dynamics and Challenges for India." Thesis, Central University of Punjab, 2019. http://hdl.handle.net/10603/254872.

Larkin, Bruce. *China and Africa 1949–1970: The Foreign Policy of the People's Republic of China.* Berkeley, California: University of California Press, 1971, p. 16.

Lin, Song-Huann (Gary) Lin. "The Relations between the Republic of China and the Republic of South Africa, 1948–1998." PhD Thesis, University of Pretoria, 2001, p. 69.

Martin, Guy. *African in World Politics: A Pan-African Perspective.* Trenton, NJ: Africa World Press, Inc., 2002.

Obiaga, Ndubisi. *The Politics of Humanitarian Organizations Intervention.* New York: University Press of America, 2004.

Rich, Timothy S. Rich, and Bajerjee Vasabjit. "Running Out of Time? The Evolution of Taiwan's Relations in Africa." *Journal of Current Chinese Affairs* 44 (2015): 146.

Scalapino, Robert A. "Sino-Soviet Competition." *Foreign Affairs* 42 (1964): 4.

Stahl, Anna K. "Trilateral Development Cooperation between the European Union, China and Africa: What Prospects for South Africa?" CCS Discussion Paper, no. 4, Centre for Chinese Studies (CCS), Stellenbosch University, Stellenbosch, South Africa (2012): 11.

Taylor, Ian. "Taiwan's Foreign Policy and Africa: The Limitations of Dollar Diplomacy." *Journal of Contemporary China* 11 (2002): 129.

Utomi, Pat. "China in Nigeria Center for Strategic & International Studies." http://csis .org/files/media/csis/pubs/080603_utomi_nigeriachina.pdf.

Yu, George T. "China's Role in Africa." *The Annals of the American Academy of Political and Social* Science 432 (1977): 103.

Zedong, Mao. "Africa's Task Is to Struggle against Imperialism (speech, Beijing, China, February 21, 1959)." https://digitalarchive.wilsoncenter.org/document /118423.

Chapter 3

China's Foreign Policy toward Africa, 1949–1970

Andrew Michael Mashingaidze

INTRODUCTION

Although contact between China and Africa before 1949 was negligible, focused on trade and movement of labor, China's passive interest in Africa changed after 1949 when the Chinese Communist Party (CCP) gained control of a unified China (PRC). The CCP's rise to power ignited an active and thriving foreign policy that has gained momentous traction to this day. What compelled China to direct its diplomatic focus on Africa? What strategies did Beijing put in place to accomplish this goal and to what end? These questions and many more have occupied the minds and discussions of Chinese watchers and analysts old and new. To address these questions, the chapter states that the period 1949–1970 constitutes a crucial period in China's Africa policy. Studying this period helps one understand better China's contemporary relations with Africa. The chapter argues that China's Africa policy, during this time, was premised on China's grand political strategy to reform world politics and ensure the survival of the CCP as the sole and legitimate authority in China. Africa, from China's perspective, was a perfect opportunity for Beijing to assert itself in global politics.

The chapter is divided into five sections. The first section explores China's worldview, specifically the factors that shaped China's foreign policy starting from 1949 going forward. This section also reflects on why Africa has become the focal point of China's foreign policy. The second section discusses the motivations and strategies implemented by China in the formative years of its foreign policy toward Africa. This section explores the alliances and organizations that China participated in as a way of both trying to understand African states and soliciting their partnership to advance its foreign policy objectives. The next section delves into CCP's core interest of being the sole and legitimate representative of China. Not only does this goal manifest in an aggressive diplomatic race with the Republic of China Taiwan (ROC), but it was also a significant factor in China's need to challenge dominant imperialist and colonialist powers of the time. The fourth section discusses China's shift from a conciliatory approach, as discussed in the second section of this chapter, to adopt a more systematic and methodical revolutionary approach. China believed that staging a successful revolution in Africa would deliver a huge blow to its two main enemies, the United States and the Soviet Union. Lastly, China's diplomatic maneuvers in Africa were without challenges.

Analyzing the challenges that China faced in formulating its Africa policy, in some way, reaffirms or reiterates the objective of this chapter that set out to show China's desire to reform the structure and functioning of the international system. However, a closer look at these different goals of Beijing's foreign policy shows that there are inherent contradictions in China's policy goals. For instance, the chapter will show how China sought diplomatic support from the ruling regimes in Africa so the PRC could be admitted into the United Nations (UN); however, this diplomatic move contradicts Beijing's support for revolutionary movements that sought to overthrow the ruling regimes.

SITUATING AFRICA IN CHINA'S FOREIGN POLICY WORLDVIEW

Although some China-Africa analysts have deployed historical narratives dating as far back as the Ming and Tang Dynasties, particularly the voyages of Eunuch Zheng He as proof of China's contact with Africa,[1] such narratives do not establish why Africa became so important to China. To gain a nuanced understanding of Africa's position in China's foreign policy strategy after 1949, it is crucial to have a firm grasp of China's worldview at the time. China's foreign policy interests, just like any other state, are a function of its position in the international community of states. The post-1949 political environment in China was a complex and conflictual period in which Chinese leaders sought to reconcile past experiences with an imagined political environment that they envisioned during this time. A leader's personal traits have a great impact on a state's foreign policy processes and outcomes. These traits include style, beliefs, values, and goals or motives.[2] By this reasoning, it would follow that China, due to its experiences with colonial powers complemented by Chairman Mao Zedong's beliefs, had the goal of restructuring world politics in an effort to regain its long-lost powerful status and to the benefit of the formerly colonized states,[3] a category of states that China perceived itself to be a leading member.[4]

To what extent, then, does China's worldview shapes its foreign policy behavior toward Africa? Exploring this question has the effect of exposing China's goals and objectives of pursuing an Africa-oriented policy. It is indisputable that China's foreign policy toward Africa, or any other state or region for that matter, is specifically meant to preserve or advance the CCP's legitimate hold on political authority in China. This implies that the narratives used by the CCP to rationalize Chinese foreign policy in Africa are a means of preserving its legitimate rule. This also entails that narratives that are not fixed narratives can be modified, emphasized, or downplayed to fit varying circumstances and interests of the CCP at any given time. However, these narratives are not the only factors that shape Chinese foreign policy.[5] Events that were unfolding in the international environment, specifically the Cold War and domestic issues such as the influence of party leaders on the policy-making processes, guided the formulation of China's Africa policy at the time.[6]

A state's identity has a significant bearing on the kind of foreign policy that the state adopts. A state's foreign policy practices, that is, its interaction with other states in the international community, become the primary way through which it establishes its position in the international system. This approach to foreign policy entails that a state's identity becomes a "site in which political struggles are enacted."[7] Just like in any other state where foreign policy behavior is guided by its interactions in the community of states, China's foreign policy toward Africa in the first two decades after the CCP's ascendency to power was guided by its identity in relation to other Western states that dominated the international system and with the Third World.

Up until the late eighteenth century, China identified itself as an important player in the international system and as a middle kingdom, which was a powerful force in Asia. As such, it is a commonly held belief in China that since Beijing was a strong and respectable global actor in the past, it is natural and rightful that China regains this role. Such a belief provides insight into China's worldview relative to other states during this period. Three elements of China's worldview help understand Beijing's foreign policy from 1949 to 1970. These are history as identity, China's century of humiliation, and China's inherent and unchanging cultural characteristics.

To understand how China perceives itself in the international system one must grasp the functions of the tribute system that was part of China's interaction with other states until the end of the nineteenth century. For nearly two thousand years, China presided over a system that guided trade and diplomatic contact with its neighbors and other distant states that sought economic or political interaction with China. The tribute system saw states that desired to collaborate with China, paying tribute in the form of economic payments to China and in return, they would be accorded economic benefits or political security. The system was meant to ensure stability within a region of autonomous states. This historical narrative or the use of history as destiny in China was crucial in creating loyalty and legitimacy for the CCP as the only party that can rejuvenate China's leading role in the international system.[8]

However, China's glory days coincided with the rapid industrialization and increasing military strength of Great Britain, instigating a period of confrontation. While Chinese tea was in great demand in Britain, China, which was self-sufficient, was in turn reluctant to buy large quantities of products from Britain. In trying to balance the trade deficit between the two, Britain began selling opium produced in India, which was controlled by the British East India Company. When the Chinese rulers banned opium consumption in the kingdom in 1839 citing addiction problems, the stage was set for the First Opium War. This confrontation with the British marked the beginning of what is now known as the "century of humiliation" (1839–1949) for China—a period in which China's imperial system collapsed; territorial control shrunk; and civil wars, uprisings, and invasions became commonplace. In essence, the century of humiliation describes how China's central role in world affairs dwindled. China's conception of "international" rapidly changed from being at the center of the tributary system to become a member of a global system of power dynamics beyond China's control.[9]

The Qing dynasty intellectuals considered China's experiences during the century of humiliation as a sign of China's lack of knowledge and resources necessary for it to integrate into the international system. Many Western texts on economics, political systems, and business were imported as part of the Qing intellectuals' efforts to understand how powerful states operated. These intellectuals were particularly concerned with two questions: What was the Chinese weakness that made it fail to adapt to Western incursion? What is it that China had to do in order for it to regain its central position in Asia and in the world? Although the first question is important, it is the second question that is crucial and relevant to the chapter's aim of understanding China's view and aspirations in the international system. The Qing intellectuals were of the view that nation-states in the international system interacted with each other in a certain way that was foreign or unfamiliar to China. This unfamiliarity with the operation or culture necessary for a state to survive in the international system saw China lagging as Western states and Japan dominated the international system. Liang Qichao was among the Chinese scholars who combined the liberal, statist, evolutionary, and Confucian theories to come up with competing views of how the international system in which China had been prematurely thrust into work. The scholars concluded that human history, including the history of nations, was "driven by a competitive dynamic." This implies that evolutionary competition between groups was a necessary and natural feature of interaction between states and a foundation of conflict and expansionism. States that successfully took part in this evolutionary competition gained dominance and the privilege to dictate terms of engagement with other states. Thus, the intellectuals considered the international system as a conflictual, zero-sum field wherein some states have to be down for others to be up. This characterization of the international system uncovered the inequality of nation-states, a feature that Chinese elites sought to redress.[10]

The aggression that characterizes the interaction of states in the international system, as postulated by Chinese scholars earlier, brings this discussion to the third but less familiar Chinese worldview, which places China's inherent and unchanging cultural characteristics right at the center of China's worldview. This commonly held attitude or belief not only informs how China relates to other states but also influences the formulation of its foreign policies. This view, although rhetorical since all states have some great things or virtues to say about their foreign policy, considers China as an inherently peaceful state that has never been aggressive or expansionist in the past. This belief is based on the fact that the notion of peace in China has been carried down over generations and generations. Confucian benevolence, forbearance, trustfulness, and equality sum up the unchanging values behind China's foreign policy. These values are embodied in the "Five Principles of Peaceful Coexistence" guiding China's conduct with other states. Thus, China is expected to act in the same manner in the future.[11]

In as much as China's belief in peace and peaceful coexistence suggests that its behavior toward other states is nonaggressive, this does not also imply that China does not intend to review the structure and functioning of the international system. China's expectation is for the five principles of peaceful coexistence to apply to all states, becoming the basis upon which the new international system functions. What this means is that, instead of adopting or implementing the militaristic or expansionist policies of Western states (and later Soviets), China seeks to create and lead a new international order through appealing morally to other states.[12]

Further, China's interest in Africa soon after 1949 can also be understood through exploring Mao Zedong's views on the Third World. The central tenant of Mao's Third World theory is the concept of a united front strategy that has its origins in the 1920's cooperation between the CCP and the Nationalist Party against regional warlords. Mao also advocated this united front strategy during the anti-Japanese fight and in the war against Chiang Kai-shek's Nationalist Party. The essence of Mao's strategy was on concentrating efforts of various groups in attacking the central enemy. Mao applied this rationality in categorizing global states into First, Second, and Third World states. The First World denoting the two superpowers—the United States and the Soviet Union; the Third World denoted the developing states in Asia, Africa, Latin America; and the Second World referred to developed states between the First and the Third Worlds. China did not apply a fixed formula in determining these three categories. Instead, these categories were born out of Chinese leader's view of the global situation vis-à-vis their place in it. If there is no fixed formula, it also entails that the composition of these categories can be modified to adapt to changing situations in the international system. For instance, the Soviet Union was, in the early years, China's ally but later became China's main political enemy. Further, China's global ambition to change the international order becomes apparent when China identifies itself as a part of the Third World.[13]

FORMATIVE YEARS OF CHINA'S AFRICA POLICY: BEIJING'S HISTORICAL IDENTITY AND PEACEFUL COEXISTENCE STRATEGY

At the time the CCP ascended to power in 1949, Africa was not high on China's foreign policy agenda. Bruce Larkin described China's contact with Africa as "few and scattered."[14] Beijing was at the time primarily concerned with ensuring stability within its territorial borders through unifying all the regions under its control and resolving border disputes with Xinjiang, Tibet, and Manchuria. Further, China's foreign policy interests, at the time, were focused on neighboring Asian states, the Soviet Union, and the United States. The CCP prioritized relations and or policies that advanced the perpetual authority of the Communist Party.[15] Although Africa was not a priority at this time, Beijing acknowledged the central role Africa would play in its foreign policy in the future,[16] implying that the CCP's strategic thinking could see events in the world beyond its history and experiences.[17]

China's limited contact with Africa, at the time, is also evident in the occasional high-ranking diplomatic visits from the two continents. Chinese officials, specifically Liao Ch'eng-chih and Lui Ning-I, only met with African officials through Soviet-organized international organizations. On the African side, a few African top officials including Walter Sisulu of South Africa's African National Congress and Félix-Roland Moumié of the Union des Populations du Cameroun were among the few top officials who had visited China. In addition to the lack of diplomatic contact between the two, China's comments on African affairs were neither persistent nor worthy of atten-tion. Lastly, the fact that none of the four independent African states, Egypt, Liberia, Ethiopia, and South Africa, recognized China portrays the distant and insignificant relationship that China and Africa had during the first few years of the CCP's coming to power.[18]

In the early 1950s, contact between China and Africa was through various front groups established by the CCP to engage like-minded groups in Africa. These groups also presented China with an opportunity to culture its actions and perceptions of Africa in a way that was consistent with the Chinese ideology at the time. The party-based mass organizations, united front groups, and people's organizations were created to boost the CCP's relations with Africa's liberation movements and or political organizations. The All-China Student Federation, All-China Youth Federation, the Afro-Asia People's Solidarity Organisation (AAPSO), and the China-Africa People's Friendship Association are some of the prominent organizations tasked by the CCP to solicit, maintain, and advance China's relations in Africa.[19]

Of all these organizations, the AAPSO played a dominant role in China's diplomacy in Africa. Given the fact that China's contact and activities in Africa during these early days were low, the AAPSO became the main channel through which China conducted its diplomatic relations and political outreach in Africa.[20] Although branches of the Soviet-controlled World Peace Movement first proposed the establishment of the AAPSO in 1955 at the Conference for the Relaxation of International Tensions convened in New Delhi, the organization was officially established on December 26, 1957, during the Solidarity Conference of Afro-Asian Peoples held in Egypt, as an extension of the Bandung Conference discussed here.[21] At this time, China had not pronounced its Africa policy and its perceptions and involvement with Africa were all done in close cooperation with the Soviet Union. This means that China's anti-imperialism, pro-independence, and pro-revolutionary policies in the Third World and Africa in particular were developed in coordination with the Soviet Union and channeled to Africa through the AAPSO.[22] The significance that this organization had in the formulation of China's Africa policy is that it presented an already established network of political organizations that had the same anticolonialist objectives. By the time the AAPSO was established, the African Association was gaining strength in both its numbers and reputation for African decolonization. All China had to do was tap into the association's infrastructure and networks to deliver China's political ambitions across the continent. Print and broadcast propaganda became China's main tools for encouraging a radical revolutionary strategy on the continent.[23] Furthermore, China's participation or contribution to the AAPSO magnifies contradictions in China's Africa policy. The use of propaganda to call for a radical revolution (presumably Mao-style communist revolution) contradicts the Bandung spirit of peaceful coexistence between states.

The fact that the CCP played a major role in the creation or functioning of these organizations implies that the CCP directed these organizations' mandate albeit in varying degrees. For instance, the constitution of the All-China Youth Federation, which was a CCP mass organization, appointed members of the Union of Chinese Writers, which was a front group. In addition, the All-China Youth Federation was bound by its constitution to support the CCP's anti-imperialism and anticolonialism struggle. The Union of Chinese Writers was responsible for the Liaison Committee of the Permanent Bureau of the Afro-Asian Writers Conference. Further, China's creation of political networks in Africa was also pursued through media publications. The *World Culture*, a CCP magazine, published an article on October 25, 1954, titled "Foreign Relations of New China during the Past Five Years" that called for the CCP to adopt an active approach to global affairs. The article identified the common trait among African, Asian, and Latin American states to oppose colonialism and imperialism as an opportunity for China to take proactive steps in reaching out to African political organizations.[24]

If Africa was not immediately crucial in China's foreign policy strategy in the first few years after 1949,[25] what changes prompted China to turn its focus toward Africa. One plausible response to Beijing's policy shifts to prioritize Africa and the developing world in general rests in the significant benefits to its overall foreign policy objectives that its partnership with African states would bring.

The Bandung Conference of 1955 was a seminal moment for China's outreach in Africa.[26] This Asia-African Conference cosponsored by the governments of Burma, India, Indonesia, Pakistan, and Sri Lanka brought together, in one venue, representatives of African states or liberation movements and CCP officials, creating an opportunity for China to create itself a favorable image in the eyes of African states, an image or model of self-reliance through struggle. Out of the twenty-nine states that attended the conference, six were African countries—Egypt, Ethiopia, Ghana, Liberia, Libya, and Sudan. This unique opportunity further presented China with a chance to advance its international ambitions of creating like-minded states based on past injustices under Western colonialism, to put together a force that would bring about a new international order. This Asian and African coalition force was guided by the principle of peaceful coexistence that was adopted at the conference.[27]

Further, the principles of peaceful coexistence agreed upon at the Bandung Conference sought to tackle issues surrounding self-determination, decolonization, economic cooperation, and global peace. These principles included nonintervention in the internal affairs of other states, nonaggression, mutual respect, respect for sovereignty, and equality among global states.[28] A closer look at these principles reveals an underlying desire by these Asian and

African states to see a change in the way the international system operated. All the principles reflect a higher degree of opposition to Western aggression and colonialism, seeking a new era in which all peoples regardless of race were treated equally. As such, the Bandung Conference was an attempt by the Third World states of Asia and Africa to construct a common ideology that would champion the creation of new postcolonial world order[29] and China assumed a leadership role for this group of states. Nevertheless, it is crucial to point out that, from the very beginning, some of the principles contradicted China's own ideological urge for world revolution. China went for these principles when it was vulnerable and worried about Western interference in China itself.

Considering the geographical separateness and the differing colonial experiences that the attending states had, it is no surprise that conflictual interests would arise. China in particular, due to its participation in Soviet-sponsored organizations and events, considered the conference as an opportunity to create a network of similar-minded states that had a similar background crucial in China's goal of exporting revolution across the globe.[30] Even though most conference participants feared the prospects of war and revolution held by China, which was at the center of world attention at the time, Premier Zhou Enlai managed to calm the situation stressing that China had no intention to go to war against the United States.[31] Zhou's remarkable handling of the situation, placing Beijing as ready to negotiate with its main enemy, the United States, on the ROC issue gained China a good reputation of being reasonable and accommodating. The prestigious personal diplomatic skills exhibited by Zhou at the conference enhanced China's image in the eyes of participating states, creating a platform from which China presented its Third World credentials. These Third World credentials form the backbone of China's Africa policy.[32] However, the fact that other conference participants became uneasy with the motives behind China's participation is a good indicator of the policy stance that China took vis-à-vis the prevailing international system.[33]

Further, the failure to convene a second Bandung Conference in 1965 was primarily due to these conflicting interests. The Bandung spirit that had emerged in the first conference was overshadowed by radical demands by some states, including China, that called for the reconfiguration of colonial relations and the capitalist system that sustained them. These radical calls departed from the initial national-democratic aspirations agreed in the first conference that sought the reconstitution of the Third World states that had endured unequal treatment during colonialism.[34]

China's radical aspirations to reconfigure the international order found fertile ground in Africa after the Bandung Conference. China's sudden prioritization of Africa was motivated by the fact that Africa had the potential of making the most impact in its anti-imperialist campaign as compared to Asia. Of all the African states that attended Bandung, as mentioned before, only five were independent. Thus, approximately forty-five African states at that time were still under some form of colonialism. By exporting revolution to these colonized African states, China saw an opportunity to ensure the greatest damage to Western colonialism and Soviet revisionism. Acting on this strategy, the Chinese government created a ministry specifically dedicated to Asian and African Affairs and in 1958 established the Chinese Commission for Cultural Relations with Foreign Countries.[35]

The post-Bandung period saw a gradual rise in China's involvement in Africa, concentrating first with Egypt in North Africa. China's prioritization of Egypt was because Gamal Abdel Nasser was the only president of an independent African state who attended the first Bandung Conference. Beijing entered agreements with Egypt that provided for trade in cotton and with military assistance during the Suez Crisis of 1956. China's anticolonial campaign further extended to Algeria, where it ran Algeria's propaganda as well as supplied ammunition and training to the National Liberation Front in its conflict with France. Ethiopia, Morocco, Sudan, and Tunisia were no exceptions to Beijing's charm offensive during this time. Participation in international conferences has become China's diplomatic weapon in Africa. For instance, the Afro-Asian Peoples' Solidarity Conference was held in Egypt in 1957 and the First Conference of Independent African States convened in Ghana in 1958.[36] The Chinese-African People's Friendship Association established in 1960 assumed the responsibility of organizing visits by African diplomats to China and vice versa. The organization moved fast, putting together a ten-member Chinese diplomatic team that extensively toured West Africa (visiting Guinea, Ghana, Mali, Niger, Upper Volta, Senegal, Togo, and Dahomey) in 1961.[37]

Africa's relevance to China's grand political strategy further deepened during the 1960s, facilitated by the breaking down of relations between Beijing and the Soviet Union.[38] Several interpretations of the conflict that eventually led to the Sino-Soviet split have been suggested. These include unresolved territorial issues, differing ideological interpretations of Marxism-Leninism, conflicting ambitions in the communist movement and the developing world, and personality differences among Russian and Chinese elites.[39] The disastrous Great Leap Forward implemented under Chairman Mao from 1958 to 1962 brewed an intraparty factional fight within the CCP which resulted in the rapid deterioration of the relationship between the CCP and the Communist Party of the Soviet Union (CPSU). Because of this fallout, the CCP adopted an anti-Soviet stance in its interactions with African organizations. China's then defense minister Peng Dehuai's July 14 letter that called for the reassessment of the losses of the Great Leap Forward, which was interpreted in the same light as Khrushchev's admission of the failures of the CPSU's experiments with the commune system, led Mao to suspect Peng of being a Soviet agent. As a result, Mao condemned Peng's antiparty comments and his criticism of the Great Leap Forward, accusing him of aiding the Soviets in a coup attempt. When the Soviets withdrew their experts and aid from China, a full-blown confrontation between the two communist organizations began. Thus, China's anti-Soviet stance was a political move to solidify Mao's position in the party in relation to his rivals who disagreed with the Great Leap Forward.[40]

However, this chapter focuses on the international dimension of the conflict in which Beijing accused the Soviet Union of revisionism or betraying the socialist revolution, after its policy rapprochement toward the West. China was determined to uphold its revolutionary policy that would serve as a model for independence-seeking Third World countries, but the Soviets had shifted their policy position, adopting an antirevolutionary stance. The Soviet Union, during this time, believed underdeveloped states were not yet ready for the kind of revolution that would make a difference in the international system of governance. Without the Soviet Union as the leader of the communist revolution, China believed that its model, based on its experiences with oppression, would provide an alternative model to champion the socialist revolution.[41]

Chairman Mao's ambition to see through the fall of imperialism, colonialism, and the restructuring of the international order manifested in his Third World theory. Mao's theory had the effect of enticing African states, winning them over to Beijing's side on the one hand, and on the other hand, it clearly expressed Beijing's opposition to the West and the Soviet Union. The Third World theory served to create a mutual identity between China and African states as well as other states in the developing world, and identity starkly opposed to that of the First and Second World categories. By considering itself as part of the developing world, China sought to assume a leadership role in reforming the world system through fighting for equality among states. Because of this political stance, China gained significant political mileage in Africa between 1960 and 1965.[42]

In the same way, that China developed its Africa policy in coordination with the Soviet Union through the AAPSO, the Sino-Soviet dispute became an open affair within the AAPSO and its offshoots, with the two communist giants trading "vituperative attacks and counterattacks." Beijing moved to dictate the policy position of the AAPSO, insisting that the organization adopt as its resolutions China's formulas on "national revolution and the necessity of armed struggle." Such a move meant that the Soviet's policies of coexistence and disarmament were not to be entertained in the organization.[43]

China's deepening relations with Africa saw an increase in high-level diplomatic visits. Guinea's Ahmed Sékou Touré became the first African president to visit China marking the genesis of an increasing frequency of African diplomats arriving in China. On the other hand, the much-publicized Zhou Enlai's 1963 tour of ten African states, also known as Zhou's "Safaris," was both a clear indication of the increasing importance that Africa was becoming to China and a way of selling China's benevolent image across the continent. Fourteen of Africa's newly independent states (Ghana, Mali, Zaire, Uganda, Burundi, Kenya, Benin, Somalia, Central African Republic, Congo-Brazzaville, Tanzania, Tunisia, Zambia, and Mauritania) entered diplomatic relations with China during this period.[44]

THE "ONE CHINA POLICY": A BID TO BLOCK TAIWAN IN AFRICA

The 1960s were a significant period in Africa's international politics. It was a period in which most African states became independent and were admitted as full members of the UN. This development meant that African states, due to their numbers and high probability of banding together when voting, had a significant role to play in the UN. The strategic position that African states had assumed saw the PRC and ROC intensifying their zero-sum competition to win over as many African allies as possible. Since 1949, the two Chinas jostled for influence internationally. For the PRC, winning over African states would see it taking over the UN seat that had been held by the ROC, a goal it achieved in 1971. As a permanent member of the UN, the PRC would be in a greater position to further its desires of confronting superpower hegemony, thereby reforming the international system. As for the ROC, maintaining or increasing its African allies was more a matter of recognition, a necessary standard in the modern state system.[45]

Foreign aid assistance to Africa became one of the major tools through which the two Chinas used to compete for legitimacy in Africa. For the PRC, economic aid was the most influential foreign policy instrument for winning over African allies. Although the PRC's aid was meant to serve its economic and political self-interests, it also had a great impact in Africa since it was provided generously with no strings attached. By giving out assistance to African states, China helped capacitate these states to free themselves from Western imperialism and colonialism. In essence, the PRC used aid to Africa as a weapon to further its foreign policy ambitions. Although China, at the time, was not strong economically, its dispute with the Soviet Union and ROC inevitably drew China into the "aid war" in Africa.[46] This "aid war" saw the PRC using foreign aid as a mechanism to isolate ROC destroying its status internationally.

For ROC, aid was a means of survival as a globally recognized state. ROC's foreign assistance was distributed to its African allies under "Operation Vanguard." Operation Vanguard was designed to capacitate African states with sustainable food production. The ROC dispatched technicians to teach and assist in the modernization of African farming methods. This operation had its successes evidenced by the fact that twenty-two African states had established diplomatic relations with ROC by 1969. However, ROC's diplomatic successes in Africa were short lived as most of these African allies switched to the PRC when the PRC took over the UN Security Council seat in 1971.[47]

What we have observed so far is that the CCP through Mao's Third World theory sought to lead the coalition of the colonized and formerly colonized states; it sought to lead the democratic revolution in the Sino-Soviet dispute and the conflict with ROC and the PRC sought to be the sole legitimate representatives of China. It follows that leadership is at the core of China's foreign policy. The same could be said about China's ambitions in the international system. Further, China's aid race in Africa must have been motivated by the fact that Taiwan's aid was funded by an American surplus from the sale of agricultural products. Thus, the PRC's successes in winning over African allies through providing more aid and other measures can be interpreted as PRC win over the United States.[48] By the time ROC was replaced by the PRC at the UN, African allies were somewhat evenly split between the two states, with ROC having twenty-two allies as compared to twenty-two for the PRC. Today, all African states have shifted diplomatic recognition from ROC to PRC except for one, the small Kingdom of Eswatini.[49]

CONSTRUCTIVE POLICIES: CHINA'S SUPPORT FOR AFRICAN SELF-RELIANCE THROUGH REVOLUTION

The increasing tensions between Beijing and the Soviet Union in the early 1960s and the increasing number of independent states on the African continent created an environment in which Beijing abandoned its conciliatory and peaceful coexistence approach to foreign policy in favor of a more revolutionary attitude. The increasing independence of African states in the 1960s implied that African states were open to adopting a new social and economic model. This increased Beijing's enthusiasm to put its revolutionary policy into practice. Beijing was of the view that if Africans understand the Chinese revolutionary experiences they might be able to deal with their problems. This belief held by China had the effect of universalizing its historical experiences across the Third World. The Chinese elites were so confident that their experiences would greatly benefit African states to the extent that they proposed teaching Africans Chinese history. Foreign minister Chen Yi reiterated this claim by stating that "our yesterday is their today and our today is their tomorrow."[50]

Beijing's revolutionary policy in Africa was based on two approaches: support for revolutionary movements or states fighting for freedom against colonial powers and promoting self-reliance. China's adoption of these two approaches shows Beijing's increasing intentions to challenge global powers that were engaged in colonial activities on the continent. At this point, China's confrontational intentions became clear, replacing the somewhat ambiguous and disjointed peaceful coexistence stance in favor of a methodical and concrete revolutionary strategy.[51]

In supporting African revolutionary movements, China provided symbolic as well as substantive support to African states. Symbolically, the CCP sought to instill a favorable image of itself in the minds of Africans. As such, the party reached out to Africans to take up higher education opportunities in China. Upon arrival, the African delegates were treated with absolute respect, paraded through streets, and mingled with top-ranking CCP officials. Through this gesture, the African delegates would adopt a positive view of China, which in turn helped advance Beijing's diplomacy and soft power in Africa. China's desire to rally African allies extended beyond symbolic gestures to include material support to African revolutionary movements fighting for their freedoms against colonialism and imperialism. Throughout the 1960s–1970s, China provided $22 billion in the form of aid and loans to African revolutionary parties. Beijing's commitment to this policy is evident given the fact that China itself was in a poor economic state at the time; however, it sacrificed the little resources that it had, overlooking its domestic challenges, to support Africa's quest for independence. China's conduct here, often captured as a case of "the poor helping the poor," implies that the freedom of African states had a significant bearing on China's foreign policy calculations.

In China's view, freedom is not fully achieved unless it is preceded by self-reliance. Having developed a positive view of China, African elites were expected to sever relations with Western imperialism and its systems as well as Soviet revisionism. In other words, the successful implementation of revolutionary democracy, led by China, in Africa would have changed not only the power configuration of the international system but its principles and values as well. Zhou Enlai's tour of Africa in 1963–1964 carried this message of self-reliance to every corner of the African continent. Zhou's message was positively received in Africa, as shown by the increasing number of African states that established diplomatic relations with China increased from the 1960s going forward.[52]

DESTRUCTIVE AMBITIONS: CHALLENGES TO CHINA'S POLICY STRATEGY IN AFRICA

Without any doubt, China's campaign in Africa was achieving remarkable results in the early 1960s. Beijing's rising popularity on the continent was supported by the fact that by 1965 half of the thirty-six independent African states had established diplomatic contact with Beijing. However, China's successes in Africa were interrupted by unforeseen circumstances in China's strategic conduct in Africa. The postponement of the second Asian-African conference scheduled for Algiers in 1965 delivered a major blow to China's diplomatic offensive. Some of the participating states did not quite understand China's actual objectives, particularly its aggressive revolutionary policies toward Africa. What resulted was a postponement of the conference and dwindling popularity of China in Africa evidenced by two African states, the Central African Republic and Dahomey, breaking diplomatic relations with Beijing while relations with Ghana and Kenya became severely strained.[53]

Africa's warning diplomatic relations with China came about due to the circumstances surrounding China's policies in the Congo. After abandoning the peaceful coexistence approach in favor of an active revolutionary approach, China's pursuit of its foreign policy goals to end imperialism and colonialism became too ambitious. The switch from peaceful coexistence to radical revolutions was logical from the perspective of the CCP's revolutionary ideology at the time. State diplomacy needed peaceful coexistence, but the CCP ideology called for a world revolution (of a Maoist violent kind). China, as a party-state, was doing a delicate balancing act. China's efforts to simultaneously pursue a united front-from-above and a united front-from-below policy, an overambitious yet highly risky policy attempt to achieve contradictory interests at the same time, did not inspire any confidence among African states. The Congo situation uncovers the fact that China was too impatient and overzealous to effect damaging change to imperialist states changing the structure of international politics. Due to its geographic location and size, the Congo presented a good opportunity, to stage a revolution that would serve as an example for other states in fighting imperialism. On the other hand, China was not willing to be identified as helping the rebels, as this would scare off other African governments that had already established normal relations with Beijing.[54]

The most damaging accusation to China's reputation was the accusation that Beijing was propping up various opposition groups in the Congo through military training and providing arms. Of particular note is China's support for Pierre Mulele, who formerly served in Patrice Lumumba's government, and Gaston Soumialot, former justice minister in the Gizenga government in 1961. In 1963, Mulele led the National Liberation Committee in launching guerrilla attacks in the Kwilu Province based on the Chinese model, from where he had received military training. The same accusations were also leveled against China's relations with Soumialot's group that was based in neighboring Burundi and operated in Kivu and Katanga Provinces.[55]

Although China "regarded it as [its] unshakable and honorable internationalist duty to support the struggle of all oppressed nations and peoples," it desired to keep its activities in the Congo a secret. If compared to the amount of aid provided by the American government to the Congolese government, China's material support to the rebels was sparing and insignificant. Yet China received the most critics from African states for assisting rebel groups. Africans argued that if China supported dissident groups in the Congo to further its policy interests, what guarantees that it will not support opposition groups in their own countries. Because of China's actions in the Congo, its reputation in Africa slumped. The then Nigerian prime minister Sir Abubakar Tafawa Balewa cited China's revolutionary policies in the Congo as one of the major reasons why Nigeria recognized the Soviet Union instead of China.[56]

China's policy objective of bending African states to suit its ambitions of becoming a world power not only led to its disruptive alliance with dissident individuals and groups in the Congo but also its support for dissident Tutsi refugees expelled from Rwanda into Burundi. The Tutsi Inyezi or Cockroaches, named after their behavior of raiding during the night, were financed and trained by China resulting in the escalation of raids in 1963. African elites considered China's actions in Burundi as "pragmatism taken too far," and the silence of Africa's founding fathers like Julius Nyerere and Sékou Touré on this issue was interpreted as a gesture of dissatisfaction. Although no proof was available to implicate China in subversive activities in Burundi, including the assassination of Pierre Ngendandumwe who had succeeded Albin Nyamoya who was removed from office due to his close alliance with China, diplomatic relations between the two were indefinitely suspended. Burundi accused the Chinese ambassador of sabotaging Burundi's efforts at reuniting its peoples. China's opportunistic behavior and poorly thought-out subversive activities in Africa were not only resented in the Congo and Burundi as discussed earlier but such activities have also been detected and denounced in Kenya, Ethiopia, Sudan, Egypt, Central African Republic, Dahomey (now Benin), Upper Volta (now Burkina Faso), and Ghana. African leaders' distaste of

China's disruptive activities was best captured in the words of Jomo Kenyatta when he denounced communism in 1964.[57]

I warn those in our country who seek to create confusion. It is true that we have passed through many years of Western imperialism. It is natural that we should detest Western colonialism, and associate the word imperialism with the West. . . . It is naïve to think that there is no danger of imperialism from the East. In world politics, the East has many designs upon us as the West and would like us serve their own interests. That is why we reject communism. It is in fact the reason why we have chosen ourselves the policy of non-alignment and African socialism. To us communism is as bad as imperialism.[58]

Given the numerous challenges China encountered in Africa during the mid-1960s, it is fair to assert that China pursued an ambition to challenge and undermine the then world powers without the requisite strength. After the Korean War, China challenged America in Vietnam, Japan, Pakistan, and Latin America. Further, China did not hesitate to break ties with the Soviets when they dragged their feet on counter-imperialist policies and with India when it emerged as the leader of the non-aligned movement. In fact, Africa became a perfect platform for Beijing to destroy the influence and reputation of the Soviets and India together with the West. This of course does not imply that China was, during this time, the only state that had a stake in instability in Africa and other parts of the developing world. Rather, it is an attempt to bring forth the Chinese elites' belief that "the road to great power-hood lies through creating and maintaining chaos and instability in large parts of the world over a long enough period in which they can quietly build up their strength to match their global ambitions."[59]

CONCLUSION

In summary, the period 1949–1970 was significant in China's foreign policy toward Africa and the Third World in general. It was a period in which the Chinese communist government reemerged in international politics. Motivated by the need to undo past injustices at the hands of imperialist and colonial powers and the fact that China was once a powerful and central kingdom, China's Africa policy was developed as a means to achieve its foreign policy goals of restructuring the configuration of power in the international system. In other words, China's Africa policies were part of a grand foreign policy strategy to challenge US imperialism and Soviet revisionism to restore China's status as a powerful global actor.

Although China's foreign policy objectives were clear, its foreign policy toward Africa was not instantly pronounced after 1949. Instead, China developed its policies gradually experimenting and learning from its experiences. In the first decade after 1949, China was particularly interested in establishing relations with African states or political organizations. This was motivated by the fact that China considered Africa as the perfect platform from which it can fight and defeat Western imperialism, colonialism, and later Soviet revisionism. As part of its strategy to win over African allies, Beijing took part in international organizations like the AAPSO and participated in conferences like the Bandung Conference that advocated for Third Word freedoms. This presented China with an opportunity to work with and later influence African elites. Domestic considerations, particularly the CCP's quest to be regarded as the sole and legitimate representative of the people, emerged as a major concern driving China's Africa policy. Such a desire saw Beijing battling the ROC for diplomatic recognition in Africa. Thus, if one combines China's need to challenge imperialism and colonialism with the need to maintain its status as the legitimate representative of China, a more confrontational and systematic policy would be inevitable. The period from 1960 to 1970 saw China instituting a more revolutionary foreign policy toward Africa, assisting in the form of aid and loans to states and political movements that were willing to rise against colonial powers and against independent regimes that were not to the CCP's ideological liking on the continent. Although China encountered challenges in the process of developing and pronouncing its Africa policy, as was the case in the Congo, Beijing's impatience and double standards show the level of determination China had against the international dominance of the imperialist United States and revisionist Soviets. By the end of this period, China was a winner in state diplomacy, namely African states supported China in its UN bidding, replacing the ROC. However, this support at the state level came after Mao's China became less zealous in urging violent revolution in Africa. After all, Beijing started to mend fences with the United States beginning in 1970.

NOTES

1. Marcus Power, Giles Mohan and May Tan-Mullins, "Contextualizing China–Africa Relations," in *China's Resource Diplomacy in Africa*. International Political Economy Series (London: Palgrave Macmillan, 2012): 30, https://doi.org/10.1057/9781137033666_2.

2. David. G Winter, "Leadership Personality Characteristics and Foreign Policy," in *Oxford Bibliographies in International Relations* (New York: Oxford University Press, 2019). doi: 10.1093/OBO/9780199743292-0256.

3. Merriden Varrall, "Chinese Worldviews and China's Foreign Policy," Lowy Institute, November 26, 2015, https://www.lowyinstitute.org/publications/chinese-worldviews-and-china-s-foreign-policy.

4. George T. Yu, "China and the Third World," *Asian Survey* 17, no. 11 (1977): 1036.

5. Varrall, "Chinese Worldviews and China's Foreign Policy."

6. Stuart Harris, *China's Foreign Policy* (Cambridge, UK: Polity Press, 2014).

7. Adel Altoraifi, "Understanding the Role of State Identity in Foreign Policy Decision-Making: The Rise and Demise of Saudi–Iranian Rapprochement (1997–2009)," (PhD Dissertation, London School of Economics and Political Science, 2012), 46–48.

8. Varrall, "Chinese Worldviews and China's Foreign Policy."

9. Alison Adcock Kaufman, "The 'Century of Humiliation,' Then and Now: Chinese Perceptions of the International Order," *Pacific Focus* 25, no. 1 (2010): 1–2, doi: 10.1111/j.1976-5118.2010.01039.x.

10. Kaufman, "The 'Century of Humiliation,' Then and Now," 6–10.

11. Varrall, "Chinese Worldviews and China's Foreign Policy."

12. Chris Alden and Ana Cristina Alves, "History & Identity in the Construction of China's Africa Policy," *Review of African Political Economy* 35, no. 115 (2008): 45.

13. Herbert S. Yee, "The Three World Theory and Post-Mao China's Global Strategy," *International Affairs* 59, no. 2 (1983): 240–243.

14. Bruce D. Larkin, *China and Africa 1949–1970: The Foreign Policy of the People's Republic of China* (Berkeley: University of California, 1973), 15.

15. Alan Hutchison, *China's African Revolution* (Boulder, CO: Westview Press, 1976).

16. Larkin, *China and Africa 1949–1970*, 1.

17. Charles Neuhausen, *Third World Politics: China and the Afro-Asian Peoples Solidarity Organisation*, 2nd ed. (Cambridge: Harvard University Press, 1970), 33.

18. Larkin, *China and Africa 1949–1970*, 14–15.

19. David Hamilton Shinn and Joshua Eisenman, *China and Africa* (Philadelphia: University of Pennsylvania Press, 2012).

20. Chris Alden and Cristina Alves, "History & Identity in the Construction of China's Africa Policy," *Review of African Political Economy* 35, no. 115 (2008): 43–58, doi: 10.1080/03056240802011436.

21. Hutchison, *China's African Revolution*, 37–40.

22. Alden and Alves, "History & Identity in the Construction of China's Africa Policy," 43–58.

23. Reem Abou-El-Fadl, "Building Egypt's Afro-Asian Hub: Infrastructures of Solidarity and the 1957 Cairo Conference," *Journal of World History* 30, no. 1–2 (2019): 183–190. doi: 10.1353/jwh.2019.0048.

24. Joshua Eisenman, "Comrades-in-Arms: The Chinese Communist Party's Relations with African Political Organisations in the Mao Era, 1949–76," *Cold War History* (2018): 3. doi: 10.1080/14682745.2018.1440549.

25. Eisenman, "Comrades-in-Arms," 3.

26. Eisenman, "Comrades-in-Arms," 3.

27. Alden and Alves, "History & Identity in the Construction of China's Africa Policy," 47.

28. Tukumbi Lumumba-Kasongo, "Rethinking the Bandung Conference in an Era of 'Unipolar Liberal Globalization' and Movements toward a 'Multipolar Politics,'" *Bandung: Journal of the Global South* 2, no. 1 (2015): 1. doi: 10.1186/s40728-014-0012-4.

29. Frank Gerits, "Bandung as the Call for a Better Development Project: US, British, French and Gold Coast Perceptions of the Afro-Asian Conference (1955)," *Cold War History* 16, no. 3 (2016): 255–256. doi: 10.1080/14682745.2016.1189412.

30. Alden and Alves, "History & Identity in the Construction of China's Africa Policy," 47.

31. Lumumba-Kasongo, "Rethinking the Bandung Conference in an Era of 'Unipolar Liberal Globalization' and Movements toward a 'Multipolar Politics,'" 11.

32. Sandra Gillespie, "Diplomacy on a South-South Dimension: The Legacy of Mao's Three-Worlds Theory and the Evolution of Sino-Africa Relations," in *Intercultural Communication and Diplomacy* (Geneva: DiploFoundation, 2004), 113–114.

33. Tukumbi Lumumba-Kasongo, "Rethinking the Bandung Conference in an Era of 'Unipolar Liberal Globalization' and Movements toward a 'Multipolar Politics,'" *Bandung: Journal of the Global South* 2, no. 1 (2015): 11. doi: 10.1186/s40728-014-0012-4.

34. Arif Dirlik, "The Bandung Legacy and the People's Republic of China in the Perspective of Global Modernity," *Inter-Asia Cultural Studies* 16, no. 4 (2015): 619–621, doi: 10.1080/14649373.2015.1103024.

35. Hutchison, *China's African Revolution*.

36. Ian Taylor, *China and Africa: Engagement and Compromise* (London: Routledge, 2006).

37. Hutchison, *China's African Revolution*, 49.

38. Yu, "China and the Third World," 1037–1038.

39. Donald S. Zagoria, "Mao's Role in the Sino-Soviet Conflict," *Pacific Affairs* 47, no. 2 (1974): 139, doi: 10.2307/2755604.

40. Eisenman, "Comrades-in-Arms," 3.

41. Taylor, *China and Africa: Engagement and Compromise*.

42. Taylor, *China and Africa: Engagement and Compromise*.

43. Neuhausen, *Third World Politics*, 30–39.

44. Taylor, *China and Africa: Engagement and Compromise*.

45. San-shiun Tseng, "The Republic of China's Foreign Policy towards Africa: The Case of ROC-RSA Relations" (PhD dissertation, University of Witwatersrand, 2008).

46. Hutchison, *China's African Revolution*, 205–206.

47. Tseng, "The Republic of China's Foreign Policy towards Africa," 5–6.

48. Natasha Skidmore, "Taiwanese Development Aid in Africa," *South African Institute of International Affairs* 43 (2002): 3–4.

49. Rich and Banerjee, "Running Out Of Time? The Evolution of Taiwan's Relations in Africa," *Journal of Current Chinese Affairs* 44 (2015): 146.

50. Gillespie, "Diplomacy on a South-South Dimension," 113–120.

51. Gillespie, "Diplomacy on a South-South Dimension," 113–120.

52. Gillespie, "Diplomacy on a South-South Dimension," 113–120.

53. George T Yu, "China's Failure in Africa," *Asian Survey* 6, no. 8 (1966): 463–464.

54. Hutchison, *China's African Revolution*, 110–114.

55. Mohamed A. El-Khawas, "China's Changing Policies in Africa," *Issue: A Journal of Opinion* 3, no. 1 (1973): 24, doi: 10.2307/1166311.

56. Hutchison, *China's African Revolution*, 110–114.

57. Hutchison, *China's African Revolution*, 110–123.

58. Hutchison, *China's African Revolution*, 117.

59. "China's Methods of Subversion," *China Report* 2, no. 1 (1966): 20, doi: 10.1177/000944556600200105.

BIBLIOGRAPHY

Abou-El-Fadl, Reem. "Building Egypt's Afro-Asian Hub: Infrastructures of Solidarity and the 1957 Cairo Conference." *Journal of World History* 30, nos. 1–2 (2019): 157–192. doi: 10.1353/jwh.2019.0048.

Alden, Chris, and Cristina Alves. "History & Identity in the Construction of China's Africa Policy." *Review of African Political Economy* 35, no. 115 (2008): 43–58. doi: 10.1080/03056240802011436.

Altoraifi, Adel. "Understanding the Role of State Identity in Foreign Policy Decision Making: The Rise and Demise of Saudi–Iranian Rapprochement (1997–2009)." PhD Dissertation, London School of Economics and Political Science, 2012.

"China's Methods of Subversion." *China Report* 2, no. 1 (1966): 20–22. doi: 10.1177/000944556600200105.

Dirlik, Arif. "The Bandung Legacy and the People's Republic of China in the Perspective of Global Modernity." *Inter-Asia Cultural Studies* 16, no. 4 (2015): 615–630. doi: 10.1080/14649373.2015.1103024.

Eisenman, Joshua. "Comrades-in-Arms: The Chinese Communist Party's Relations with African Political Organizations in the Mao Era, 1949–76." *Cold War History* 2018: 1–17. doi: 10.1080/14682745.2018.1440549.

El-Khawas, Mohamed A. "China's Changing Policies in Africa." *Issue: A Journal of Opinion* 3, no. 1 (1973): 24. doi: 10.2307/1166311.

Gerits, Frank. "Bandung as the Call for a Better Development Project: US, British, French and Gold Coast Perceptions of the Afro-Asian Conference (1955)." *Cold War History* 16, no. 3 (2016): 255–272. doi: 10.1080/14682745.2016.1189412.

Harris, Stuart. *China's Foreign Policy*. Cambridge, UK: Polity Press, 2014.

Hutchison, Alan. *China's African Revolution*. Boulder, CO: Westview Press, 1976.

Kaufman, Alison Adcock. "The "Century of Humiliation: Then and Now: Chinese Perceptions of the International Order." *Pacific Focus* 25, no. 1 (2010): 1–33. doi: 10.1111/j.1976-5118.2010.01039.x.

Larkin, Bruce D. *China and Africa 1949–1970: The Foreign Policy of the People's Republic of China.* Berkeley, CA: University of California, 1973.

Lumumba-Kasongo, Tukumbi. "Rethinking the Bandung Conference in an Era of 'Unipolar Liberal Globalization' and Movements toward a 'Multipolar Politics.'" *Bandung: Journal of The Global South* 2, no. 1 (2015): 1–17. doi: 10.1186/s40728-014-0012-4.

Neuhausen, Charles. *Third World Politics: China and the Afro-Asian Peoples Solidarity Organization.* 2nd ed. Cambridge: Harvard University Press, 1970.

Rich, Timothy S., and Vasabjit Banerjee. "Running Out of Time? The Evolution of Taiwan's Relations in Africa." *Journal of Current Chinese Affairs* 44, no. 1 (2015): 141–161. doi: 10.1177/186810261504400106.

Skidmore, Natasha. "Taiwanese Development Aid in Africa." *South African Institute of International Affairs* 43 (2002): 1–22.

Taylor, Ian. *China and Africa: Engagement and Compromise.* London: Routledge, 2006.

Tseng, San-shiun. "The Republic of China's Foreign Policy towards Africa: The Case of ROC-RSA Relations." PhD, University of Witwatersrand, 2008.

Varrall, Merriden. "Chinese Worldviews and China's Foreign Policy." Lowy Institute, 2015. https://www.lowyinstitute.org/publications/chinese-worldviews-and-china-s-foreign-policy.

Winter, David G. "Leadership Personality Characteristics and Foreign Policy." In *Oxford Bibliographies in International Relations.* New York, NY: Oxford University Press, 2019. doi: 10.1093/OBO/9780199743292-0256.

Yee, Herbert S. "The Three World Theory and Post-Mao China's Global Strategy." *International Affairs* 59, no. 2 (1983): 240–243.

Yu, George T. "China and the Third World." *Asian Survey* 17, no. 11 (1977): 1037–1038.

Zagoria, Donald S. "Mao's Role in the Sino-Soviet Conflict." *Pacific Affairs* 47, no. 2 (1974): 139. doi: 10.2307/2755604.

Chapter 4

Building Community of Practices

China's Relations with Africa, 1971 to Date

Emmanuel Ezi Obuah and Charles
Sikibo Ijuye-Dagogo

INTRODUCTION

The People's Republic of China (PRC) was one of the founding members of the United Nations (UN) in 1945 as well as a member of the UN Security Council (UNSC) but was excluded from UNSC during the Cold War between 1949 and 1971. A civil war broke out in 1945 between the ROC and the Communist Party of China (CPC). The CPC emerged victorious and forced the ROC government to retreat to Taiwan in 1949. This resulted in a contest for legitimate representation of the Chinese people at the UN between the PRC and the ROC. In 1971, the twenty-sixth session of the UN General Assembly adopted Resolution 2758 replacing Taiwan with the PRC. Seventy-six UN member countries voted for China's readmission, thirty-five voted against, and seventeen abstained. The emergence of the PRC was in no small part because of the growing number of developing countries, particularly African countries in the UN following the wind of decolonization. Out of the seventy-six votes for the PRC, twenty-six were from African countries.[1] In the words of Chairman Mao Zedong, "It was our African brothers, the small and medium-sized countries that carried us into the United Nations with a sedan chair."[2]

Following China's readmission into the UN in 1971, China's relations with Africa can be divided into the post-readmission era (1971–1990), an era of reinvigorated engagement (1990–2000), and an era of vigorous engagement symbolized by the creation of the Forum on China-Africa Cooperation (FOCAC) (2000 to date).

During the readmission era, China's diplomatic missions in Africa increased from thirteen in 1967 to thirty in 1974.[3] China positioned itself as the representative of the Third World at the UN and spared no efforts in winning diplomatic support from African countries. China continued its support for Africa's independence, uniting Africa against colonialism, imperialism, and racism by providing technical assistance and infrastructure. Following the Cultural Revolution and the death of Mao Zedong in 1976, China embarked on internal reforms to reposition its declining economy. This forced China to withdraw from its tradition of unconditional support for Africa. China's domestic reforms in the late 1970s and early 1980s led to the adoption of the policy of socialist modernization.[4] China was more concerned about how diplomacy would serve its economic needs. The old policy of unconditional assistance to Africa was replaced with a more pragmatic and mutually beneficial one.

China's "Father Christmas policy" toward Africa waned until the Tiananmen Square incident in 1989. It was faced with massive condemnation from Western countries for human rights abuses. China had to turn back to Africa for its economic needs. The renewed emphasis on China-African cooperation signaled the beginning of the post–Cold War era, a reinvigoration of China-African relations. From the early 1990s, China broadened its relationship with Africa in finance, investment, trade, development assistance, technology transfers and training, tourism, and cultural exchange. China resumed its high-profile visits.[5]

During the twenty-first century, China's engagement with Africa became vigorous with the creation of FOCAC in 2000.[6] The FOCAC was created to promote trade and investments between China and Africa. With its triennial meetings, the FOCAC was established as a platform for collective consultation and pragmatic cooperation between China and Africa.[7] The new era of China's engagement led to an increase in trade, investments, and aid. Just three years following the first FOCAC conference in 2000, trade between China and Africa grew from 10 billion USD to 39 billion USD,[8] and by 2008 trade figures were put at 107 billion USD.[9] By 2004 nearly seven hundred Chinese companies were operating in forty-nine African countries.[10] China supports Africa with needed infrastructure, debt cancellations, medical teams, and scholarships. Another mechanism China used to facilitate its engagement with Africa is the Belt and Road Initiative (BRI) for promoting trade and investments.[11]

China needs Africa and Africa needs China. China needs Africa for its natural resources, large market, and political support in multilateral organizations. Africa, on the other hand, is in dire need of infrastructure, technology transfer, and investments, which China is willing to provide. However, China's engagement in Africa has come under criticism. Critics have labeled China a rogue donor, opportunistic lender, colonizer, anti-environmentalist, and exploiter.[12] The pessimism surrounding China's engagement with Africa would make one conclude that China is but a resource-hungry vampire. Despite strong criticism and warnings, African leaders welcome China's policy practices. A former Liberian finance minister noted that "in Africa, we have a lot to learn from China, beyond financial capacity to assist, China has made the most progress over the past several decades in reducing poverty. That experience is of great interest to us."[13]

Faced with the pros and cons of China's Africa policy, this chapter examined China-Africa relations from 1971 to date. It explores the possibility of building a community of practices from China's policy toward Africa. The chapter looks at the concept of community of practices, exploring its origins and application. A chronology of China-Africa relations from 1971 to date is reviewed.

COMMUNITIES OF PRACTICE APPROACH (CPA)

"Communities of practice" is a concept derived from the practices of a group of people who have a similar passion, concerns, or a set of problems regarding a specific topic. They interact regularly to have a deeper understanding and expertise, and to learn how to do things better.[14] Communities of practice are units of analysis that cut across formal organizations, institutions, and other forms of association such as social movements. Simply put, a set of relations among people doing things together. Communities of practice are groups of people informally linked by shared expertise and passion for a common enterprise.

The origin of CPA is commonly associated with the works of Etienne Wenger and Jean Lave. In 1991 Wenger coauthored a book with Jean Lave titled *Situated Learning: Legitimate Peripheral Participation.*[15] In 1998 Wenger's work *Communities of Practice: Learning, Meaning and Identity* set the foundations of the CPA.[16] Wenger worked as a researcher at the Institute for Research on Learning (IRL) in Palo Alto, California. The IRL was a multidisciplinary institute that worked with the philosophy that people learn more through social interactions than formal instructions. Wenger following the same philosophy based his works on the relationship between "learning" and "doing." Wenger and Lave defined communities as vessels that host competence and facilitate practical learning. It allows them to investigate the informal organization of different learning practices. Learning is a practical activity, while knowledge requires "doing" as part of the socialization process. The socialization process is called "legitimate peripheral participation."[17] This means that a certain route of learning must be followed to become a competent community member. That means learning through a form of apprenticeship.

John Seely Brown and Paul Duguid corroborated Wenger and Lave's position in their review of CPA in science and technology studies. They see the tradition of separating knowledge from practice as an anomaly and support Wenger's position for a practice-based approach to learning.[18]

The CPA was first adapted to International Relations (IRs) in Emanuel Adler's *Communitarian International Relations* published in 2005. According to Adler, the CPA is a "pragmatist understanding of International Relations that is based on learning and highlights the dynamic social process by which collective meanings evolve within communities of like-minded, become attached to material objects, and persist in time as new and renewed social institutions and practices."[19] Adler took CPA beyond private organizations to identify national, international, and global communities of practice. These communities include diplomats, traders, environmentalists, human rights activists, security communities, epistemic communities and global public policy networks, and transnational advocacy networks.[20] They are communities because of what they do.

CPA in IRs does not just deal with abstract discussions about theories but involves practices toward social change. As Adler and Pouliot explained:

> The community of practice concept encompasses not only the conscious and discursive dimensions and the actual doing of social change, but also the social space where structure and agency overlap and where knowledge, power, and community intersect. Communities of practice are intersubjective social structures that constitute the normative and epistemic ground for action, but they also are agents, made up of real people, who affect political, economic, and social events.[21]

What does China want from Africa and in what ways does China make itself appeal to African states? China wants to become a dominant force in Africa's political economy and security architecture. It wants to be a major defender and protector of Africa's interests in international platforms. To this end, it is combining the use of soft power with building communities of practices that African states will emulate. These practices are in various areas, such as trade, investment, aid, multilateral forums, diplomacy and security, and cultural exchanges. These vessels of communities of practices are intended to create structural linkages between the various sectors of the Chinese economy and sectors in the African economy.

CHINA-AFRICA RELATIONS, 1971–1990

In 1971, China with the help of African countries successfully replaced Taiwan in the UN and UNSC. This was made possible following years of China courting Africa with aid and anticolonial support. In the early 1970s, China positioned itself as the leader of the South in the UN and a representative of Third World countries in the UNSC.

China's Africa policy focused on ideology and the need to maintain diplomatic ties against Taiwan. China promoted its style of communism in Africa. China's Africa policy countered the recognition of Taiwan and curbed the West's and Soviet Union's influence in Africa.[22] China carried out prestigious projects like the Tanzania-Zambia Railway, which was the biggest aid project to Africa at the time. Other loyal African countries received federal buildings, stadiums, factories, infrastructure, medical teams, and student exchange programs. China also reiterated its support for anticolonial movements in Africa, especially in South Africa.[23]

Following the death of Chairman Mao Zedong and the Cultural Revolution, China was faced with serious economic challenges. The economic decline forced Premier Deng Xiaoping to carry out reforms that included what Li Anshan called the policy of socialist modernization[24] or what Alden called a capitalist-oriented development policy.[25] The socialist modernization was characterized by a focus on China's economic development and a foreign policy of independence and peace.[26] China's foreign policy focus shifted from "ideological dogmatism towards eclectic pragmatism, from extreme totalitarianism toward liberalized authoritarianism, from a command economy toward market socialism, and autarky isolationism toward international interdependence."[27] China's socialist modernization policy forced it to reduce its engagement with Africa and turned to the West for much-needed revenue and technology for economic reconstruction and recovery. Between 1976 and 1980 China's aid to Africa totaled $94 million, trade figures at the end of 1980 were a meager $1.1 billion, and China did not send doctors between 1979 and 1980.[28]

In 1982, the Chinese premier Zhao Ziyang visited eleven African countries to promote the four principles that would guide China's Africa policy henceforth. They included equality and mutual benefit, emphasis on practical results, diversity in form, and economic development.[29] China turned away from its previous aid gratis policy to a more pragmatic and mutually beneficial Africa policy. China's self-imposed status as the leader of the Third World began to fade. China did not have the financial resources to be Africa's "Father Christmas."

However, in the 1990s, China turned back to Africa following the events at Tiananmen Square and Taiwan's advances toward African countries.[30] China also needed raw materials and energy to service its burgeoning economy. African countries faced with drowning debts and diminished revenues welcomed China's renewed engagement. In 1989, African countries were disillusioned with the so-called Washington Consensus policies. China was perceived as an alternative because it focused on ameliorating poverty than imposing institutional reforms.[31]

REINVIGORATION OF CHINA-AFRICA RELATIONS, 1990–2000

In 1990, China returned to Africa to curb the diplomatic advances of Taiwan and meet its economic needs. Taiwan dished out aid to African states to recover its lost UN seat. On the other hand, some African countries used their allegiance as a bargaining chip to attract funds. In 1995, the Gambia received $48 million when it moved its embassy from Beijing to Taipei. The following year Senegal moved its embassy from Beijing to Taipei after receiving a large development aid package from Taiwan. In response to these developments, China used foreign aid, military assistance, access to its markets, and its status as a permanent member of the UNSC to deter African countries from having diplomatic relations with Taiwan.

In 1996, China's president Jiang Zemin made a six-nation African tour and made promises of aid. During the trip, China offered Zaire $10 million for cobalt and copper mining projects, plus a $3.6 million cash gift. China also announced a $24 million investment in Sudan's gold mine.[32] President Nelson Mandela made efforts toward dual recognition of China and Taiwan. In response to this policy, Taipei promised to invest $3.5 billion in a petrochemical complex in the economically depressed Eastern Cape. Beijing countered this offer with an $18 billion industrial complex in South Africa's Northern Province that would create 500,000 jobs. When it was all said and done, South Africa went with the highest bidder and severed its ties with Taiwan.[33]

China's economic growth led to increased manufacturing and the Chinese people became wealthier, increasing the demand for consumer goods such as cars and fridges. As a result, China's industries needed energy and the country turned to Africa to meet this need.[34] China carried out several reforms that shaped its current Africa policy. China partially separated its state-owned enterprises (SOEs) from their parent ministries to make them more profit oriented. In 1994, the China Development Bank, the China Agricultural Bank, and the China Export-Import Bank (EximBank) were created. These banks were state-owned institutions but were given the mandate to make profits. This brought an era of aggressive domestic and international financing that fed China's economic boom. The China EximBank grew to become the leading institution for extending buyer's credit and concessional loans to developing countries.[35]

In 1995, China introduced concessional loans. This policy was communicated by Vice Premier Zhu and Vice Premier Li in their thirteen African countries tour. In the same year Premiers Zhu Rongji, Qian Qichen, and Li Lanqing visited eighteen African countries to introduce a joint venture approach to aid projects. Eleven intergovernmental framework agreements for concessional loans were signed with Zimbabwe and Sudan, among other countries. In May 1996, President Jiang Zemin presented a five-point proposal for the development of a twenty-first-century long-term China-Africa cooperation plan. On the one hand, China desired an institutional platform to promote in-depth cooperation with Africa. On the other hand, Africa was disillusioned by the development promises from Western countries and their institutions and saw China as a more favorable alternative. African countries requested a mechanism for China-Africa cooperation. China obliged and in 2000 the first FOCAC ministerial conference was held with the theme, "building a new international political and economic order and China-Africa economic and trade cooperation for the 21st century."[36]

BUILDING COMMUNITY OF PRACTICE

China's engagement with Africa reached an unprecedented high in the twenty-first century. In this new era of China-Africa relations, China combines aid, trade, investments, security, and cultural exchange to form a policy of mutual benefit and development. China uses these tools at its disposal to secure access to Africa's natural resources and markets. Africa sees China as a willing source of revenue and infrastructure. A community of practice can be built from China's Africa policy in the areas of trade, investments, aid, diplomacy, security, and cultural exchanges. A major development that facilitated China-Africa relations is the creation of the FOCAC.

The FOCAC

In the year 2000, over forty African states with eighty foreign ministers, as well as seventeen international and regional organizations, NGOs, and entrepreneurs, met in Beijing to mark the creation of the FOCAC. The agenda of the meeting was to discuss South-South cooperation, North-South dialogue, debt relief, and China's economic cooperation with African states. The grand conference produced two documents: the Beijing Declaration and the Program for China-Africa Cooperation in Economics and Social

Development. The latter covered Chinese investments in Africa, financial cooperation between China and the African Development Bank, debt relief and cancellation, agricultural cooperation, natural resources and energy, education, and multilateral cooperation.[37]

The FOCAC was established as a mechanism for collective consultation and pragmatic cooperation between China and Africa. The FOCAC conference holds every three years and the venue is interchanged between Beijing and Africa. Since its inception, seven ministerial conferences have been held. Beijing hosted the first (2000), third (2006), fifth (2012), and seventh (2018) conferences. The second conference was held in Addis Ababa (2003), the fourth in Sharm el-Sheikh (2009), and the sixth in Johannesburg (2015).[38]

The FOCAC has recorded several successes in debt relief, trade, investments, aid, human resources development, agricultural development, healthcare, peace, and security. The 2000 FOCAC conference declared the exemption of RMB10 billion worth of debts for different African countries. In the 2003 Addis Ababa conference, China promised to train 10,000 Africans in various professions.[39]

At the 2006 FOCAC, China and forty-three African heads of state met to discuss further economic, political, and social cooperation. President Hu Jintao pledged to double China's aid to Africa by 2009. The promises made at the conference included: preferential loans and credits to Africa totaling $5 billion; a promise to increase two-way trade to over $100 billion by 2010; a Chinese-Africa investment fund of $5 billion; debt forgiveness to the least developed African countries; doubling of African exports to China, as well as zero tariffs on exports from the least developed African countries; construction of 30 hospitals, 30 malaria treatment centers, and 100 schools in rural Africa.[40]

At the fourth ministerial conference in 2009, China decided to gradually give tariff-free treatments to 95% of imported goods from the least developed African countries having diplomatic relations with it. China announced the addition of RMB500 million worth of medical equipment and antimalaria supplies for previously established health centers.[41] Concessional loans and preferential buyer's credit were increased to $10 billion. China pledged to train 20,000 Africans between 2010 and 2012.[42]

In 2012 and 2015 FOCAC, respectively, China created the Initiative on China-Africa Cooperative Partnership for Peace and Security and the China-Africa Peace and Security Plan to support the AU's peacekeeping operations. China also promised to provide $60 million in free assistance to the AU to support the building and operation of African standby force and the African Capacity for Immediate Response to Crises. In 2015 FOCAC President Xi Jingping promised $60 billion in various loans, grants and special funds, various assistance in industrialization, agricultural modernization, infrastructure, financial services, trade and investments facilitation, poverty reduction, and peace and security. Similarly, in the 2018 FOCAC, China promised a $60 billion development financing until 2021.[43]

Diplomacy

The principles of China's relations with Africa are contained in what is popularly called the Beijing Consensus. The Beijing Consensus is an antithesis of the Washington and Post-Washington Consensus. It is a multifaceted policy set that spearheads constant innovation as a development strategy instead of a blanket development strategy for the entire heterogeneous countries of the South. It measures development with quality of life measures rather than just economic growth. It supports development within the peculiarities of Third World countries without superimposing a philosophy of what development should look like.[44] The Beijing Consensus is an attractive alternative to the Washington and Post-Washington Consensus because the strings attached to aid are less stringent and investments are primarily in infrastructure and human capital rather than primary products. It addresses development challenges that cannot be resolved by the laws of demand and supply.

China's diplomacy with Africa includes the use of high-profiled visits to African countries. In 1982, Premier Zhao Ziyang visited eleven African countries to promote four principles of China's Africa policy: equality and mutual benefits, emphasis on practical results, diversity in form, and economic development.[45] In 1995, Vice Premier Zhu Rongji visited Africa and kick-started a new era of the "African boom" in China.[46] In 1996 and 2002, President Jiang Zemin visited Africa a total of six times and proposed that China-Africa relations would be guided by sincere friendship, equal treatment, common development, solidarity and cooperation, and futuristic. Similarly, Premier Wen Jiabao visited seven African countries in 2006.[47] In 2019, State Councilor and Foreign Minister Wang Yi's toured Ethiopia, Burkina Faso, the Gambia, and Senegal to boost the traditional friendship with nations of the continent and implement the consensus Chinese and African leaders reached at the 2018 Beijing Summit of the FOCAC.[48]

High-profile visits also include an exchange of development experience with African leaders. In 1996, the "Understanding China Symposium" was created. It was a window for Africa to understand China's past and present. The symposium included classes in China's history, culture, arts, and a tour of the rich and poor regions of China. The symposium was held from 1996 to 2004, with 161 young African diplomats attending nine symposia. In 2003, China hosted twenty-two officials from different economic and financial units of sixteen African countries, including seven officials of the African

Development Bank, who attended a Seminar on Economic Reform and Development Strategies.[49]

China uses public diplomacy to build a positive image among Africans. Chinese state media has increased its footprint in Africa. In 2006, StarTimes bought major shares in South Africa's Top TV. In the same year, China's Radio International began broadcasting from Nairobi. In 2012, Chinese Central Television began operations in Africa. The same year China created an African edition of *China Daily*. A distinctive feature of China's public diplomacy is that China provides the media and communication infrastructure for Africa. China doesn't only transmit its good image but it also gives Africans the technology to receive the transmissions. China provided loans and grants for media and communication infrastructure to state-owned broadcasting houses that include the Zambia National Broadcasting Corporation, the Zimbabwe Broadcasting Holdings, and National Radio of Equatorial Guinea. In Malawi, a fiber optic communication project worth $22.94 million was commissioned. In 2002, Zambia received FM transmitters for seven provinces.[50]

China's diplomacy in Africa also includes the provincial diplomatic initiative. Provincial and municipal officials carry out relations with their counterparts in Africa. For example, Jiangsu Province and the Lagos State Government signed a Memorandum of Understanding (MoU) to promote the Lekki Free Trade Zone in 2006. Henan Province opened discussions about setting up a Chinese bank in Nigeria. Sichuan Province and Ogun State government signed a $50 million deal to build a pharmaceutical manufacturing plant.[51]

Trade

China's trade with Africa is guided by the former's need for natural resources and access to the latter's huge markets. China's growing demand for oil is a result of its rapidly growing economy. In 1993, China became a net importer of oil. China's oil needs are estimated to grow by 156% between 2010 and 2025. On its part, Africa accounts for 8.4% of the world's oil reserves and 10.4% of the world's oil production. China is the world's second-largest consumer of crude oil, with more than 25% of its oil needs coming from the Gulf of Guinea and Sudan.[52] Critics of China's Africa policy see China as an oil-thirsty vampire. However, 2006 figures showed that China got only 9% of Africa's petroleum exports, while the United States and European Union purchased 33% and 36%, respectively. China seeks oil to feed its industries but also aims to position itself as an important player in the international oil market.[53]

Oil is not the only natural resource China requires from Africa. China also turns to Africa for timber which it gets from Cameroon, Central African

Republic, Equatorial Guinea, Liberia, and Nigeria. China is the world's leading exporter of textiles but still requires cotton from Burkina Faso, the Republic of Benin, Mali, Guinea, Nigeria, Togo, and the Central African Republic.[54]

With a population of about 1.3 billion people, China has found in Africa a ready market for its low-quality consumer products. These consumer products are cheap and of satisfactory quality for the African market. Chinese exports to Africa include household utensils, mechanical and electrical products, textiles, and clothes. China focuses exports to South Africa, Nigeria, Egypt, Morocco, and Algeria because of their relatively higher purchasing power.[55]

China's trade with Africa has grown rapidly since the creation of FOCAC in 2000. More than forty trade agreements had been signed, doubling trade from $10 billion in 2000 to more than $20 billion in 2004.[56] The following year trade grew to $39 billion.[57] By 2008, total trade was $107 billion.[58] In 2018, China's total exports to Africa grew from $10.12 billion in 2003 to over $104.95 billion in 2018. Imports grew from $7.41 billion in 2003 to $80.34 billion in 2018.[59] China is currently Africa's third-largest trading partner after the United States and France.

China's African trade policies aim to achieve win-win trade relations. China declared tariff exemptions on goods from twenty-five least developed African countries. The zero-tariff goods totaled $340 million in 2005.[60] At the 2006 Beijing Summit, the number of tariff-free imported goods from thirty least developed countries having diplomatic relations with China increased from 190 items to 440. The fourth ministerial conference in 2009 decided on a gradual tariff-free treatment to 95% of imported goods from the least developed African countries. At the 2015 FOCAC conference, China announced the implementation of fifty trade promotion and aid projects as well as the expansion of Africa's exports.[61]

In 2013, President Xi Jinping created China's BRI as one of the most ambitious infrastructure projects ever conceived. The BRI is a transcontinental long-term policy and investment program which aims at infrastructure development to promote unimpeded trade among other objectives.[62] China seeks to invest in port development along the Indian Ocean, from Southeast Asia to East Africa and parts of Europe. China already spent $200 billion on the BRI and is estimated to spend $1.2–1.3 trillion by 2027.[63] Forty-nine out of forty-four African countries have signed the Memoranda of Understanding on the BRI. Twenty-two of the MoU was signed with West African countries, twelve with East African countries, nine with North African countries, and six with Southern African countries.[64] As a result of the BRI, Ethiopia and Djibouti are now bridged through the Addis Ababa-Djibouti railway and Ethiopia-Djibouti pipeline.[65] Mali signed an $11 billion agreement with

China to finance two cross-country rail projects to link the landlocked country to the coast.[66]

Investment

Africa is in dire need of foreign investments to fill one of the gaps for economic growth. Chinese capital provides the badly needed funds for Africa's development. According to Uchehara, China's investment is determined by the need to acquire natural resources, energy supplies, and export markets to sustain its economic growth. China uses its investments to promote its development model in Africa. Investments are also tools to strengthen China's diplomatic alliances to support its global ambitions.[67] Considerable investments have been made in oil fields in Sudan, Nigeria, Angola, and Gabon. China's National Petroleum Corporation beginning in 1996 has transformed the Sudanese oil sector after years of war. China's investments also include logging in Equatorial Guinea and Liberia, cotton and sisal plantation agriculture in Tanzania, and textile manufacturing in Zambia and Kenya. Some of these investments are carried out by Chinese small and medium enterprises (SMEs). In 2004, Nigeria's non-oil exports were over $500 million because of Chinese investments and joint ventures in products like cotton and timber.[68]

The China EximBank actively provides incentives for China's SOEs to invest in Africa. In 2006, China provided $3 billion preferential loans and $2 billion in preferential buyer credits and set up a $5 billion China-Africa Development Fund to support Chinese firms to invest in Africa.[69] China uses the EximBank and other financial institutions to encourage Chinese SOEs to invest in processing industrial and agricultural products, extracting natural resources, and investing in infrastructure, power supply, and real estate. Chinese FDI has grown over the decades. China's FDI flows have grown from $78.81 million in 2003 to $5.389 billion in 2018: 32% in construction, 22.7% in mining, 13% in manufacturing, 11% in financial intermediation, 6.4% in leasing and commercial services, and 14.9% in other sectors.[70] One key strategy China's SOEs use to outbid competitors is slicing their profit margin. While local and international foreign construction companies operate on a profit margin of 15–25%, China's SOEs operate below 10%.[71]

China invests in African countries and areas that have been overlooked by the West, in some cases abandoned investments. Zambia's Chambishi copper mines, Gabon's supposedly exhausted oil reserves, and Ghana's Bui Dam are some examples. In Ethiopia, China's investments are in telecommunication; in the Democratic Republic of the Congo, it has invested in the Geca Mine, the state-owned mining company; and in Nigeria, China launched Nigeria's first space satellite. China invested in the unexploited and supposedly barren Muglad oil fields in Southern Sudan. In 2009, 50% of the crude from Southern Sudan goes to China. Thirteen out of fifteen most important companies in Sudan are owned by the Chinese. Top on the list are the China Petroleum Corporation and the Zhongyuan Petroleum Corporation.[72]

Aid

China's aid to Africa prior to the post-Maoist era was more or less gratis. Aid was an ideological tool given to build friendly relations and political support against Taiwan in Africa. However, China restructured its aid policies in the post-Maoist era. Interest-free loans became discount loans, and grants have been replaced by joint ventures. Toward the end of the 1990s, China had established 480 joint ventures in forty-seven African countries. China's aid to Africa is used as a tool for mutual economic benefits. In the twenty-first century, China's aid to Africa has been growing rapidly and is used to secure new investments and natural resources. China's aid includes concessional or low-interest loans and government backed subsidized investments in infrastructure and natural resources, technical assistance, development grants, humanitarian assistance, food aid, military and security-related assistance.[73]

China's aid figures are shrouded in secrecy. China is a developing country that administers aid in an ad hoc fashion, without a centralized administrative agency or regularized funding schedule. Some scholars suggest that the secrecy in China's aid figures is because as an aid recipient China doesn't want to be perceived as a major aid donor.[74] However Lum et al cited a New York University's Wagner School study on China's foreign aid stated that China funded projects in Africa are worth a combined total of $25 billion: 66% was provided as concessional loans or credit lines, 29% represented state-sponsored investments, and 5% included grants, debt cancellation or debt relief, and in-kind aid.[75] Africa is the largest recipient of China's aid, receiving 44% of annual aid flows. China uses billions of dollars in aid to secure oil contracts and outbid competitors for rights to Africa's petroleum resources. In 2004, India was on the verge of closing a $620 million oil deal with Angola when China announced a $2 billion increase in project aid to Angola. In 2007, China gave Congo $5 billion for infrastructure development to gain access to the country's timber, cobalt, and copper reserves.[76] The $2 billion credit line given to Angola in 2004 for infrastructure was guaranteed by the sale of oil from a field that generated 10,000 bpd.[77]

China is willing to transfer technology and technical know-how to African countries. As part of the China-Africa cooperation plan for agricultural modernization, China implemented the "Enriching People with Agriculture" project in 100 African villages and the "10+10" cooperation mechanism between Chinese and African agro-scientific research institutes.[78] In October 2020, China launched the Luban Workshop Facility at the University of Abuja in Nigeria. It included course majors in Urban Rail Transit Traffic Management, Urban Rail Transit Vehicles, and Railway Bridges and Tunnels. The facility was established with the support of Tianjin Sino-German University.[79]

China deals with Africa like a partner rather than a subject. Unlike major donors, China does not impose its development ideals on Africa as superior. China offers aid with little or no precondition in line with the needs of the recipient.[80] China sees economic rights and rights of subsistence as more important than the Western notions of personal and individual rights. President Wen Jiabao was quoted saying, "We do offer our assistance with the deepest sincerity and without any political conditions."[81] Notwithstanding, Chinese loans are not unconditional there is still the long-standing condition of "no diplomatic relations with Taiwan."

Peace and Security

China believes that Africa's peace and security can be assured when poverty is reduced and the standard of living of the average African is improved.[82] This policy was expressed by China's foreign minister Yang Jiechi when he suggested that "we (China) believe that development is the foundation of peace in Africa. Conflict and poverty often come hand in hand and form a vicious cycle. If Africa is to achieve durable peace and stability, it needs to speed up economic and social development and let all the people share the benefits of development."[83]

China began contributing personnel to the United Nations Peacekeeping Operations (UNPKO) in 1989 to support the United Nations Transition Assistance Group in Namibia. Since then, Chinese blue helmets have been seen in UN Observer Mission in Liberia, UN Operation in Mozambique, UN Observer Mission in Sierra Leone, UN Mission in Ethiopia and Eritrea, UN Operation in Burundi, UN Organization Mission in the Democratic Republic of the Congo, UN Mission in Sudan, UN Mission in Liberia, among others.[84]

More than 2,500 Chinese peacekeepers are carrying out UN missions in Africa. China is the second-largest contributor to the UN peacekeeping expenditure. Chinese peacekeepers are not just a force of peace but are also agents of development. In September 2015, China had 2,420 troops, 171 police, and 26 experts attached to seven UN peacekeeping operations in Africa. The majority of the units are noncombatant soldiers, including engineers, doctors, and other professionals. They engaged in training the local population on basic development enhancement techniques. The combat units also carried out training for local security forces on confidence-building measures, problem-solving, and peaceful conflict resolution strategies.

Chinese peacekeepers have renovated and built 110,000 kilometers of road and over 300 bridges. They have diffused 9,400 landmines and explosives, shipped 1.1 million tons of materials, completed 450 patrols and 230 convoys, and treated 149,000 patients. In 2016, Chinese peacekeepers opened a Chinese language class for orphans in the Democratic Republic of the Congo.[85] In Mali, Chinese peacekeepers were tasked with completing the construction of the hospital in Gao as well as road constructions, building security checkpoints, providing drinking water, and building fences around public schools in Gao.[86]

China is reluctant when it comes to direct interference in African conflicts. China proffers a regional or multilateral approach to peace and security in Africa. In 2012 and 2015, China created the Initiative on China-Africa Cooperative Partnership for Peace and Security and the China-Africa Peace and Security Plan to support AU peacekeeping operations. China continues to support peacekeeping efforts and capacity building in African countries' national defense, antiterrorism, antiriot, customs supervision, and immigration control.[87] In 2015, China promised to provide $60 million in free assistance to the AU to support the building and operation of the African Standby Force and an African capacity for intermediate response to a crisis.[88]

Cultural Exchanges

China uses scholarships, student exchange programs, and the Confucius Institute (CI) as an avenue of cultural exchanges with African countries. China contributes to the development of human resources in Africa. Africans go to China to gain technical knowledge. From 1956 to 1999, 5,582 Africans studied at Chinese universities. In 2002, there were 1,646 African students in China. New students in 2004 numbered 332. China provides 1,500 scholarships annually to Africans and by 2004, 17,860 had benefited from the scholarship.[89] In 2006, 600 Africans were trained, and 1,500 students visited China on educational exchange programs.[90] Chinese scholarships to Africa have grown from 2,000 a year in 2006 to 10,000 in 2018.[91] While brain drain is a major concern with African migration patterns to the West, the China-Africa migration pattern is less detrimental. There are many Chinese living in Africa but few Africans living in China. The vast majority of Africans in China are students bound to return in four to five years.[92]

The CI, also known as Hanban, was established in 2004 as a cluster of nonprofit educational organizations charged with the responsibility of promoting the Chinese language and culture outside China. In 2012 FOCAC Beijing Plan of Action, China and Africa agreed to the establishment of more CIs and Confucius Classrooms in Africa.[93] By 2017, there were 525 CIs and 1,113 Confucius Classrooms in 146 countries and territories around the world. The CIs are normally affiliated with universities, schools, cultural organizations, and community centers outside China. They are jointly established by the host institution and their Chinese partner institution (Universities in China).

The CI conducts several cultural activities, including tai chi, film screenings, calligraphy, paper cutting, and traditional Chinese medicine for interested audiences. They also organized photo exhibitions, Chinese song competitions, lectures, and seminars with academics and Chinese experts. In South Africa, the Stellenbosch Confucius Institute organized seventy cultural activities and academic conferences in 2013. In the same year, the institute organized the Annual Rhodes University China Week on the Chinese experience in South Africa and hosted the visiting Students Art Troupe from Zhejiang National University.[94] The CI also provides information for African students who want to take advantage of Chinese scholarships to study in China. China's cultural relations with Africa also included the China-Mali Spring Festival Evening Gala in January 2019. It featured Chinese medical teams, workers at the CI, and Chinese speakers.[95]

CONCLUSION

In IRs, communities of practices involve not just the intellectual discourse but also the actions that cause social change. It involves states who affect political, economic, and social events. It emphasizes not just what state officials say but what states do. This chapter explored the various dimensions of China's relations with Africa. The aim was to expose the features of China's Africa policy that can be regarded as building a community of practice.

A community of practice can be built from China's relations with Africa in the areas of diplomacy, trade, investments, aid, security, and cultural exchange. China's diplomacy with Africa includes high-profiled visits by Chinese officials to build a sense of kinship with African countries. China also utilizes public diplomacy to influence the perceptions of ordinary Africans. China does not only use media broadcast to Africa but also plays a huge role in providing the technology and infrastructure necessary to receive such broadcasts and transmissions. China also uses provincial-level diplomacy to allow subnational units to conduct diplomacy with their counterparts in Africa.

China attempts to level the playing field in trade by providing tariff exemptions to the least developed African countries. China also contributes to the necessary infrastructure Africa needs to promote its trade through the BRI. In terms of investments, China uses institutions such as the EximBank to encourage Chinese SOEs and SMEs to invest in Africa. China also invests in areas that are overlooked by developed countries like the Biu Dam in Ghana and the Muglad oil fields in Southern Sudan.

China's aid figures are shrouded in secrecy because China as an aid recipient does not want to be tagged as major aid donor. China uses aid to Africa to secure investments and access to natural resources. China's aid policy toward Africa is geared toward mutual benefit and development. China doesn't care much for institutional changes in Africa but focuses on providing much-needed infrastructure to Africa. Nevertheless, China does not compromise its stance against Taiwan's recognition when dishing out aid.

Peace and security in Africa can only be ensured when Africa is developed. Therefore, China sends more noncombat peacekeepers than combat peacekeepers. Chinese peacekeepers are regarded as agents of development, providing medical, infrastructure, and educational aid to conflict zones. China also believes that states should use a multilateral approach to solving Africa's conflicts. China spared no effort in contributing peacekeepers to the UNPKO and providing financial and technical support to the AU peace and security initiatives.

China's cultural policy toward Africa is expressed through scholarships, student exchange, and the CIs. China's scholarship and student exchange programs are free from the brain drain syndrome. This is because China is strict with its education visa policies. The CIs, on the other hand, promote China's culture and language. The CIs create room for African institutions to take part in its administration. China is in the process of building a community of practice in diplomacy, trade, investment, aid, peace and security, and cultural exchange. It is recommended that the pros of China's practices with Africa be emulated and not completely condemned in the future.

NOTES

1. Cheema, Iqtidar Karamat. "Sino-African Relationship in Past, Present and Future Perspective," in *China-Africa: New Types of Exchange, Cultural Identity and Emerging Relations in a Globalized World*, eds. Ivo Carneiro de Sousa, Ansoumane Douty Diakite, and Ojo Olukayode Iwaloye (Philadelphia: Saint Joseph Academic Press, 2011), 59.

2. Niu, "A Historical Overview," 67.

3. Van de Looy, *Judith, Africa and China: A Strategic Partnership?* (Leiden: African Studies Centre, 2006), 2.

4. Kieran E. Uchehara, "China-Africa Relations in the 21st Century: Engagement, Compromise and Controversy," *Uluslararası İlişkiler* 6, no. 23 (2009): 98.

5. David Haroz, "China in Africa: Symbiosis of Exploitation," *Fletcher Forum World Affairs*, no. 35 (2011): 68.

6. Karen Foerstel, "China in Africa: Is China Gaining Control of Africa's Resources," *CQ Global Researcher* 2, no. 1 (2008): 15.

7. Zeng Aiping and Shu Zhan. "Origin, Achievements, and the Prospects of the Forum on China-Africa Cooperation," *China International Studies* 72 (2018): 88.

8. Barry Sautman, "Friends and Interests: China's Distinctive Links with Africa," Centre on China's transnational relations, Working Paper no. 12, 9.

9. Haroz, "China and Africa: Symbiosis or Exploitation," 74.

10. Van de Looy, *Africa and China: A Strategic Partnership?*, 26.

11. Andrew Chatzky and James McBride, "China's Massive Belt and Road Initiative," *Council on Foreign Relations* 21 (2019): 1.

12. Deborah Brautigam, *The Dragon's Gift: The Real Story behind China in Africa* (New York: Oxford University Press, 2009), 3.

13. Haroz, "China and Africa: Symbiosis or Exploitation," 75.

14. Haradhan Kumar Mohajan, "Roles of Communities of Practice for the Development of the Society," *Journal of Economic Development, Environment and People* 6, no. 3 (2017): 1.

15. Jean Lave and Etienne Wenger, *Situated Learning: Legitimate Peripheral Participation* (New York: Cambridge University Press, 1991).

16. Etienne Wenger, *Communities of Practice: Learning, Meaning, and Identity* (New York: Cambridge University Press, 1998).

17. Christian Breuger, "Communities of Practice in World Politics: Theory or Technology?" *International Studies Association Annual Conference* (2012): 4–5.

18. John Seely Brown and Paul Duguid, "Organizational Learning and Communities-of-Practice: Toward a Unified View of Working, Learning, and Innovation," *Organization Science* 2, no. 1 (1991): 50.

19. Emanuel Adler, *Communitarian International Relations: The Epistemic Foundations of International Relations* (London/New York: Psychology Press, 2005), 12.

20. Adler, *Communitarian International Relations*, 7.

21. Emanuel Adler and Vincent Pouliot. "International Practices," *International Theory* 3, no. 1 (2011): 18–19.

22. Deborah Brautigam, "China's Foreign Aid in Africa: What Do We Know?," *China into Africa: Trade, Aid and Influence* (2008): 209.

23. Van de Looy, *Africa and China*, 4.

24. Li Anshan, *Transformation of China's African Policy: When, Why and What* (Beijing: Xinchu Publishers, 2007), 3.

25. Alden, *China in Africa*, 10.

26. Anshan, *Transformation of China's African Policy*, 3.

27. Anas Elochukwu, "China's Peace Efforts in Africa Since the End of the Cold War," *Covenant University Journal of Politics and International Affairs* 3, no. 2 (2016): 17.

28. Anshan, *Transformation of China's African Policy*, 7.

29. Uchehara, *China-Africa Relations in the 21st Century: Engagement*, 18.

30. Van de Looy, *Africa and China*, 6.

31. Foerstel, *China in Africa: Is China Gaining Control*, 15.

32. Foerstel, *China in Africa: Is China Gaining Control*, 15.

33. Alden, *China in Africa*, 10.

34. Van de Looy, *Africa and China*, 9.

35. Haroz, *China in Africa, Symbiosis or Exploitation*, 69.

36. Aiping, *Origin, Achievements*, 89–90.

37. Van de Looy, *Africa and China*, 10.

38. Aiping, *Origin, Achievements*, 88.

39. Aiping, *Origin, Achievements*, 92.

40. Forestal, *China in Africa: Is China Gaining Control*, 3.

41. Aiping, *Origin, Achievements*, 94.

42. Haroz, *China in Africa, Symbiosis or Exploitation*, 74.

43. Lokanathan Venkateswaran. "China's Belt and Road Initiative: Implications in Africa," (2020): 1.

44. Sautman, *Friends and Interests*, 18.

45. Van de Looy, *Africa and China*, 5.

46. Anshan, *Transformation of China's African Policy*, 4.

47. Emmanuel Ezi Obuah, *Understanding the Dynamics of Sino-Africa Relations: Building Communities of Practice* (Germany: Lambert Academic Publishing, 2013), 76.

48. Cao Desheng, *Wang to Begin Five Days of African Visits*, Last modified January 2, 2019, https://www.chinadaily.com.cn/a/201901/02/WS5c2bfd44a310d 91214051f39.html

49. Anshan, *Transformation of China's African Policy*, 4.

50. M Leslie, "The Dragon Shapes Its Image: A Study of Chinese Media Influence Strategies in Africa," *African Studies Quarterly* 16, no. 3 (2016): 164.

51. Alden, *China in Africa*, 29.

52. Uchehara, *China-Africa Relations in the 21st Century*, 102.

53. Foerstel, *China in Africa: Is China Gaining Control*, 9.

54. Van de Looy, *Africa and China*, 20.

55. Van de Looy, *Africa and China*, 24.

56. Uchehara, *China-Africa Relations in the 21st Century*, 102.

57. Sautman, *Friends and Interests*, 18.

58. Haroz, *China in Africa, Symbiosis or Exploitation*, 74.

59. John Hopkins China-Africa Research Initiative, "China Exports to African Countries," (2020): 12.

60. Anshan, *Transformation of China's African Policy*, 11.

61. Aiping, *Origin, Achievements*, 94.

62. About Belt and Road Initiative, Belt and Road Initiative, accessed November 11, 2020, beltroad-initiative.com/belt-and-road/

63. Chatzky and McBride, *China's Massive Belt and Road Initiative*, 5.

64. Venkateswaran, *China Belt and Road Initiative*, Accessed November 11, 2020, https://www.orfonline.org/research/chinas-belt-and-road-initiative-implications-in -africa/,34

65. BBC, *Kenya Opens Nairobi-Mombasa.*

66. Venkateswaran, *China Belt and Road Initiative*, 34.

67. Kieran E. Uchehara, "China-Africa Cooperation in the 21st Century: Analysis of the Obstacles and Challenges to Good Cooperation," *Journal of Global Strategic Management* 6 (2009): 9.

68. Alden, *China in Africa*, 14.

69. Cheung, Jakob, Xingwang, and Shu, "China's Outward Direct Investment," 201.

70. John Hopkins, *China Exports to African Countries*, 15.

71. Uchehara, *China-Africa Relations in the 21st Century: Analysis*, 7.

72. Uchehara, *China-Africa Relations in the 21st Century: Engagement*, 106.

73. Linda Lönnqvist, "China's Aid to Africa: Implications for Civil Society," *Policy Briefing Paper* 17 (2008): 1&4.

74. Lum, Fischer, Gomez-Granger, and Leland, *China's Foreign Aid Activities in Africa*, 1.

75. Lum, Fischer, Gomez-Granger, and Leland, *China's Foreign Aid Activities in Africa*, 3–4.

76. Forestal, *China in Africa: Is China Gaining Control*, 17.

77. Barry Sautman and Yan Hairong. "Trade, Investment, Power and the China-in-Africa Discourse" (2009): 26.

78. Aiping, *Origin, Achievements*, 93.

79. Xinhua, *Chinese Luban Workshop Facility Launched in Nigeria.*

80. Forestal, *China in Africa: Is China Gaining Control*, 6.

81. Alden, *China in Africa*, 15.

82. Leslie, *China–Africa Relations: Political and Economic Engagement and Media Strategies*, 1.

83. Benebdallah, *China's Peace and Security in Africa*, 19.

84. Elochukwu, *China's Peace Efforts in Africa since the End of the Cold War*, 21.

85. Benebdallah, *China's Peace and Security in Africa*, 25.

86. Banabdallah and Large, *Development, Security and China's Role in Mali*, 14.

87. Aiping, *Origin, Achievements*, 96.

88. Leslie, *China–Africa Relations: Political and Economic Engagement and Media Strategies*, 1.

89. Sautman, *Friends and Int*, 22.

90. Van de Looy, *Africa and China*, 7.

91. Aiping, *Origin, Achievements*, 93.

92. Sautman, *Friends and Interests*, 31.

93. Falk Hartig, "The Globalization of Chinese Soft Power: Confucius Institutes in South Africa," in *Confucius Institutes and the Globalization of China's Soft Power*, eds. R.S. Zaharna, J. Hubbert, and F. Hartig (Los Angeles: The University of Southern California Center for Public Diplomacy Perspectives on Public Diplomacy, 2014), 53.

94. Hartig, *The Globalization of Chinese Soft Power*, 56.

95. Banabdallah and Large, *Development, Security and China's Role in Mali*, 9.

BIBLIOGRAPHY

Adler, Emanuel. *Communitarian International Relations: The Epistemic Foundations of International Relations.* Vol. 20. New York: Psychology Press, 2005.

Adler, Emanuel, and Vincent Pouliot. "International Practices." *International Theory* 3, no. 1 (2011): 1–36.

Aiping, Zeng, and Shu Zhan. "Origin, Achievements, and the Prospects of the Forum on China-Africa Cooperation." *China Int'l Studies* 72 (2018): 88.

Asche, Helmut. "Contours of China's 'Africa Mode' and Who May Benefit." *Journal of Current Chinese Affairs—China aktuell* 37, no. 3 (2008): 165–180.

BBC News. "Kenya Opens Nairobi-Mombasa Madaraka Express Railway." May 31, 2017. bbc.com/news/world-africa-40098219:text: Kenya%20opened.

Benabdallah, Lina. "China's Peace and Security Strategies in Africa: Building Capacity Is Building Peace?" *African Studies Quarterly* 16 (2016): 17–34.

Benabdallah, Lina, and Daniel Large. "Development, Security, and China's Evolving Role in Mali." 2020.

Brautigam, Deborah. *The Dragon's Gift: The Real Story behind China in Africa.* New York: Oxford University Press, 2009.

Brautigam, Deborah. "China's Foreign Aid in Africa: What Do We Know?" *China into Africa: Trade, Aid and Influence* (2008): 197–216.

Brown, John Seely, and Paul Duguid. "Organizational Learning and Communities-of-Practice: Toward a Unified View of Working, Learning, and Innovation." *Organization Science* 2, no. 1 (1991): 40–57.

Bueger, Christian. "Communities of Practice in World Politics—Theory or Technology." In *International Studies Association Annual Conference*, pp. 16–19, 2012.

Carol, Lancaster. *The Chinese Aid System.* Washington, DC: Centre for Global Development, 2007. http://www.cgdev.org/files/13953_file_Chinese_aid.pdf (accessed November 29, 2020).

Chatzky, Andrew, and James McBride. "China's Massive Belt and Road Initiative." *Council on Foreign Relations*, May 21, 2019.

Cheema, Iqtidar Karamat. "Sino-African Relationship in Past, Present and Future Perspective." In *China-Africa: New Types of Exchange, Cultural Identity and Emerging Relations in a Globalized World*, edited by Ivo Carneiro de Sousa, Ansoumane Douty Diakite, and Ojo Olukayode Iwaloye, 56–68. Philadelphia: Saint Joseph Academic Press, 2011.

Cheung, Yin-Wong, Jakob De Haan, Xingwang Qian, and Shu Yu. "China's Outward Direct Investment in Africa." *Review of International Economics* 20, no. 2 (2012): 200–221.

Desheng, Cao. "Wang to Begin Five Days of African Visits." Last Modified January 2, 2019. https://www.chinadaily.com.cn/a/201901/02/WS5c2bfd44a310d9121 4051f39.html.

Elochukwu, Anas. "China's Peace Efforts in Africa since the End of the Cold War." *Covenant University Journal of Politics and International Affairs* 3, no. 2 (2016): 15–28.

Ferdjani, Hannane. *African Students in China: An Exploration of Increasing Numbers and Their Motivations in Beijing.* South Africa: Center for Chinese Studies, Stellenbosch University, 2012.

Foerstel, Karen. *China in Africa: Is China Gaining Control of Africa's Resources?* Washington, DC: CQ Press, 2008.

Haroz, David. "China in Africa: Symbiosis of Exploitation." Fletcher F. World Aff. 35 (2011): 65.

Hartig, Falk. "The Globalization of Chinese Soft Power: Confucius Institutes in South Africa." In *Confucius Institutes and the Globalization of China's Soft Power*, edited by R. S. Zaharna, J. Hubbert, and F. Hartig, Vol. 3, pp. 47–66. Los Angeles, CA: The University of Southern California Center for Public Diplomacy Perspectives on Public Diplomacy, 2014.

John Hopkins China-Africa Research Institute. "China Exports to African Countries." 2020. sais-cari.org/data_china_africa_trade (Accessed November 16, 2020).

Katsouris, Christina. "Africa's Oil and Gas Potential." London: Chatham House. http://www.chathamholuse.org/sites/default/files/public/Research/Africa/1611 11katsouris.pdf. (accessed November 28, 2020). (n.d.).

Lave, Jean, and Etienne Wenger. *Situated Learning: Legitimate Peripheral Participation.* Cambridge: Cambridge University Press, 1991.

Leslie, Agnes Ngoma. "Introduction: China-Africa Relations: Political and Economic Engagement and Media Strategies." *African Studies Quarterly* 16, no. 3/4 (2016): 1.

Lönnqvist, Linda. "China's Aid to Africa: Implications for Civil Society." Policy Briefing Paper 17 (2008).

Lum, Thomas, Hannah Fischer, Julissa Gomez-Granger, and Anne Leland. "China's Foreign Aid Activities in Africa, Latin America, and Southeast Asia." *Russia China and Eurasia—Social Historical and Cultural Issues* 25, no. 2 (2009): 175.

Mohajan, Haradhan Kumar. "Roles of Communities of Practice for the Development of the Society." *Journal of Economic Development, Environment and People* 6, no. 3 (2017): 27–46.

Niu, Zhongjun. "A Historical Overview of China-UN Relations." *Journal of Asia-Pacific Studies*, no. 2 (2018): 65.

Obuah, Emmanuel Ezi. *Understanding the Dynamics of Sino-Africa Relations: Building Communities of Practice.* Germany: Lambert Academic Publishing, 2013.

Sautman, Barry. "Friends and Interests: China's Distinctive Links With Africa." Centre on China's Transnational Relations, Working Paper No. 12. 2006. https://www.cctr.ust.uk/materials/working_paper/workingpaper12.pdf (Accessed November 1, 2020).

Sautman, Barry, and Hairong Yan. "Trade, Investment, Power and the China-in-Africa Discourse." 2009.

Tao, Yu, and Jiayi Wang. "Confucius Institutes." *Oxford Bibliographies in Chinese Studies* (2018): 149.

Uchehara, Kieran E. "China-Africa Cooperation in the 21st Century: Analysis of the Obstacles and Challenges to Good Cooperation." *Journal of Global Strategic Management* 6 (2009): 5–16.

Uchehara, Kieran E. "China-Africa Relations in the 21st Century: Engagement, Compromise and Controversy." *Uluslararası İlişkiler/International Relations* (2009): 95–111.

USAID. *Knowledge for Development Strategy 2004–2008.* Washington, DC: US Agency for International Development. 2004. http://www.dec.org/pdf_docs/PDACA224.pdf.

Van de Looy, Judith, and Leo de Haan. "Africa and China: A Strategic Partnership? Institute for Defence Studies and Analysis." *Strategic Analysis* 30, no. 3 (2006): 562–575.

Venkateswaran, Lakshmi. "China's Belt and Road Initiative: Implications in Africa." Orfonline.org/research/china_belt_and_road_initiative_implications_in_Africa/ (Accessed August 24, 2020).

Wenger, Etienne. *Communities of Practice: Learning, Meaning, and Identity.* Cambridge: Cambridge University Press, 1998.

Chapter 5

African Relations with China and Taiwan

A Web of Anticolonialism, Cold War, Recognition Politics, and Debt Trap

Priye S. Torulagha

INTRODUCTION

International politics is generally considered anarchic and amoral because of how states pursue their interests. As a result, it is not unusual for states to openly declare their support for human rights and democracy while actively perpetrating human rights abuses. It is also not unusual for them to deny actions that they have just taken. They behave in such a contradictory manner because they are sovereign entities and are motivated primarily to enhance their national interest.[1] Consequently, states pursue their self-interests through the doctrines of reason of state, expediency, and rationalism. The reason of state can be defined as the right of a state to take whatever action or decision it deemed necessary to ensure its existence. The doctrine of expediency hinges on the view that a state has a right to take any action or decision that is least painful or costly to its national interest. Rationalism in international relations is predicated upon the assumption that every state act based on a logical appraisal of any given situation to maximize its interest.[2]

Based on the aforementioned three principles of international relations, one particular issue that demonstrates the anarchic nature of international politics is the question of the two Chinas. There is the People's Republic of China (PRC) on the mainland and the Republic of China (ROC) in Taiwan. For the purpose of this discourse, the PRC is hereafter referred to as China and the ROC as Taiwan. Before 1949, only one China existed, and it was globally recognized. The ROC participated actively in major multilateral meetings, including the 1943 Moscow and the 1944 Dumbarton Oaks conferences which culminated in the establishment of the United Nations (UN) on October 24, 1945. It was a charter member of the UN and served as a permanent member of the Security Council.[3] However, the political fate of the country changed in 1949 when the communists, led by Mao Zedong, defeated the nationalist government of Gen. Chiang Kai-shek. Following the defeat, the nationalists moved to Taiwan (Formosa) and continued to operate as the ROC. The communists established the PRC on the mainland and insisted that there is only one China and not two. This issue remains unresolved even today.

The purpose here is to (1) explore the factors which contributed to the emergence of the two Chinas; (2) identify the factors which motivated African states to derecognize Taiwan and support China; (3) determine whether African states are beholden to China due to massive indebtedness that threatens their sovereign right to do business with Taiwan; and (4) determine whether China's assertive effort in isolating Taiwan could backfire as its actions are increasingly being viewed as exploitative, hegemonic, and racist in Africa.

FACTORS THAT CONTRIBUTED TO THE EMERGENCE OF TWO CHINAS

To identify the factors which contributed to the emergence of the Two-China issue, it is necessary to examine (1) the historical source of the Cold War and (2) China's One-China policy.

Historical Source of the Cold War on China

The end of World War II in 1945 ushered in an intense Cold War rivalry between the Union of Soviet Socialist Republics (USSR) and the United States as the two powers competed to spread their ideologies and dominate the world. The rivalry was predictable since both powers embraced contradictory ideologies (capitalism and communism) that made their relationship mutually suspicious. Hence, when Stalin in 1942 sent a memorandum to the Western allies demanding the opening of a second front to reduce the German military pressure on the Soviet Union in the Eastern front and Winston Churchill of Britain did not respond positively to the request,[4] Stalin's suspicion grew. With such mutual suspicion, the Soviet Union strategically incorporated the countries it liberated from Nazi Germany and turned them into communist countries in Eastern and Central Europe. Likewise, wherever the Soviet Union assisted domestic elements to resist Japanese and German military offensives during the war, it was forced to identify with the communist bloc. Hence, North Korea and North Vietnam, like the Chinese communists, identified with the Soviet Union while South Korea and South Vietnam, like the Chinese nationalists, identified with the United States.

Consequently, the struggle to liberate China from Japanese military occupation during World War II resulted in an ideological split among the Chinese. The Chinese nationalist government headed by Gen. Chiang Kai-shek, an anticommunist and a staunch ally of the United States, had a fallout with the communists led by Mao Zedong. The split resulted in a civil war between the government and the communists. The communists defeated the nationalists in 1949. Fearful of annihilation, Chiang Kai-shek and his supporters moved to the island of Taiwan (Formosa) and set up a parallel government that still bore the name ROC. On the mainland, the communists set up a new government known as the PRC. By moving to Taiwan, the nationalists escaped total defeat while the communists felt that total victory had been snatched away from them. The United States continued to support and strengthen the resolve of the nationalists to operate as the ROC. Thus, the end of the civil war between the two factions resulted in the emergence of two Chinas.

Hence the United States was very hostile to China while doing everything possible to protect and sustain Taiwan. The protection prevented the communists from completely winning the war since they could not capture the leaders of the nationalists or compelled them to sign an instrument of surrender that would have demonstrated the physical and psychological ending of the civil war. On the other hand, the escape to Taiwan enabled the nationalists to feel that they were not defeated at all since they were able to set up a parallel government of China in Taiwan. Due to American protection, the communists could not extend the war to Taiwan or go there to stop the nationalists from claiming to represent China. This resulted in a stalemate that continues to heighten the China/Taiwan issue today.

Due to the ideological coloration of the China matter, China which had defeated the nationalist government of Chiang Kai-shek was denied admission into the UN by the United States and its allies. President Harry Truman declared:

> We shall refuse to recognize any government imposed upon a nation by the force of any foreign power. In some cases, it may be impossible to prevent the forceful imposition of such a government. But the United States will not recognize any such government.[5]

Resultantly, Taiwan held the China seat in the UN until 1971 before China replaced it. Among the African states, twenty-seven voted for the resolution which removed Taiwan from the UN while twelve voted against the resolution since they were aligned with the United States and the West.[6] The twenty-seven states which supported the resolution were oriented toward liberating the continent from Western colonialism. Nigeria's minister of foreign affairs under the Buhari administration, Mr. Geoffrey Onyeama, explained:

> Of course, Nigeria and Africa also played an important role in getting China to be admitted as a member of the United Nations because before then, it was Taiwan that was considered and had a seat at the Security Council of the UN. So, China has always been very grateful to Africa and Nigeria for the role they played in making it to become a UN member and a member of the Security Council.[7]

The African response to the UN resolution to remove Taiwan was influenced by anticolonialism, antiapartheid, and the Cold War as many African states aligned with the Eastern bloc against the Western bloc. It was this alliance that culminated in the war of independence in Algeria, Angola, Guinea-Bissau, Mozambique, Namibia, and Zimbabwe. Egypt was the first African country to recognize China on May 30, 1956, and Morocco followed on November 1, 1958. Like a bandwagon, other newly independent African countries followed suit. The most recent countries to do so included Eritrea (May 24, 1993), South Africa (January 1, 1998), and South Sudan (July 9, 2011). Nigeria's minister of foreign affairs, Mr. Geoffrey Onyeama, explained the influence of the Cold War on Nigerian relations with China:

> First, in the early days of the relationship, we had a cold war in the world, and we had the developing countries that were non-aligned. Nigeria was a non-aligned country and we always had the support of China and worked together at the multi-lateral level—United Nations and other multilateral organizations.[8]

The One-China Foreign Policy of China

Following its humiliating experiences dealing with the West during the Opium Wars in the mid-nineteenth century and how some of its territories were taken and colonized, China vowed to reintegrate all Chinese territories to ensure that there is only one China. Driven by this goal, a major facet of its foreign policy has been to prevent Taiwan from becoming an independent state. In fact, in 2005, China enacted the anti-secession law which states categorically its right to use non-peaceful means to stop Taiwan if it declares independence. It convinced the world to accept the notion of one China, which requires the reintegration of Taiwan with the mainland. Even the UN agrees with this view.[9] Using its enormous economic and financial clout, it has dissuaded almost all African states to cut off relations with Taiwan since there can be only one China. China's second goal is to recoup its past glory and become a superglobal power by spreading its tentacles across the world. A possible third goal is to embrace Africa to secure natural resources for its industries while at the same time, establishing a market for its finished goods.

On the other hand, Taiwan has shifted from the 1947 "One-China Principle" it embraced to seek independence and become a soverign state. However, it does not want to embroil itself in a hot war with its mainland sister since the balance of military power is lopsidedly in favor of China. Moreover, it does not want to embroil the United States into a war with China that is capable of degenerating into a nuclear conflagration. As a result, it operates tactically as an independent entity even though it does not use the term per se. To reduce any possibility of conflict, both China and Taiwan refer to their conflicting interests as cross-strait relations.[10] Despite the pressure mounted by China to persuade other countries from establishing relations with Taiwan, the island continues to maintain diplomatic and economic relations with about twenty states. These states recognize it as an independent nation. In addition, it maintains nondiplomatic relations with about fifty-seven states and the European Union (EU).[11]

While China has achieved so much in scientific, technological, economic, and infrastructural development, Taiwan too has a remarkable record of growth in those spheres. As such, it has a robust free-market economy and a high standard of living, with a democratic political system that allows for freedom of speech and the right to vote.

FACTORS THAT MOTIVATED AFRICAN STATES TO DERECOGNIZE TAIWAN AND SUPPORT CHINA

Under international law, to attain statehood, four conditions must be met: (1) an indigenous population, (2) a defined territory, (3) a self-ruling government, and (4) an ability to establish relations with other states.[12] If these conditions were applied to China and Taiwan, it is obvious that both meet the basic requirements for statehood. However, due to sovereignty, individual states determine on their own accord whether to recognize or not an independent-seeking nation or group. Therefore, even though Taiwan meets the conditions for statehood, strategic considerations have persuaded many countries to refuse to recognize or broke diplomatic relations with it while emphatically recognizing China. In particular, African countries have been very emphatic in recognizing China while breaking diplomatic relations with Taiwan. What factors prompted these states to do so? Six major factors could be identified for having influenced African states to derecognize Taiwan and support China: (a) strong anticolonial and antiapartheid sentiments and the need for liberation, (b) Western hesitation in engaging in substantial infrastructural development and modernization of African economies, (c) the high interest rates that Western governments and financial institutions charge for providing financial loans to African states, (d) the caretaker (care takerism) model of rulership in Africa, (e) the begging (beggarism) syndrome emanating from care takerism, and (f) necessity doctrine and expediency.

Strong Anticolonial and Antiapartheid Sentiments and the Need for Liberation

First, immediately after World War II ended, the demand for decolonization and independence increased in the colonies, not only in Africa but throughout the world. While some colonial powers were willing to grant independence, others were not so eager to do so. The hesitation, especially by France, Belgium, and Portugal, forced many early African nationalists to look toward the Soviet Union and the communist bloc for assistance in equipping, training, and financing liberation fighters, especially in Algeria, Angola, Guinea-Bissau, Mozambique, Namibia, Rhodesia, South Africa, and so forth. As they increasingly looked toward the Eastern bloc for assistance, they established relations with communist and socialist states, including the USSR, Cuba, East Germany, Czechoslovakia, Yugoslavia, and so forth. Since China became a communist state after the communist victory in the civil war against the nationalists in 1949, it was sympathetic to the liberation struggles in Africa. Chairman Mao Zedong of the PRC recognized the affinity between his country and the liberation fighters by referring to them as "partners in the struggle against imperialism."[13] It should be noted that during the move toward China, Taiwan had more diplomatic relations with African states than China. Around 1963, Taiwan had relations with about twenty-three African countries while China had diplomatic relations with only five. This was possible because many African countries in the late 1950s and early 1960s gained independence through negotiated settlements with their former colonial masters. As such, they were not hostile to the West and Taiwan appeared to have benefited from the warm relationship.

However, since the situations in Algeria, Angola, Guinea-Bissau, Mozambique, Namibia, South Africa, and Zimbabwe necessitated a liberation war, many Pan-African states supported the establishment of armed groups to fight and liberate the aforementioned territories from colonialism and the apartheid system in South Africa. Since communist and socialist countries supported the liberation of colonial territories, the Soviet Union, East Germany, Cuba, China, and Czechoslovakia got involved in the African liberation struggles. Again, Geoffrey Onyeama, Nigeria's foreign minister in Muhammadu Buhari's administration, explained:

We worked with them at the anti-colonial level and in the struggle against Apartheid. China was always supportive of Africa and as you know, Nigeria was considered the frontline state in the struggle to dismantle Apartheid and colonialism in Africa. We have built-up relationships with them over time, believing that as developing countries, we had shared interests. This relationship also occurred in the multi-lateral organizations, such as the UN and it was very instrumental in making developing countries have a Secretary Generalship of the United Nations.[14]

On the other hand, since the colonial powers, including Belgium, Britain, France, Netherlands, Portugal, and Spain, were allies of the United States, which was engaged in the Cold War against the Soviet Union, they opposed the African liberation struggle. They believed that the liberation struggle was a strategic tool by the communist bloc to spread communism and take over Africa from Western control. As a result, the United States was not at the forefront of the abolition of colonialism since it did not want to antagonize its Western allies. Instead, it enunciated a containment policy intended to checkmate the expansion of communist influence in the world. The policy contributed to the US support for apartheid South Africa against the interest of Africa.[15] Communist China benefited from the fact that Africans sought independence from Western colonialism. Therefore, it was quite easy for the anticolonial fighters to establish relations with the communists and Socialists since they agreed in totality with the need for independence of the colonies. In fact, between 1960 and 1977, China supported and supplied arms and money to African liberation movements like the Soviet Union and Cuba.[16]

On the other hand, Taiwan being a staunch anticommunist nation had the unfortunate circumstance of being aligned with the United States which was not comfortable with the anticolonial stance of many African nationalists. Moreover, the United States, like Britain, worked cooperatively with the South African government to sustain the apartheid system in its effort to resist communist influence in Africa. Taiwan agreed with the anticommunist stance of the United States and South Africa by establishing diplomatic relations with South Africa in 1949. H. K. Yang, the Taiwanese ambassador to South Africa, justified his country's position by saying, "South Africa and my country are joined in the fight against communism, democracy, and freedom."[17] This meant that Taiwan was not sensitive to the African concern about the apartheid system in South Africa. Instead, it reinforced the alliance between the two nations by establishing a bilateral nuclear agreement which required the country to supply about 4,000 tons of uranium to South Africa.[18] However, as communist China identified more with the anticolonial struggle, an increasing number of African countries began to transfer their recognition from Taiwan to China. The tilt toward the PRC not only in Africa but in other parts of the world eventually led to the removal of Taiwan and its replacement by China in the UN in 1971. Among the states that voted to eject Taiwan from the UN twenty-seven were African entities.[19] It should be noted that the 1970s were noted for intensive anticolonial wars in Africa.

Therefore, from having a relationship with about thirty African countries in the past, Taiwan in 2021 has a diplomatic relationship with only Eswatini (former Swaziland). This means that almost all independent African states now have diplomatic relations with China and not with Taiwan. The shift from Taiwan to China could have been greatly influenced by the One-China policy and the fact that China has invested extensively in Africa. It is estimated that from 2000 to 2018, China provided $152 billion loans to African states, thereby compelling them to be obligated to China.[20] The top ten debtor states in Africa are as follows: Angola ($25 billion), Ethiopia ($13.5 billion), Kenya ($7.9 billion), the Republic of the Congo ($7.3 billion), Sudan (6.4 billion), Zambia ($6 billion), Cameroon ($5.5 billion), Nigeria ($4.8 billion), Ghana ($3.5 billion), and the Democratic Republic of the Congo (DRC) ($3.4 billion).[21]

Western Hesitation in Supporting Substantive Infrastructural Development and Modernization of the African Economy

Having gained independence, African states expected their former colonial powers to provide some assistance in ensuring their infrastructural development. Unfortunately, the European nations seemed uninterested in doing so to ensure African industrialization. Rather, their actions tended to create the impression that they prefer African states to remain as mere producers of cash crops and raw materials. For instance, Ghana's effort to build the Volta Dam resulted in an exploitative relationship when, through the prodding of the United States, Kaiser Industries agreed to build a smelter but set the price for obtaining electricity to run the project so low. Moreover, the United States introduced Cold War politics into the matter so much that the project became a financial quagmire for Ghana.[22] Likewise, in an effort to develop the transportation infrastructure, Tanzania and Zambia agreed to build the TANZAM railway to connect the two countries. They sought financial and technical assistance from Western nations and the Soviet Union but were turned down in the 1960s. China accepted the proposition and completed the project in 1975 with interest-free loans.[23] To facilitate the movement of goods and people, Ethiopia and Djibouti agreed to build the Addis Ababa to Djibouti railway, and it was China that built it and not a Western country, even though Ethiopia had a long-term relationship with the West.[24]

Perhaps, to ensure perpetual underdevelopment, many infrastructural development activities that Western nations supported in Africa in the 1960s,

1970s, and 1980s were capital-intensive industrial projects with prohibitive conditions that resulted in massive corruption and debt.[25] The failed projects contributed to the retarding of economic development in sub-Saharan Africa.

While the West hesitated, China plunged headlong in carrying out massive infrastructural development projects in Africa. The projects involve energy, telecommunications industries, public health, railway construction, technical assistance, power plants, optical networks, port facilities, dam construction, medical training, public buildings, hydropower, and offshore oil development. These infrastructural projects are capable of transforming Africa into a major economic powerhouse in the future. Hence, Sella Oneko and Philipp Sandner noted, "For Africa, the relationship to the world's second-biggest economy, China, has meant an alternative to relying on the former colonial powers of the West."[26]

The High Interest Rates Charged by Western Governments and Financial Institutions on Financial Loans That Lead to Debt Trap

In contemporary times, the concept of debt trap or debt book has become the catchy terminology for describing China's methodology for doing business with African countries. So, what is a debt trap? The debt trap is generally defined as a means whereby a "creditor country intentionally extends excessive credit to debtor country, thereby inducing the debtor into a debt trap. This is done with the intention of extracting economic or political concessions from the debtor country when it is unable to meet its debt repayment obligations."[27] In short, a debt trap is a business strategy whereby a state or an organization intentionally entraps a borrower by providing generous financial loans or investments to enable a borrower to borrow to a point of being incapable of repaying the debt incurred. By failing to meet the terms of the loans or contracts, the creditor uses the opportunity to impose its will on the borrower, thereby subjecting it to whatever demands the creditor wants. The concept of the debt trap was first developed in 2017 by Brahma Chellaney who studied the manner in which China does business to reinforce its Belt and Road Initiative (BRI).[28] Concerning the issue of the debt trap, it is necessary to trace the African experience in dealing with it.

First, although the notion of a debt trap is now linked with China's business practices, nonetheless, the country is not responsible for initiating the strategy for entrapping potential victim states. It was Western nations and major international business organizations which initiated business practices that entrapped countries that wanted to develop their economies. It should be recalled that when African countries gained independence, almost all the former colonial powers instituted preconditions that prevented them from doing business with other countries. As a result, former British colonies were prevented from doing business with France and other countries. France made sure that its former colonies only do business with France and not with other countries. In fact, France still maintains a two-currency policy in which eight of its former colonies are tied to the West African Economic and Monetary Union, and six others are attached to the Central African Economic and Monetary Community. The arrangement compels the fourteen African countries to do business with the Bank of France by depositing 50% of their foreign exchange reserves there.[29]

Almost all the newly independent African states were prevented from doing business with socialist and communist countries in the 1960s, 1970s, and 1980s. This accounted for why Patrice Lumumba was killed and replaced because he was thought to be a socialist. Kwame Nkrumah of Ghana was looked upon suspiciously for being too friendly with Socialist and communist countries. Guinea suffered during the rulership of Sékou Touré because the country refused to sign the French Constitution and the French wrecked the country's infrastructure as much as possible.[30] Africa is filled with numerous cases where political and military rulers were overthrown because they attempted to establish political and economic relations with countries that the former colonial powers did not want them to associate with.

Second, most Western foreign aids and assistance programs are intended to cause a debt trap for African countries. The reason being that for every aid or assistance program sent to Africa, conditions are attached to the extent that the receiving countries end up paying more. Hence, following a report by a group of nongovernmental organizations, Mark Anderson wrote: "The report says that while Western countries send about $30bn in development aid to Africa every year, more than six times that amount leaves the continent 'mainly to the same countries providing that aid.'"[31]

Third, newly independent African countries in the 1960s, 1970s, and 1980s had no choice but to go along with business practices that rewarded their former colonial powers and their companies while indebting themselves. This was how the Royal Shell dominated the oil business in Nigeria. Britain had made sure that only Shell could engage in oil exploration in Nigeria through its Mineral Ordinances which prevented the indigenes of the Niger Delta from engaging in petroleum exploration.[32] Even in the twenty-first century the oil business in Nigeria, Cameroon, Angola, Gabon, and others are dominated by giant multinational corporations and the countries have little or no say in how much oil is being produced. Overall, multinational companies take away from Africa about $46 billion annually without paying commensurate taxes to the African countries.[33]

Fourth, it was a common practice to make it exceedingly difficult for Third World countries, especially those in Africa, to borrow loans to invest in their infrastructural development. By making it excessively difficult, the would-be-borrower country was forced to borrow loans or obtain contracts at very high interest rates. Even when the borrower realized that the interest on the loan was excessive, it was left with no other option but to accept the high rate if it wanted to develop its infrastructure and the economy. Left with little or no option, the borrower was trapped and compelled to meet conditions that tended to threaten its sovereignty. In fact, in the 1970s and 1980s, many countries in Africa and Latin America defaulted on loans they borrowed from Western financial institutions like the International Monetary Fund and World Bank.[34] It is not surprising that in 2017, Ghana spent about 30% of its revenue on debt repayment. In Mozambique, an aluminum smelter built with loans and a supposed foreign aid is reported to be costing substantially in financial repayment.[35]

It is costly for African countries to do business with Western countries and companies because Western lenders charge about 50–55% interest on borrowed loans. Such high interest rates result in a debt trap. In fact, a major reason which influenced African countries to seek business relations with China is the low interest rates that it offers. China's enterprises charge about 17% interest on borrowed loans.[36]

Therefore, if the United States and other Western nations are really committed to reducing the debt trap as the US bipartisan group of sixteen senators in August 2018 stated: "It is imperative that the United States counters China's attempts to hold other countries financially hostage and force ransoms that further its geostrategic goal," they should first put pressure on their own financial institutions to stop charging high interest rates on financial loans.[37] Likewise, while former US vice president Mike Pence suggested in a 2018 speech about the importance of providing "foreign nations a just and transparent alternative to China's debt-trap diplomacy," he should realize that the debt trap practices of Western lending institutions are responsible for persuading many developing countries to seek economic and financial ties with China.

The Caretaker Model of Rulership in Africa

Although modern African rulers claim to be leaders of sovereign states, nevertheless, they tend to behave as if they are merely caretakers who are taking care of the territorial properties of their former colonial masters. As a result, they do not act as leaders who are committed to advancing the lives of their citizens. Marcus T. Cicero, the Roman political thinker, believes that leaders must be just, maintain a good reputation by avoiding suspicious and corrupting circumstances, protect their citizens over their personal interests, avoid burdensome taxation on the citizens, and ensure that they have necessities of life. Moreover, leaders must have the ability to persuade rather than threaten or intimidate.[38] Cicero's view of good leadership is supported by John of Salisbury who believes that a leader (prince) must obey the law and must serve the people and not his personal interest.[39] Modern African rulers can hardly qualify under Cicero and John's criteria for good leadership since they act as caretakers. Caretakerism can be defined as political behavior in which a ruler behaves as if he or she is not a leader but someone who is taking care of another person's property in the hope of being compensated or rewarded. African rulers act as caretakers in various ways.

First, after the colonies gained independence, the rulers did not take practical steps to redraw the boundaries of the states to ensure territorial compatibility with the geographical distribution of the ethnic groups. The rulers simply adopted the arbitrary colonial boundaries without adjusting them to ensure ethnic compatibility. As a result, some African countries would never be stable because of the way the ethnic groups are distributed. For instance, the Fulanis are spread into Senegal, Mali, Guinea, Chad, Mauretania, Niger, Nigeria, Cameroon, Ghana, Benin, Burkina Faso, and possibly Central African Republic. The Tuaregs are found in Algeria, Burkina Faso, Mali, Niger, Chad, and Libya. The Berbers are in Algeria, Egypt, Libya, Mali, Mauretania, Morocco, and Tunisia. The Masai are found in Kenya and Tanzania. The Tutsis are found in Burundi, the DRC, Rwanda, and possibly Uganda. The Somalis are found in Somalia, Somaliland, Kenya, Djibouti, and Ethiopia. The Akan people are found in Ghana and Ivory Coast (Côte d'Ivoire). The Hausas are in Benin, Cameroon, Chad, Ivory Coast, Ghana, Niger, Nigeria, and possibly Togo. The Yorubas are in Nigeria, Benin, and Togo. Territorial problems affect most African states to the point that when something happens in one state, it spreads to other states because of the spread of ethnic groups. Neither the African Union nor the regional organizations have made any effort to redraw territorial boundaries to reflect African ethnic realities.

Second, African rulers have not made any serious attempt to Africanize their states to reflect the cultures, traditions, and institutions of their citizens. Resultantly, almost all modern African states have political, judicial, governmental, educational, and religious systems that are borrowed from their former colonial masters and conquering powers. Therefore, there is nothing in these states to show that they are African political entities. If African rulers were true leaders, they would have reshaped their states to reflect African cultural principles, traditions, and institutions of governance.

Third, most African rulers do not seem to care about the issue of governance. As a result, they pay little or no attention to the potential implications of their policies and actions, which often contribute to the destabilization of their countries. For instance, on assuming office as Nigeria's head of state in May

2015, President Muhammadu Buhari appointed mostly members of his ethnic group, region, and religion into high-level national security positions in a country that has about three hundred or more ethnic groups, thereby inflaming political passions to a degree in which many ethnic groups are calling for restructuring. Like caretakers, instead of serving as leaders, African rulers tend to focus primarily on self-preservation, hence surround themselves with mostly members of their families, ethnic groups, regions, religious affiliations, and political parties. The tendency toward personalization, tribalization, and regionalization of governance contributes to separatist and irredentist conflicts. Burkina Faso, Ivory Coast, Mozambique, Cameroon, Central African Republic, Libya, Ethiopia, Nigeria, the DRC, Ivory Coast, Liberia, Mali, Sierra Leone, Uganda, Somalia, Chad, and many others face irredentist and separatist threats regularly.

Fourth, many African rulers have no respect for the constitutions of their countries. They amend them at will and rig elections endlessly to remain in power and threaten opposition parties and candidates. Generally, most African rulers detest leaving office after completing their constitutional term limits. Therefore, Algeria, Tunisia, Equatorial Guinea, Libya, Uganda, Djibouti, Congo-Brazzaville, Cameroon, Chad, Togo, and so forth, have had rulers who ruled for fifteen or more years. The sit-tight behavior of rulers like President Teodoro Obiang Nguema Mbasogo of Equatorial Guinea, President Paul Biya of Cameroon, President Yoweri Museveni of Uganda, President Faure Gnassingbe Eyadema of Togo, and others contribute to political instability in their respective countries.

Fifth, many African rulers and their surrogates engage in massive pilfering of public funds. Generally, the embezzled funds end up in banks that are in the home countries of their former colonial masters. The former colonial powers used the embezzled funds to enhance their economies while the African economy is stunted. Nick Dearden of Al Jazeera reported a 2014 estimate which indicated that rich Africans ferreted away about $500 billion in tax havens.[40]

Sixth, almost all African rulers tend to send their children to school overseas while the children of the masses remain at home. They refuse to build modern medical facilities that can provide quality healthcare services to their citizens while they and their families receive healthcare services abroad and are paid for by the state. Some African rulers, including Umaru Musa Yar'Adua of Nigeria, Robert Mugabe of Zimbabwe, Ali Bongo Ondimba of Gabon, Levy Mwanawasa and Michael Sata of Zambia, Malam Bacai Sanha of Guinea-Bissau, and Meles Zenawi of Ethiopia, died in overseas hospitals.[41]

Seventh, most African rulers tend to look for an easy way out instead of tightening their belt and developing economic structures that can result in the industrialization of their states. Consequently, they scout the globe for foreign powers that would offer them foreign aid and help them to pretend to develop their countries. Thus, the core foreign policy goals of many African rulers seem to be focused on looking for foreign aid, international loans, and bilateral and multilateral relations that are likely to result in self-enrichment. They generally do not mind sacrificing the interest of their citizens to satisfy their personal financial needs by signing agreements that impact their countries negatively. As a result, it was not difficult for many of them to cut diplomatic ties with Taiwan and establish relations with China as the country became a major global economic and financial powerhouse. China suffered humiliation at the hands of foreign powers and its leaders decided not to allow such experience to repeat itself, so its leaders developed and modernized the country. On the other hand, Africa suffered from slavery, religious and military conquest, and colonialism, yet African rulers have not been sufficiently motivated to develop their own states the way the Chinese have done in China and Taiwan. Instead, they are busy looking for outside assistance. Hence, it was very easy for China to woo African countries away from Taiwan.

The Beggar Syndrome Emanating from Caretakerism

Originating from the caretaker style of rulership, it seems that a sizable number of African rulers do not want to transform themselves into leaders. Instead, they behave as if they are beggars. As such, they prefer to sit on the sidelines and expect foreign states, companies, and individuals to come and assist them to develop instead of mobilizing their citizens to ensure self-development. In doing so, they sacrifice the interest of their citizens and the abundance of natural resources in their territories. The following provide ways in which they behave as beggars instead of as leaders: (1) they put more faith in development plans put forward by experts from their former colonial powers and the developed countries, (2) they are more likely to award major contracts to companies and consultants from foreign countries in the hope that they would be individually rewarded by the home countries of those contractors, (3) they are always eager to sign contracts with foreign powers in the hope that they would be rewarded personally, (4) they sign atrocious business deals with multinational corporations that exploit their states but enrich themselves, and (5) they are willing to sign military pacts with powerful states that reward and protect them personally while threatening the sovereignty of their states.

First, most African rulers seem to put more faith in development plans put forward by experts from their former colonial powers and the developed countries and ignore the experts in their own countries. They are probably prompted to do so to avoid antagonizing their former colonial masters whom they think could instigate instability resulting in their being kicked out of office. It is not surprising that about fourteen Francophone African countries have a politico-economic and financial deal with France that turns them into semiautonomous states rather than independent entities. As a result, the rulers of these states always turn to France and possibly Belgium to assist them to remain in power. Hence, France has an extensive military presence in many Francophone states. Even Nigeria that claims to be the leader of sub-Saharan Africa is still largely dependent upon Britain in many ways. It was Britain that actively intervened to assist the federal side against Biafra during the civil war (1967–1970). It was also Britain that assisted Nigeria to clean its image over the allegations of human rights abuses during the civil war when a UN Observer Team was sent to investigate the matter. The leader of the observer team was a British military officer. Due to the difficulty on the part of the Nigerian Army to end the Boko Haram War, some Nigerians are suggesting that the country should seek foreign military assistance. The United States, France, and Britain are currently involved in fighting terrorist groups in the continent. China has a military base in Djibouti.

Second, African rulers are more likely to award major contracts to contractors and consultants from foreign countries in the hope that they would be individually rewarded by the home countries of the contractors. Some African rulers intentionally seek contractors and professional advice from outside consultants as a means to establish a conduit for ferreting out embezzled public funds. Tom Burgis noted that in the DRC, the Kabila regimes (father and son) transferred mining assets worth $5 billion from state control to private ownership, thereby depriving the state and their citizens the right to the wealth generated. This arrangement benefited the political leadership and the private companies.[42] There are large deposits of gold and diamond in many African countries, but the rulers allow foreign citizens, including the Chinese, to exploit the resources to the dismay of the indigenous populations.

Third, African rulers are always eager to sign bilateral and multilateral treaties with foreign powers in the hope that they would be personally rewarded with all kinds of favors. By so doing, they stunt the growth of their states in terms of scientific, technological, and economic development. Increasingly, reports indicate that many contracts that African governments signed with China are done with a high degree of secrecy to the extent that most citizens of these states have no understanding of the terms of the contracts. Due to the secrecy, the cost of goods and projects is inflated to enrich the African officials who negotiate the deals on behalf of their states. Kingsley Jeremiah of the *Nigerian Guardian* wrote:

> While Nigeria and China have in recent times entered into funding deals reportedly standing at $47 billion and spread across 22 major infrastructural

projects, the current agitations backed by some civil society organizations are coming at a time when other African countries, including Kenya, are unraveling massive corruption in loans and contracts led by China.[43]

Okiya Omtata, a Kenyan activist, went to court in 2013 to know the details of contracts signed between Kenya and China over various projects, including the standard gauge railway line that was estimated to cost $3.2 billion.[44] Okiya Omtata, a Kenyan activist, went to court in 2013 to know the details of contracts signed involving Kenya and China over various projects, including the standard gauge railway line that was estimated to cost $3.2 billion. The waiver allowed the company to import items that are available in Nigeria, thereby arousing suspicion about what prompted the Nigeria Customs Service to grant such a waiver.[45]

Fourth, acting as beggars, they sign atrocious business deals with multinational corporations that exploit their states but enrich themselves. The rulers and their high-level officials sign such atrocious business deals that allow multinational companies to exploit their resources in the hope that the companies will reward them personally. A typical example of a country where multinational corporations gain tremendously at the disadvantage of the citizens is Nigeria. Even though Nigeria claims to be the superpower of Africa, its relationships with multinational oil corporations are unbelievably in favor of the oil corporations and the ruling elite.

Generally, in almost all African countries, the indigenes of the resource-rich regions have no say in decisions about the exploration and management of the resources. Similarly, the indigenes of the resource-rich regions are marginalized, deprived, and cheated from gaining from the wealth. The lopsided arrangements that favor the international corporations are purposely done to reward the political and military rulers and their high-level officials that sign the contracts. The rulers get rich, and the citizens get poorer.[46] This is why many African countries are mired in poverty and conflict. A report in 2014 indicated that about $46 billion were siphoned off from Africa by multinational corporations. At the same time, about $35 billion were taken out of Africa into a tax haven overseas.[47]

Fifth, acting as beggars who are always looking for easy handouts, many African rulers are willing to sacrifice their economies by signing bilateral and multilateral economic treaties that impoverish their citizens and stunt economic growth. Some countries signed free trade deals with the EU under the European Union Economic Partnership Agreements that allow European countries to export their government-subsidized goods and services in the continent, thereby making it difficult for domestic producers of such goods to thrive. The result is that many local producers give up as their products cannot compete with the cheap imports. Ghana provides a typical example of a situation where the national government signed a free trade deal with the EU, thereby enabling European countries to export their tomato products into the country. Likewise, many Ghanaian traders import tomatoes from Burkina Faso. The cheap imports contribute to the destruction of the local tomato industry.[48]

Generally, African farmers and producers of various goods suffer from free trade deals that allow foreign products to pour into their countries, thereby making it difficult for domestic farmers and producers to prosper because their products are incapable of competing with the subsidized foreign products. The situation got so bad that Nigeria had to close its borders in 2018 suspecting that many foreign goods were pouring into the country through other West African states.[49] Kenya, Rwanda, and other African countries too had closed their borders at various times.

Sixth, African rulers are willing to sign military pacts with powerful states that can subvert the sovereignty of their countries but reward them personally through security protection. Instead of taking proactive measures to develop their industrial sector and produce their military equipment, most African rulers prefer to beg for arms from foreign countries. As a result, Africa is probably the only continent in which most states, except for South Africa, do not produce their own military technology. This means that almost all African countries rely on imported weapons to ensure their security. The failure of African rulers to embark on domestic production of arms clearly indicates that they do not act as leaders because they are always looking for easy handouts, thereby solidifying the theory of beggarism. On the other hand, Malaysia, Singapore, South Korea, Taiwan, India, Brazil, Israel, and so forth are producing and exporting weapons to earn foreign exchange. Moreover, North Korea, India, and Pakistan, like China, have nuclear weapons.

Thus, the need to get easy loans forced many African rulers to rush to China in the hope that the country would assist them to develop their countries, instead of working hard to ensure self-development. In doing so, they forget that in international politics, there is no free lunch since the system is anarchic and Machiavellian. Therefore, China should not be held accountable for whatever happens in Africa since national interest dictates that states apply whatever means necessary to ensure their strategic interests.

The Application of the Doctrine of Expediency by African Rulers to Emphasize National Interest

While African rulers might be accused of acting like caretakers and beggars, on the one hand, they could be said to be strategic in their thinking on the other hand. By utilizing the doctrine of expediency to move away from the Western economic orbit, cut ties with Taiwan, and embrace China, they act as leaders on the international scene. They seemed to have rationalized that their states have more to gain by establishing relations with China rather than with Taiwan. Nigeria's foreign minister, Geoffrey Onyeama, again explained:

> At the international level, we cooperate with China and also have their support. As we seek, for instance, to reform the United Nations and the Security Council, China has been very supportive of that endeavor for Africa to be better represented on the Security Council. A lot of our businesspeople also go to China now to source their products. So, it is a people-to-people relationship that keeps growing considering that a large number of Nigerians and Chinese are symbiotically involved in business.[50]

By aligning with China, they gain a strategic advantage in the sense that no Western country can threaten China in Africa without weighing the enormous risks involved. By so doing, African rulers are increasingly carving out an independent path different from the road map that Western nations might have propounded for them. Therefore, African rulers could be said to be as crafty as leaders of other states in the world since they are playing international politics in a manner that rewards their states. According to a common African expression, it is now a medicine after death for Western nations to scramble to alert the world about China's debt trap and possible colonization of Africa since they had decades of opportunity to contribute positively toward the infrastructural development of the continent and failed. On the other hand, China is actively contributing to the infrastructural development of Africa which ultimately may result in the industrialization of the continent's economy. Already, Africa had the fastest developed economy in 2019 due to the massive infrastructural projects that are enhancing economic mobilization. The development prompted Wade Shepard of Forbes to write:

> The attention of the world is now drifting towards Africa, with comparisons to 1990s-era-China are no longer coming off as a radical projection. China has likewise become a central player in Africa's urbanization push, as a huge percentage of the continent's infrastructure initiatives are being driven by Chinese companies and/or backed by Chinese funding. China is now Africa's biggest trade partner, with Sino-African trade topping $200 billion per year.[51]

Therefore, in terms of gaining from the economics of large scale, it was strategically advantageous for African states to cut ties with Taiwan and establish relations with China. Nigeria's foreign minister, Geoffrey Onyeama, noted, "China developed rapidly economically and technologically, faster than any country has done historically and became a superpower. During that period, the nature of relationships also changed, especially as Africa has been growing."[52] However, the expediency argument is dampened by the massive debt incurred, thereby subjecting the continent to the possibility of Chinese colonization.

MASSIVE INDEBTEDNESS THAT THREATENS STATES' RIGHT TO DO BUSINESS WITH TAIWAN

While Taiwan continues to hold its own and makes its presence known internationally, due to a buoyant economy, it has not been able to compete with China's ability to influence other countries in its sphere of influence. On the other hand, to ensure that Taiwan's global presence is significantly reduced, China literally flooded the world with enormous financial, technological, and development resources to push countries away from doing business with it. Due to the eagerness with which China invests in the continent, almost all African countries now do business with PRC and not with Taiwan. In fact, in 2018, Burkina Faso broke diplomatic ties with Taiwan and reestablished relations with China. A spokesperson of China's foreign ministry stated, "We welcome Burkina Faso's return to the big family of China-Africa friendly cooperation based on the one-China principle." On the other hand, the spokesperson of Taiwan's Foreign Ministry referred to the decision as a "sad situation."[53]

In Africa, there is no doubt that China has created a greater impact in the last thirty or more years in infrastructural development activities than the Western countries which actually established most of the African states. Therefore, it is predictable that a vast majority of African states will continue to align with China due to the extensive Sino-African relationship. Moreover, some of the projects that are being carried out in the continent involve long-term payback plans. Some African observers have expressed concern that China has replaced Western nations and is increasingly behaving like a colonial overlord in Africa. This further means that Taiwan's ability to reestablish an active working relationship with African countries will be almost impossible in the immediate future because it cannot engage in large-scale financial investment and infrastructural development projects that Africa needs.

Additionally, China does not hesitate to flex its enormous political, financial, and economic muzzle against any state that attempts to do business with Taiwan. It reacts very quickly whenever any of its allies try to do business with Taiwan by cutting off diplomatic relations. Breaking off diplomatic relations also means terminating economic and financial relationships. For African countries, China's policy of cutting off relations with any country that does business with Taiwan is a serious threat since most of them owe China billions of dollars in loans. This means that most

African countries are locked into China's orbit since they cannot afford to annoy the country at a time when they need a dependable financier and developer. Hence, to avoid antagonizing China, South Africa prevented the Dai Lama of Tibet from attending a World Summit of Nobel Peace laureates in the country. The refusal provoked Bishop Desmond Tutu to criticize the government.[54]

A second way China flexes its muzzle is by using its veto power in the Security Council of the UN. Although it rarely exercises this extraordinary power, nevertheless, it does not hesitate to veto any action that enhances the capability of any country which recognizes or does business with Taiwan. Consequently, when Macedonia in 1999 recognized Taiwan, China vetoed a peace-keeping mission in the Balkans, thereby exposing Macedonia to regional conflict.[55]

While China's threat against most African countries is real, the Caribbean and Central American states can act in a manner that ensures their ability to do business with Taiwan. The implication is that the American countries in the two subregions did not rush to China the way African countries did, hence can get from both China and Taiwan. This forces China to compete with Taiwan for attention.[56] In rushing to do massive business with China, some African states might sacrifice their independence due to indebtedness. However, Nigeria's foreign minister, Geoffrey Onyeama, seems to disagree with the view that Africa might suffer from a debt trap by explaining:

> First, every country is out to protect its interest and promote its own development. No country or government is there only for the benefit of other countries. The primary concern and responsibility are for the wellbeing of the country and its citizens. So, when we go into these agreements and cooperation with other countries, China inclusive, it is incumbent on us. Nothing is forced on us. We sign agreements that we can live with and that are beneficial to us. China will also do the same on their side. That is the reason it is called an agreement. So, it is either you both agree, or you don't because it is not by force.[57]

CHINA'S ASSERTIVE EFFORTS TO ISOLATE TAIWAN COULD BACKFIRE DUE TO HEGEMONIC TENDENCIES

As a world power, China has numerous strategic advantages over Taiwan; nonetheless, the situation is not hopeless for Taiwan in Africa, even though only one state now recognizes it. Taiwan might be able to recoup its diplomatic relations with some African countries if China miscalculates or overplays its goal of isolating it. The undermentioned circumstances and considerations are some strategic missteps that have already taken place and those that may take place in the immediate future which could compel some African countries to reestablish relations with Taiwan.

First, due to its abundant critical raw materials, massive size, and sudden emergence as a technological, economic, and military superpower, it is increasingly being viewed as a big tiger that is working frantically to turn resource-rich African states into its captured dominions. Moreover, its sudden rise has ushered in a change in the global power structure, resulting in a shift from a unipolar power system dominated by the United States following the collapse of the Soviet Union into a tripolar system in which the United States, Russia, and China now compete for hegemonic control of the world, even though India is not far behind. China is now gravitating from being a gentle giant to becoming an assertive tiger. Consequently, it is increasingly displaying behaviors that are characteristic of hegemonic states which often impose their will on other states. The clearest example of its determination to assert its will is the tactical control of the South China Sea by creating islands in the middle of the ocean, building military installations, and claiming the right to own the area in such a manner that threatens its neighbors, including Vietnam and the Philippines. Another evidence of China's determination to assert its influence globally is its actualization of its BRI through the spreading of economic and financial investments in a manner that entangles Africa in its hegemonic umbrella.

Second, as a growing superpower, China's wooing of African countries through the massive pouring of financial loans and infrastructural development contracts seems to create the impression that it is trying to colonize the continent to maximize its presence and have unrestricted access to the abundant critical raw materials. The development is prompting some Africans to wonder whether China is attempting to replace European powers as the next colonial master in the continent. Indeed, the speed at which most African states broke diplomatic relations with Taiwan indicates that China is unquestionably spreading its influence geometrically.

Third, the unrestrained way it dishes out loans and engages in massive infrastructural activities tends to create the perception that China is strategically attempting to entrap African states with massive debt to compel them to be obligated to it for a very long time. As a result, a sizable number of Africans seemed apprehensive about China's motives. There is an increasing concern that many African countries could technically forfeit their sovereignty if they are unable to pay back the enormous loans they borrowed, thereby necessitating China's taking over of some of their critical assets. Currently, Zambia presents a worrisome scenario that is capable of replicating in other states if they are unable to pay back the loans they borrowed from China. It should be noted that Zambia ran into financial difficulty when it defaulted in paying back $40 million that was due to the creditor in October 2020. To reduce the financial pressure on Zambia, the China Development Bank provided a six-month delay in the repayment plan.[58] The Zambian default raised concern that China might be compelled to take over certain assets of the country. In fact, China indirectly took possession of the Zambia National Broadcasting Corporation by controlling the cash flow and the broadcast signal of the organization.[59] The Zambian situation compelled Nigerian legislators and citizens to question the series of loans that Nigeria borrowed from China to build various infrastructural development projects. Nigerians, like Zambians, are perturbed that if Nigeria defaults on the massive loans it borrowed, China could be compelled to seize Nigerian assets, especially the oil and gas fields in the Niger Delta/South-South zone. The fear prompted Nigeria's National Assembly to question the country's Minister of Transportation, Mr. Chibuike Rotimi Amaechi, about alleged secret arrangements made with China that are unknown to the public.[60] Due to the COVID-19 epidemic, other African countries, including Angola, Sudan, and the Republic of the Congo, face financial difficulties.

Fourth, an increasingly worrisome aspect of China's presence in Africa is that the country is even sending down ordinary Chinese workers (drivers, construction workers, plumbers, etc.) to work in Chinese firms, thereby preventing African citizens from gaining employment in those firms. People wonder why China should be sending ordinary workers to Africa to compete for employment when Africa has a huge population of jobless individuals.[61] In 1996, there were about 160,000 Chinese in Africa. The number climbed to about 1.1 million in 2012.[62] The number includes workers and nonworkers. However, the China Africa Research Institute of John Hopkins University reported that there were 182,745 Chinese workers in Africa in 2019, with most located in Algeria, Angola, Nigeria, Zambia, and Kenya.[63]

Fifth, the labor practices of Chinese companies in Africa are not something to be admired. The companies seem to engage in exploitative management practices that arouse anger among African workers. There was a particular case in Kenya where a Chinese supervisor literally slapped a Kenyan employee, thereby prompting the individual to slap the manager in retaliation. In Zambia, it was alleged that Chinese employers even locked down Zambian workers on their job premises to prevent them from going home as a preventive measure.[64] In 2006, Michael Sata, an opposition presidential candidate, threatened to recognize Taiwan if he wins the Zambian presidential election due to China's labor practices and its alliance with the ruling Zambian political party. In reaction, the Chinese ambassador threatened to withhold investment in the country if Sata wins the presidential election.[65] The issue of Chinese employment practices is a recurring theme in Sino-African relations.

Sixth, apart from the perception that companies from China do not treat their African workers with dignity nor pay them appropriately, there is an increasing feeling that in China, African citizens are treated disdainfully. In fact, during the early phase of the COVID-19 pandemic in April 2019, a video was flashed throughout the world, showing how Chinese officials and landlords violated the rights of Africans who lived in the city of Guangzhou. The ill-treatment aroused anger in Africa to the point that some African countries, including Nigeria, had to send their diplomats to discuss the matter with Chinese officials. Going back to 1979, clashes between Africans and Chinese occurred regularly in China. Hence, in 1986, about two hundred African students demonstrated in Beijing over their maltreatment.[66]

Increasingly, allegations of racism are being launched against the Chinese in Africa. For instance, a Chinese employer allegedly compared Africans to monkeys in Kenya. Likewise, some Chinese businesses in Kenya discriminated against their African employees.[67] In Zambia, the racial situation became volatile to the point where three Chinese, including Mrs. Cao Guifang, Bao Junbin, and Fan Minje, were killed by three Zambians. Likewise, Mayor Miles Sampa of Lusaka had to revoke the licenses of some Chinese businesses for racial discrimination.[68] Some Africans have insisted that Chinese workers should be sent back to China.

Seventh, if the China/Taiwan matter continues to drag on, a time may come in which some African states might react toward China's hegemonic tendency by rejecting it and reestablishing relations with Taiwan. In other words, some African states could be compelled to reestablish relations with Taiwan. Therefore, China must pay attention to the manner its officials, citizens, and companies treat Africans in Africa and China. It must also be very cautious in responding to the African debt matter.

CONCLUSION

In peroration, some significant inferences are drawn from the analytical study of the African relations with China and Taiwan. First, the Chinese Civil War between the communists and nationalists which began during World War II has not ended and continues to create tension in the world. Second, the civil war continues to be clothed with all the dynamic ingredients of the Cold War. Third, China is driven to achieve three principal goals, including integrating Taiwan with the mainland, spreading its influence globally through its BRI, and guaranteeing an uninterrupted supply of raw materials to feed its gigantic industrial machines as well as create a market for its products in Africa. Fourth, China is aided in achieving its goals by African states whose historical past compels them to reduce their economic relationship with the West and seeks a more fulfilling economic relationship with China, thereby opening their vast natural resources to China's massive industries. Fifth, the Sino-African relationship has the potential of turning Africa into a global economic powerhouse; however, the danger of a debt trap is a worrisome development. Sixth, African rulers tend to act as if they are caretakers and beggars instead of as leaders of states with vast critical natural resources that can turn Africa into a major economic and industrial power in the world. Due to their lack of appreciation, they easily give away their advantages by establishing bilateral and multilateral business agreements that allow others to exploit them and their citizens. Seventh, Taiwan will continue to seek various diplomatic means to achieve independence even though the odds are lopsidedly against it. It competes with a much bigger and boisterous tiger that has enormous economics of large scale to attract African states to its orbit. However, African relations with China are filled with fraught as the continent faces the possibility of being indebted to the country in the foreseeable future, thereby creating a possibility for Chinese colonization.

Globally, the One-China Policy seems to be a violation of international law because it threatens the sovereign rights of states to freely determine their right to recognize and establish diplomatic relations with any nation in the world. Due to its economic clout, China has forced African states to choose between doing business with it or recognize Taiwan. Following the doctrine of expediency, most African states choose to do business with China and derecognize Taiwan, even though the nation possesses the requisite characteristics that qualify it for statehood. The question is if China were not a major global power, would the African states, the UN, and most countries in the world agree to violate their right to determine whether they agree with the One-China Policy or not? It is maintained that the African relationship with China and Taiwan in the foreseeable future will be determined by China's behavior concerning the management of the huge African debt.

NOTES

1. Robert J. Art and Robert Jervis, *International Politics: Enduring Concepts and Contemporary Issues* (Pearson/Longman, 2005).

2. James H. Wolf, *Modern International Law: An Introduction to the Law of Nations* (Upper Saddle River, NJ: Prentice-Hall, 2002).

3. John Pickles and Jeff Woods, "Taiwanese Investment in South Africa," *African Affairs* 88, no. 353 (October 1989): 507–528.

4. Andrew Glass, "Stalin Pressures Allies to Open Second Front in Europe." *Politico*, August 13, 2017, https://www.politico.com/story/2017/13/stalin-pressures -allies-to-open-second-front-in-europe (accessed March 2021).

5. Warren Christopher, Normalization of Diplomatic Relations, Bureau of Public Affairs, Department of State (June 11, 1977).

6. Salem Solomon, "Once Influential in Africa, Taiwan Loses All but One Ally," *Voice of America*, May 26, 2018, https://www.voanews.com/africa/once-influential-africa-taiwan-loses-aall-one-ally (accessed September 25, 2020).

7. Bridget Chiedu Onochie, "Nigeria, China Relationship: We Sign Deals with Our Eyes Open, Says Onyeama," *The Guardian*, February 15, 2021, https:www.guardian.ng/politics/nigeria-china-relationships-we-sign-deals-with-our-eyes-open-says-onyeama/ (accesses March 12, 2021).

8. Ibid.

9. Kimutai Gilbert, "Countries That Recognize Taiwan," *World Atlas*, May 29, 2018, https://www.worlddatals.com/articles/which-countries-recogize-taiwan-as-a-country.html (accessed October 16, 2020).

10. Ibid.

11. Ibid.

12. Wolf, *Modern International Law.*

13. Timothy S. Rich and Vasabjit Banerjee, "The Chinese Presence in Africa: A Learning Process," *Journal of Current Chinese Affairs* 44, no. 1 (2015): 141–161.

14. Bridget Chiedu Onochie, "Nigeria, China Relationship: We Sign Deals with Our Eyes Open."

15. John T. Rourke and Mark A. Boyer, *World Politics*, 3rd ed. (Dushkin/McGraw-Hill, 2000), 33.

16. Richard H. Immerman and Petra Goedde, *The Oxford Handbook of the Cold War* (Oxford University Press, 2013).

17. Pickles and Woods, "Taiwanese Investment in South Africa."

18. Ibid.

19. Solomon, "Once Influential in Africa, Taiwan Loses All but One Ally."

20. Laura He, "China Is Promising to Write Off Some Loans to Africa," *CNN Business*, June 19, 2020, cnn.com/2020/06/19/economy/china-xi-jinping-africa-intl-hnk/index.html (accessed October 12, 2020).

21. Takudzwa Chiwanza Hillary, "The Top Ten African Countries with the Largest Chinese Debt," *The African Exponent*. Archived from the original on May 18, 2019.

22. Peter Calvert and Susan Calvert, *Politics and Society in the Developing World*, 3rd ed. (Pearson/Longman, 2007).

23. Tanzania – Zambia Railway Authority, "Our History." n.d., www.tazarasite.com/our-history (accessed February 23, 2021).

24. Sophie Morhn-Yron, "All Aboard! The Chinese-Funded Railways Linking East Africa," CNN, January 17, 2017, www.edition.cnn.com/2016/11/21/africa/chinese-funded-railways-in-africa (accessed March 4, 2021).

25. Calvert and Calvert, *Politics and Society.*

26. Sella Oneko and Philipp Sandner, "Africa Diplomatic Battleground for China and Taiwan." *DW*, April 15, 2016, www.dw.com/en/Africa-diplomatic-battleground-for-china-and-taiwan-19192069).

27. Peter Fabricius, "Is COVID-19 Enabling Debt-Trap Diplomacy?" *Institute for Security Studies*, April 30, 2020, issafrica.org/iss-today/is-covid-19-enabling-debt-trap-diplomacy (accessed March 10, 2021).

28. Brahma Chellaney, "China's Debt Trap Diplomacy," *Project Syndicate*, January 25, 2017. Chellaney.net/2017/01/25/chinas-debt-trap-diplomacy (accessed March 20, 2021).

29. Owei Lakemfa, "Italy Tells France the Truth, but Africa Isn't Listening," *Vanguard*, February 15. 2019, https://www.vanguardngr.com/2019/02/italy-tells-france-the-trith-but-africa-ins't-liste... (accessed August 14, 2020).

30. Calvert and Calvert, *Politics and Society*, 152.

31. Mark Anderson, "Aid to Africa: Donations from West Mask '$60 bn Looting' of Continent," *The Guardian*, March 6, 2021. www.theguardian.com/global-development/2014/July/15/aid-africa-west-looting-continent) (accessed March 6, 2021).

32. A. O. Y Raji, I. Grundlingh and T. S. Abejide, T. S. (2013, October). "The Politics of Resource Control in Nigeria: Example of Niger Delta Region 1990s–2010." *Kuwait Chapter of Arabian Journal of Business and Management Review* 3, no. 2 (October 2013). http//citeseerx.ist.psu.edu/viewdoc/download?doi=10.1.1.1073.42568&rep=rep1&type=pdf (accessed October 6, 2020).

33. MarkAnderson, "Aid to Africa: Donations from West mask '$60 bn Looting' of Continent."

34. Calvert and Calvert, *Politics and Society.*

35. Nick Dearden, "Africa Is Not Poor, We Are Stealing Its Wealth," *Al Jazeera*, May 24, 2017, www.aljazeera.com/opinion/2011/524/africaa-is-not-poor—wwe-are-stealing—ts-wealth (accessed September 19, 2020).

36. Deborah Brautigam, "Opinion: Is China the World's Loan Shark?" *The New York Times*. April 26, 2019. Archived from the original on April 30, 2019).

37. "US Senators 'Concerned' over Possible IMF Loan to Pakistan," *The Tribune*, April 11, 2018, www.tribune.com-pk/story/1778787/1-us-senators-concerned-possible-imf-loan-pakistan (accessed March 4, 2021).

38. Donald G. Tannenbaum and David Schultz, *Inventors of Ideas: An Introduction to Western Political Philosophy* (Bedford/St. Martin's, 1998), 68.

39. John of Salisbury, *Politicraticus*, ed. and trans. C. J. Nederman (New York: Cambridge University Press, 1990), 25.

40. Anderson, "Africa Is Not Poor, We Are Stealing Its Wealth."

41. Tebada Mmota, "African Leaders Prefer Overseas to Local Health Care," *Mail Guardian*, October 7, 2019, www.mg.co.uk.za/article/2019-10-07-00-african-leaders-prefer-overseas-to-local-health-care/ (accessed March 10, 2021); "African Politicians Seeking Medical Help Abroad Is Shameful, and Harms Health Care," *The Conversation*, August 24, 2017, https://theconversation.com/Africa-poloticians-seeking-medical-help-abroad-is-shameful-and-harms-health-care—82771 (January 22, 2021).

42. Tom Burgis, *The Looting Machine: Warlords, Oligarchs, Corporations, Smugglers, and the Theft of Africa's Wealth* (New York: Public Affairs, 2015).

43. Kingsley Jeremiah, "Stakeholders Demand Terms for %47b Chinese Loan, Project Execution," *The Guardian*, March 3, 2020, https://guardian.ng/news/stakeholders-demand-term-for-47b-chinese-loan-projects-execution (accessed March 2, 2021).

44. Ibid.

45. Levinus Nwabughiogu, "Chinese Loan: Reps Uncover Illegal Waivers for Chinese Firm," *Vanguard*, February 4, 2021, www.vanguardngr.com/2021/02/Chinese-loan-reps-uncover-n5bn-ilegal-waivers-for-chinese-firm/(accessed February 20, 2021).

46. Burgis. *The Looting Machine.*

47. Mark Anderson, "Aid to Africa: Donations from West Mask $60bn Looting of Continent."

48. Emmanuel F. Boamah and James Sumberg, "The Long Overhang of Bad Decisions in Agro-industrial Development: Sugar and Tomato Paste in Ghana," *Science Direct* 89 (December, 2019): 101786 (accessed December 20, 2020).

49. "Customs Reveal Why Nigeria's Borders Will Remain Closed," *Vanguard*, September 12, 2019, www.vanguardngr./2019/09/customs-reveals-why-nigerias-borrders-will-remain-closed/ (accessed March 4, 2021).

50. Bridget Chiedu Onochie, "Nigeria, China Relationship: We Sign Deals with Our Eyes Open."

51. Wade Shepard, "What China Is Really Up to in Africa," *Forbes*, October 3, 2019. www.forbes.com/sites/wadeshepard/2019/10/03/what-china-is-reallly-up-to-in-africa?sh=4f20de995930 (accessed December 12, 2020).

52. Bridget Chiedu Onochie, "Nigeria, China Relationship: We Sign Deals with Our Eyes Open."

53. Solomon, "Once Influential in Africa, Taiwan Loses All but One Ally."

54. Sella Oneko and Philipp Sandner, "Africa: Diplomatic Battleground for China and Taiwan."

55. Joshua S.S. Goldstein, *International Relations*, 5th ed. (Longman, 2004), 83.

56. Ibid.

57. Bridget Chiedu Onochie, "Nigeria, China Relationship: We Sign Deals with Our Eyes Open."

58. "Zambia on Brink of Defaulting on Foreign Debt," *BBC News*, November 13, 2020, www.bbc.com/news/world-africa=549288356 (accessed September 23, 2020).

59. "Chinese Take-Over of Zambia's Assets." *News Diggers*, September 16, 2018, www.diggers.news/opinion/2018/09/16/chineese-takeover-of-zambias-assets-is-rea/ (accessed November 10, 2020).

60. Jeremiah, "Stakeholders Demand Terms for $47b Chinese Loan; Project Execution."

61. Brenan J. Cannon, "Is China Undermining Its Own Success in Africa," *The Diplomat*, February 8, 2019. www.thediplomat.com/2019/02/is-china-undermining-its-own-success-in-africa/ (accessed August 3, 2020).

62. Su Zhou, 2017, "Number of Chinese Immigrants in Africa Rapidly Increasing," *China Daily*, January 14, 2017, www.chinadaily.com.cn.world/2017/14/content_27952426.htm) (accessed June 20, 2020).

63. China Africa Research Institute, "Data: Chinese workers in Africa," School of Advanced International Studies, John Hopkins University (2020), sais-cari.org/data-chinese-workers-in-africa (accessed March 4, 2021).

64. Jenni Marsh and Chiwoyu Sinyangwe, "Three Chinese Nationals Were Murdered and Burned in Zambia," CNN, 2020, June 5. cnn.com/2020/06/05/china-zambia-murder-inl-ink/index.htm (accessed March 4, 2021).

65. Timothy S. Rich and Vasabjit Banerjee, "The Evolution of Taiwan's Relations in Africa."

66. Jenni Marsh, "China Says It Has a 'zero-tolerance policy' for Racism, but Discrimination towards Africans Goes Back Decades." *CNN*. May 25, 2020. www .cnn.com/2020/05/25/asia/china-anti-african-attacks-history-hink-int/index.html (accessed March 6, 2021).

67. Cannon, "Is China Undermining Its Own Success in Africa."

68. Marsh, "Three Chinese National Were Murdered and Burned in Zambia."

BIBLIOGRAPHY

Anderson, Mark. "Aid to Africa: Donations from West Mask '$60 bn Looting' of the Continent." *The Guardian*, March 6, 2021. theguardian.com/global-development/ 2014/July/15/aid-africa-west-looting-continent (accessed March 6, 2021).

Art, Robert J., and Robert Jervis. *International Politics: Enduring Concepts and Contemporary Issues*. New York: Pearson/Longman, 2005.

BBC News. "Zambia on Brink of Defaulting on Foreign Debt." November 13, 2020. bbc.com/news/world-africa=549288356 (accessed January 25, 2021).

Boamah, Emmanuel F., and James Sumberg. "The Long Overhang of Bad Decisions in Agro Industrial Development: Sugar and Tomato Paste in Ghana." *Science Direct* 89, December 2019. 101786.sicencedirect.com/science/article/pii/S03069 19219306086 (accessed March 6, 2021).

Brautigan, Deborah. "Opinion: Is China the World's Loan Shark?" *The New York Times*, April 26, 2019. Archived from the Original on 2019, April 30 (accessed March 4, 2021).

Calvert, Peter, and Susan Calvert. *Politics and Society in the Developing World*, 3rd ed. New York: Pearson/Longman, 2007.

Cannon, Brenan J. "Is China Undermining Its Own Success in Africa?" *The Diplomat*, February 8, 2019. thediplomat.com/2019/02/is-china-undermining-its-own-success -in-africa/ (accessed March 4, 2021).

Chellaney, Brahma. "China's Debt Trap Diplomacy." *Project Syndicate*, January 25, 2017. Chellaney.net/2017/01/25/chinas-debt-trap-diplomacy (accessed March 20, 2021).

China Africa Research Institute. "Data: Chinese Workers in Africa." School of Advanced International Studies, John Hopkins University. 2020. sais-cari.org/data -chinese-workers-in-africa (accessed March 4, 2021).

Christopher, Warren. "Normalization of Diplomatic Relations, Bureau of Public Affairs, Department of State." June 11, 1977.

Dearden, Nick. "Africa Is Not Poor, We Are Stealing Its Wealth." *Al Jazeera*, May 25, 2011. https://aljazeera.com/opinions/2011/5//24/Africa-is-not-poor-we -are-stealing-its-wealth/.

Fabricius, Peter. "Is COVID-19 Enabling Debt Trap Diplomacy?" *Institute for Security Studies*, April 30, 2020. https://isafrica.org/iss-covid-19-enabling-debt -trap-diplomacy.

Gilbert, Kimutai. "Countries That Recognize Taiwan." *World Atlas*, May 29, 2018. Worldatlas.com/articles/which=countries-recognize-taiwan-as-a-country.html.

Goldstein, Joshua S. *International Relations*, 5th ed. New York: Longman, 2004.

He, Laura. "China Is Promising to Write-Off Some Loans to Africa." *CNN Business*, June 10, 2020. CNN.com/2020/06/19/economy/china-xi-jinping-africa-intl-hnk/ index.html.

Jeremiah, Kingsley. "Stakeholders Demand Terms for %47b Chinese Loan, Project Execution." *The Guardian*, March 3, 2020. Guardian.ng/news/stakeholders-deman d-term-for-47b-chinese-loan-projects-execution (accessed March 2, 2021).

John of Salisbury. Politicraticus, ed. and trans. C. J. Nederman. New York: Cambridge University Press, 1990.

Lakemfa, Owei. "Italy Tells France the Truth, But Africa Isn't Listening." *Vanguard*, February 15, 2019. https://www.vanguardngr.com/2019/02/italy-tells-france-the -truth-but-africa-ins't-liste (accessed September 10, 2020).

Lakemfa, Owei. "Opinion: The African Road to China." *African Examiner*, August 24, 2018. https://www.africaexaminer.com/opinion-the-african-road-to-china-by -owei-lakemfa/.

Marsh, Jenni, and Chiwoyu Sinyangwe. "Three Chinese Nationals Were Murdered and Burned in Zambia. In a Week When Racial Tension Were Running High." *CNN*, June 5, 2020. https://cnn.com/2020/06/05/china-zaambia-murder-inl-ink/ index.html (accessed March 4, 2021).

Mmota, Tebada. "African Leaders Prefer Overseas to Local Health Care." *Mail Guardian*, October 7, 2019. Mg.co.uk.za/article/2019-10-07-00-african-leaders- prefer-overseas-to-local-health-care/.

Morlin-Yron, Sophie. "All Aboard! The Chinese-Funded Railways Linking East Africa." *CNN*, January 17, 2017. www.edition.cnn.com/2016/11/21/africa/chinese -funded-railways-in-africa (accessed March 4, 2021).

News Diggers, "Chinese Take-Over of Zambia's Assets." September 16, 2018. digge rs.news/opinion/2018/09/16/chineese-takeover-of-zambias-assets-is-rea/ (accessed February 10, 2021).

Nwabughiogu, Levinus. "Chinese Loans: Reps Uncover Illegal Waivers for Chinese Firm." *Vanguard*, February 4, 2021. Vanguardngr.com/2021/02/Chinese-loans-re ps-uncover-n5bn-illegal-waivers-for-chinese-firm/.

Oneko, Sella, Philipp Sandner, Sella Oneko, and Philipp Sandner. "Africa: Diplomatic Battleground for China and Taiwan, April 15, 2016." *DW*. dw.com /en/Africa-diplomatic-battleground-for-china-and-taiwan/a-19192069 (accessed Mach 10, 2021).

Onochie, Bridget Chiedu. "Nigeria, China Relationship: We Sign Deals with Our Eyes Open, Says Onyeama." *The Guardian*, February 2021. Guardian.ng/politics/ Nigeria-china-relationships-we-sign-deals-with-our-eyesoppen-says-onyeama/.

Pickles, John, and Jeff Woods. "Taiwanese Investment in South Africa." *African Affairs* 88, no. 353 (October 1989): 507–528.

Raji, A. O. Y, I. Grundlingh, and T. S. Abejide. "The Politics of Resource Control in Nigeria: Example of Niger Delta Region 1990s–2010." *Kuwait Chapter of Arabian Journal of Business and Management Review* 3, no. 2 (October 2013). http//citeseerx.ist.psu.edu/viewdoc/download?doi=10.1.1.1073.42568&rep=rep1&type=pdf (accessed October 6, 2020).

Rich, Timothy S., and Vasabjit Banerjee. "Running Out of Time? The Evolution of Taiwan's Relations in Africa." *Journal of Current Chinese Affairs* 44, no. 1 (2015): 141–161. https://doi.ord/10-1177/186810261504400106.

Rourke, John T., and Mark A. Boyer. *World Politics*, 3rd ed. New York: Dushkin/McGraw-Hill, 2000.

School of Advanced International, China Africa Research Institute. "Data: Chinese Workers in Africa." School of Advanced International, John Hopkins University. 2020. Sais-cari.org/data-chinese-workers-in-africa.

Shepard, Wade. "What China Is Really Up to in Africa." *Forbes*, October 3, 2019. forbes.com/sites/wadeshepard/2019/10/03/what-china-is-reallly-up-to-in-africa?sh=4f20de995930 (accessed February 29, 2021).

Solomon, Salem. "Once Influential in Africa, Taiwan Loses All but One Ally." *Voice of America*, May 26, 2018. https://www.voanews.com/africa/once-influential-afriica-taiwan-loses-all-one-ally (accessed September 25, 2020).

Tannenbaum, Donald G., and David Schultz. *Inventors of Ideas an Introduction to Western Political Philosophy*. New York: Bedford/St. Martin's, 1998.

Tanzania – Zambia Railway Authority. "Our History." n.d. www.tazarasite.com/our-history (accessed February 23, 2021).

The Iowa Times. "Senators Warn against China's Debt-Trap Diplomacy During COVID-19 Crisis." April 24, 2020. Theiowastandard.com/senators-warn-against-china-debt-trapdiplomacy-during-covide-19-crisis (accessed March 4, 2021).

The Nation Guard. "Top Ten African Countries Indebted to China." June 8, 2020. www.nationguardnews.com/2020/06/08/top-ten-african-countries-indebted-to-china/ (accessed February 17, 2021).

The Tribune. "US Senators 'Concerned' Over Possible IMF Loan to Pakistan." April 11, 2018. www.tribune.com-pk/story/1778787/1-us-senators-concerned-possible-imf-loan-pakistan (accessed March 4, 2021).

Vanguard. "Customs Reveal Why Nigeria's Borders Will Remain Closed." September 12, 2019. vanguardngr. /2019/09/customs-reveals-why-nigerias-borrders-will-remain-closed/ (accessed March 4, 2021).

Wolfe, James. *Modern International Law: An Introduction to the Law of Nations*. Upper Saddle River, NJ: Prentice-Hall, 2002.

Zhou, Su. "Number of Chinese Immigrants in Africa Rapidly Increasing." *China Daily*, January 14, 2017. Chinadaily.com.cn/world/2017-01/14/content_27952426.html.

Part II

ISSUES AND STRATEGIES

Chapter 6

China, Taiwan, and the African University

Abdul-Gafar Tobi Oshodi, Abdul-Wasi Babatunde
Moshood, and Mary Chinelo Ubabudu

INTRODUCTION

Universities are not only arenas for academic conversation. Beyond *thin* functionality which limits their role to "teaching, research, and community service (TRC),"[1] the *thick* perspective of universities accommodates much broader roles. The latter perspective considers universities "as arenas to shape discourses, project power and circulate ideologies to its audience,"[2] while also mirroring a country, serving as "a microcosm and a symptom"[3] of relationships. They become a lens to understand, construct, and deconstruct relationships among and between societies. Within a thick conceptualization, universities are thus arenas for international relations and struggles, a point that is illustrated in this chapter. In agreeing with Ali Mazrui that the African University can be a manifestation of, and response to, an external power[4]—or in our case tension between contesting territories—our chapter adopts a thick perspective of the university that views it both as a center for TRC and beyond. The African University—used in this chapter in its singular form not to present them as equals or on the same level in terms of size and outputs, but used to amplify similarities across many historical, geographical, and institutional settings on the continent—offers an important lens to deepen our understanding of Africa's shift to China and the decline of Taiwan.

By focusing on the African University, we offer a glimpse and snapshot of how China's rise and Taiwan's decline manifest in a context that is not necessarily statist, in that universities—even where they are publicly owned—are not often assumed to be entrapped in international relations. Thus, we shed light on an important non-state institution in Africa involved in international relations. Although "China's rising influence amid Taiwan's decline in Africa has also generated responses in African universities,"[5] academic interests in unpacking the implications of this for African countries, China, or Taiwan have been abysmally low. This dearth of interest is, however, problematic given that the universities in Africa, as elsewhere, are often the producers of future leaders and arenas of scholarship. Bearing in mind the limited academic commentaries on the subject, our chapter contributes by drawing the attention of scholars of Taiwan and China's global contestations to happenings on the African University campus.

Developing an argument first espoused in an op-ed entitled "Beijing's Rise and Taiwan's Decline in Africa: What Does the African University Tell Us?"[6] written in the University of Nottingham's *Taiwan Insight* in 2019, our chapter addresses two questions: (i) What are manifestations of China and Taiwan on the African University campus? (ii) What are the implications of these manifestations for China, Taiwan, and the African University? To answer both questions, the rest of our chapter is divided into four sections. The second section presents a theoretical and contextual framework within which our argument is located. The third section highlights some manifestations of China and Taiwan on the African University. The fourth section discusses the implications of these manifestations for China, Taiwan, and African University. This is followed by a conclusion.

THICKNESS: BRIEF COMMENT ON THEORY AND CONTEXT

Regardless of whether a thin or a thick conceptualization of the university is adopted, it is first an institution within a state. Conceptually, we describe the university as the network of individuals, processes, and structure that represents higher education. It is an aspect of a broader educational subsystem that is itself in turn a small component within the State System. Based on the works of Talcott Parsons and Gabriel Almond, the systems theory argues that society is a network of interconnected parts. Our discourse, thus, adopts a systems approach for two reasons that speak to the theory's flexibility: first, because we contend that the (in)actions of the universities have in the main reflected Africa's slanted relations with the two countries. While there are instances, as will be highlighted here, where Taiwan has played some roles, this is as infinitesimal as Taiwan's dwindling support on the continent. In this sense, the university can be a stabilizing institution, executing the convictions of the state in the system. This must not be constructed to be an African representation. An example can be situated in the China-US relations and how that has impacted American universities. China spent an estimated $158 million[7] on the about 100 Confucius Institutes that are mainly based in US universities between 2006 and 2019, but this has not stopped some universities from closing or threatening to close the institutes in the United States in the wake of the frosty China-US relations under the Donald Trump presidency. Confucius Institutes fell from 103 in 2017 to 55 in 2021, with some of the universities citing reasons to include "concerns about academic freedom; the potential for Chinese government influence and risks to U.S. national security," among others.[8] This exemplifies American universities playing the system stabilizing role.

Second, systems theory fits our analysis because it envisages and allows us to accommodate destabilization. Universities, as in all systems, may not reflect the views of the state or play a stabilizing role in the State System, at least this is the case in several African countries. There are instances, demonstrated in the histories of groups like the Academic Staff Union of Universities and University Teachers Association of Ghana, where members of the university community have disagreed with the state, protested and called on national strikes, and sometimes successfully forced governments to change course or revert policies.[9] In South Africa, "Rhodes Must Fall" and "Fees Must Fall" were largely university projects that demanded a change in the workings or policies of the state. In this context, the university becomes an arena for challenging the system, engaging in tenacious conversations with the state. An understanding of the African University—that is, staff and students—is elemental for a critical grasp of the postcolonial struggles on the African continent, especially as buttressed in the popular struggle against the structural adjustment programs in African countries. The university can therefore be a destabilizing element in the State System.

As indicated in the previous section, we adopt a thick conceptualization of the university. Beyond the TRC, this thickness suggests that the universities occupy an even more important position—although sometimes in terms of its potentialities—in the development equation of the continent. It is generally acknowledged that higher education (and university education in particular) can play a crucial role in national development in African countries.[10] For Africa to develop—or, as Mkandawire puts it, *run* while others *walk*—it "requires a revitalization of the African University, its internal functioning and its relationships with the global world of knowledge."[11] Convinced of their centrality to Africa's development, Mamdani notes that "there can be no independent thought—indeed no independence—without institutions to sustain independent research and produce relevant knowledge. The key institution is the research university."[12] While the role—or rightly, the potentials—of the African University is not in doubt, there is an increasing manifestation of China on its campuses. Policy and media reports of these manifestations appear to be common and continuing while the academic study is largely lagging. Yet, the responses, implications, and agency of the

African University in the emerging context are less understood and thus ripe for academic research. The case of China's multidimensional footprints and the limited Taiwanese presence is another example of how universities are an arena for international struggle. This is not unique to Africa.

Recent relationships between universities in the United States and Europe with China and Chinese entities have been complicated by the tenuous relationship between Beijing and their capitals. For instance, on June 21, 2014, the *Washington Post* in its editorial of June 21, 2014, reported that while in 2009 an event that invited the Dalai Lama, "a Tibetan spiritual leader whom China considers a traitor," to North Carolina State University was reportedly canceled, by 2014 the American Association of University Professors had called on universities in the United States to reexamine their ties with China's Confucius Institutes based on their view that the institutes "function as an arm of the Chinese state and are allowed to ignore academic freedom."[13] Although one study suggested that concerns over the impact of Confucius Institutes on the views of Americans studying in them are "overblown,"[14] this has not stopped critical views about China in universities. Within a few years, top institutions became entangled in the frosty relationship between the United States and China, with European countries taking the former's side. Oxford and Massachusetts Institute of Technology suspended collaboration with Chinese telecoms giant, Huawei and Zhongxing Telecommunication Equipment Corporation, in 2019,[15] while Australia on August 28 of the same year introduced the University Foreign Interference Taskforce to "provide better protection for universities against foreign interference."[16]

These complications in the relationship between universities in the United States and Europe and China coincide with a period when the perception of China as a major threat in Western geopolitics increased, expanding under the anti-Chinese policies and rhetoric of Trump.[17] But things were sharply different in Africa, as highlighted in the next section. In the case of the African University, the Chinese presence is illustrated in both hard (physical) and soft forms.[18] This growing presence calls for the timely attention of scholars of Africa-China relations. Although the Ain Shams University in Egypt was already "teaching Chinese from 1958,"[19] only a handful of scholars have been drawn to this dimension of Africa-China relations.[20] Yet, the November 2009 Forum on China-Africa Cooperation held at Sharm el-Sheikh in Egypt set in motion "the partnership between twenty leading African and twenty leading Chinese universities,"[21] a development that was followed by the trilateral "UNESCO-China-Africa University Leaders Meeting" on October 24–25, 2011. The next section discusses the manifestations of China on the African campus, contrasting it with Taiwan.

CHINA AND TAIWAN ON THE AFRICAN CAMPUS

Taiwan's decline and recognition of China in Africa are not in doubt. As of 2021, all countries in Africa recognize China—except Eswatini, a small kingdom formerly referred to as Swaziland in Southern Africa. To arrive at this situation, countries that hitherto recognized Taiwan shifted their support to China, generating or limiting relationship that goes beyond the sphere of the governments. In Africa, the shift has impacted non-state actors and institutions, with the African University offering an example to illustrate. In this section, we show that while China's presence is growing on the African University campus, Taiwan is minuscule. To demonstrate this, we contrast the main manifestations of China and Taiwan on the African campus.

Five manifestations of China in the African University are worth highlighting. First, the introduction of Confucius Institutes is arguably the most visible manifestation of China in African universities. The first and second Confucius Institutes outside China were established in Seoul, South Korea, and the University of Maryland, the United States, in 2004 and 2005, respectively.[22] Since first introducing one in the University of Nairobi in 2005, they have become a major manifestation of China on university campuses in Africa, although lagging behind those in Europe.[23] These institutes are usually located in universities in the capital or commercial cities in Africa. As of 2019, forty-five African countries have at least one on their university campus. Countries like South Africa have a disproportionately high number with six, followed by four in Kenya and three in Morocco.

Three important points must be stressed at this juncture. (1) It appears that population or trade relations may not be the main incentive for setting up the Confucius Institutes. For instance, while Nigeria, Africa's most populous country, has two institutes, less populated countries like Ghana and Tanzania have the same number. South Africa with less population than Nigeria has six. Similarly, even though Angola is one of the top trading partners of China, it has only one institute. (2) The list in table 6.1 demonstrates that the establishment of Confucius Institutes in African universities by China is linked to one element: the acceptance of the One-China Policy by the host country. Burkina Faso is the latest country to shift from Taiwan to China in 2018; by 2019 it got its own Confucius Institute.[24] (3) Confucius Institutes are not merely existing on the African campus; they are linked to a Chinese university. Although the roles of these universities are often unstated in the functioning of the institutes, they are a potentially powerful element in China's soft power, a future tool to deepen Africa-China relations when they are expanded beyond popularizing Chinese culture and language in countries.[25]

Table 6.1   Confucius Institutes in African Universities

Country and Number of CIs	University	Location	Partner Chinese University	Year
Angola (1)	Agostinho Neto University	Luanda	Harbin Normal University, CITIC	2015
Benin (1)	University of Abomey-Calavi	Porto-Novo	Chongqing Jiaotong University	2009
Botswana (1)	University of Botswana	Gaborone	Shanghai Normal University	2009
Burkina Faso (1)	Bobo-Dioulasso Polytechnic University	Bobo-Dioulasso	Tianjin Polytechnic University	2019
Burundi (1)	University of Burundi	Bujumbura	Bohai University	2012
Cameroon (1)	University of Yaounde II	Yaounde	Zhejiang Normal University	2007
Cape Verde (1)	University of Cabo Verde	Praia	Guangdong University of Foreign Studies	2015
Central African Republic (1)	University of Bangui	Bangui	–	2019
Chad (1)	University of N'Djamena	N'Djamena	–	2019
Comoro (1)	University of Comoro	Moroni	Dalian University	2018
Congo (1)	Marien Ngouabi University	Brazzaville	University of Jinan	2012
DR Congo (1)	Diplomatic University of Democratic Republic of Congo	Kinshasa	Central South University	2017
Egypt (2)	Cairo University	Cairo	Peking University	2008
	Suez Canal University	Ismailia	Beijing Language and Culture University	2007
Equatorial Guinea (1)	National University of Equatorial Guinea	Malabo	Zhejiang International Studies University	2014
Ethiopia (1)	Addis Ababa University	Addis	Tianjin Vocational Technology Normal University	2013
Gabon (1)	Omar Bongo University	Libreville	Tianjin Foreign Studies University	2017
Ghana (2)	University of Ghana	Accra	Zhejiang University of Technology	2013
	University of Cape Coast	Cape Coast	Hunan City University	2016
Guinea (1)	Gamal Abdel Nasser University of Conakry	Conakry	Linyi University	2017
Ivory Coast (1)	Université Félix Houphouët-Boigny	Abidjan	Tianjin University of Technology	2015
Kenya (4)	University of Nairobi	Nairobi	Tianjin Normal University	2005
	Kenyatta University	Nairobi	Shandong Normal University	2008
	Egerton University	Nakuru	Nanjing Agricultural University	2012
	Moi University	Eldoret	Donghua University	2014
Liberia (1)	University of Liberia	Monrovia	Changsha University of Science and Technology	2008
Madagascar (2)	Antananarivo University	Antananarivo	Jiangxi Normal University	2006
	University of Toamasina	Toamasina	Ningbo University	2014
Malawi (1)	University of Malawi	Lilongwe	University of International Business and Economics	2013

Country	African University	City	Chinese Partner University	Year
Mali (1)	University of Letters and Human Science of Bamako	Bamako	Southwest Forestry University	2017
Mauritania (1)	Nouakchott University	Nouakchott	Hebei University	2018
Mauritius (1)	University of Mauritius	Port Louis	Zhejiang Sci-Tech University	2015
Morocco (3)	University Mohammed V-Agdal	Rabat	Beijing International Studies University	2009
	University Hassan II	Casablanca	Shanghai International Studies University	2012
	Abdelmalek Essaadi University	Tangier	Jiangxi Science and Technology Normal University	2016
Mozambique (1)	Eduardo Mondlane University	Maputo	Zhejiang Normal University	2012
Namibia (1)	University of Namibia	Windhoek	China University of Geosciences (Beijing)	2013
Nigeria (2)	University of Lagos	Lagos	Beijing Institute of Technology	2009
	Nnamdi Azikiwe University	Akwa	Xiamen University	2009
Republic of Congo (1)	Marien Ngouabi University	Brazzaville	University of Jinan	2013
Rwanda (1)	University of Rwanda	Kigali	Chong Qing Normal University	2009
São Tomé and Príncipe (1)	University of São Tomé and Príncipe	São Tomé	Hubei University	2018
Senegal (1)	University of Dakar	Dakar	Liaoning University	2012
Seychelles (1)	University of Seychelles	Victoria	Dalian University	2015
Sierra Leone (1)	University of Sierra Leone	Freetown	Gannan Normal University	2012
South Africa (6)	Stellenbosch University	Western Cape	Xiamen University	2009
	University of Cape Town	Cape Town	Sun Yat-sen University	2007
	Rhodes University	Grahamstown	Jinan University	2007
			Fujian Agriculture and Forestry University	
	Durban University of Technology	Durban	Nanjing University of Technology	2013
	University of Johannesburg	Johannesburg	Zhejiang Normal University	2014
	University of Western Cape	Cape Town	Chinese Medical University	2018
Sudan (1)	University of Khartoum	Khartoum	Northwest Normal University	2009
Tanzania (2)	University of Dar es Salaam	Dar es Salaam	Zhejiang Normal University	2013
	University of Dodoma	Dodoma	Zhengzhou Institute of Aeronautical Industry	2013
The Gambia (1)	University of the Gambia	Banjul	Guizhou University	2017
Togo (1)	University of Lome	Lome, Togo	Sichuan International Studies University	2009
Tunisia (1)	University of Carthage	Tunis	Dalian University of Foreign Languages	2018
Uganda (1)	Makerere University	Kampala	Xiangtan University	2014
Zambia (1)	University of Zambia	Lusaka	Hebei University of Economics and Business	2010
Zimbabwe (1)	University of Zimbabwe	Harare	Renmin University of China	2007

Source: Created by Author from Oshodi, A. T. (2019) and Various Data Points.

It is noteworthy to stress that although there was a UNESCO-China-Africa University Leaders Meeting[26] on October 24–25, 2011, the establishment of Confucius Institutes has, arguably, remained one of the most visible manifestations of Africa-China university collaboration. Nonetheless, Chinese universities are collaborating with their African counterparts. Stellenbosch University offers an example of this collaboration that ranges from student exchanges to other institutional partnerships. The fifteen Chinese universities and institutions that partner with Stellenbosch University include the following: Beijing Jiaotong University, Capital Normal University, North China University of Water Conservancy and Electric Power, Chinese University of Hong Kong, Guangdong Academy of Agricultural Sciences, Hunan University, Institute of West-Asian and African Studies in the Chinese Academy of Social Sciences, Nanjing University, Ningxia University, Renmin University of China, University of Hong Kong, Xiamen University, Yunnan University, Zhejiang Normal University, and Fudan University.

Second, Chinese manifestation on the African campus is in construction. Chinese companies are major players in the construction industry in Africa, a reality manifesting in African universities. Chinese companies have been involved in the construction of the entire university and single projects like libraries and faculties. For instance, at the Lagos State University in Nigeria, the Senate Building (a central edifice that hosts the Vice Chancellor's Office and those of other principal and senior administrative staff, the periodic meeting of the professors, and the other administrative offices), the Faculty of Management Annex, the main library that could be one of the largest in Nigeria, and a university gate are either already completed or are being built by a Chinese company China Civil Engineering Construction Corporation (CCECC). Other landmark construction project includes the 40 million USD library in the University of Dar es Salaam in Tanzania, once described as "Africa's largest university library."[27]

At the University of Health and Allied Sciences in Ghana that started operation in 2012, after completing Phase I of the university's construction and handing it over in 2015, China signed another agreement with the Ghanaian government for a grant worth about 60 million USD (or 400 million Yuan) for Phase II construction.[28] Phase I—which covered 10,386 square meters, and included all the equipment for the School of Basic and Biomedical Sciences, libraries, lecture halls, senior staff residents, and students' hostels—cost 104 million Yuan, about one-fourth of the cost for Phase II.[29] Phase II covers 29,200 square meters and would include the "Central Administration block, the School of Nursing and Midwifery and the Duty and Equipment Rooms as well as supporting facilities such as desks, chairs, computers, and some teaching aids for a medical specialty."[30] Nigeria's Transportation University is being built by the CCECC, a major construction company operating in the country. The $50 million university is being constructed as the company's corporate social responsibility.[31] It is also not new for Chinese companies to build the Confucius Institutes located on the African University campus, as was the case with the construction of the institute at the University of Ghana by Changxin International Engineering (Ghana) Limited.

Third is the Chinese scholarship in African universities. There are variations in the scholarships. While some of the scholarships are offered to support students in their local institutions, others, including those given by Chinese companies, are taken in institutions in China. Some scholarships are given by Chinese embassies in Africa. Examples include the "Chinese Ambassador Scholarship Award," introduced in 2017 and given to students of the Confucius Institute in the University of Cape Coast and its teaching points in Ghana[32] and the "October 1st Scholarship for China-Nigeria Friendship," symbolizing China's National Day and Nigeria's Independence Day, that is awarded to the students with the highest cumulative grade point average in their disciplines in Ahmadu Bello University.[33] While some scholarships are linked to the Confucius Institutes, others are from Chinese companies and government for programs other than learning Chinese culture and language. As of the end of 2019, for instance, the CCECC was training "at least 150 young Nigerian students in railway engineering in China."[34] This must be understood against the background of an increasing number of African students in China. One estimate reports that "China's government is offering more university scholarships to African students than the leading western governments combined."[35] In 2018, China had over 60,000 African students, making China the second-highest destination after France.[36] China's role in education in Africa is growing, and these scholarships awarded to university students in Africa are elemental to it.

Fourth, Chinese companies are becoming involved in on-campus training in African universities. The Chinese multinational, Huawei, is leading others in this regard.[37] From inaugurating an estimated 6 million USD Innovation and Experience Centre on a 500 square meter in 2016 on the campus of University of Lagos campus[38] in Nigeria to collaborating with Rain to establish Africa's first 5G Innovation Lab at the University of the Witwatersrand[39] in South Africa in 2020, Huawei's footprint on the African University is no longer news. Aside from periodic competition for students and invitation for lecturers to visit the company's headquarters in China, the Huawei Authorized Information and Network Academy (HAINA) and the "Seed for the Future" are elemental to the company's program for African universities as elsewhere. As noted on the company's website, the Seeds for the Future program "works with local governments and universities to send students overseas to provide work experience with the world's best ICT equipment."[40] As of 2016, over 30,000 students from 280 universities in

96 countries have benefited from the program.[41] While some universities in Europe and America have raised concerns about collaborations with Huawei, several African universities have signed a memorandum of understanding with the Chinese telecommunication multinational.

Fifth is the discursive dimension of China in the African University.[42] Aside from Confucius Institutes, this relates to the teaching of China on campus. Universities are beginning to respond to the growing Africa-China relations in their program. This ranges from the establishment of centers to inaugurating projects. In South Africa, for example, Stellenbosch University established a Centre for Chinese Studies following a "South Africa-Chinese Bi-national Commission held in June 2004"[43] in 2009[44] while the University of the Witwatersrand's Africa-China Reporting Project "aims to improve the quality of reporting on Africa-China issues by providing facilitation and capacity building for journalists via reporting grants, workshops, and other opportunities."[45] In 2018, the University of Lagos set up the Institute of Nigeria-China Development Studies, "a research institute established to inject new vitality into Nigeria-China development as well as collaboration in order to strengthen the relationship between both countries."[46] In Kenya, the Sino-Africa Joint Research Center (SAJOREC) located on Jomo Kenyatta University of Agriculture and Technology was set up in 2013 to, among other things, serve "as the platform and bridge of scientific cooperation between the Chinese and the African scientists in a wide range of fields."[47] Since its establishment, SAJOREC has initiated over "45 joint research programs focusing on biodiversity investigation, pathogenic microorganism detection, geographic science and remote sensing, high-yield and high-quality crop cultivation demonstration, and land and water resources management."[48] Meanwhile, like their counterparts outside the continent,[49] universities in Africa have also incorporated "China in Africa" as a component of their social sciences and humanities courses.[50] Conferences on China in/and Africa have also been organized on some campuses.

The five manifestations underscore China's growing presence as well as influence on the continent. More importantly, it underscores the decline and limitations of Taiwan on the continent. First, Taiwan is limited in terms of the number of countries—or territory, as in the case of Somaliland[51]—that recognize it on the continent. One result of this limitation is that the tendency for a Taiwanese and host government's sanctioned presence is reduced. Second, Taiwan is limited by the small number of African universities that are willing to relate with its indifference to their government's position on the One-China Policy. Many universities in Africa are public owned and state funded, making an independent relationship with Taiwan or Taiwanese entities difficult. Notwithstanding, a few manifestations of Taiwan on the African University campus are worth noting. One of these manifestations is reflected in the cordial relationship Taiwan has with Eswatini, the only country that recognizes the former in Africa. For instance, the private and faith-based Southern Africa Nazarene University in Eswatini is affiliated with the Taipei Medical University.[52] In addition to the case of Eswatini, two other examples of Taiwan's presence on the African University are worth discussing: one within a territory that is not (yet) a country, the other in a university in a country that does not recognize Taiwan.

Just as in Eswatini, Taiwan's relationship with Somaliland also manifests in the university. Somaliland and Taiwan announced they had a "bilateral accord" on July 1, 2020, which "will see Somaliland open a representative office in Taipei and Taiwan open a representative office in Hargeisa," after earlier signing the accord on February 28, 2020, in Taiwan.[53] By December of the same year, Somaliland's University of Hargeisa signed an agreement with the Chung Yuan Christian University (CYCU) in Taiwan to "cooperate on research, exchange students and teachers program," declaring themselves "Sister Universities."[54] Following up on the December 2020 Hargeisa-CYCU agreement, the Taiwan deputy representative to Somaliland, Nabil Chen-Chu Wu, visited the University of Hargeisa on January 6, 2021, requesting that "the University encourage its students to apply to the Taiwan Scholarship Programs open this year 2021 particularly in the fields of Engineering, Fisheries and Marine Management, Healthcare, and Medicine."[55] Before 2020, the government of Taiwan—through Somaliland's representative in the United Arab Emirates, Bashe Awil Omer—in August 2016 gave five universities in Somaliland fifty laptops. Receiving ten laptops each, the benefiting universities include the following: Nugaal University, Burco University, Berbera Maritime University, Tima-ade University, and the Erigavo University.[56] Through its university diplomacy, Taiwan is therefore not only aiming to solidify its partnership with Somaliland, but also it is aiming to deepen people-to-people relationships with the territory's universities. Like its main competitor, China, scholarships are being used as an incentive to invite African students to study in Taiwan.

One unusual manifestation of Taiwan on the African University campus is in a country that recognizes China. South Africa is China's major partner in Africa. Apart from their trade and investment relations, both countries belong to the club of emerging economies: that is, BRICS[57] economies. As earlier noted in the op-ed in *Taiwan Insight*, the example of Stellenbosch University suggests that the African University has "an ability to swim against the tide."[58] Although Stellenbosch University is in partnership with numerous Chinese Universities and had established one of the earliest centers of Chinese Studies and Confucius Institutes in Africa, it nonetheless entered a partnership with Taiwan's top university, the National Taiwan University (NTU). Both universities signed two agreements: (a) "Agreement on

Scholarly Exchange and Collaboration between Stellenbosch University and National Taiwan University" in 2012–2022, and (b) "Agreement on Student Exchange Program between Stellenbosch University and National Taiwan University"[59] in 2012–2022. The NTU-Stellenbosch partnership is unique, but it is not comparable to those with Chinese universities. In some sense, the fifteen Chinese universities against one Taiwanese are partnering with Stellenbosch to buttresses the point that China is the country recognized by South Africa. Although South Africa allows for the establishment of a Taipei Economic and Cultural Representative Office "where Taiwan can issue visas and serve expatriates in the country,"[60] China is recognized, a recognition that is starkly captured on campus.

SOME IMPLICATIONS FOR THE PRESENT AND FUTURE

Virtually all states in Africa recognize China—and not Taiwan. The more pronounced presence of China as compared to the limited manifestations of Taiwan on university campuses in Africa demonstrates that the former's influence goes beyond the sphere of governments. Thus, the main implication of the current situation is that state recognition appears to be trickling down to non-state actors, in this case, the African University. The competition between Taiwan and China is being lost on campus, underscoring Chinese dominance. This offers China the opportunity to deepen the people-to-people relationship, something that will benefit China in the short and long term. Scholarships to university students and the inauguration of training hubs on campuses in Africa are soft power symbolisms that China can rely on in the future discourse of its relationship with African countries. For instance, the construction of the TAZARA railway (when other potential financiers declined to support it) remains a powerful landmark. It offers China the opportunity to refer to an episode where it was willing to support the development of the TAZARA railway when its economy was confronted by its own challenges. China's construction of libraries, universities, and 5G hub in African universities will offer the same discursive power in years to come. This discursive power ultimately represents an emerging but powerful evolution of Chinese soft power on the continent.

With regard to Taiwan, the current situation is both a demonstration of its decline and a lesson. The decline is such that even the African University mirrors its limitations in Africa, a continent that it once had supporters. The lesson is such that the universities are also important elements in their struggle with China for recognition. In this competition, the rise of one is naturally the demise of the other. Although some argue that "Taiwan can offer high-quality Mandarin education, subsidize overseas trips by teachers and certify language instructors"[61] following the closure of Confucius Institutes in countries like the United States and Australia, this will be a difficult task given the scale and cost—that is, even if it is assumed there is a similar vacuum in the African University. Taiwan lacks the financial muscles to fill the vacuum that could be left in the African University—even if China decides to exist. In African universities, things become even more difficult where the buildings are constructed by China. In any case, though popular in universities in Africa, the institutes are only a part of the broader manifestations of China in Africa. Yet, the relationship between African governments and China is strong, and not affected by the sentiments currently developing in the West. In the nearest future, Taiwan's aspirations in the African University remain bleak and limited as discussed earlier.

Given the challenge of funding confronting African universities, the entry of China as a major player in Africa's educational system offers African students within the continent numerous opportunities. Furthermore, aside from training programs like HAINA and other Chinese-built centers that offer students excellent opportunities, universities in China could also become a destination of choice not only for short-term student exchange but also for postgraduate training as well. The collaboration between African and Chinese universities holds enormous prospects. For instance, African universities could increase the number of their early and mid-career academic staff studying in China, thereby increasing the prospects for scientific network (i.e., academic collaboration with their Chinese counterpart). In doing this, disciplines or focus of collaboration could be prioritized as demonstrated in the example of SAJOREC in Jomo Kenyatta University of Agriculture and Technology highlighted earlier. The emergence of China as a funder in Africa offers an alternative to Western countries, agencies, and philanthropists that have hitherto dominated the international funding landscape. However, given that China is not necessarily guided by the same socioeconomic and political considerations as may be in operation in the host African countries, time will tell whether or if academic freedom will be affected as have been alleged by universities outside Africa.

CONCLUSION: THINKING ABOUT THE UNANSWERED QUESTIONS

Our chapter demonstrates that China's rise and Taiwan's decline have ramifications that go beyond the recognitions by African states; they trickle into the university campus. Both Asian countries have sought to expand their presence in African universities. In the case of China, Confucius Institutes and interuniversity collaborations, construction projects, scholarships, Chinese companies, and the discursive element are important manifestations in the African University. Taiwan, though limited, is also offering scholarships and gifts. Taiwanese universities also collaborate with their African counterparts, but this is not comparable to those by Chinese universities. It can be concluded that just as virtually all countries in Africa (except Eswatini, and Somaliland, an independent country that is not recognized by other countries) now recognize China and have shifted from Taiwan, China is strongly consolidating its growing popularity on the continent by investing in and building networks within African universities. China's strategy of expanding people-to-people relationships on the African University campus strongly supports its One-China Policy in that it is already building useful connections among students, who may become the next generation of African leaders. Though Taiwan is also adopting the same strategy of targeting and investing in the next generation of African leaders through scholarship and friendly relations with their universities, its ability to catch up with China is difficult in the current circumstances.

Despite demonstrating in this chapter that China's manifestation on the African campus surpasses Taiwan's, we are mindful that we have only focused on relatively modern manifestations. For instance, our chapter did not focus on the relationship between African universities and Taiwan prior to[62] the 1971 resolution that marked a turning point in many African countries' relationship with China. This could shed more light on whether China's focus on the African University is unique to the modern era or a historically evolving strategy common to it and Taiwan. Also, that China has more visibility on university campuses does not answer the question of how "the relationship between China and Taiwan is captured in the curriculum (i.e., the Teaching of China in Africa—TeChA)."[63] How is the relationship between China and Taiwan captured in the curriculum (i.e., TeChA) in the African University? The extent both Taiwan and Chinese university diplomacy permeates the views of stakeholders like students and teachers in African universities is open to further research. Yet, in all the cases identified, no in-depth interview was conducted to make a deeper sense of the decisions of stakeholders and gauge the extent to which their specific contexts impacted these decisions. Therefore, we have only offered a snapshot of the manifestations and implications of China and Taiwan in the African University. To this end, the African University is still ripe for a rigorous and multidisciplinary study that can further engage the unanswered aspects of Taiwan and China in the African University.

NOTES

1. Oshodi, A.T. (2019). "Beijing's Rise and Taiwan's Decline in Africa: What Does the African University Tell Us?" *Taiwan Insight*, University of Nottingham, UK,

14 August: https://taiwaninsight.org/2019/08/14/beijings-rise-and-taiwans-decline-in-africa-what-does-the-african-university-tell-us/

2. Ibid.

3. Moshood, A. B. & Oshodi, A. T. (2018). "Breaking the Ice: The Nigerian University System and Its Funding Challenges." In: Olanrewaju Fagbohun & Adewale Aderemi (eds.), *Global Aids and Tertiary Education in Nigeria*. Lagos: Profemative Concepts Int'l, p. 63.

4. Mazrui, Ali. (1975). "The African University as a Multinational Corporation: Problems of Penetration and Dependency," *Harvard Educational Review*.

5. Oshodi (2019). "Beijing's Rise and Taiwan's Decline in Africa: What Does the African University Tell Us?"

6. Abdul-Gafar Tobi Oshodi is grateful to Chun-Yi Lee, Karolina Wysoczanska, and the Taiwan Insight team for granting permission to expand his original article written in their magazine. He is also grateful to the Social Science Research Council's NextGen Fellowship program for sponsoring aspects of this chapter in a paper entitled "Has—or, how has—the African University responded to China in Africa?" presented at the international conference on *Africa-Asia, A New Axis of Knowledge*, University of Dar es Salaam, Tanzania, 20–22 September 2018. He is also grateful to the Centre of African Studies at the University of Edinburgh for the Catalyst Fellowship he received in 2019 that allowed him present a paper entitled "In whose interest? China in African universities" at the *Eighth European Conference of African Studies (ECAS)*, hosted in Edinburgh, 12–14 June 2019. He is grateful for all the comments made by participants at the *Toyin Falola @ 65 Conference* on *African Knowledges and Alternative Futures*, held at the University of Ibadan, Nigeria, 29–31 January 2018 where he presented a paper entitled "Engaging the Dragon without Blindfolds: Reflections on the African University and the Ecologies of China in Africa." Finally, he is grateful for the comments made by participants at the International Studies Association (ISA) conference on Exploring the Agency of the Global South in International Studies, held at the Legon Centre for International Affairs and Diplomacy, Accra, Ghana, 1–3 August 2019 where he presented a paper entitled "The African University and China in Africa: Understanding the Agency and Contradictions in a Complex South-South Engagement.

7. Congressional Research Service (2021). "Confucius Institutes in the United States: Selected Issues," 18 March, https://fas.org/sgp/crs/row/IF11180.pdf

8. Ibid.

9. Oshodi, A.T. (2019). "The African University and China in Africa: Understanding the Agency and Contradictions in a Complex South-South Engagement," *International Studies Association (ISA) International Conference* on 'Exploring the agency of the global south in international studies,' the Legon Centre for International Affairs and Diplomacy, Accra, Ghana, 1–3 August.

10. Mamdani, M. (2007). *Scholars in the Marketplace: The Dilemmas of Neo-liberal Reform at Makerere University, 1989–2005*. Dakar: CODESRIA; See also Mkandawire, T. (2011). "Running While Others Walk: Knowledge and the Challenge

of Africa's Development." *Africa Development*, 36(2), 1–36; Godin, B., & Gingras, Y. (2000). "The Place of Universities in the System of Knowledge Production," *Research Policy*, 29(2), 273–278.

11. Mkandawire, T. (2011). "Running While Others Walk: Knowledge and the Challenge of Africa's Development," *Africa Development*, p. 25.

12. Mamdani, M. (2007). *Scholars in the Marketplace: The Dilemmas of Neoliberal Reform at Makerere University, 1989–2005*. Dakar: CODESRIA, p. xvi.

13. *Washington Post* (2014). "The Price of Confucius Institutes," *Editorial*, 21 June, https://www.washingtonpost.com/opinions/the-price-of-confucius-institutes /2014/06/21/4d7598f2-f7b6-11e3-a3a5-42be35962a52_story.html?itid=lk_inline _manual_15

14. Green-Riley, Naima (2020). "The State Department Labeled China's Confucius Programs a Bad Influence on U.S. Students. What's the Story?" *The Washington Post*, 25 August, https://www.washingtonpost.com/politics/2020/08/24/state-department -labeled-chinas-confucius-programs-bad-influence-us-students-whats-story/

15. Oshodi (2019). "Beijing's Rise and Taiwan's Decline in Africa: What Does the African University Tell Us?"

16. Tehan, D. (2019). "Taskforce to Protect Universities from Foreign Interference," Wednesday 28 August, Media Release, https://www.dese.gov.au/uncategorised/ resources/development-university-foreign-interference-taskforce-media-release

17. President Trump campaigned on an anti-Chinese and nationalists view that sort to make America great again. His administration pursued anti-Chinese policies that affected Chinese companies and introduced punitive tariffs on Chinese goods. China retaliated by introducing its own tariffs.

18. Oshodi, A.T. (2019). "In Whose Interest? China in African Universities," the *Eighth European Conference of African Studies (ECAS)*, University of Edinburgh, UK, 12–14 June.

19. King, K. (2013). *China's Aid and Soft Power in Africa: The Case of Education and Training*. Suffolk and New York: James Currey, p. 90.

20. Ibid. See also Carayannis, T., & Olin, N. (2012, January). *A Preliminary Mapping of China-Africa Knowledge Networks*. Retrieved June 16, 2019, from Social Science Research Council: https://s3.amazonaws.com/ssrc-cdn1/crmuploads/new _publication_3/a-preliminary-mapping-of-china-africa-knowledge-networks.pdf

21. King (2013). *China's Aid and Soft Power in Africa: The Case of Education and Training*, p. 167.

22. Congressional Research Service (2021). "Confucius Institutes in the United States: Selected Issues," 18 March, https://fas.org/sgp/crs/row/IF11180.pdf

23. Oshodi, A.T. (2019). "Does the Location of Confucius Institutes in African and European Universities Tell Us Anything about China's Strategy in Africa?" Faculty of Social Science Conference on *Africa in the Competitive 21ˢᵗ Century: Towards an Agenda for Urgent Repositioning*, Lagos State University, Nigeria, 17–20 November.

24. Ibid.

25. Ibid.

26. The 2011 trilateral meeting had forty-four participating universities and set out to promote partnerships and collaborations among parties. See UNESCO (2011).

2011 UNESCO-China-Africa University Leaders Meeting: Prospects for Future Collaboration, 24 October, http://www.unesco.org/new/fileadmin/MULTIMEDIA/ HQ/ED/pdf/China-Africa-concept%20note.pdf

27. Havergal, C. (2016). "China Funds Construction of Africa's Largest University Library," *Times Higher Education*, 8 June, https://www.timeshighereducation.com/ news/china-funds-construction-africas-largest-university-library

28. See Ghana MOF (2019). "Ghana Government and the People's Republic of China sign Exchange of Note for the Construction of Phase II of the University of Health and Allied Sciences," *Ghana Ministry of Finance Website*, 15 January, https://www.mofep.gov.gh/news-and-events/2019-01-15/ghana-government-and-the -people-republic-of-china-sign-exchange-of-note-for-the-construction-of-phase-ii-of -the-university-of-health-and-allied-sciences

29. Ibid.

30. Ibid.

31. BBC (2019). "University of Transportation Daura: Wetin You Suppose Sabi About Dis First Special University Inside Nigeria," 2 December, https://www.bbc .com/pidgin/world-50617657

32. Chinese Embassy Ghana (2019). "Chinese Ambassador Scholarship Inspires Ghanaian Students," Embassy Website, 5 January, http://gh.china-embassy.org/eng/ zjgx/jylx/t1627182.htm

33. ABU (2019). "China Embassy Awards Scholarships to 48 ABU Students," *ABU website*, 26 April, https://www.abu.edu.ng/news-and-events/news/full-news .php?token=china-embassy-awards-scholarships-to-48-abu-students

34. *Xinhua* (2019). "Nigeria Builds Nation's First Transportation University with Chinese Support," 3 December, http://www.xinhuanet.com/english/2019-12/03/c _138602919.htm

35. Jack, A. (2020). "China Surpasses Western Government African University Scholarships," *Financial Times*, 23 June, https://www.ft.com/content/4b2e6c1c-83cf -448a-9112-477be01d2eee

36. Makundi, Hezron. (2018). "I Asked Tanzanians about Studying in China: Here's What They Said," *The Conversation*, 23 January, https://theconversation.com /i-asked-tanzanians-about-studying-in-china-heres-what-they-said-129358

37. Tsui, Benjamin (2016). "Do Huawei's Training Programs and Centers Transfer Skills to Africa?" *SAIS-CARI Policy Brief*, no. 14, July, https://static1 .squarespace.com/static/5652847de4b033f56d2bdc29/t/578e94e83e00be65954feb3f /1468962026573/Tsui+brief+v.5.pdf

38. Huawei (2016). "Huawei Inaugurates Innovation and Experience Center in Nigeria," 8 October, https://www.huawei.com/en/news/2016/10/huawei-innovation -experience-center-nigeria

39. Huawei (2020). "Huawei, Rain and Wits University Open Africa's First 5G Innovation Lab," 3 October, https://www.huawei.com/za/news/za/2020/huawei-rain -and-wits-university-open-africas-first-5g-innovation-lab

40. Huawei (2015). "Huawei to Train 1,000 African Students Over the Next Five Years through the Seeds for the Future Program," 5 June, https://www.huawei.com/ en/news/2015/06/hw_437649

41. See https://www.huawei.com/en/sustainability/win-win-development/social -contribution/seeds-for-the-future/south-africa

42. Oshodi (2019). "The African University and China in Africa: Understanding the Agency and Contradictions in a Complex South-South Engagement."

43. See http://www0.sun.ac.za/ccs/?cat=17

44. Carayannis, T., & Olin, N. (2012, January). *A Preliminary Mapping of China-Africa Knowledge Networks.* Retrieved June 16, 2019, from Social Science Research Council: https://s3.amazonaws.com/ssrc-cdn1/crmuploads/new_publication _3/a-preliminary-mapping-of-china-africa-knowledge-networks.pdf

45. See http://africachinareporting.co.za/about/

46. Maria Diamond, Maria (2018). "Institute of Nigeria-China Development Studies Makes Debut at UNILAG," *The Guardian*, 15 November, https://guardian.ng /features/institute-of-nigeria-china-development-studies-makes-debut-at-unilag/

47. See http://www.sinafrica.cas.cn/English/About/Introduction/

48. Ibid.

49. Oshodi, A.T. (2018). "Engaging the Dragon without Blindfolds: Reflections on the African University and the Ecologies of China in Africa," *The Toyin Falola @ 65 Conference* on *African Knowledges and Alternative Futures*, the University of Ibadan, Nigeria, 29–31 January; see also Carayannis, T., & Olin, N. (2012, January). *A Preliminary Mapping of China-Africa Knowledge Networks*, from Social Science Research Council: https://s3.amazonaws.com/ssrc-cdn1/ crmuploads/new_publication_3/a-preliminary-mapping-of-china-africa-knowledge -networks.pdf

50. Carayannis, T., & Olin, N. (2012, January). *A Preliminary Mapping of China-Africa Knowledge Networks.* Retrieved June 16, 2019, from Social Science Research Council: https://s3.amazonaws.com/ssrc-cdn1/crmuploads/new_publication _3/a-preliminary-mapping-of-china-africa-knowledge-networks.pdf

51. Just like China considers Taiwan as part of it, Somalia views Somaliland as a component unit although the later declared independence in 1991. See BBC (2021). "Somaliland and Taiwan: Two Territories with Few Friends but Each Other," 13 April, https://www.bbc.com/news/world-africa-56719409

52. See http://www.sanu.ac.sz/accreditations/

53. Pegg, Scott (2020). "The Somaliland-Taiwan Partnership: A New Frontier in De Facto State Diplomacy?" *De Facto States Research Unit*, 14 August, https:// defactostates.ut.ee/blog/somaliland-taiwan-partnership-new-frontier-de-facto-state -diplomacy

54. Ivudria, Godfrey (2020). "Hargeisa University and CYCU of Taiwan Sign Partnership Agreement," *EABW News*, 2 December, https://www.busiweek.com/ hargeisa-university-and-cycu-of-taiwan-sign-partnership-agreement/

55. See http://www.uoh-edu.net/the-taiwan-deputy-representative-to-somaliland -paid-a-visit-to-the-university-of-hargeisa/

56. *Somtribune* (2016). "Somaliland: Taiwan Donates Computers to 5 Universities," 28 August, https://www.somtribune.com/2016/08/28/somaliland-taiwan-donates -computers/

57. The BRICS stands for Brazil, Russia, India, China, and South Africa.

58. Oshodi (2019). "Beijing's Rise and Taiwan's Decline in Africa: What Does the African University Tell Us?"

59. See https://oia.ntu.edu.tw/en/agreement/country/school/3235

60. See Solomon, Salem (2018). "Once Influential in Africa, Taiwan Loses All but One Ally," *VOA*, 26 May, https://www.voanews.com/africa/once-influential -africa-taiwan-loses-all-one-ally; see also https://www.roc-taiwan.org/za_en/ index.html

61. Po-hsuan, Wu (2021). "Closing Confucius Centers Boon for Taiwan: Experts," *Taipei Times*, 23 March, https://www.taipeitimes.com/News/taiwan/archives/2021 /03/23/2003754325; see also Aspinwall, Nick (2021). "US Asks Taiwan to Fill Void as Confucius Institutes Close," *Nikkei Asia*, 2 February, https://asia.nikkei.com/ Business/Education/US-asks-Taiwan-to-fill-void-as-Confucius-Institutes-close

62. Between 1960 and 1963, thirteen of twenty-three African countries recognized Taiwan while China had five. Central African Republic, Côte d'Ivoire, Ethiopia, Niger, and Sierra Leone did not recognize both. See Rich, Timothy S. and Banerjee, Vasabjit (2015). "Running Out of Time? The Evolution of Taiwan's Relations in Africa," *Journal of Current Chinese Affairs*, 44(1), 141–161.

63. Oshodi (2019). "Beijing's Rise and Taiwan's Decline in Africa: What Does the African University Tell Us?"

BIBLIOGRAPHY

ABU. (2019). "China Embassy Awards Scholarships to 48 ABU Students." *ABU Website*, 26 April. https://www.abu.edu.ng/news-and-events/news/full-news.php ?token=china-embassy-awards-scholarships-to-48-abu-students.

Aspinwall, Nick. (2021). "US Asks Taiwan to Fill Void as Confucius Institutes Close." *Nikkei Asia*, 2 February. https://asia.nikkei.com/Business/Education/US -asks-Taiwan-to-fill-void-as-Confucius-Institutes-close.

BBC. (2019). "University of Transportation Daura: Wetin You Suppose Sabi About Dis First Special University Inside Nigeria." 2 December. https://www.bbc.com/ pidgin/world-50617657.

BBC. (2021). "Somaliland and Taiwan: Two Territories with Few Friends but Each Other." 13 April. https://www.bbc.com/news/world-africa-56719409.

Carayannis, T., and N. Olin. (2012, January). *A Preliminary Mapping of China-Africa Knowledge Networks*. Social Science Research Council. https://s3.amazonaws.com /ssrc-cdn1/crmuploads/new_publication_3/a-preliminary-mapping-of-china-africa -knowledge-networks.pdf.

Chinese Embassy Ghana. (2019). "Chinese Ambassador Scholarship Inspires Ghanaian Students." *Embassy Website*, 5 January. http://gh.china-embassy.org/eng /zjgx/jylx/t1627182.htm.

Congressional Research Service. (2021). "Confucius Institutes in the United States: Selected Issues." 18 March. https://fas.org/sgp/crs/row/IF11180.pdf.

Ghana MOF. (2019). "Ghana Government and the People's Republic of China Sign Exchange of Note for the Construction of Phase II of the University of Health and

Allied Sciences." *Ghana Ministry of Finance*, 15 January. https://www.mofep .gov.gh/news-and-events/2019-01-15/ghana-government-and-the-people-republic -of-china-sign-exchange-of-note-for-the-construction-of-phase-ii-of-the-university -of-health-and-allied-sciences.

Godin, B., and Y. Gingras. (2000). "The Place of Universities in the System of Knowledge Production." *Research Policy* 29, no. 2: 273–278.

Green-Riley, Naima. (2020). "The State Department Labeled China's Confucius Programs a Bad Influence on U.S. Students. What's the Story?" *The Washington Post*, 25 August. https://www.washingtonpost.com/politics/2020/08/24/state -department-labeled-chinas-confucius-programs-bad-influence-us-students-whats -story/.

Havergal, C. (2016). "China Funds Construction of Africa's Largest University Library." *Times Higher Education*, 8 June. https://www.timeshighereducation.com /news/china-funds-construction-africas-largest-university-library.

Huawei. (2015). "Huawei to Train 1,000 African Students Over the Next Five Years through the Seeds for the Future Program." 5 June. https://www.huawei.com/en/ news/2015/06/hw_437649.

Huawei. (2016). "Huawei Inaugurates Innovation and Experience Center in Nigeria." 8 October. https://www.huawei.com/en/news/2016/10/huawei-innovation -experience-center-nigeria.

Huawei. (2020). "Huawei, Rain and Wits University Open Africa's First 5G Innovation Lab." 3 October. https://www.huawei.com/za/news/za/2020/huawei -rain-and-wits-university-open-africas-first-5g-innovation-lab.

Jack, A. (2020). "China Surpasses Western Government African University Scholarships." *Financial Times*, 23 June. https://www.ft.com/content/4b2e6c1c -83cf-448a-9112-477be01d2eee.

King, K. (2013). *China's Aid and Soft Power in Africa: The Case of Education and Training.* Suffolk and New York: James Currey.

Makundi, Hezron. (2018). "I Asked Tanzanians about Studying in China: Here's What They Said." *The Conversation*, 23 January. https://theconversation.com/i -asked-tanzanians-about-studying-in-china-heres-what-they-said-129358.

Mamdani, M. (2007). *Scholars in the Marketplace: The Dilemmas of Neo-Liberal Reform at Makerere University, 1989–2005.* Dakar: CODESRIA.

Maria Diamond, Maria. (2018). "Institute of Nigeria-China Development Studies Makes Debut at UNILAG." *The Guardian*, 15 November. https://guardian.ng/fea- tures/institute-of-nigeria-china-development-studies-makes-debut-at-unilag/.

Mazrui, Ali. (1975). "The African University as a Multinational Corporation: Problems of Penetration and Dependency." *Harvard Educational Review* 45, no. 2: 191–210.

Mkandawire, T. (2011). "Running While Others Walk: Knowledge and the Challenge of Africa's Development." *Africa Development* 36, no. 2: 1–36.

Moshood, A. B., and A. T. Oshodi. (2018). "Breaking the Ice: The Nigerian University System and Its Funding Challenges." In *Global Aids and Tertiary Education in Nigeria*, edited by Olanrewaju Fagbohun and Adewale Aderemi, 61–93. Lagos: Profemative Concepts Int'l.

Oshodi, A. T. (2018). "Engaging the Dragon without Blindfolds: Reflections on the African University and the Ecologies of China in Africa." *The Toyin Falola @ 65 Conference* on *African Knowledges and Alternative Futures*, The University of Ibadan, Nigeria, 29–31 January.

Oshodi, A. T. (2019a). "Beijing's Rise and Taiwan's Decline in Africa: What Does the African University Tell Us?" *Taiwan Insight.* University of Nottingham, UK, 14 August: https://taiwaninsight.org/2019/08/14/beijings-rise-and-taiwans-decline -in-africa-what-does-the-african-university-tell-us/.

Oshodi, A. T. (2019b). "Does the Location of Confucius Institutes in African and European Universities Tell Us Anything about China's Strategy in Africa?" Faculty of Social Science Conference on *Africa in the competitive 21st Century: Towards an Agenda for Urgent Repositioning*, Lagos State University, Nigeria, 17–20 November.

Oshodi, A. T. (2019c). "The African University and China in Africa: Understanding the Agency and Contradictions in a Complex South-South Engagement." *International Studies Association (ISA) International Conference* on 'Exploring the Agency of the Global South in International Studies,' The Legon Centre for International Affairs and Diplomacy, Accra, Ghana, 1–3 August.

Pegg, Scott. (2020). "The Somaliland-Taiwan Partnership: A New Frontier in De Facto State Diplomacy?" *De Facto States Research Unit*, 14 August. https:// defactostates.ut.ee/blog/somaliland-taiwan-partnership-new-frontier-de-facto-state -diplomacy.

Po-hsuan, Wu. (2021). "Closing Confucius Centers Boon for Taiwan: Experts." *Taipei Times*, 23 March. https://www.taipeitimes.com/News/taiwan/archives/2021 /03/23/2003754325.

Rich, Timothy S., and Vasabjit Banerjee. (2015). "Running Out of Time? The Evolution of Taiwan's Relations in Africa." *Journal of Current Chinese Affairs* 44, no. 1: 141–161.

Solomon, Salem. (2018). "Once Influential in Africa, Taiwan Loses All but One Ally." *VOA*, 26 May. https://www.voanews.com/africa/once-influential-africa -taiwan-loses-all-one-ally.

Somtribune. (2016). "Somaliland: Taiwan Donates Computers to 5 Universities." 28 August. https://www.somtribune.com/2016/08/28/somaliland-taiwan-donates -computers/.

Tehan, D. (2019). "Taskforce to Protect Universities from Foreign Interference." Wednesday 28 August, Media Release. https://www.dese.gov.au/uncategorised /resources/development-university-foreign-interference-taskforce-media-release.

Tsui, Benjamin. (2016). "Do Huawei's Training Programs and Centers Transfer Skills to Africa?" *SAIS-CARI Policy Brief*, No. 14, July. https://static1.squarespace .com/static/5652847de4b033f56d2bdc29/t/578e94e83e00be65954feb3f /1468962026573/Tsui+brief+v.5.pdf.

UNESCO. (2011). *2011 UNESCO-China-Africa University Leaders Meeting: Prospects for Future Collaboration*, 24 October. http://www.unesco.org/new/ fileadmin/MULTIMEDIA/HQ/ED/pdf/China-Africa-concept%20note.pdf.

Washington Post. (2014). "The Price of Confucius Institutes." Editorial, 21 June. https://www.washingtonpost.com/opinions/the-price-of-confucius-institutes/2014/06/21/4d7598f2-f7b6-11e3-a3a5-42be35962a52_story.html?itid=lk_inline_manual_15.

Xinhua. (2019). "Nigeria Builds Nation's First Transportation University with Chinese Support." 3 December. http://www.xinhuanet.com/english/2019-12/03/c_138602919.htm.

Chapter 7

China's Emerging Security Diplomacy and Its Implications for Taiwan in Africa

Isaac Owusu Frimpong

INTRODUCTION

The end of the Cold War and the emergence of new security threats, includ-ing political violence, economic nationalism, competition over natural resources, transnational crime, and global health crises, are important factors that have influenced China's strategic thinking over the past three decades.[1] Meanwhile, China's engagement in contemporary Africa is being defined by its increasing role in peace and security issues. Given China's stated respect for the principles of state sovereignty and "noninterference" that have guided its bilateral relations with African states since the end of the Cold War, this is generating controversy, to say the least. As such, Beijing has been intensify-ing its military presence on the continent by establishing permanent facilities for the People's Liberation Army (PLA), expanded its role within United Nations (UN) operations in Africa, and has actively engaged the African Union (AU) to address peace and security issues on the continent. As a result, security is gaining policy traction in China's engagement with Africa in what I refer to as China's emerging "security diplomacy" in Africa. At the same time, African support for Taiwan's presence on the continent is waning amid its efforts to build diplomatic ties on the continent.

This chapter discusses China's emerging "security diplomacy" as part of its overall foreign policy strategy toward Africa contra the dwindling influence of Taiwan. I argue that this evolving security diplomacy seeks to advance and defend Chinese interests in Africa and other parts of the world. I argue further that China's evolving security diplomacy is not intended to achieve great power status only but to influence the international system to strategically isolate Taiwan as the latter seeks to establish itself as an independent state by seeking ties in Africa.

Although Taiwan is not the main target, I argue that this emerging security diplomacy has the potential to eliminate the dwindled influence/presence of Taiwan on the continent. This is because all of China's actions and inactions domestically or internationally have implications for Taiwan, either explicitly or implicitly. As such, the Chinese government (Chinese Communist Party [CCP]) believes that the rise, progress, and stability of China are intrinsically linked with the unification (if not annexation) of Taiwan. Besides, Beijing has also demonstrated intentions to use force as an instrument to achieve this objective, supported by its 2005 Anti-Secession Law which specifically authorizes the use of military force in case Taiwan declares formal independence.[2] This was reiterated by President Xi Jinping in January 2019 when he called on Taiwanese leaders to accept peaceful reunification, but made it clear at the same time that China reserved the option of using force if Taiwan didn't go along.[3] Some scholars argue that China's economic and political clout explains its aggressive policy and posture toward Taiwan.[4] Indeed, as Mearsheimer asserts, "given the difficulty of determining how much power is enough for today and tomorrow, great powers recognize that the best way to ensure their security is to achieve hegemony now, thus eliminating any possibility of a challenge by another great power,"[5] it is important for China to cement its position and place in the international order as a rising superpower.

The chapter proceeds by providing a historical account of China-Taiwan diplomatic and military completion, followed by a discussion of Chinese security practices in Africa. The chapter also defines the concept of security diplomacy. I employ neoclassical realism to explain how systemic factors and domestic constraints/concerns are shaping China's emerging security diplomacy in its engagement with Africa. This is because neoclassical realism incorporates first, second, and third image variables in its analysis. The chapter ends with a discussion on the implications of such a move for China-Taiwan engagement on the African continent.

HISTORICAL, DIPLOMATIC, AND MILITARY COMPETITION BETWEEN PRC AND ROC

The Republic of China (ROC) was established on the mainland in 1911 after the ruling party of the ROC, the Chinese Nationalist Party (KMT, or the nationalists), overthrew the last dynastic regime. The nationalist regime itself was toppled by the CCP in a ten-year Civil War, leading ROC president Chiang Kai-shek to flee to China's island province of Taiwan in 1949 with almost 2 million followers (mainly soldiers, bureaucrats, and their families). A new battle began between the two "states" as each competed for diplomatic and international recognition, and most importantly, a seat at the UN. This new battle was later referred to as the "cross-strait" tension or relation. Africa became an overseas "battleground" for diplomatic recognition between the PRC, otherwise referred to as mainland, and the ROC, also known as Taiwan. During this time, China-Africa relations were largely insignificant and none of the four independent African states at the time (Egypt, Liberia, Ethiopia, and South Africa) recognized nor had any diplomatic relations with China.[6] However, the battle for diplomatic recognition, international relations, and a seat within the UN gave both the PRC and ROC a reason to focus their attention on Africa. This was because decolonization presented an opportunity and a competition for both the PRC and the ROC to increase and solidify their respective diplomatic relations with many newly independent African countries.

One of the major challenges the PRC faced at its inception in 1949 was the support of the United States and Western allies for Taiwan. During the Cold War, countries were forced to choose between Beijing and Taipei as the sole legitimate central government representing the whole of China as both parties considered the tension as an absolute zero-sum game. This typically reflects the traditional Chinese political culture of *han zei bu liang li*, meaning men and bandits don't coexist. Although Taiwan outpaced China initially, most African countries switched their support to the latter resulting in Taiwan's loss of its status as an internationally recognized independent country when the PRC joined the UN following a 1971 UN resolution. Within a few years, most UN member states had switched their diplomatic recognition to the PRC based on the "One-China" principle. By the 1990s, Taiwan's overt quest for international recognition resulted in huge investments in Africa in return for diplomatic ties. The PRC pursued a policy to constrain and marginalize the ROC on the international stage,[7] as it intensified its own influence.

The normalization of US-China relations and Beijing's own return to the international stage contributed to the narrowing of Taiwan's international space.[8] China's declaration of 2006 as the "Year of Africa" elevated its relations with Africa to a higher degree of prominence. The year climaxed with the Third Forum on China-Africa Cooperation (FOCAC) meeting held in Beijing which was attended by forty-eight African leaders. Meanwhile, Taiwan's version of an African Summit in September 2007, held in Taipei, went largely unnoticed.[9] The contrast between Taipei in September 2007 and Beijing in November 2006 is what some have described as the ascendancy of China and the terminal decline of Taiwan in Africa.[10] Beijing has combined several strategies not only to compete against Taipei but also to eliminate its presence in Africa. These include economic means, diplomacy, and "soft power." China has used economic incentives or "Chinese dollar diplomacy" to persuade the so-called friends of Taiwan to switch diplomatic ties in favor of Beijing,[11] further abandoning the island. In 2018, Alpha Barry, Burkina Faso's minister of foreign affairs, mentioned that China had offered his country $500 million in return for the establishment and recognition of diplomatic relations.[12] Diplomatically, China has pursued the "One-China" principle which prohibits countries to recognize or establish diplomatic relations with both Beijing and Taipei at the same time.

In recent times, China has combined intentions and capabilities, as evidenced by the modernization of its military, to deter Taipei in matters on the Taiwan Straits in Asia. This military modernization and power projection has been extended into Africa more recently, which I argue has the potential to further deter Taiwan's waning presence and diplomatic recognition on the continent. As of the time of writing, only one African country, Eswatini, had diplomatic relations with Taiwan. This is non-consequential for Chinese interests as Eswatini does not wield much political and economic clout. A more recent and "controversial" relationship between Taiwan and Somaliland is discussed further in this chapter. China's attempt to enhance its military prowess globally has "unintended" consequences for Taiwan's continuous quest for independent statehood. Meanwhile, China's actions resonate with Thucydides's telling of the ancient Athenians' subjugation of the island of Melos—"The strong do what they can and the weak suffer what they must."[13] China is showing itself as the strong one and Taiwan as the weak one which must suffer. Taiwan is recognized by China as a renegade province and insists that it is inseparable from the mainland PRC. For its part, Taiwan rejects the social and political structure of mainland China and the narrative about its "rebel province status."

Nevertheless, global political developments have gradually marginalized Taiwan. The PRC is intent on minimizing Taiwan's international presence and does not recognize activities that might imply Taiwanese sovereignty, a development that makes Taiwan's quest for independence very complicated within the international environment. Indeed, Taiwan has been struggling to maintain its "independent" position by any means possible, including attempts to establish diplomatic relations with other states, while the number of countries that diplomatically recognize Taiwan keeps declining. Between 2016 and 2018 alone, Taiwan lost the support of Burkina Faso, the Dominican Republic, El Salvador, Panama, the Gambia, and São Tomé and Príncipe. As of December 2018, Taiwan had diplomatic relations with only seventeen countries globally which further reduced to thirteen in recent times. Moreover, Taipei has either covertly or overtly responded to all or most of China's actions on the international scene with regard to matters that concern its sovereignty. For instance, despite the Taiwanese government's claim that its organization of the Africa Summit in 2007 was not intended to rival Beijing's FOCAC, such comparisons were inevitably made by observers and policy analysts which the former tried to downplay.[14]

Military tension undercurrents have also characterized the cross-strait issue over the years. By the 1990s, a standoff with the United States over Taiwan tested the PLA's preparedness to defend the interests of Beijing.[15] One of the lessons Beijing learned from its military retreat following America's dispatch of two carrier-led battle groups as a result of this standoff in 1996 was that a country's ability to operate in the maritime domain was vital in modern warfare.[16] This lesson greatly inspired the transformation and modernization of the PLA, including the establishment of military facilities overseas. During the Cold War, "China refused to view international power competition solely as a superpower 'zero-sum' game where its fate would be determined by the outcome of the East-West power struggle."[17] On the contrary, however, China viewed the cross-strait tension as an absolute "zero-sum" game as mentioned earlier and has persisted in and intensified its stance on this issue despite Taiwan's desertion of the traditional "one China" rivalry.

In 2006, Chad, one of Taiwan's allies, switched diplomatic ties in favor of Beijing citing security reasons.[18] The president of Chad explained to the Taiwanese premier, who was scheduled to visit Chad, that the switch was necessary "for the survival of Chad" amid fears of Chinese-backed rebels based in Sudan who were preparing to attack N'Djamena. Meanwhile, it is reported that in the year 2000 China had sent troops to Khartoum to protect China National Petroleum Corporation's investments in the oilfields in southern Sudan and involved themselves in the ongoing civil war, partly confirming the suspicion and worry of the Chadian president.[19] The relationship between Chad and Beijing consequently thickened and featured a military collaboration and assistance program from China. Shen Dingli, a renowned Fudan University scholar, published an article in 2010 that sought to encourage China to consider establishing military bases overseas. Shen argued that these military bases could enable China to respond to threats from any country that attempted to block China's trade routes and to deter any secessionist intentions from the mainland, including Taiwan and Hong Kong. He argued further that such military facilities could enhance Beijing's opportunities to retaliate against an attack from within the host country. He summed his arguments up by suggesting that these bases were necessary to enhance the ability of the Chinese navy to restrict potential enemies' access to international waterways.[20] Although this suggestion was dismissed by Chinese policymakers at the time, Beijing opened its first foreign military base at Djibouti in 2017, almost a decade after Shen's suggestion.

CHINA'S EVOLVING SECURITY
PRACTICES IN AFRICA

While some scholars argue that Chinese presence in Africa is part of its strategy of global influence,[21] I argue that China's increasing security engagement in Africa is part of its global strategic reorientation as a new or emerging superpower. In addition to protecting its citizens and defending its interests, I also argue that this deepening security engagement is a strategic move to strengthen its "one-China" policy and to diffuse and possibly eliminate Taiwan's presence and/or influence on the continent. This move is further meant to project China's growing military prowess to deter others. Admittedly, one of the key attributes of a great power status is its ability to project power beyond its regional sphere of influence to pursue its national interests, unimpeded by other great powers.[22] China has been in pursuit of this great/global power status, and in 2017 opened its first foreign military base in Djibouti, drawing concern from scholars and analysts both within and outside the African continent. This combination of military expansion and economic development evidenced in Djibouti is paralleled in other African countries, including China Harbour Engineering Company's port expansion of Namibia's Walvis Bay on the Atlantic Ocean, with intentions of building a Chinese naval base there, and, reportedly, a Chinese 10 billion USD port facility and special economic zone project under construction in Tanzania's coastal town of Bagamoyo.[23] China has also expanded its role (both personnel and financial contribution) within UN peacekeeping operations with about half of the organization's missions located in Africa as of August 2019.[24] Further to this, China's construction (gift) of the AU headquarters complex[25] in Addis Ababa and its willingness to support the African Peace and Security Architecture demonstrate its commitment to the course of the union.

China's "military diplomacy" is part of its wider diplomacy and that aspects related to building the image of the PLA can be considered as an extension of its public diplomacy.[26] The author argues further that this military diplomacy undertaken by the PLA is essentially a set of activities and initiatives that align with regular diplomacy, mainly regarding foreign armies in harmony while endorsing and pursuing the agenda set by Chinese foreign policymakers in its own autonomous way. Meanwhile, Chinese officials have attempted to defend the motivation for the establishment of the military base in Djibouti and have indicated that it is meant to provide logistics and respite for Chinese troops and naval vessels and to also participate in UN peacekeeping operations.[27] They further claim that it is designed to assist in noncombatant evacuation operations and provide support for the Belt and Road Initiative.[28]

China's military base in Djibouti was set up to support five mission areas: (i) counter-piracy in the Gulf of Aden, (ii) intelligence collection on other countries, (iii) noncombat evacuation of Chinese citizens in East Africa, (iv) international peacekeeping operations where Chinese soldiers are deployed, and (v) counterterrorism operations.[29] The author further argues that although foreign troops are generally deployed to counter threats to international peace, subdue terror groups and pirates, and support foreign security initiatives in Africa, other motivations explain these enterprises. These include protection of commercial interests, aligning with friendly regimes, and expressing dominance on a continent that is the focus of rising global competition.

CONCEPTUALIZING CHINESE SECURITY DIPLOMACY IN AFRICA

Scholars have attempted to discuss China's military engagement with other countries under the title "military diplomacy." Much of the discourse on military diplomacy focuses on the activities, operations, and initiatives of the PLA or the Chinese military with other militaries. Other scholars have deliberated on China's "naval diplomacy" in East Asia and beyond. Naval diplomacy has been defined as the "use of naval forces in a manner short of combat operations to primarily fulfill some foreign policy-related goal."[30] The 2011 edition of *PLA Military Terminology* of the Chinese military's authoritative lexicon defined military diplomacy as the

> external relationships pertaining to the military and related affairs between countries and groups of countries, including military personnel exchange, military negotiations, arms control negotiations, military aid, military intelligence cooperation, military technology cooperation, international peacekeeping, military alliance activities, etc. Military diplomacy is an important component of a country's foreign relations.[31]

Military diplomacy has also been defined "as a broad, overarching concept that connects all of the military's foreign affairs work to the nation's diplomacy."[32] Also, Matsuda Yasuhiro classifies China's military diplomacy by geopolitical strategy into six categories—strategic partnership, strategic placement, co-opting surrounding countries, co-opting advanced countries, restraining, and conflict avoidance. This classification focuses essentially on the military exchanges between the PLA and the military of other countries, like the United States and Russia. These definitions tend to narrow the broader issues that are related to security architecture across the globe, and Africa in particular. In addition to that, the discourse on military diplomacy does not include the government-led or state-to-state engagement on security-related issues. Nevertheless, the PLA is among the most active partners of African militaries. These bilateral military-to-military ties are based on arms sales, equipment donations, and training and education programs. China was the second-largest supplier of weapons to sub-Saharan Africa after Russia in 2015, accounting for 22% of arms transfers to the region.[33]

This chapter, therefore, attempts to conceptualize/define "Security Diplomacy" as a broader foreign policy concept and discusses what China intends to achieve with this emerging "tool." I define Chinese "security diplomacy" as the "government-led initiative with other states that are aimed at establishing security partnership for the common good of both parties essentially spearheaded by the Chinese state (CCP) and not necessarily the PLA or the military." It includes China's bilateral/unilateral security engagement with specific countries, its continental dialogue with the AU at the regional level, as well as Beijing's active and expanding role within the UN framework aimed at the security landscape in Africa. Further, this *security diplomacy* also includes the establishment of permanent Chinese military facilities and the projection of its military prowess in Africa. However, it must be mentioned that the PLA (and its auxiliary units) plays a key role in this security diplomacy as a unit mandated to act in the overall interest of the Chinese state. Although the PLA has not been involved in any direct conflict since the end of the Cold War, it remains an important political actor in China's government and continues to contribute significantly to the country's foreign relations.[34] As such, Zhou Bo has noted that all the PLA's overseas involvement, including peacekeeping, counter-piracy, noncombatant evacuation, or disaster relief, is found in Africa. He argues further that Beijing's approach to dealing with such nontraditional threats has been underpinned by a desire to help, rather than police the world.[35] This makes it imperative for scholars and policymakers to understand the scope, rationale, and operations of the PLA in Africa. Despite the increasing number of foreign policy actors, the PLA still plays a vital role in crafting China's foreign policy.[36] Thus, this emerging security diplomacy has two main actors, bureaucrats (including government officials and appointees, scholars, and analysts) and the PLA. I argue that China's *security diplomacy* aims to achieve the following: (i) influence; (ii) form alliances; and (iii) serve as a deterrent to other states, especially Taiwan.

Influence

China's security diplomacy in Africa is designed to influence or shape security discourse on the continent to its favor. This strategy is to allay the apprehensions African states may exhibit with regard to China's rapid military expansion and project its intentions in a positive light. This has the potential to diminish Taiwan's activities and interests on the continent in the process. A former deputy head of the military building department of the PLA Academy of Military Science, Yang Chunchang, argued that "military 'soft power' is marked by an ability to influence the non-coercive nature (*fei qiangzhi xing*) of specific targets and non-material nature grounded on 'hard power,' and an ability to penetrate and constrain people's thinking and mentality."[37] It has been indicated that China's invitation of high-ranking military representatives from fifty African countries to the first China-Africa Defense and Security Forum at the instance of China's Ministry of National Defense is an attempt to emphasize Beijing's strategic interest in Africa.[38] I argue such gestures provide China with a powerful but benign way to control and influence military thinking on the continent. This is also part of its long-term strategy to influence and shape security architecture on the continent. Hitherto, these officers attended such courses in Western countries, which have largely shaped military doctrines on the continent.

Since China's "threat theories" started gaining attention, China realized that its rise coupled with its military modernization was becoming a matter of concern for many countries, providing a basis for critics to develop powerful anti-China propaganda.[39] China made it a point to project its military modernization as nonthreatening and benign, and also to create a discourse of a peaceful military that strives for global harmony and cooperation among militaries.[40] In recent years, Chinese leaders have authorized the People's Liberation Army Navy (PLAN) to carry out tasks related to naval diplomacy beyond maritime East Asia, in the "far seas," designed to directly support its broader strategic and foreign policy objectives.[41] In January 2009, the PLAN embarked on an UN-sanctioned counter-piracy mission in the Gulf of Aden to protect and defend its interests in that region.[42] Aside from Africa, China's deployment of the *Peace Ark*[43] hospital ship to Grenada was also part of its attempts to weaken Taiwan's diplomatic ties with the latter, which in itself demonstrates how "naval diplomacy"[44] can in some cases aim, in part, to strengthen and influence the CCP's political narrative and vision of unification and/or the takeover of Taiwan.

Alliance Formation

Characteristically, a superpower must have allies or build alliances with countries across the globe. In 2016, Zhou Bo, an honorary fellow at the PLA's Academy of Military Science, argued China did not need allies to survive.[45] Also, some commentators argue that President Xi believes that international relations should be premised on partnerships rather than alliances and that alliances are an outmoded relic of the Cold War.[46] Partnership here is taken to mean a "win-win" dialogue or engagement between sovereign and equal states, while alliances have to do with the "asymmetric" relationship that characterized global politics during the Cold War. On the contrary, I argue that China's emerging security diplomacy in Africa is intended to build alliance(s) on the continent. As an emerging global power, China needs to build an alliance in other places far from its region to sustain and advance its superpower ambitions. In the aftermath of events that forced the Chinese military to evacuate some of its citizens from Libya in 2011 and Yemen in 2015, discussion on Beijing's historical reluctance to establish foreign military bases and formal alliances was revived among scholars and officials in China.[47] The establishment of the PLA's overseas military base in Djibouti has been described by some analysts as the initial attempt by Beijing to build a formal system of allies.

China's engagement in Africa, just as elsewhere, is linked to its quest to obtain superpower status. Indeed, as much as African countries rely on China for several reasons, China in turn depends on the continent, not only for economic reasons but for its growing global ambitions. China needs the support of African countries in its quest to become a superpower. One of the cardinal areas of this quest is to be reunited with Taiwan by "every means necessary." I argue that China's emerging security diplomacy in Africa is to help Beijing build alliances with African countries, and as an unintended or implied consequence, contribute to diminishing Taiwan's presence and interests on the continent. This alliance will make it difficult and unattractive for African countries to switch diplomatic ties to Taiwan as was evident in the 1960s and 1970s. Some Chinese analysts have viewed Beijing's "naval diplomacy" as an important instrument for enabling the CCP's central leadership to achieve its foreign policy goals, including promoting stability and enabling efforts to shape global rules and norms.[48] I argue that these efforts have a long-term goal or objective to help China build allies, not only in Africa but in other parts of the world.

Deterrence and Defense

As an emerging superpower, China needs to have the capacity to deter competitors and that its capacity must not be limited to its immediate region (within Asia only) but must extend to other parts of the world. I, therefore, submit that Chinese security diplomacy in Africa will eventually deter Taiwan's pursuit of diplomatic recognition on the continent. Indeed, this security diplomacy tends to enforce the "one-China" policy in Africa. Some scholars contend that "in the future, a more blue-water capable PLAN could serve more overtly coercive functions to defend and advance China's rapidly growing overseas interests when operating abroad."[49] Also, the concept of "naval diplomacy" is gaining attention among scholars and policy analysts in China. Yang Zhen and Cai Liang (2016),[50] writing on the subject, recommended cooperated practices (joint military exercises and exchanges) but at the same time emphasized the importance of deterrence when necessary. Professor Xu Lite of Jilin University (China) authored an article on naval diplomacy in a Central Party School journal that affirmed deterrence as a key principle, upholding the "safeguarding of national security and development interests" as a key consideration. His appeal of "development interests" suggests deterrence could be applied to the protection of economic interests in the far seas, *including in Africa.*[51]

Aside from deterrence, the Chinese government, and for that matter, the CCP leadership needs to prove the capacity of the state to defend its interests externally. Arguably, the protection of Chinese citizens and interests abroad has been a distinct trademark of Xi Jinping's foreign policy. In Ethiopia, Chinese nationals became proxy targets for the opposition members and rebel movements to register their dissatisfaction with the ruling government and Beijing's association with that government.[52] These incidents, and others, have raised concerns about the ability of the ruling CCP to protect its citizens and investments overseas. These developments are generating a growing concern among policy analysts and scholars about the country's substantial national economic and other interests that are being exposed to danger and risk in Africa due to persistent conflicts. Admittedly, the Libyan crisis generated public outcry on the inability of the ruling government to protect its citizens and national interests abroad. Thus, Chinese emerging security diplomacy is not intended to deter other states only, but also to project the country's ability to defend its interests and citizens overseas. China has extended its quest to deter Taiwan from Asia to other parts of the world, as is evidenced in Africa.

NEOCLASSICAL REALISTS' EXPLANATIONS

Taiwan's competitive edge over China over the years has dwindled considerably in Africa. In the past, Taipei used its economic clout, appealing liberal democratic political structure, advanced technology plus what others refer to as genuine altruistic motivation to win allies on the continent.[53] However, China has risen to the occasion and managed to exterminate Taiwan's interest in Africa. This section analyzes the International Relations theory that best explains this paradigm shift. Since there are both domestic and international factors emanating from China's perspective, I shall employ neoclassical realists' arguments to explain China's emerging security diplomacy in Africa. "Neoclassical realists share with neorealist and classical realists the view that a country's foreign policy is primarily formed by its place in the international system and in particular by its relative material capabilities. However, these theorists also argue that the impact of systemic factors on a given country's foreign policy will be indirect and more complex than neorealists have assumed since such features can affect policy only through factors on the domestic level."[54]

For neoclassical realists, it is relative material power that determines the basic parameters within which a state can formulate its foreign policy. Neoclassical realism provides a theoretically inspired framework that strives to expound the foreign policies of different states facing similar external restraints or the foreign policy of the same state over time. They also recognize that systemic pressures and incentives may guide the general direction of a state's foreign policy, but that these forces are not so incisive as to determine the intricacies of state behavior. Meanwhile, it has been argued that the evolving area of neoclassical realism attempts to reintroduce domestic level actors and issues, such as internal Chinese politics, economic issues, government-military relations, and the factions within the CCP, as important variables in understanding the trajectory of Chinese foreign policy.[55] This is affirmed by others who contend that China's expanding security involvement in Africa is a consequence of its strategic objective—sustaining its economic growth and creating a Sino-African "community of common destiny."[56]

Importantly, neoclassical realism advances a well-defined causal chain comprising of three steps—first, the independent or the exogenous variable or a country's relative material power in the anarchical international system. Second is the intervening or the endogenous variable or the domestic level "transmission belt" which sieves systemic forces. The third is the foreign policy outcome or the dependent variable. Proponents of neoclassical realism argue that a country's relative power—political, economic, and military power (hard power)—influences and constrains its position in the anarchical international system. Thus, as the relative material power capabilities of a country rise in an anarchical international system, its aims, objectives, and the ability to achieve the objectives will also rise. They further argue such power capabilities have an indirect and complex influence on foreign policy. This is because the pressure exerted by the system must be interpreted through an intervening variable(s) at the unit level.[57] This theory argues further that, while systemic balance of power (or overall international environment) matters in the formulation of a state's foreign policy, the real final policy is the result of domestic political elite processing such systemic conditions and assessing how the state's interests (domestic and international) can be fulfilled under the circumstances. In a state like the PRC, this means the leader's role is vital—his or her vision and ideas steer the foreign policy. I argue that President Xi (as an individual) acts as the most important intervening variable shaping China's foreign policy in this era. Neoclassical realism incorporates first, second, and third image variables, which are discussed to explain China's emerging security diplomacy in Africa. The first image has to do with the role of individuals in determining or shaping the course of a country's foreign policy. The second image focuses on the fundamental role of states as principal actors, while the third image refers to the "anarchical" international system (environment) within which states operate.

First Image Analysis

Arguably, the current president of China, Xi Jinping, is one of the most influential leaders the PRC has had, and his stated desire to shape and/or reshape the international system using China's power and influence aligns with neoclassical analysis at the "first image" or individual level. He is among the first to have signaled China's new status in the global order. He has also stated and exhibited a desire to shape the international system using China's power to influence others and to establish or revise the global rules of engagement. Indeed, history reveals how some individuals have been very instrumental in influencing the course of events in the international system.[58] At a meeting with the country's military and foreign policy elites in November 2014, President Xi outlined his intention to move China from its status as an emerging or regional power to that of a global power.[59] To achieve this, President Xi began reforms as the head of the Central Military Commission that commands China's armed forces. These reforms sought to shift the focus and buildup of the PLA power to naval, air, and missile forces, which are vital for his ambitions to enforce territorial claims in Asia and protect China's increasing economic interests overseas,[60] *and possibly deter Taiwan*.[61] The goal of this reform is to enable the PLA to conduct complex joint operations combining air, sea, and ground forces with information technology—akin to operations undertaken by the United States.[62] In one of his earlier speeches as president, President Xi is reported to have said that one of the reasons for the collapse of the Soviet Union was that its armed forces were under the control of the state, which accounted for its inaction. For him, the Chinese PLA would remain very much the armed forces of the Communist Party to prevent such an occurrence.[63] In 2019, President Xi Jinping redefined the 1992 Consensus[64] as an understanding that "the two sides of the Taiwan Strait belong to one China, jointly seeking to achieve cross-strait unification." His appeal and occasional threats to Taiwan demonstrate his desire for reunification, making him an important intervening variable in this discourse.

Second Image Analysis

The second image variable discusses the internal processes and interactions among various actors which shape the foreign policy of countries. There have been a growing number of agencies, groups, and organizations that are contributing to Chinese foreign policymaking over the last few years. Although there has been a greater concentration of political power in the Chinese government, including in the area of foreign policy, under Xi Jinping, however, the number of actors who contribute to foreign policymaking continues to grow both within the Chinese government and increasingly outside of it.[65] This is a development that elucidates the influential role of domestic actors in foreign policy. As such, there is growing consensus among many in China for the CCP government to make good its promise of unifying the "two China." This pressure has been exacerbated by calls from the Chinese youth for the government to make good on their bluster and to take Taiwan by force if necessary.[66] Meanwhile, it has been observed that several social media commentators in China called on the government to invade Taiwan amid the COVID-19 pandemic.[67] Although Beijing has not ruled out this option, analysts say the CCP leadership did not want to be rushed on this matter, but rather took steps to calm the "Nationalist fever."[68]

Third Image Analysis

The third image variable analyzes the impact of the international system on a state's foreign policy. Since its founding in 1949, the PRC has risen and/or is rising to be one of the most powerful countries in the world. There is no doubt today that China is a global power. It is currently the world's first or second-largest economy after the United States depending on the indices one uses to measure—that is whether in nominal or purchasing power parity terms.[69] At the same time, China's military prowess and capacity are rising to reflect its status as a global power and boasts the world's largest standing army. It is also among one of only five designated nuclear weapons states under the Non-Proliferation Treaty. China's ability to defend itself and to project power afield is significant and growing due to its investments in aircraft carriers, stealth fighter jets, and one of the world's few antiship ballistic missiles. Its military spending ranks second only to that of the United States. To further project its military power and standing as a global power, China put up its first foreign military base at Djibouti in 2017—a development that raises doubts on its avowed principle of noninterference. China has also created five artificial islands in the South China Sea. These developments are attributed to the influential role of President Xi.

Also, there are ongoing debates about the "seeming" decline of US global power and/or its indifference toward global affairs, with the 2008/2009 global financial crises being the pinnacle of these debates. The crises caused the American economy to fall into a deep recession. China, on the other hand, remained unscathed by these events. A situation that made Chinese policymakers and officials assert that the financial crunch represented an inflection point in world history, albeit the decline of the United States and the rise of China.[70] This seeming shift in the direction of the balance of power in China's favor was noted at the CCP's Central Work Conference on Foreign Affairs in July 2009.[71] Remarkably, some analysts note that the conference called for a radical shift from Deng Xiaoping's famous maxim for keeping a low profile (*Taoguang Yanghui*, meaning "hide and bide") and called for a more active foreign policy,[72] not to say a more assertive one. An emerging foreign policy orientation labelled in both China and the West as "Wolf Warrior diplomacy" as a result of this assertive stance of Beijing in recent times. The United States has been committed to ROC's security against PRC's aggression (even after Sino-US rapprochement during the 1970s) ever since China's division, while also advising the ROC against provoking the mainland, entrenching the division of a historically unified China in the process. The perceived decline of US influence, and perhaps its "isolation" from global issues, gives China more room to assert its stance on Taiwan. At least, the silence of the United States and other Western countries over the Hong Kong crises is a case in point.

In addition to the so-called American decline, Chinese leaders felt that its relative power in the international system had increased substantially.[73] As a result, a famous adviser to Chinese leaders, Wang Jisi, asserted that "many Chinese officials believe that their nation has ascended to be a first-class power in the world and should be treated as such."[74] The sentiment—"the West is declining, and China is rising"—became particularly pronounced in 2020 due to the apparent relative success of China in controlling COVID-19. This message was also contained in Beijing's virus diplomacy. Still, on matters related to COVID-19, China successfully prevented Taiwan from attending the World Health Assembly's[75] meeting in 2020 as an observer.[76] Some analysts aptly contend that China's power has grown apace with its ability to buy and coerce the world into pretending Taiwan's independent government does not exist.[77]

It is noteworthy to mention the support and willingness of African leaders and governments toward Chinese policies and its rising security initiatives on the continent. Arguably, Africa's embrace of China's increasing security engagement on the continent is part of the systemic variables that contribute to this emerging security diplomacy. Others have also argued in support of this assertion that African elites have embraced China's growing role in international affairs more than other regions of the world, first as a counterbalance to the West and more recently as a development model to be emulated.[78] Thus, Xi Jinping's role at the individual level, changing domestic conditions within China at the state level, calling for greater participation of Beijing in international affairs, and its growing aspiration to modify global norms at the systemic level fit into neoclassical realists' arguments. Invariably, all these elements bear the impact of President Xi as a "vision-ary totalitarian leader," making him the most important intervening variable responsible for China's current foreign policy toward Africa with serious implications for Taiwan.

IMPLICATIONS FOR TAIWAN

Given China's success over Taiwan for diplomatic ties, and its increasing influence on the continent, this section discusses the implications of these developments on Taiwan's quest for recognition in Africa. It is clear from the preceding discussion that China will continue to "squeeze" Taipei's quest for diplomatic recognition on the continent. Economically, the trusted strategy of "dollar diplomacy" employed by Taiwan to establish diplomatic relations is no longer tenable, or unattractive at best, to many African countries due to the economic prowess of China. Besides, it is costly for African states to be on the wrong side of China as this may lead to dire consequences—diplomatic tension, withdrawal of Chinese economic sup-port, and a possible military confrontation. Moreover, China's pursuit of a foreign policy orientation which has been labeled in both China and the West as "Wolf Warrior diplomacy" under President Xi's administration, which appears caused some havoc on Australian exports recently, may likely be replicated by Beijing to its African counterparts if the need arises. It appears that China is making Taiwan's quest "unattractive" or unachievable in Africa. Under these circumstances, Taiwan can continue to maintain, and possibly expand, its economic presence (partnership) on the continent like what it has currently with South Africa to keep its hopes alive. In the mean-time, the Biden administration in the United States could provide Taiwan a ray of hope if it decides to pursue the Obama administration's "Pivot to Asia" policy. However, the recent verbal barbs between the new Biden administration and Chinese officials in Alaska over US-China respective views about neoliberal values such as human rights mark a significant shift in China's so-called peaceful rise. The outcome of the meeting demonstrates China's willingness to stand against what it considers unfair allegations or foreign aggression.

CONCLUSION

This chapter has discussed China's emerging "security diplomacy" in Africa and how this affects Taiwan's continuous quest for independent statehood and recognition on the continent. Importantly, the chapter argues that this emerging security diplomacy is a broader concept that is intended to replace, if not complement, the erstwhile military diplomacy spear-headed by the PLA and its auxiliary units. At the same time, the security diplomacy is intended to influence, deter its foes, and defend its interests as well as to build alliances for Beijing's expanding interest and engagement in Africa. The chapter also provided the historical basis influencing this move, and China's evolving security (military) practices on the continent to fend off Taiwan. Arguably, the chapter discusses the role of African leaders and maintains that Africa's continuous support and partnership with China remain a setback in Taiwan's interest in the continent. The chapter proposes and adopts neoclassical realism to explain this evolving security disposition emanating from Beijing. Specifically, the chapter combines the three image variables—first (*role of individuals*), second (*role of the state and other domestic factors*), and third (*anarchic international environment*), as well as the intervening variable (*responsible for interpreting pressure from the system*)—as proposed by neoclassical realists to explain this development.

NOTES

1. Lanteigne, Marc. "China's Military and Emerging Security Concerns." Chap. 5 In *Chinese Foreign Policy: An Introduction*, 29. London: Routledge, 2020.

2. Schreer, Benjamin. "The Double-Edged Sword of Coercion: Cross-Strait Relations after the 2016 Taiwan Elections."*Asian Politics & Policy* 9, no. 1 (2017): 50–65.

3. Wees, van der Gerrit. "How President Xi Jinping Is Misreading Taiwan." *The Diplomat* (2019). Published electronically January 3, 2019. https://thediplomat.com /2019/01/how-president-xi-jinping-is-misreading-taiwan/.

4. Taylor, Ian. "Taiwan's Foreign Policy and Africa: The Limitations of Dollar Diplomacy." *Journal of Contemporary China* 11, no. 30 (2002): 125–40.

5. Elman, Colin, and Michael Jensen. *The Realism Reader*. London: Routledge, 2014, p. 185.

6. Larkin, Bruce D. *China and Africa, 1949–1970 : The Foreign Policy of the People's Republic of China*. Berkeley: University of California Press, 1971.

7. Taylor, "Taiwan's Foreign Policy and Africa," 125–40.

8. Fell, Dafydd. "Taiwan's External Relations: Balancing International Space and Cross-Strait Relations." Chap. 9 In *Government and Politics in Taiwan*, edited by Dafydd Fell, 171–95. New York: Routledge, 2018.

9. It was attended by only six African countries that still had diplomatic relations with Taiwan.

10. Large, Dan, and Shiuh-Shen Chien. "China Rising in Africa: Whither Taiwan." Paper presented at the Conference paper, Charles University, Prague, 2008.

11. Šárka, Waisová. "China's Strategy Vis-a-Vis Taiwan's Diplomatic Friends: Is Beijing Using Dollar Diplomacy? 1." *Journal of Comparative Politics* 13, no. 1 (2020): 76–101.

12. Bax, Pauline, Simon Gongo, and Lungile Dlamini. "Chinese Billions Fail to Sway Taiwan's Last Two Allies in Africa." *Bloomberg*, 2017. Available at: https://www. bloomberg. com/news/articles/2017-01-24/chinese-billions-fail-to-sway-taiwan-s-last-two-allies-in-africa (accessed 9 August 2020).

13. Quote cited in Robert D. Kaplan, "The South China Sea Is the Future of Conflict," *Foreign Policy*, no. 188 (Sep/Oct2011): 1–8.

14. Large and Chien, "China Rising in Africa: Whither Taiwan."

15. Page, Jeremy. "President Xi Jinping's Most Dangerous Venture Yet: Remaking China's Military." *Wall Street Journal* 25 (2016).

16. Yahuda, Michael. "China: The Ascent to Global Economic, Political and Military Influence." Chap. 5 In *The International Politics of the Asia-Pacific*, 140–83. Taylor & Francis Group, 2019.

17. Tow, William T. "China and the International Strategic System." Chap. 6 In *Chinese Foreign Policy : Theory and Practice*, edited by Thomas W. Robinson and David L. Shambaugh. Studies on Contemporary China. Oxford: Clarendon Press, 1994. p. 120.

18. Large and Chien, "China Rising in Africa: Whither Taiwan."

19. Taylor, "Taiwan's Foreign Policy and Africa," 125–40.

20. Dingli, Shen. "Don't Shun the Idea of Setting up Overseas Military Bases." *China.org.cn* 28 (2010).

21. Large, Dan. *Chinas Role in the Mediation and Resolution of Conflict in Africa.* Norway: Centre for Humanitarian Dialogue, 2008, pp. 35–41.

22. Antwi-Boateng, Osman. "New World Order Neo-Colonialism: A Contextual Comparison of Contemporary China and European Colonization in Africa." *The Journal of Pan African Studies* 10, no. 2 (2017): 177–95.

23. Strategic Comments, 2018.

24. UN Peacekeeping Operations in Africa. Report by the Congressional Research Service, September 23, 2019.

25. China completed and presented the AU with a headquarters complex at a cost of $200 million in 2012.

26. Singh, Prashant Kumar. "China's 'Military Diplomacy': Investigating PLA's Participation in UN Peacekeeping Operations." *Strategic Analysis* 35, no. 5 (2011): 793–818.

27. Ghiselli, Andrea. "China's First Overseas Base in Djibouti, an Enabler of Its Middle East Policy." *China Brief* 16, no. 2 (2016).

28. Blanchard, Ben. "China Launches Charms Offensive for First Overseas Naval Base." *Reuters*, March 23 (2016).

29. Neethling, Theo. "Why Foreign Countries Are Scrambling to Set up Bases in Africa." *The Conversation* (2020). https://theconversation.com/why-foreign-countries-are-scrambling-to-set-up-bases-in-africa-146032.

30. Heath, Timothy R. "China Maritime Report No. 8: Winning Friends and Influencing People: Naval Diplomacy with Chinese Characteristics." (2020). p. 5.

31. Quote cited in Timothy R. Heath (2020), "China Maritime Report No. 8: Winning Friends and Influencing People: Naval Diplomacy with Chinese Characteristics." p. 5.

32. Heath, Timothy R. "China Maritime Report No. 8: Winning Friends and Influencing People: Naval Diplomacy with Chinese Characteristics." (2020). p. 6.

33. Duchâtel, Mathieu, Richard Gowan, and Manuel Lafont Rapnouil. "Into Africa: China's Global Security Shift." *European Council on Foreign Relations* (2016).

34. Lanteigne, "China's Military and Emerging Security Concerns," p. 29.

35. Zhou Bo is an honorary fellow with the PLA Academy of Military Science in China. https://www.scmp.com/comment/opinion/article/3021745/africa-test-lab-how -china-approaches-international-security-and

36. Lanteigne, "China's Military and Emerging Security Concerns," p. 29.

37. Quote cited in Singh (2011), "China's 'Military Diplomacy': Investigating PLA's Participation in UN Peacekeeping Operations," p. 3.

38. Spross, Hans. "Why Has China Invited African Army Chiefs to Beijing?" (2018). Published electronically June 29, 2018. https://www.dw.com/en/why-has -china-invited-african-army-chiefs-to-beijing/a-44462013.

39. Singh, "China's 'Military Diplomacy': Investigating PLA's Participation in UN Peacekeeping Operations," 793–818.

40. Roy, Denny. "The 'China Threat' Issue: Major Arguments." *Asian Survey* 36, no. 8 (1996): 758–71.

41. Heath, Timothy R. "China Maritime Report No. 8: Winning Friends and Influencing People: Naval Diplomacy with Chinese Characteristics." (2020).

42. Susanne, Kamerling, and Frans-Paul van der Putten. "An Overseas Naval Presence without Overseas Bases: China's Counter-Piracy Operation in the Gulf of Aden." *Journal of Current Chinese Affairs* 40, no. 4 (2011): 119–46.

43. Peace Ark is one of the hospital ships of the PLAN, which embarked on two separate voyages to Grenada between 2015 and 2018.

44. I argue in this chapter that naval diplomacy is contained in China's overall emerging security diplomacy.

45. https://www.scmp.com/comment/insight-opinion/article/1974414/us-right -china-has-no-allies-because-it-doesnt-need-them

46. Limin, Zheng. "Xi's World Vision: A Community of Common Destiny, a Shared Home for Humanity." *English.cctv.com* 1 (2017).

47. Economy, Elizabeth C. "The Lion Awakens." In *The Third Revolution: Xi Jinping and the New Chinese State*. Oxford: Oxford University Press, Incorporated, 2018.

48. Heath, Timothy R. "China Maritime Report No. 8: Winning Friends and Influencing People: Naval Diplomacy with Chinese Characteristics." (2020).

49. Heath, Timothy R. "China Maritime Report No. 8: Winning Friends and Influencing People: Naval Diplomacy with Chinese Characteristics." (2020), p. 3.

50. Cited in Heath Timothy (2020), "China Maritime Report No. 8: Winning Friends and Influencing People: Naval Diplomacy with Chinese Characteristics."

51. Italics mine.

52. Aidoo, Richard, and Steve Hess. "Non-Interference 2.0: China's Evolving Foreign Policy towards a Changing Africa." *Journal of Current Chinese Affairs* 44, no. 1 (2015): 107–39.

53. Large and Chien, "China Rising in Africa: Whither Taiwan."

54. Rose, Gideon. "Neoclassical Realism and Theories of Foreign Policy." *World Politics (Online)* 51, no. 1 (1998): 144–72.

55. Lanteigne, Marc. "Introduction: The Reconstruction (and Expansion) of Chinese Foreign Policy." Chap. 1 In *Chinese Foreign Policy: An Introduction*: Taylor & Francis Group, 2020.

56. Yu, Lei. "China's Expanding Security Involvement in Africa: A Pillar for 'China–Africa Community of Common Destiny.'" *Global Policy* 9, no. 4 (2018): 489–500.

57. Rose, "Neoclassical Realism and Theories of Foreign Policy," 144–72.

58. Frimpong, Isaac Owusu. "Response of the International Community to the Boko Haram Insurgency in Nigeria." *Korea and Global Affairs* 3, no. 1 (2019): 24.

59. Economy, "The Lion Awakens."

60. Page, "President Xi Jinping's Most Dangerous Venture Yet."

61. Italics mine.

62. Page, Jeremy. "President Xi Jinping's Most Dangerous Venture Yet: Remaking China's Military." Wall Street Journal 25 (2016).

63. Yahuda, "China: The Ascent to Global Economic, Political and Military Influence," 140–83.

64. An informal agreement between the KMT and the CCP that there is one China, but that each side can have its own definition of what that might mean.

65. Lanteigne, "Introduction: The Reconstruction (and Expansion) of Chinese Foreign Policy."

66. Eisenman, Josuha, and Sean King. "Beijing Is Pushing the Taiwanese toward Independence Hard and Fast." *Foreign Policy* (2020). Published electronically May 18, 2020. https://foreignpolicy.com/2020/05/18/beijing-pushing-taiwan-toward -independence/.

67. Chan, Minnie. "China Tries to Calm 'Nationalist Fever' as Calls for Invasion of Taiwan Grow."*South China Morning Post* (2020). Published electronically May 10, 2020. https://www.scmp.com/news/china/politics/article/3083696/china-tries -calm-nationalist-fever-calls-invasion-taiwan-grow.

68. Ibid.

69. Economy, "The Lion Awakens."

70. Economy, "The Lion Awakens."

71. Yahuda, "China: The Ascent to Global Economic, Political and Military Influence," 140–83.

72. Glaser, Bonnie S, and Benjamin Dooley. "China's 11th Ambassadorial Conference Signals Continuity and Change in Foreign Policy." *China Brief* 9, no. 22 (2009): 8–12.

73. Yahuda, "China: The Ascent to Global Economic, Political and Military Influence," 140–83.

74. Cited in Christopher A. Ford, *China Looks at the West* (2015), p. 335.

75. This is the decision making body of the World Health Organisation.
76. Josuha and King. "Beijing Is Pushing the Taiwanese toward Independence Hard and Fast"; Harrison, Mark. "Taiwan's Exclusion from World Health Assembly Threatens Global Pandemic Response."*Australian Strategic Policy Institute* (2020). Published electronically November 12, 2020. https://www.aspistrategist.org.au/taiwans-exclusion-from-world-health-assembly-threatens-global-pandemic-response/.
77. Eisenman and King. "Beijing Is Pushing the Taiwanese toward Independence Hard and Fast."
78. Alden, Chris, and Daniel Large. "On Becoming a Norms Maker: Chinese Foreign Policy, Norms Evolution and the Challenges of Security in Africa." *The China Quarterly*, no. 221 (2015): 123.

BIBLIOGRAPHY

Aidoo, Richard, and Steve Hess. "Non-Interference 2.0: China's Evolving Foreign Policy towards a Changing Africa." *Journal of Current Chinese Affairs* 44, no. 1 (2015): 107–139.

Alden, Chris, and Daniel Large. "On Becoming a Norms Maker: Chinese Foreign Policy, Norms Evolution and the Challenges of Security in Africa." *The China Quarterly*, no. 221 (2015): 123.

Antwi-Boateng, Osman. "New World Order Neo-Colonialism: A Contextual Comparison of Contemporary China and European Colonization in Africa." *The Journal of Pan African Studies* 10, no. 2 (2017): 177–195.

Bax, Pauline, Simon Gongo, and Lungile Dlamini. "Chinese Billions Fail to Sway Taiwan's Last Two Allies in Africa." *Bloomberg*. 2017. https://www.bloomberg.com/news/articles/2017-01-24/chinese-billions-fail-to-sway-taiwan-s-last-two-allies-in-africa (accessed 9 August 2020).

Blanchard, Ben. "China Launches Charms Offensive for First Overseas Naval Base." *Reuters*, March 23, 2016.

Chan, Minnie. "China Tries to Calm 'Nationalist Fever' as Calls for Invasion of Taiwan Grow." *South China Morning Post*. 2020. Published Electronically May 10, 2020. https://www.scmp.com/news/china/politics/article/3083696/china-tries-calm-nationalist-fever-calls-invasion-taiwan-grow.

Dingli, Shen. "Don't Shun the Idea of Setting Up Overseas Military Bases." *China.org.cn* 28 (2010).

Duchâtel, Mathieu, Richard Gowan, and Manuel Lafont Rapnouil. "Into Africa: China's Global Security Shift." *European Council on Foreign Relations*. 2016.

Economy, Elizabeth C. "The Lion Awakens." In *The Third Revolution: Xi Jinping and the New Chinese State*. Oxford: Oxford University Press, Incorporated, 2018.

Eisenman, Josuha, and Sean King. "Beijing Is Pushing the Taiwanese toward Independence Hard and Fast." *Foreign Policy*. 2020. Published Electronically May 18, 2020. https://foreignpolicy.com/2020/05/18/beijing-pushing-taiwan-toward-independence/.

Elman, Colin, and Michael Jensen. *The Realism Reader*. London: Routledge, 2014. doi: 10.4324/9781315858579.

Fell, Dafydd. "Chapter 9: Taiwan's External Relations: Balancing International Space and Cross-Strait Relations." In *Government and Politics in Taiwan*, edited by Dafydd Fell, 171–195. New York: Routledge, 2018.

Frimpong, Isaac Owusu. "Response of the International Community to the Boko Haram Insurgency in Nigeria." *Korea and Global Affairs* 3, no. 1 (2019): 24.

Ghiselli, Andrea. "China's First Overseas Base in Djibouti, an Enabler of Its Middle East Policy." *China Brief* 16, no. 2 (2016): 6–9.

Glaser, Bonnie S., and Benjamin Dooley. "China's 11th Ambassadorial Conference Signals Continuity and Change in Foreign Policy." *China Brief* 9, no. 22 (2009): 8–12.

Harrison, Mark. "Taiwan's Exclusion from World Health Assembly Threatens Global Pandemic Response." *Australian Strategic Policy Institute*. 2020. Published Electronically November 12, 2020. https://www.aspistrategist.org.au/taiwans-exclusion-from-world-health-assembly-threatens-global-pandemic-response/.

Heath, Timothy R. "China Maritime Report No. 8: Winning Friends and Influencing People: Naval Diplomacy with Chinese Characteristics." 2020.

Lanteigne, Marc. "Chapter 1: Introduction: The Reconstruction (and Expansion) of Chinese Foreign Policy." In *Chinese Foreign Policy: An Introduction*. Taylor & Francis Group, 2020.

Lanteigne, Marc. "Chapter 5: China's Military and Emerging Security Concerns." In *Chinese Foreign Policy: An Introduction*, Vol. 29. London: Routledge, 2020.

Large, Dan. *China's Role in the Mediation and Resolution of Conflict in Africa*, pp. 35–41. Norway: Centre for Humanitarian Dialogue, 2008.

Large, Dan, and Shiuh-Shen Chien. "China Rising in Africa: Whither Taiwan." Paper Presented at the Conference Paper, Charles University, Prague, 2008.

Larkin, Bruce D. *China and Africa, 1949–1970: The Foreign Policy of the People's Republic of China*. Berkeley: University of California Press, 1971.

Limin, Zheng. "Xi's World Vision: A Community of Common Destiny, a Shared Home for Humanity." *English.cctv.com* 1 (2017).

Neethling, Theo. "Why Foreign Countries Are Scrambling to Set Up Bases in Africa." *The Conversation*. 2020. https://theconversation.com/why-foreign-countries-are-scrambling-to-set-up-bases-in-africa-146032.

Page, Jeremy. "President Xi Jinping's Most Dangerous Venture Yet: Remaking China's Military." *Wall Street Journal* 25 (2016).

Rose, Gideon. "Neoclassical Realism and Theories of Foreign Policy." *World Politics (Online)* 51, no. 1 (1998): 144–172.

Roy, Denny. *China's Foreign Relations*. Houndmills, England: Macmillan, 1998.

Roy, Denny. "The 'China Threat' Issue: Major Arguments." *Asian Survey* 36, no. 8 (1996): 758–771.

Šárka, Waisová. "China's Strategy Vis-a-Vis Taiwan's Diplomatic Friends: Is Beijing Using Dollar Diplomacy? 1." *Journal of Comparative Politics* 13, no. 1 (2020): 76–101.

Schreer, Benjamin. "The Double-Edged Sword of Coercion: Cross-Strait Relations after the 2016 Taiwan Elections." *Asian Politics & Policy* 9, no. 1 (2017): 50–65.

Singh, Prashant Kumar. "China's 'Military Diplomacy': Investigating PLA's Participation in UN Peacekeeping Operations." *Strategic Analysis* 35, no. 5 (2011): 793–818.

Spross, Hans. "Why Has China Invited African Army Chiefs to Beijing?" 2018. Published Electronically June 29, 2018. https://www.dw.com/en/why-has-china -invited-african-army-chiefs-to-beijing/a-44462013.

Susanne, Kamerling, and Frans-Paul van der Putten. "An Overseas Naval Presence without Overseas Bases: China's Counter-Piracy Operation in the Gulf of Aden." *Journal of Current Chinese Affairs* 40, no. 4 (2011): 119–146.

Taylor, Ian. "Taiwan's Foreign Policy and Africa: The Limitations of Dollar Diplomacy." *Journal of Contemporary China* 11, no. 30 (2002): 125–140.

Tow, William T. "Chapter 6: China and the International Strategic System." In *Chinese Foreign Policy: Theory and Practice*, edited by Thomas W. Robinson and David L. Shambaugh. Studies on Contemporary China. Oxford: Clarendon Press, 1994.

Wees, van der Gerrit. "How President Xi Jinping Is Misreading Taiwan." *The Diplomat.* 2019. Published Electronically January 3, 2019. https://thediplomat.com /2019/01/how-president-xi-jinping-is-misreading-taiwan/.

Yahuda, Michael. "Chapter 5: China: The Ascent to Global Economic, Political and Military Influence." In *The International Politics of the Asia-Pacific*, 140–183. Taylor & Francis Group, 2019.

Yu, Lei. "China's Expanding Security Involvement in Africa: A Pillar for China–Africa Community of Common Destiny." *Global Policy* 9, no. 4 (2018): 489–500.

Chapter 8

How Taiwan Lost Africa, and What the Future Holds for Its Last Remaining Alliance with Eswatini

Kristina Kironska and Thiombiano Dramane

INTRODUCTION: THE AFRICAN STATE

Taiwan, officially the Republic of China (ROC), is a unique country, both politically and economically. Politically, it transitioned from an autocratic, incompetent, and frustrating regime, which lost the Chinese Civil War, to a solid democracy. Economically, it moved from being backward and poor to one of the world's greatest economies. In 2018, Taiwan was ranked by the WTO as the eighteenth-largest exporter and the seventeenth-largest importer of merchandise, as well as the largest holder of foreign reserves.[1]

However, when looked at in terms of the international world system, Taiwan is an isolated island. The Taiwanese government has domestically accepted control of its territory[2] (internal sovereignty), but the country lacks formal diplomatic relations with most independent countries (external sovereignty). Although Taiwan has a little problem establishing unofficial ties, it faces problems due to China's efforts to block its entry into official relationships. Its remaining diplomatic allies are all comparatively weak countries in the developing world, except for the Vatican, with only one ally on the whole African continent.

China, officially the People's Republic of China (PRC), has used its relations in Africa to enhance its position vis-à-vis Taiwan, a so-called weapon in cross-strait relations. And we can say that Taiwan has essentially lost its diplomatic battle with China in Africa and must look for alternative sources of legitimacy in the twenty-first century. Altogether thirty African countries at one time or another maintained formal relations with Taiwan, but today the country is a politically marginalized actor with a minuscule presence mostly confined to the pursuit of economic interests. The only

African country that currently maintains diplomatic relations with Taiwan is Eswatini, formerly known as Swaziland. China—the world's second-biggest economy—has attracted one African country after another to its side, but Eswatini has stuck with Taiwan. Why?

The answers can be found in the characteristics of the African state and its patterns of functioning. "The prevailing African state, in all African countries, is an implant from the European countries whose colony each African country was. The present postcolonial State in Africa did not grow organically out of the body of Africa: it is an implant on the African body, hence the grotesque features of some nation-states."[3] This quote eloquently shows the nature of the African state; it is not African in origin and has been imported if not imposed on Africans by former colonial powers after independence. Except for a few countries, the African elite that inherited the state was chosen by the former colonial powers. The colonial state was predatory, divisive, and exploitative, and worked to destroy the establishment of civil society in Africa.[4] As argued by Mueni wa Muiu and Guy Martin, during colonialism, the African state no longer served the interests of the people concerning food, security, and shelter. Instead, it became a coercive force.[5] As a continuity of the colonial state, the modern African state contains some remnants of colonialism. The leaders who inherited the colonial state did not alter it to meet the priorities and needs of Africans and thus did not focus on continental unity; self-determination; and freedom from conflict, fear, and hunger. Instead, they Africanized colonial institutions, appropriated the state, stealing from it, and ignoring indigenous institutions. The state in Africa is characterized by patterns of predation, neo-paternalism, and rent-seeking, whereby the elite takes hold of the state resources for private use. African political power after independence is thus characterized by patrimonialism, clientelism, corruption, and power. In this atmosphere, state elites use their status to gain resources and strengthen their economic and political power. In Africa, this is called "the politics of the belly."[6]

Examples of this patrimonial appropriation of public resources are common in Africa. For instance, the late president of the DRC Mobutu Sese Seko embezzled foreign aid funds from Western countries such as the United States, one of his biggest allies.[7] Zimbabwe, under the leadership of Robert Mugabe, is also another striking eloquent example. In Burkina Faso, under the Compaoré regime, the funds from Taiwanese aid were managed by the Presidential Office and not channeled directly to the bodies concerned with the different development projects.

Some scholars argue that the disconnection of African states from their citizens is exacerbated by the provision of foreign aid that destroys the accountability of the leaders to their populations. As Dambisa Moyo posits: "When governments don't rely on taxes for revenue, leaders don't feel they owe their people anything, and the people don't expect anything from their leaders. This opens the door to corruption. And despite ostensible 'conditionalities' on aid, in reality, the money flows with virtually no strings attached, so corrupt leaders eschew much-needed infrastructure projects and instead partake in reckless consumption."[8]

In Eswatini—an absolute monarchy—the king has the last word on every decision. And so, since he supports Taiwan, it is unlikely that Eswatini will sever ties with the country while he remains the leader. This was the same for countries like Liberia, Burkina Faso, and the Gambia, where the leaders—often dictators or soft dictators, such as Charles Taylor of Liberia, Yahya Jammeh of the Gambia, or Blaise Compaoré of Burkina Faso—supported Taiwan because of the personal economic benefits they received in return.

Drawing evidence from the existing literature, newspaper reports, and in-depth interviews with key informants[9] in Taiwan, this chapter examines the evolution of Taiwan's relations with Africa, with a special focus on its last diplomatic ally—Eswatini. Some limitations of this study include the limited access to key informants, such as the Eswatini Embassy in Taiwan (which never responded to any emails or calls) or the Africa Department of the MOFA (which turned down an interview).

After having given a brief introduction and explained the nature of the African state, we then continue by describing Taiwan's relations with Africa—from the postindependence and Cold War relations, through post–Cold War pragmatic diplomacy initiatives to twenty-first-century relations, in which Taiwan has embarked on the quest of finding new alternatives to traditional diplomatic relations. We then turn to the Taiwan-Eswatini relations, a topic that has not received much attention in academic circles, followed by the conclusion. Among other data, the appendix includes a comprehensive table listing all the African countries and stating their connections to Taiwan and China.

TAIWAN'S RELATIONS WITH AFRICA

Postindependence and Cold War Relations—
Competing with China for UN Support

In the 1950s–1960s, many countries on the African continent gained independence and were courted by both China and Taiwan. Both asserted themselves as the sole legitimate representative of China and used diplomatic allies in Africa to support their claims—which were mutually exclusive, making diplomatic recognition a zero-sum game.[10] Directly after 1949, several countries had no relations with either side, as they were waiting for a final settlement.

Taiwan first made a connection with South Africa, then one of three independent African countries. South Africa was a staunch anticommunist country strongly opposed to the PRC's admission to the UN.[11] Between 1960 and 1963, Taiwan received recognition from thirteen of twenty-three African countries, while China only did so from five (CAR, Ethiopia, Côte d'Ivoire, Niger, and Sierra Leone), while five recognized neither.[12] Cold War rationales initially benefited Taiwan; newly independent countries such as Zaire were suspicious of communism and moved to recognize Taiwan.

The ROC's strategy emphasized providing agriculture and technical training and assistance to newly independent countries (in exchange for diplomatic recognition). The first technical cooperation agreement was signed with Liberia in 1960. From 1961 through 1972, eighteen phases of technical training were undertaken in African countries with more than 45,000 people receiving nonagricultural technical training.[13] At the same time, an agency in charge of agricultural cooperation with Africa was established to provide agricultural training to farmers. Medical teams were also sent to countries such as Libya to provide medical assistance. Several African students were also sent to Taiwan to receive training in human resources and agricultural techniques. From 1965 through 1970, Taiwan sent agricultural teams to provide technical training to farmers in Upper Volta (Burkina Faso), Chad, Malawi, the Gambia, and Swaziland (Eswatini).[14]

These countries were impressed by the increased output of rice production in Libya and the miracle of rice cultivation in the Libyan Desert and hoped to reach food sufficiency through Taiwanese technical assistance. About a thousand people from Taiwan were thus dispatched to provide technical assistance in farming to African countries—projects that fell into this category include rice production in Burkina Faso, the Gambia; rice and vegetable farming in Chad, Liberia, Senegal, and São Tomé and Príncipe; corn, sweet potato, and vegetable production in Malawi; broiler raising in São Tomé and Príncipe; corn production in Swaziland; and freshwater fish farming in Senegal.[15]

From the outset, Taipei's pursuit of economic diplomacy was stimulated by self-interest—seeking to isolate Beijing and gain support at the UN. Taipei initiated economic diplomacy—with a whole range of economic instruments, including trade, aid, and investment—despite its reliance on US aid.[16] However, it should be noted that Taiwanese technical assistance to Africa was done under the instigation of the United States, which saw it as a cheaper way to aid Africa and contain the spread of communism.[17]

Taiwan's aid and technical assistance helped increase the number of allies in Africa from one (Egypt) in 1955 to twenty-two in 1969 (see appendix

1), and African states voting for the ROC at the UN from three in 1955 to twenty-one (the most ever) in 1969, and fifteen in the fateful October of 1971 (see appendix 2). Exact numbers concerning the amount of money allocated are unknown given that Taiwan's aid allocations have been kept secret; furthermore, the Legislative Yuan only decided on the total foreign aid budget as a lump sum.

After 1960, the number of UN members increased with the admission of other countries that gained independence. This resulted in a decline in Western influence, with the regional powers having until then dominated the UN, and the gradual desire of several members to renegotiate the issue of Chinese representation. Beijing achieved this in part with its so-called banquet diplomacy—inviting prominent representatives of Western and African countries to visit the PRC. Conversely, China also sent representatives to visit other countries. In 1971 alone, 290 delegations from 80 countries were invited to the PRC, while 70 Chinese delegations visited 40 countries.[18] That year, the PRC finally managed to gain admission to the UN as the legitimate representative of China—including with the help of African votes.

At that time, the African continent was roughly evenly split—Taiwan was recognized by twenty countries while China by twenty-two. However, the PRC endeavor to marginalize Taiwan on the international stage, coupled with the United States switching recognition in 1979 from the ROC to the PRC, led many countries to follow suit, and between 1971 and 1979 forty-six states came to recognize the PRC instead of the ROC,[19] and only five out of all fifty African countries recognized the ROC in 1979.[20] Taiwan not only lost its UN seat but also found itself abandoned diplomatically.

In the 1980s, after Taiwan had lost most of its African allies, the country scaled down its technical assistance program to Africa and shifted its economic assistance to Latin America, where many of its diplomatic allies were located. Furthermore, soft loans replaced technical assistance as the main component of Taiwan's foreign aid.[21]

Post–Cold War Relations—Pragmatic Diplomacy

In the late 1980s, President Lee Teng-hui declared a new direction for Taiwan's diplomacy, a so-called pragmatic diplomacy which emphasized consolidation of existing diplomatic ties and winning new allies through economic cooperation, development of substantive ties with China's allies, and participation in intergovernmental organizations.[22]

There was the China External Trade Development Council (later renamed the Taiwan External Trade Development Council, TAITRA), established by the Ministry of Economic Affairs in the 1970s, which promoted Taiwan's foreign aid and acted as MOFA's front for sensitive diplomatic communication with China's allies. In the late 1980s, a new fund (the International Economic Cooperation Development Fund) was established to promote more comprehensive cooperation with partner countries and allocate aid and economic assistance to allies. In 1996, this became the International Cooperation and Development Fund (ICDF), which is managed by the Taiwanese MOFA.[23] Before the ICDF, the agency overlooking cooperation with African nations was the Sino-Africa Technical Cooperation Committee, a permanent agency responsible for agricultural cooperation. In 1972, it would become the Committee of International Technical Cooperation, in charge of the ROC's foreign technical cooperation activities, assisting partner nations with their agricultural development.

After the Tiananmen massacre in 1989, China was criticized and isolated by most countries on the international stage. The country's main focus thus became regaining respectability, and thus it was less effective in obstructing Taiwanese diplomatic activities. In 1989 and 1990, Taiwan used its economic might to increase its presence in Africa and elsewhere. In exchange for millions of dollars in soft loans, it managed to woo seven new allies, four of which were in Africa—Liberia, Lesotho, Guinea-Bissau, and CAR.

After the end of the Cold War, the ideological rationale (anticommunism) for diplomatic recognition became obsolete, as did the rationale for many countries to maintain relations with Taiwan. Countries now often switched support without any clear ideological or political rationale. Moreover, Beijing's position was always, and remains, to unconditionally sever relations with any state that establishes diplomatic relations with the ROC. A major foreign objective for China in Africa was and still is the One China principle, a fundamental exception to China's "no-strings-attached policy."[24] With that, diplomatic recognition has become an easily politicized dynamic in African politics, and African ruling elites have learned to play Beijing against Taipei. For example, Senegal, Liberia, and CAR each switched five times since originally forging ties with Taiwan in 1962, and there are another six countries that switched three times. Liberia is one of the few nations that established ties with both the PRC and the ROC at the same time—between 1993 and 1997 both Beijing and Taipei ran embassies in Liberia. In 1997, however, Monrovia proclaimed that it would recognize "two Chinas" and the PRC subsequently severed diplomatic relations. And then there is the peculiar case of the Gambia, which in 2013 unilaterally broke relations with Taiwan although it has subsequently not courted China for recognition.

Taiwan was able to maintain diplomatic relations with South Africa until 1998 (due to its financial support for the African National Congress during the 1994 elections and beyond),[25] and Taipei's economic power enabled it to win recognition from several other countries in need of cash. This practice of providing financial assistance in exchange for diplomatic recognition was termed "dollar diplomacy," and this tug of war for diplomatic recognition was adopted by both Taiwan and China, being particularly acute during times of cross-strait tensions, such as the 1995–1996 Taiwan Strait Crisis. Throughout this period five countries severed ties with China to the detriment of Taiwan—Burkina Faso, the Gambia, Senegal, São Tomé and Príncipe, and Chad.[26] At the same period, China managed to attract four countries—Lesotho (1994), Niger (1996), the CAR (1998), and Guinea-Bissau (1998).[27] Aid from Taiwan was provided as deemed necessary—São Tomé and Príncipe received 30 million USD in loans, Chad 125 million USD in loans,[28] the Gambia 35 million USD in assistance, and when Malawi suddenly switched recognition in 2008, aid intended for this country was transferred to Swaziland (now Eswatini).[29]

As Taiwan was losing allies, China was gaining allies. How did China further its influence in Africa? Two important arguments attracted newly independent countries. The first is that both China and Africa were victims of Western colonialism; therefore, they shared the same bitter history of Western imperialism. This argument of common colonial history is part of what has led African countries to vote in favor of China taking over the UN seat and expelling Taiwan. In a now unearthed tape released by the US archives, Ronald Reagan, then governor of California and staunch supporter of Taiwan, expressed his frustration and anger to then-president Nixon, calling African delegates cannibals: "To see those . . . monkeys from those African countries—damn them, they're still uncomfortable wearing shoes."[30] The second argument is the necessity of creating a unified non-aligned movement that would neither lean toward the West nor the East; however, in the 1990s, after China undertook reforms and experienced double-digit GDP growth, ideological motives made way for economic ones. Beijing used its economic might to woo Taiwan's most significant allies—Saudi Arabia, South Korea, and South Africa, leaving Taiwan with a group of small and impoverished states.[31]

Twenty-First-Century Relations—Finding Alternatives

The beginning of the twenty-first century coincided with a major political event in Taiwan: the 2000 presidential election when Chen Shui-bian of the Democratic Progressive Party (DPP) won the presidential election. This was the first time that power had been transferred from the ruling party to the opposition in Taiwan, and it had happened peacefully. It ended the half-century dominance of the Kuomintang in Taiwan. The new president sought to assert the country's position on the world stage and after taking office undertook state visits to diplomatic allies in Africa and Central America to strengthen relations.[32] Under Chen Shui-bian's administration, Taiwan was successfully admitted to the World Trade Organization as its 144th member in 2002. Chen undertook two important diplomatic visits to all African allies—in 2000 and again in 2003—to increase awareness of Taiwan in Africa in particular, and on the international stage in general.

However, this diplomatic endeavor to assert Taiwan's presence in Africa would not prevent its African allies from switching to China for economic and development reasons (see table 8.1). Liberia, the Gambia, and Burkina Faso—new democracies on the continent in the twenty-first century—switched to China within a few years of democratizing; Chad and Malawi switched to China within a year after elections following the declining performance of their incumbent leaders.[33] Senegal changed amid a growing economy when it received an invitation by China to attend the Forum on China-Africa Cooperation (FOCAC) summit of 2006 (while it was still recognizing Taiwan); after the switch, the country's China-bound exports grew quite substantially and the nation gained interest-free loans from China. São Tomé and Príncipe also moved to recognize China after its request for financial support was rejected; however, even before that, the tiny archipelago was more economically dependent on China than Taiwan.

China sees Africa as an important source of natural resources and a potential market for Chinese businesses. Its soft power and active foreign policy have also helped win over many countries on the continent. For example, China has joined peacekeeping missions throughout Africa, supported UN reforms that would grant an African country a permanent seat in the Security Council, in 2000 created a platform for meeting and discussions between African leaders and China—the FOCAC, and in 2007 created China-Africa Development fund.[34] Moreover, it is now a tradition that the first trip made each year by the PRC Minister of Foreign Affairs is to an African country.[35]

In 2006, the third FOCAC meeting in Beijing was attended by a record number of African leaders, even those from Taiwan-recognizing countries (invited as observers).[36] In response, Taipei the following year organized its first Taiwan-Africa summit in Taipei.[37] It was attended by five states that still

Table 8.1   African Countries Switching Recognition in the Twenty-First Century

Country	Switch from ROC Recognition to PRC Recognition
Liberia	2003
Senegal	2005
Chad	2006
Malawi	2008
The Gambia	2013
São Tomé and Príncipe	2016
Burkina Faso	2018

Source: Author created.

had official diplomatic relations with Taiwan and was regarded as an exercise in symbolic politics to rival the FOCAC. In the years since, China has managed to style itself as the leader of the Global South and the only African nation that still recognizes Taiwan in Eswatini. In 2018, when most African leaders gathered in Beijing for another round of FOCAC, King Mswati III was instead hosting his annual traditional reed dance, where he selected his fifteenth wife.[38]

With the second democratic transfer of power in Taiwan in 2008, when the Kuomintang won the elections, relations between China and Taiwan warmed, and a tacit diplomatic truce between the two was agreed upon. Under this, both Taiwan and China agreed to not pursue formal relations with those recognizing the other, thus preventing countries from essentially offering diplomatic recognition to the highest bidder.[39] For instance, in 2009, Panama attempted to ditch Taiwan and extend recognition to China, but this was met with China's refusal because it did not want to antagonize Taiwanese president Ma Ying-jeou, who was working on improving cross-strait relations.[40] The same case occurred after the Gambia severed ties with Taiwan and moved to recognize China. As expected, China did not recognize the Gambia in 2013 when it cut ties with Taiwan because of the diplomatic truce with the Ma administration. However, when the pro-independence DPP came to power, China immediately established relations with the Gambia.[41]

The twenty-first century has so far been characterized by Taiwan's dwindling presence in Africa, due to China's economic power and the impressive work it has done by lifting millions out of poverty, thus presenting an attractive model for the continent. Today, China has fifty-four allies out of fifty-five countries in Africa. Only one country still recognizes Taiwan—Eswatini, once known as Swaziland. Zhang Baohui, a professor of political science in Hong Kong, notes: "In the 1990s, they (Taiwan and China) still had a fair fight because China was not so rich. Now there is no longer any contest. China can offer a tremendous amount of economic incentives to woo countries."[42]

To resolve the issue of its dwindling presence on the international stage in general and Africa in particular, Taiwan had to settle for a different strategy—establishing unofficial bilateral links. According to the Global Diplomacy Index, in 2021 Taiwan had 110 postings around the world, both embassy level (with diplomatic allies) and representative offices (in states with which it does not have official diplomatic ties).[43] In Africa, besides the embassy in Eswatini, Taiwan has only three representative offices—in South Africa, Somaliland, and Nigeria (plus negotiations are underway with Egypt)—although it has enjoyed more diplomatic privileges and exemptions over the past few years.

Building multiple channels of contact has been the strategy adopted by Taiwan to expand its foreign relations. As argued by Keohane and Nye, international society is connected through various actors, including government officials, agencies stationed in foreign countries, the private elite, and transnational corporations.[44] Globalization of issues such as environmental damage and human rights abuses, as well as developments in online communication, has led to the growing importance of transnational actors, thus ending the monopoly of state actors on the world stage.[45] In this vein, Taiwan has several initiatives going on in Africa. TAITRA currently has five offices on the continent: Egypt, Kenya, South Africa, Nigeria, and Algeria. Furthermore, the Africa Taiwan Economic Forum—founded in 2003—is a platform jointly held by African embassies and trade offices in Taiwan and the MOFA, established to solve the issue of trade imbalances between Taiwan and Africa. It aims to inform potential Taiwanese investors in Africa and promote intercultural communication and tourism between Taiwan and African nations.[46]

According to Megan Liu from the TATPO under the Ministry of Economic Affairs, when Taiwan loses allies, this does not mean that it also loses business with them. Investors will usually face more pressure in countries with no political ties, and Taiwanese businesses that have already established a presence in a certain country are not significantly affected if that nation then withdraws official ties with the ROC, although new investors will face a lot of challenges.[47] Most Taiwanese business in Africa is conducted in Egypt, Nigeria, and South Africa, the three more important economies on the continent. Besides this, CPC Corporation—the Taiwanese state-owned petroleum, natural gas, and gasoline company—has (after thirty years of exploring) found oil reserves/crude in Chad, so business is also expected to pick up with this country.[48]

How important is Africa for Taiwan? Retrospectively, looking at the relation between Taiwan and African countries, one thing that is striking is the nature of this relationship. Economic relations between the two have always been insignificant, even for countries in which Taiwan had (and one still has) diplomatic ties. For instance, in Burkina Faso, economic relations with Taiwan amounted to 2.4 million USD in 1995, whereas this figure was 5 million USD with China. This gap continued to widen, and in 2011 economic relations with Taiwan were valued at 19 million USD, compared to 381 million USD with China.[49] Not one African country features in the list of the top 10 trading partners of Taiwan.[50] In contrast, China is Africa's biggest trading partner, with trade worth 200 billion USD per year.[51] In addition, more than ten thousand Chinese-owned firms are doing business on the continent.[52] The clear contrast between these two sets of figures explains why most countries in Africa moved toward China. Moreover, Africa was always of more symbolic value to Taiwan, as a potential support base for its foreign policy objectives—such as its bids to join the UN, the WTO, and other organizations.

For Taiwan, the only diplomatic connection left in Africa is that with Eswatini. In the introduction, we have briefly outlined the rationale for this connection, but the nature of this relationship will now be examined in the following chapter.

TAIWAN-ESWATINI RELATIONS IN FOCUS

As of 2021, Eswatini (formerly known as the Kingdom of Swaziland) is the only African country that maintains formal diplomatic relations with Taiwan, and it has never had relations with the PRC. This unlikely alliance has lasted half a century since Taiwan recognized Swaziland right after it gained independence from Britain in 1968. Taiwan set up an embassy in Mbabane the same year, while the Embassy of the Kingdom of Swaziland (later Eswatini) in Taiwan officially opened in Taipei in 2000.[53]

Eswatini's King Mswati III is Africa's last absolute monarch, and the so-called politics of the belly can be found in this small landlocked country, where the king rules by decree over his 1.3 million subjects, most of whom live in the countryside. Eswatini does not have relations with China, and Taipei has poured millions of investment and donation dollars into the country—funding schools, hospitals, businesses, rural electrification, and infrastructure projects, such as a new airport. According to the opposition in Eswatini, however, the king, the royal family, and the elites have used their ties with Taiwan to enrich themselves while most of the population remains impoverished. According to the World Bank, almost 40% of the population lives in extreme poverty.[54]

The king has been a regular visitor to Taiwan, making seventeen trips to date. All the state visits were "at the invitation" of Taiwan and thus subsidized by Taipei.[55] He last visited in 2018, along with several ministers.[56] While in Taiwan, the king accepted an honorary degree in management at the same university from which his son had graduated.[57] That year President Tsai Ing-wen also visited Eswatini and pledged to strengthen cooperation.[58] By the end of the year, the Economic Cooperation Agreement between Taiwan and Eswatini went into effect—setting the framework for future cooperation, while at the same time reducing the tariffs on 153 commodities.[59]

For the last ten years, Eswatini has only ranked as Taiwan's 149th largest trading partner, with a trade share well below 1%.[60] Taiwan today exports machinery and semifinished products to Eswatini, while it imports beef (2020 was the trial year for this), textiles, and fruit, mostly citruses. In 2018, trade between the two countries jumped 40% to reach over 10 million USD, with Taiwan's exports to Eswatini constituting most of this sum, and Taiwan's imports from Eswatini only a little more than 400,000 USD.

Eswatini is a developing country with a small agricultural economy (GDP per capita is 4,145 USD),[61] and the biggest industries there include forestry, labor-intensive textiles, sugar (and other agricultural) production, and cattle production (the beef is exported mostly to Europe). TAITRA conducts trade missions (now online due to COVID-19), research trips researching business opportunities (one such mission was conducted in 2019),[62] followed by awareness campaigns in Taiwan. These campaigns are aimed at investors and highlight the fact that Eswatini is an English-speaking country, much safer than other African countries, labor is cheap, and there is a big market nearby—South Africa, with which it has a free trade agreement (Eswatini is a member of both the Southern African Customs Union and the Common Market for Eastern and Southern Africa), meaning that there is a free flow of people and goods between these two countries.[63]

There are, however, several problems with the aforementioned commodities. The national cattle herd in Eswatini currently stands at around 600,000 heads, with a relatively limited average number of cattle slaughtered annually for the domestic and export markets,[64] so it is questionable if it could provide a higher volume of exports to Taiwan. Given the limited amount of grassland available, raising a sufficient number of cattle would require an increase in the efficiency of grass-fed beef production. The same goes for honey—although, of high quality, it is unsure if there is enough of it to export to Taiwan. As for the textile industry in Eswatini, it was encouraged by the African Growth and Opportunity Act, a trade act created by the United States in 2000 as a way to help the countries of sub-Saharan Africa increase their access to the US market. Under this act, textile products can be exported to the United States with no or a low tax, which has attracted quite a few investors. However, under the Obama presidency, due to work rights problems, textiles produced in Eswatini were excluded from this scheme and Taiwanese textile manufacturers now sell to South Africa, having established a supply chain with brands there (because South Africa has traditionally produced textile for other brands).

TAITRA alongside the aforementioned TATPO is trying to promote Africa in general and introduce Eswatini to Taiwanese businesspeople since it remains fairly unknown in Taiwan. Currently, there are only about 20–30 Taiwanese investors in Eswatini—not only in the textile business but also in the agricultural sector (e.g., producing cotton), with a total investment of 90 million USD (2019).[65] Most of them, however, are local Taiwanese from neighboring South Africa. Conversely, and to the best of the knowledge of both TAITRA and TATPO, there are no Eswatini investors in Taiwan.

However, TAITRA works with the Eswatini Embassy in Taiwan, and, for example, they invite them to various expos to promote their agricultural products. In 2019, they were invited to the Kaohsiung Food Show, Taipei Gift Show, and Taipei Food Show.[66]

In terms of academic exchange, Taiwan is very active in this area, and not only in Eswatini. In 2018, sixteen Eswatini students received a "Taiwan Scholarship" from the MOFA, another seven received the "International Advanced Human Resources Training Scholarship" from the ICDF, and nineteen received Yishou University's medical department post-bachelor special class scholarship for foreign students.[67] That year, there were more than 250 Eswatini students in Taiwan, who were all invited to a celebration dinner at EDA World in the south of Taiwan on the occasion of the king's visit.[68] Moreover, the ICDF organizes various short-term research and study seminars every year to provide opportunities in advanced studies for the government and citizens of Eswatini. There are several Taiwanese groups of volunteers from various universities and departments providing community services and medical help in Eswatini.

According to one (anonymous) MOFA official who visited Eswatini a few years ago to assess the progress of the agricultural and technical cooperation mission (see figures 8.1 and 8.2), Taiwan has dispatched several technical teams to Eswatini to implement several projects ranging from food security, through technical education and training, to e-governance and e-commerce. Taiwan has assisted with potato production, from seed development to packaging, this way making Eswatini less dependent on imports from South Africa. Taiwan has also assisted with seed breeding and fruit tree planting, for example, dragon fruit and guava, but also banana (including finding

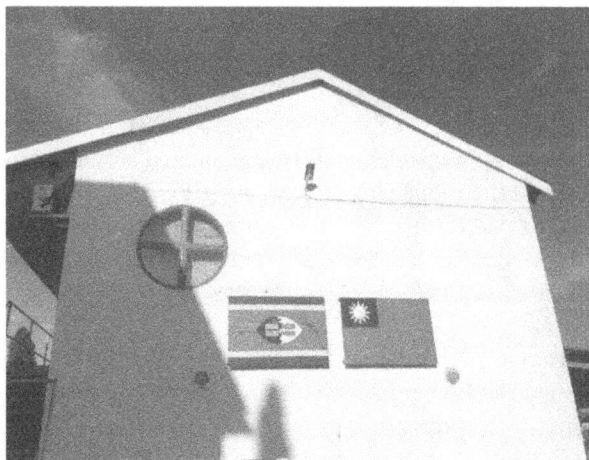

Figure 8.1   Taiwanese Technical Mission in Eswatini.

Figure 8.2   A Banana Farm in Eswatini Developed with Taiwanese Assistance.

distribution channels)—drawing on Taiwan's experience from the 1950s and 1960s, when it was one of the biggest banana exporters in the world. Many Eswatini students are enrolled in tropical agriculture studies at the National Pingtung University to prepare for work in the agricultural sector upon return home.

Taiwan has also been providing medical support to Eswatini, including pregnancy and infant health improvement planning, and sending doctors and nurses to work at the capital's government hospital (which has equipment funded by the EU) and provide training to the local staff to make the system sustainable.[69] During the pandemic, Taiwan donated surgical masks, bedside monitors, forehead thermometers, gloves, goggles, gowns, infrared scanners, pharmaceuticals, rapid testing kits, ventilators, and an ambulance, plus sent a Taiwan Can Help medical team (with four medical experts).[70]

Taiwan has created some 13,000 jobs in Eswatini,[71] with the textile company Tex-Ray (a global company with headquarters in Taiwan) being the biggest employer in the country. The chairman of the company was even awarded the Friend of Foreign Service Medal by the MOFA in 2016 to honor his contribution to the promotion of bilateral relations between Taiwan and Eswatini.[72] It is no exaggeration to say that this company is the centerpiece of the bilateral relationship between the two nations, and it is unclear what would happen if this manufacturer withdrew from Eswatini.

Taiwan's support for Eswatini has changed from mere agricultural cooperation to a more comprehensive form because Taiwan is well aware of the (symbolic) value of Eswatini as its last official diplomatic ally in Africa. While Chinese influence can also be felt in Eswatini, for now, Taiwan still dominates. Taiwan is well known in the country, and visiting Taiwanese officials are often jokingly referred to as "money wo/man,"[73] while Taiwan is the second most common destination for students after South Africa (interview with Eswatini student, December 2020). The diplomatic alliance depends very much on the king and his personal loyalty to Taiwan, most likely based on all the financial support his nation has received. Without him, many are skeptical about the future of this alliance.

CONCLUSION

Taiwan believes—whether under the Kuomintang or DPP—that a stable pool of allies is necessary to support the island's claim to (external) sovereignty. The island state has for decades been trading economic favors in exchange for diplomatic support. The growing influence of China as the world's second economy has led to Taiwan's dwindling influence on the world stage. At one time or another, Taiwan maintained formal relations with thirty African countries, but its economic diplomacy did not prevent its most significant allies from switching sides and granting recognition to the PRC. Today in Africa Taiwan has only one diplomatic ally and a few unofficial connections in the form of representative offices.

Taiwan did not always have such a limited presence in Africa as it does now. Its official relations with the continent began in 1949, shortly after the Nationalists were driven out of China by the Communists during the Chinese Civil War. It went through a period of competing with China for African allies in UN votes during the Cold War, through to a shift to more pragmatic diplomacy with both allies and non-allies, to finding alternatives for formal diplomatic relations in the twenty-first century.

Taiwan's competitive advantage vis-à-vis China in the past—a powerful economy that could use its economic might to woo poor African countries—waned in the twenty-first century, as China's economic power continued to grow. China's economic might has now given it tremendous power through its multibillion-dollar investments in trade and development. This has attracted scores of African countries to establish relations with China, leaving Taiwan with only Eswatini—a tiny country in southern Africa.

Although Taiwan has poured millions of dollars in investment and aid into Eswatini, much of this has simply supported the so-called politics of the belly—where elites take advantage of their positions to enrich themselves, blurring the lines between private and public business. As such, as long as King Mswati III is in power, it is unlikely that Taiwan will lose this alliance. However, once the king's rule ends, this is less certain.

NOTES

1. "Economy." *Government Portal of the Republic of China (Taiwan)*.

2. The ROC has given up the claim to represent the whole of China, and its sovereignty is limited to Taiwan and numerous small islands within its vicinity and off the coast of China (such as Kinmen, Matsu, and Penghu).

3. Herbert W. Vilakazi, Commissioner of the Independent Electoral Commission at the KZN Election Indaba, Durban, South Africa, September 17, 2002, http://www .ifp.org.za.

4. Mueni wa Muiu and Guy Martin, *A New Paradigm of the African State* (New York: Palgrave Macmillan, 2009), 191–210.

5. Mueni wa Muiu and Guy Martin, *A New Paradigm of the African State*, 191–210.

6. Jean-François Bayart, *The State in Africa: The Politics of the Belly*, 2nd ed. (London: Longman, 1993).

7. Jason Abbott, "Neo-Structuralism and African Political Economy," *Review of International Political Economy* 2, no. 2 (1995): 361.

8. J. Whitney, "Dambisa Moyo and Why Western Aid Is Killing Africa," *Huffpost*, May 25, 2011, https://www.huffpost.com/entry/dambisa-moyo-and-why -west_b_180964.

9. Key informants that have been interviewed: an official from MOFA who wants to remain anonymous; Eswatini students living in Taiwan who also wish to remain anonymous; an anonymous official from the West Asia and Africa Department at TAITRA; and Ms. Megan Liu, the deputy executive director of Taiwan-Africa Trade Promotion Office (TATPO) and Secretary-General at the Taiwan-Africa Business Association. Ms. Liu is identified and her interview is printed with permission.

10. Timothy S. Rich, "Status for Sale: Taiwan and the Competition for Diplomatic Recognition," *Issues & Studies* 45, no. 4 (2009): 159–188.

11. Richard J. Payne and Cassandra R Veney, "Taiwan and Africa: Taipei's Continuing Search for International Recognition," *Journal of Asian and African Studies* (n.d.): 14.

12. Timothy S. Rich and Vasabjit Banerjee, "Running Out of Time? The Evolution of Taiwan's Relations in Africa," *Journal of Current Chinese Affairs* 44, no. 1 (2015): 141–161.

13. Baikeng Tu 塗柏鏗, "Fúzhù ruòxiǎo hànwèi mínguó: Nóngyè yuán fēi gùshì扶助弱小捍衛民國：農業援非故事," *Duowei News*, 2019, https://duoweicn .dwnews.com/TW-2019%E5%B9%B4040%E6%9C%9F/10007604.html.

14. Minglai Wang王明來, "Táiwān nóngyè yuánwài de chéngxiào yǔ qiánjǐng台灣農業援外的成效與前景" *Council of Agriculture Executive Yuan*, 2005, https://www.coa.gov.tw/ws.php?id=10331.

15. IDCF. 對外技術援助的興起 (Genesis of Technical Assistance), https://www.icdf.org.tw/web_pub/20060512154443Chap%201%20Overview.pdf.

16. Czeslaw Tubilewicz, *Taiwan and Post-Communist Europe: Shopping for Allies*, 1st ed. (London: Routledge, 2007).

17. Wei-chen Lee and I-min Chang, "US aid and Taiwan," *Asian Review of World Histories* 2, no. 1 (2014): 47–80.

18. Samuel S. Kim, "The People's Republic of China in the United Nations: A Preliminary Analysis," *World Politics* 26, no. 3 (2011).

19. Ian Taylor, "Taiwan's Foreign Policy and Africa: The Limitations of Dollar Diplomacy," *Journal of Contemporary China* 11, no. 30 (2002): 125–140.

20. Rich and Banerjee, "Running Out of Time?"

21. Tubilewicz, *Taiwan and Post-Communist Europe*.

22. Tubilewicz, *Taiwan and Post-Communist Europe*.

23. "History of the Taiwan ICDF," Taiwan International Cooperation and Development Fund, December 6, 2010, https://www.icdf.org.tw/ct.asp?xItem=4582&ctNode=29843&mp=2.

24. Dan Large and Shiuh-Shen Chien, "China Rising in Africa: Whither Taiwan?" (n.d.), 18.

25. Martyn J. Davis, "South Africa and Taiwan: Managing the Post-diplomatic Relationship," *Witwatersrand: East Asia Project (EAP)*, International Relations Department and University of the Witwatersrand, 1998.

26. San-Shiun Tseng, "The Republic of China's foreign policy towards Africa: The case of ROC-RSA relations" (diss., University of the Witwatersrand, 2008).

27. Shannon Tiezzi, "Taiwan Loses Another Ally as Panama Embraces China," *The Diplomat*, June 13, 2017, https://thediplomat.com/2017/06/taiwan-loses-another-ally-as-panama-embraces-china/.

28. Large and Chien, "China Rising in Africa: Whither Taiwan?" 18.

29. Rich and Banerjee, "Running Out of Time?"

30. "Ronald Reagan Called Africans at UN 'monkeys', Tapes Reveal" *BBC*, July 31, 2019, https://www.bbc.com/news/world-us-canada-49177034.

31. Tubilewicz, *Taiwan and Post-Communist Europe*.

32. Tseng, "The Republic of China's foreign policy towards Africa."

33. Bhaso Ndzendze, "Domestic Audiences and Economic Opportunity Cost: African Democratisation as a Determinant in the Recognition of China over Taiwan, 2001–2018," *Journal of Asian and African Studies* (June 12, 2020): 002190962092653, doi: 10.1177/0021909620926531.

34. Michal Meidan, "China's Africa Policy: Business Now, Politics Later," *Asian Perspective* 30, no. 4, (n.d.): 69–93.

35. Rich and Banerjee, "Running Out of Time?"

36. Large and Chien, "China Rising in Africa: Whither Taiwan?" 18.

37. First Taiwan-Africa Heads of State Summit (September 9, 2007) and Taiwan-Africa Progressive Partnership Forum (September 10, 2007).

38. Larry Madowo, "eSwatini – Taiwan's last friend in Africa," *BBC*, January 14, 2019, https://www.bbc.com/news/world-africa-46831852.

39. Rich and Banerjee, "Running Out of Time?"

40. Tiezzi, "Taiwan Loses Another Ally as Panama Embraces China."

41. Pap Saine and Michael Gold, "Gambia to Cut Ties with Taiwan, China Says Unaware," *Reuters*, Nov. 15, 2013, https://www.reuters.com/article/us-africa-china-taiwan-idUSBRE9AE04Z20131115.

42. Chris Horton and Steven Lee Myers, "Panama Establishes Ties with China, Further Isolating Taiwan," *The New York Times*, June 13, 2017, https://www.nytimes.com/2017/06/13/world/asia/taiwan-panama-china-diplomatic-recognition.html.

43. "2019 Country Ranking," Lowy Institute Global Diplomacy Index, https://globaldiplomacyindex.lowyinstitute.org/country_rank.html.

44. Robert O. Keohane and Joseph S. Nye, "Power and Interdependence," *Survival* 15, no. 4 (July 1973): 158–65. doi: 10.1080/00396337308441409.

45. Strobe Talbott, "Globalization and Diplomacy: A Practitioner's Perspective," *Foreign Policy*, Winter 1997.

46. For more information about ETEF, please see http://www.africa.org.tw/introduction_english.asp.

47. Megan Liu, deputy executive director of TATPO, interview by Kristina Kironska, Taipei, November 2020.

48. Anonymous official from the West Asia and Africa Department, interview by Kristina Kironska, TAITRA, November 2020.

49. Guive Khan Mohammad, "The Chinese Presence in Burkina Faso: A Sino-African Cooperation from Below," *Journal of Current Chinese Affairs* 43, no. 1 (2014): 71–101.

50. The top ten trading partners of Taiwan are as follows: (1) China: 91.9 billion USD (27.9% of Taiwan's total exports); (2) the United States: $46.3 billion (14.1%); (3) Hong Kong: $40.4 billion (12.3%); (4) Japan: $23.3 billion (7.1%); (5) Singapore: $18.2 billion (5.5%); (6) South Korea: $16.9 billion (5.1%); (7) Vietnam: $10.8 billion (3.3%); (8) Malaysia: $9.4 billion (2.9%); (9) Germany: $6.5 billion (2%); (10) Philippines: $6.2 billion (1.9%). (See Daniel Workman. "Taiwan's Top Trading Partners," World's Top Exports. http://www.worldstopexports.com/taiwans-top-import-partners/.Accessed June 2020.)

51. Wade Shepard, "What China Is Really up to in Africa," *Forbes*, October 3, 2019, https://www.forbes.com/sites/wadeshepard/2019/10/03/what-china-is-really-up-to-in-africa/?sh=874b76593046.

52. Kartik Jayaram, Omid Kassiri, and Irene Yuan Sun, "Field interviews with more than 1,000 Chinese companies provide new insights into Africa–China business relationships," *McKinsey*, June 28, 2017, https://www.mckinsey.com/featured-insights/middle-east-and-africa/the-closest-look-yet-at-chinese-economic-engagement-in-africa.

53. Zhonghua minguo waijiao bu 中華民國外交部. *Zhonghua minguo 107 nian waijiao nianjian* 中華民國 *107* 年外交年鑑. Xinbeishi 新北市, 2018.

54. "Eswatini Overview," The World Bank Group, https://www.worldbank.org/en/country/eswatini/overview.

55. Taylor, "Taiwan's Foreign Policy and Africa: The limitations of dollar diplomacy."

56. Zhonghua minguo waijiao bu 中華民國外交部. *Zhonghua minguo 107 nian waijiao nianjian* 中華民國 *107* 年外交年鑑.

57. Madowo, "eSwatini – Taiwan's last friend in Africa."

58. Pei-ju Teng, "President Tsai to Taiwanese enterprises looking to expand globally, 'consider Africa,'" *Taiwan News*, March 18, 2018, https://www.taiwannews.com.tw/en/news/3408136.

59. Qiaoyan Lin, 林巧雁, "Fēizhōu jīngjì qǐfēi jīng zhǎng bào yìměi nǐ fù shǐ wǎ dì ní tóuzī 非洲經濟起飛經長爆義美擬赴史瓦帝尼投資," *Apple Daily*, May 22, 2019, https://tw.appledaily.com/property/20190522/I63ZD3BTSACNJCTPZNQZCTCOLY/.

60. "Value of Exports & Imports by Country" Bureau of Trade – Trade Statistics, https://cuswebo.trade.gov.tw/FSCE040F/FSCE040F.

61. "World Economic Outlook Databases," International Monetary Fund, https://www.imf.org/en/Publications/SPROLLs/world-economic-outlook-databases#sort=%40imfdate%20descending.

62. Usually, a trade mission includes a package of four African countries, in 2019 it was Ethiopia, Kenya, South Africa, and Eswatini—a so-called all-purpose trip for potential investors to get to know these countries and markets.

63. Anonymous Informant, interview.

64. "Beef value chain analysis in eSwatini," *Value Chain Analysis for Development – European Commission*, March 2019.

65. Liu, interview. And Anonymous Informant, "Fēizhōu jīngjì qǐfēi非洲經濟起飛."

66. Liu, interview.

67. Zhonghua minguo waijiao bu 中華民國外交部. *Zhonghua minguo 107 nian waijiao nianjian* 中華民國 *107* 年外交年鑑.

68. Anonymous, Eswatini student, interview by Kristina Kironska, Taipei, December 2020.

69. Anonymous, MOFA official, interview by Kristina Kironska, December 2020.

70. Taiwan Can Help promotional booklet found on the Taiwan Embassy in Eswatini FB page.

71. Lin, "Fēizhōu jīngjì qǐfēi非洲經濟起飛."

72. "The Friend of Foreign Service Medal," Tex-Ray Industrial Co., Ltd., https://www.texray.com/the-friend-of-foreign-service-medal/.

73. Anonymous, MOFA official, interview.

BIBLIOGRAPHY

"2019 Country Ranking." Lowy Institute Global Diplomacy Index. https://globaldiplomacyindex.lowyinstitute.org/country_rank.html.

Abbott, Jason. "Neo-Structuralism and African Political Economy." *Review of International Political Economy* 2, no. 2 (1995): 361.

Bayart, Jean-François. *The State in Africa: The Politics of the Belly* (2nd ed.). London: Longman, 1993.

"Beef Value Chain Analysis in eSwatini." *Value Chain Analysis for Development – European Commission*, March 2019.

Davis, Martyn J. "South Africa and Taiwan: Managing the Post-Diplomatic Relationship." *Witwatersrand: East Asia Project (EAP)*, International Relations Department and University of the Witwatersrand, 1998.

"Economy." *Government Portal of the Republic of China (Taiwan)*.

"Eswatini Overview." The World Bank Group. https://www.worldbank.org/en/country/eswatini/overview.

"History of the Taiwan ICDF." Taiwan International Cooperation and Development Fund, December 6, 2010. https://www.icdf.org.tw/ct.asp?xItem=4582&ctNode=29843&mp=2.

Horton, Chris, and Steven Lee Myers. "Panama Establishes Ties With China, Further Isolating Taiwan." *The New York Times*, June 13, 2017. https://www.nytimes.com/2017/06/13/world/asia/taiwan-panama-china-diplomatic-recognition.html.

IDCF. 對外技術援助的興起 (Genesis of Technical Assistance). https://www.icdf.org.tw/web_pub/20060512154443Chap%201%20Overview.pdf.

Jayaram, Kartik Omid Kassiri, and Irene Yuan Sun. "Field Interviews with More Than 1,000 Chinese Companies Provide New Insights into Africa–China Business Relationships." *McKinsey*, June 28, 2017. https://www.mckinsey.com/featured-insights/middle-east-and-africa/the-closest-look-yet-at-chinese-economic-engagement-in-africa.

Keohane, Robert O., and Joseph S. Nye. "Power and Interdependence." *Survival* 15, no. 4 (July 1973): 158–165. https://doi.org/10.1080/00396337308441409.

Kim, Samuel S. "The People's Republic of China in the United Nations: A Preliminary Analysis." *World Politics* 26, no. 3 (2011): 299–330.

Large, Dan, and Shiuh-Shen Chien. "China Rising in Africa: Whither Taiwan?" (n.d.), p. 18.

Lee, Wei-chen, and I-min Chang. "US Aid and Taiwan." *Asian Review of World Histories* 2, no. 1 (2014): 47–80.

Lin, Qiaoyan林巧雁. "Fēizhōu jīngjì qǐfēi jīng zhǎng bào yìměi nǐ fù shǐ wǎ dì ní tóuzī 非洲經濟起飛經長爆義美擬赴史瓦帝尼投資." *Apple Daily*, May 22, 2019. https://tw.appledaily.com/property/20190522/I63ZD3BTSACNJCTPZNQZCTCOLY/.

Madowo, Larry. "eSwatini – Taiwan's Last Friend in Africa." *BBC*, January 14, 2019. https://www.bbc.com/news/world-africa-46831852.

Meidan, Michal. "China's Africa Policy: Business Now, Politics Later." *Asian Perspective* 30, no. 4 (n.d.): 69–93.

Mohammad, Guive Khan. "The Chinese Presence in Burkina Faso: A Sino-African Cooperation from Below." *Journal of Current Chinese Affairs* 43, no. 1 (2014): 71–101.

Ndzendze, Bhaso. "Domestic Audiences and Economic Opportunity Cost: African Democratisation as a Determinant in the Recognition of China over

Taiwan, 2001–2018." *Journal of Asian and African Studies* (June 12, 2020): 002190962092653. https://doi.org/10.1177/0021909620926531.

Nye, Joseph S., and Robert O. Keohane. *Transnational Relations and World Politics.* Cambridge, MA: Harvard University Press, 1971.

Payne, Richard J., and Cassandra R. Veney. "Taiwan and Africa: Taipei's Continuing Search for International Recognition." *Journal of Asian and African Studies* (n.d): 14.

Rich, Timothy S. "Status for Sale: Taiwan and the Competition for Diplomatic Recognition." *Issues & Studies* 45, no. 4 (2009): 159–188.

Rich, Timothy S., and Vasabjit Banerjee. "Running Out of Time? The Evolution of Taiwan's Relations in Africa." *Journal of Current Chinese Affairs* 44, no. 1 (2015): 141–161.

"Ronald Reagan Called Africans at UN 'Monkeys', Tapes Reveal." *BBC*, July 31, 2019. https://www.bbc.com/news/world-us-canada-49177034.

Rosenau, James N. *Turbulence in World Politics: A Theory of Change and Continuity.* Princeton, NJ: Princeton University Press, 1990.

Saine, Pap, and Michael Gold. "Gambia to Cut Ties with Taiwan, China Says Unaware." *Reuters*, November 15, 2013. https://www.reuters.com/article/us-africa -china-taiwan-idUSBRE9AE04Z20131115.

Shepard, Wade. "What China Is Really up to in Africa." *Forbes*, October 3, 2019. https://www.forbes.com/sites/wadeshepard/2019/10/03/what-china-is-really-up-to -in-africa/?sh=874b76593046.

Talbott, Strobe. "Globalization and Diplomacy: A Practitioner's Perspective." *Foreign Policy*, Winter 1997.

Taylor, Ian. "Taiwan's Foreign Policy and Africa: The Limitations of Dollar Diplomacy." *Journal of Contemporary China* 11, no. 30 (2002): 125–140.

Teng, Pei-ju. "President Tsai to Taiwanese Enterprises Looking to Expand Globally, 'Consider Africa.'" *Taiwan News*, March 18, 2018. https://www.taiwannews.com .tw/en/news/3408136.

"The Friend of Foreign Service Medal." Tex-Ray Industrial Co., Ltd. https://www .texray.com/the-friend-of-foreign-service-medal/.

Tiezzi, Shannon. "Taiwan Loses Another Ally as Panama Embraces China." *The Diplomat*, June 13, 2017. https://thediplomat.com/2017/06/taiwan-loses-another -ally-as-panama-embraces-china/.

Tseng, San-Shiun. "The Republic of China's Foreign Policy towards Africa: The Case of ROC-RSA Relations." Dissertation, University of the Witwatersrand, 2008.

Tu, Baikeng塗柏鏗. "Fúzhù ruòxiǎo hànwèi mínguó: Nóngyè yuán fēi gùshì扶助弱小捍衛民國：農業援非故事." *Duowei News*, 2019. https://duoweicn .dwnews.com/TW-2019%E5%B9%B4040%E6%9C%9F/10007604.html.

Tubilewicz, Czeslaw. *Taiwan and Post-Communist Europe: Shopping for Allies* (1st ed.). London: Routledge, 2007. https://doi.org/10.4324/9780203946978.

"Value of Exports & Imports by Country." Bureau of Trade – Trade Statistics. https:// cuswebo.trade.gov.tw/FSCE040F/FSCE040F.

Vilakazi, Herbert W. "Commissioner of the Independent Electoral Commission at the KZN Election Indaba, Durban, South Africa, September 17, 2002." http://www.ifp .org.za.

Wa Muiu, M., and G. Martin. *A New Paradigm of the African State*, pp. 191–210. New York: Palgrave Macmillan, 2009.

Wang, Minglai王明來. "Táiwān nóngyè yuánwài de chéngxiào yǔ qiánjǐng台灣農業援外的成效與前景" *Council of Agriculture Executive Yuan*, 2005. https://www.coa.gov.tw/ws.php?id=10331.

Whitney, J. "Dambisa Moyo and Why Western Aid Is Killing Africa." *Huffpost*, May 25, 2011. https://www.huffpost.com/entry/dambisa-moyo-and-why-west_b _180964.

"World Economic Outlook Databases." International Monetary Fund. https://www .imf.org/en/Publications/SPROLLs/world-economic-outlook-databases#sort= %40imfdate%20descending.

Zhonghua minguo waijiao bu 中華民國外交部. *Zhonghua minguo 107 nian waijiao nianjian* 中華民國 *107* 年外交年鑑. Xinbeishi 新北市, 2018.

Chapter 9

The Future of Taiwan

A Brief Commentary

Sabella Ogbobode Abidde

INTRODUCTION

In early October 2021, sections of the US media reported President Xi Jinping of China as saying that

> Taiwan independence separatism is the biggest obstacle to achieving the reunification of the motherland, and the most serious hidden danger to national rejuvenation. No one should underestimate the Chinese people's staunch determination, firm will, and strong ability to defend national sovereignty and territorial integrity. The historical task of the complete reunification of the motherland must be fulfilled and will definitely be fulfilled.[1]

This statement was especially perilous and ominous considering China's incessant military incursions into Taiwan's waterways and airspace. The statement, although not the first of its kind in the last couple of years, seems to have jolted Taipei, the White House, and other Western capitals. Shortly thereafter, the US president, Joseph Biden, responded thus:

> I've spoken with Xi about Taiwan. We agree . . . we'll abide by the Taiwan agreement. We made it clear that I don't think he should be doing anything other than abiding by the agreement.[2]

President Biden, according to the media, appeared to be referring to Washington's long-standing "One-China Policy" under which it officially recognizes Beijing rather than Taipei, and the Taiwan Relations Act, which makes clear that the "US decision to establish diplomatic ties with Beijing instead of Taiwan rests upon the expectation that the future of Taiwan will be determined by peaceful means."[3] In this instance, China seems to believe only its can determine what "peaceful means" means and how the China-Taiwan political disagreements would be resolved. And so far—especially since the coming into office of President Tsai Ing-wen on May 20, 2016—China has unceasingly and steadily exerted all manner of pressure on the people and government of Taiwan. President Jinping statement, along with his government's actions, forced President Ing-wen to assert that

> there should be absolutely no illusions that the Taiwanese people will bow to pressure. We will continue to bolster our national defense and demonstrate our determination to defend ourselves in order to ensure that nobody can force Taiwan to take the path China has laid out for us.[4]

How to resolve this seven-decades-old suspicion and hostility between the People's Republic of China (PRC, mainland China), and the Republic of China (Taiwan) is one of the most difficult, compelling, and dangerous questions facing the international community. What will China do now or in the nearest future? And how will Taiwan react? Essentially, what is likely to happen to Taiwan within a decade or less? This chapter, then, is a brief commentary on the future of Taiwan—a country many believe would be invaded soon.[5] The United Nations (UN), along with other powerful and influential countries and governments, is doing a disservice to mankind by ignoring the China-Taiwan question. But really: What would China lose if Taiwan were to become a sovereign nation-state—recognized, accepted, and allowed into the UN system?

TAIWAN AND CHINA: AN OVERVIEW

Not long after the Kuomintang fled to Taiwan after its defeat in 1949, the party and the government developed diplomatic relations with South Africa which, at that time, was staunchly anticommunist and opposed China's admission to the UN. But as African countries gained independence from colonial Europe beginning in the late 1950s, the *balance of recognition* began to change. Beijing and Taipei lobbied for African votes at the UN in 1971. Beijing's strategic support for national liberation movements and radical regimes on the continent tilted the balance of recognition in favor of China. Also, the current Sino-Africa relations which began in the 1950s when Zhou Enlai, the first premier of the PRC, visited Africa and signed bilateral agreements with several African states elevated Beijing's status in the continent. Several decades later, only one African country has a full diplomatic relationship with Taiwan. And that's Eswatini (Swaziland). The other, Somaliland, is itself an unrecognized territory. What's Taiwan to do?

What does the future hold? The pragmatic answer is simple: "No one knows." Indeed, no one knows what the future holds for Taiwan—a country many consider one of the greatest countries in the twentieth and twenty-first centuries. The unknown or unknowable aside, one of five scenarios is likely to happen: (1) the invasion and forceful takeover of the island nation; (2) succumbing to threats and the political reality of the region, the people and government of Taiwan agree to be a part of China; (3) the continuation of the status quo; in other words, Taiwan remains a contested state just as it has been since 1949; (4) the UN member states—led by the United States or other Western nations—agree to grant Taiwan statehood and international recognition; or (5) the unilateral declaration of independence (UDI) by the government of Taiwan. The first and last options are fraught with the gravest danger. The second option would have been possible decades ago, but with a changing demographic and a changing political, social, and economic culture, surrender is out of the question, while international recognition at the UN is not a possibility primarily because of the structure of the UN which gives China a veto power.

Can Taiwan defy China and declare independence? Can the international community defy China and grant Taiwan statehood? Both are possible but come with a hefty price. In the end, only the government and people of Taiwan can decide for themselves what they want, when they want it, and how to get what they want. After all, China is not about to give up Taiwan. What's more, military and political partners do not always show up in times of crisis; and the status quo—ambiguous, restricted, contested, paralyzing, and in the shadows of China—is not sustainable beyond another decade or so. Around the world, many countries have gained independence through armed struggle, negotiation, or a combination of both. This is a historical fact: Colonizers and colonial states don't always willingly give up their prized possession. And China, in the twentieth and twenty-first century, does not have a history of willingly giving up peopled-geographic possessions.

Taiwan is a political darling of the United States and many Western countries. But one can hardly come up with a condition or scenario under which it will engage in outright war with China in defense of Taiwan. The invasion and annexation of Taiwan would be costly, very costly economically and politically. But in the end, much of the world will simply look the other way. Since 1945 or thereabout, the United States has gotten its way—mostly unchallenged. That's where China is today. Or at least that's where it is heading. Only one and one country alone can put a stop to China's march: and that's Taiwan. With external help of course. A Taiwan with nuclear armaments would have been in better shape. After all, one of the reasons why the State of Israel is still standing and thriving today is because of its nuclear capability.

TAIWAN IN US INTERMESTIC POLICY

Much the same way that the United States is Israel's most dependable ally and supporter, the United States is Taiwan's strongest ally and supporter. However, while it had in the past and is ready to continue to defend Israel's territorial integrity and well-being, it has not made such commitment, overtly or covertly, to defend Taiwan's territorial integrity and well-being. The relationship the United States had with Taipei is fundamentally different from what it has with Tel Aviv. And there are many reasons for this (many of which are beyond the scope of this brief chapter). Nevertheless, one of the most important and telling reasons is the size of the enemy involved. Besides, the internal composition and dynamics of Israel and Taiwan are vastly different. And of course, there is the issue of religion. Millions of Christians in the United States have a direct and indirect affinity with Israel. This is not the case with Taiwan. However, some of the ways the United States has helped Taiwan is in terms of moral and institutional support and by helping it shore up its defense capability. The last three decades, for instance, have witnessed US cabinet-level visits to Taiwan, that is

- Carla Hills, US Trade representative under GHW Bush administration, December 1992
- Federico Pena, secretary of Transportation under Bill Clinton, December 1994
- Phil Lader, administrator, Small Business Administration under Bill Clinton, December 1996
- Bill Richardson, secretary of Energy under Bill Clinton, November 1998
- Rodney E. Slater, secretary of Transportation under Bill Clinton, June 2000
- Gina McCarthy, administrator, Environmental Protection Agency under Barack Obama, April 2014
- Alex Azar, secretary of Health and Human Services, under Donald Trump, August 2020[6]

Beginning with President Jimmy Carter (1977–1981), every US government—Republicans and Democrats—has seen it fit to sell arms to Taiwan to booster its defense. Table 9.1 presents a sample of some of the arms sales to Taiwan. In addition, US domestic and foreign policy has firmly been in support of the Taiwanese government, this in addition to US public opinion. But unfortunately, there is no defense pact between both countries. This gap in US foreign and defense policy leaves Taiwan vulnerable to China's attacks and invasion.

Table 9.1   Sample US Arms Sale to Taiwan, 1979–2021

Date	Arms	Value in Million
1979	Northrop F-5	$240
1980	8-in. (203 mm) M110 self-propelled howitzer	$3.7
1984	Lockheed C-130 Hercules	$325
1992	RIM-66 Standard	$126
1992	General Dynamics F-16 Fighting Falcon	$6,000
2000	The Raytheon MIM-23 HAWK	$106
2000	Advanced Medium-Range Air-to-Air Missile	$150
2015	FGM-148 Javelin	$57
2015	Joint Tactical Information Distribution System	$120
2018	Spare parts for F-16, C-130H, F-5E/F	$330
2019	General Dynamics F-16 Fighting Falcon	$8,000
2020	Mark 48 and its improved advanced capability	$180
2021	M109 howitzer and related equipment	$750

Source: Created by author from various sources including the Department of Defense, State Department, and the Congressional Research Service.

WHAT AWAITS TAIWAN?

The Status Quo

One would be hard-pressed to find an observer of Chinese or cross-strait politics who believes that China would let Taiwan be or allow it to maintain its status for an indefinite period. Year after year and decade after decade Taiwan has been growing stronger politically and economically and more countries around the world seem to be open to the idea of an independent Taiwan—even if those countries have not openly said so and or act on it. Once a major European, North American, Asian, or African country speaks in favor of or confer recognition, many others are likely to follow. China seems to know this. This perhaps accounts for why Beijing has been very aggressive with penalties and or verbal warnings when a current or former political leader visits Taiwan or offers compliments. China, therefore, would not allow the status quo to continue. Taiwan, on the other hand, is not likely to allow it undermined status to continue for several more decades. Its status must be a psychological barrier to its continuing growth, development, and participation in the international system.

Also, no serious observer of Chinese or cross-strait politics believes Taiwan will not run out of patient insofar as the status quo is concerned. There are three factors to consider here: First, with a demography that is ever younger, more open, savvier, more globalized, and less patient than their parents and grandparents, they are more likely to rock the boat. Second, in another decade or two, the Taiwanese with a memory of China and Chinese would have decreased to an intangible number. Today, millions of

Taiwanese do not see themselves as Chinese and many more do not have a favorable assessment of China. For them—unlike their parents, grandparents, and great-grandparents—they are Taiwanese and not Chinese. Also, seven decades of living under China's shadow is long enough. Therefore, foreseen and unforeseen conditions may trigger a sizeable majority to rebel and in the process call China's bluff. Calling China's bluff, as Beijing has demonstrated over the years, can be dangerous.

Military Invasion

For several decades, systemic studies and conventional wisdom have pointed to a military invasion of Taiwan as the likely course of action by China. It is indeed the anticipated course of action which, many scholars and observers have predicted, may happen within a decade (before 2030). Others expect it sooner than that. China may be an emerging global hegemon with the largest population, the second-largest economy, and with the world's largest military. Still, an invasion of Taiwan is likely to be costly. In the first place, it is not as if Taiwan is a sitting duck or that it is unprepared. Or that it will simply lay there and allow China to run all over it. This is a country with a healthy military expenditure and acquisitions and with a reasonably well-trained military and defense force. Within and outside of the region, Taiwan has friends and partners, and allies—including but not limited to Japan, South Korea, Australia, and the United States—who are likely to indirectly aid Taiwan in defending itself against military assaults by China.

And because military victory is not predicated on size, stealth, and modernity, there is no guarantee that China will be outright victorious against Taiwan. There are many lessons to be learned from many of the wars the United States—with its allies—has engaged in in the last six or so decades, that is, Vietnam, Iran, and Afghanistan. Also, China as an occupying force may be confronted by guerrilla tactics or justifiable terrorism, or Taiwan may simply paralyze key military and civilian installations and centers in China which may effectively paralyze or render China ineffective. Or at least cause it to wobble painfully. Furthermore, China's economy and by extension, the global economy, would also be negatively impacted by such a war. Also, as John G. Stoessinger, in *Why Nations Go to War*, recounted, "The emperors and generals who sent their men to war in August 1914 thought in terms of weeks, not months, let alone years."[7] President Xi Jinping and the Chinese Communist Party may yet find Taiwan to be a hot potato they cannot hold on to. One of the beauties and ironies of wars is that you cannot predict the outcome.

The human, economic, and infrastructural cost of such a war may be unbearable for Taiwan, but the images on social media and outlets would be damaging to China's image which, in many parts of the world, is already suspect. Today and in the last couple of decades, China is seen as a bully in many parts of the world. To be seen bullying and dehumanizing and annexing a small island nation like Taiwan would not only cause a global uproar, but China may also not recover from it for a very long time. One of the unintended consequences of China's actions would be the opening of new fissures and the expanding and deepening of old ones within the Chinese society in mainland China. And whatever favor they may enjoy within Taiwan—among those who favor unification—would most likely disappear because of the carnage, suffering, and humiliation that are likely to follow. A second unintended consequence is that unless Taiwan and its pro-independence leaders are completely overwhelmed, they may come out of the war with more support and sympathy as many nations around the world are likely to call for outright independence for Taiwan.

Taipei Capitulates

Taiwan's capitulation may come in one of two ways. In the event of an imminent military attack, Taipei may simply capitulate or agree to Beijing's demand. At this point, it may win some concessions in addition to averting the attack. Under this scenario, the outcome may be "One China, Two Systems." In the long run, however, Taiwan may likely suffer the same fate as Hong Kong but perhaps not as severe. But if the invasion had started before Taiwan capitulates, it may not stand a good chance of winning concessions from Beijing in which case the eventual situation becomes direr than what we currently have in Hong Kong. Under this scenario, Beijing may no longer agree to the "One China, Two Systems" policy but rather, a comprehensive absorption of Taipei which would then result in something like the following:

- The detention—short or long term—of Taiwan's top military hierarchy will then be reoriented in Beijing's detention camps or military academies. Or they may simply disappear into the vastness that China is.
- The detention—short or long term—of Taiwan's top political leaders who will then be reschooled in Beijing's political academies. Or they too may simply disappear into the immensity that China is.
- The replacement of the heads of all private and public institutions in Taiwan with CCP members brought in from China.
- The entire population of Taiwan may be subjected to whatever some citizens of China are being subjected to.
- And for a while, there may be a total blackout of the formal and informal media until such a time when Beijing feels it is in control.

• A group of foreigners may be expelled and asked to reapply for reentry or expelled and forbidden to return to China's Taiwan.

After the capitulation and annexation of Taiwan, the new China is likely to be vastly different because the internal dynamics of the country would have changed leading to political and extralegal unrests, anarchy, violence, and terrorist activities. The *New Chinese*—mostly those between sixteen and fifty, who were accustomed to freedom, liberty, freethinking, and whatever else their previous country offered them—would find it extremely difficult to adjust to a life of political control, social limitations, and authoritarianism. This, in my learned view, would be the beginning of the disintegration of China. Frankly, it would get to the point where China will find it difficult to mold and control its citizens.

International Recognition

At this point in history, it is difficult to predict what might trigger, en masse, the international community to offer Taiwan international recognition at the UN, regionally, or at the state level. There are a few countries that offer Taiwan full diplomatic recognition and relationship. But that number is not enough. Should the numbers increase three or fourfold, perhaps, that would compel the UN to take up the China-Taiwan question. However, such a move on the part of ten, forty, or fifty new countries around the world would be the trigger Beijing needs to invade right away. On the other hand, an invasion would be out of the question if five or more major countries—along with those placed strategically in Asia and the Pacific Rim—publicly states they would come to Taiwan's aid militarily if attacked. Or those countries could preemptively offer Taiwan a defense pact that says something like "an attack on Taiwan is an attack on us all . . . we reserve the right to defend ourselves and our allies."

For more than fifty years, the United States, it is believed, scuttled Palestinian independence, the Palestinian statehood. And the fear of the United States is what has prevented many countries from defying and or openly supporting and or recognizing Palestine as a state. The day the United States comes around to it, the *Two-State Solution* in the Middle East will become a reality. Likewise, the fear of China—not in terms of its military might but of its reputation and economic might—is what seems to be preventing much of the world from conferring recognition and legitimacy on Taiwan. Militarily, the United States and a handful of its allies could flatten China. We know that. We also know that should the United States and a handful of its allies sternly, honestly, and openly tell Beijing to stay away from Taiwan, Beijing will comply. But at this point, much of the world—especially the West—does not know what to make of China. And no government in the Global South has the morals, the temerity, or the wherewithal to challenge Beijing. Most are beholden to China in more ways than one—especially in terms of loans, investments, and the development of their infrastructure.[8]

Unilateral Declaration of Independence?

A UDI can be tricky. Between 1776 and 1922, a total of nine countries unilaterally declared their independence. Of these, only the Philippines, in 1898, failed to achieve its aim having been denied its independence by Spain. But between 1945 and 2017, twenty-three countries unilaterally declared their independence with only four successes. In this instance, a unilateral declaration by Taiwan is likely to evoke China's anger which in turn would likely result in a quick and brutal military invasion. In addition, two other factors make this route less likely. In the first place, an untold number of Taiwanese—even if a small minority—seems to have an affinity for the *old country* and as such does not and would not support a UDI. This lack of unity of purpose and aspiration is a big challenge in Taiwan. Second, the United States and other allies and supporting countries would have over the years, directly and or indirectly, told Taipei they would not support a UDI even though a 2010 advisory opinion by the International Court of Justice asserts that UDI is legal and acceptable in international law.[9]

TRICKY PROBLEM—ABSURD SITUATION

None of the paths outlined earlier is without danger. Perhaps it is for this reason that Taiwan has been mindful of its actions and pronouncements—doing its best not to provoke China into taking actions that may not bode well for both sides. And simultaneously doing its best not to alienate its friends, partners, and allies within and outside of the region who may not think it is wise for Taiwan to prematurely embark on any course of action that might annoy Beijing. Yet, to expect a political entity, an institution, a people, or an individual to remain in an indeterminate state or continue with the status quo is not healthy. It can be frustrating and paralyzing. It is a situation that does allow Taiwan and its people to plan far ahead as many countries and governments do. The isolation must be asphyxiating.

Other than for individual and or collective pride and nationalism, what does China want from Taiwan? What would China lose by consenting to Taiwan's independence? In what ways would an independent Taiwan diminish China's rising power, its prosperity, and ascension to global dominance? The world recognizes China's power and influence around the world. No one doubts that. Not Japan. Not France. Not Britain. Not Germany or Australia. And not even the United States of America. In every conversation and all the conferences, one has participated in, it is assumed by some and believed by others that this century belongs to China. Annexing Taiwan by military might, therefore, is likely to diminish its standing around the world. A great power like China cannot and should not be seen bullying and attacking those who do not threaten its power or existence.

In the last seventy years, Taiwan has not thwarted China's enviable and illustrious growth and development and is not likely to do so anytime within the next seventy years and beyond. Pragmatic solutions don't always make sense, and not all prudent solutions are pragmatic. But what makes sense in the cross-strait and its geographical zones is a *Two-State, One People* solution: a PRC and a sovereign Republic of Taiwan. Or the Democratic Republic of Taiwan. Chinese are Chinese wherever they may be, no matter their ideological differences, geographical delineation, economic standing, or role and place in the world. China and Taiwan have the wherewithal, the attitude, and the consciousness to coexist peacefully as two independent nations but whose peoples are united in their history, experiences, dreams, and aspirations for the future. An independent Taiwan will not be a hindrance to China's rise and affluence. But if there must be a unification, it must not be forced.

The unfortunate part of this seven-plus-decade saga is that Taiwan does not have many options. Maybe there are other options one has not considered; but of the five so outlined, only the fifth option—international recognition by all the member states of the UN—is within the realm of possibility. It is the right cause of action.

It would have made a great deal of difference if Taiwan was a nuclear power. This would have made a huge difference in how Beijing approaches Taipei. Being a nuclear power is what made the biggest difference in the tension and hostility in the Middle East and is what makes the difference in the relationship between the United States and the Soviets (and now Russia). This is also true between India and Pakistan. There is something about deterrence that makes some nations explore better options. In all of these, does Taiwan have a wild card—a surprise no one knows about? It's hard to tell.

The reading of the tea leaves blowing from and within Beijing points to an imminent invasion. Still, no one can say with 100% certainty whether China will invade within a year, within half a decade, or later. President Xi Jinping himself may not know. Or may have decided not to invade but enjoy the brinkmanship. Or perhaps the CCP gets to think twice because of a recalculation in the total cost and implications of war or perhaps because, as is expected, leading world leaders have called and keep calling for China not to invade. Should this wind blow over, the world must find answers to the China-Taiwan question. And to the Israeli-Palestinian and Morocco-Western Sahara questions.

CONCLUSION

The status of Taiwan—ambiguous, contested, and undetermined—must be worrying to many scholars; diplomats; observers; and students of international relations, national security, foreign policy, and geopolitical affairs. Why has the UN denied independence to a political entity that meets all the requirements for statehood? How and why would you forbid such a country from full participation in the international system? Not only does Taiwan meet all the requirements for statehood, but it is also not a rogue state and does not breed nefarious non-state actors. It is also a liberal democracy with an open and healthy system. But more than that, it has shown a willingness to act within norms and obey international laws. Taiwan matters, not only to its region and neighbors but also to the United States, and more importantly, to the international community.[10]

Even so, we cannot and must not ignore China's concerns and ambition, its governing ideology, and its sense of pride and nationalism. The solution to cross-strait affairs seems entirely political. Not military. Therefore, China must learn from the mistakes of previous global powers. By so doing, it may avoid many of the mistakes committed by Britain, France, the United States, and others, and empires that have long faded into oblivion. The collective wishes and aspirations of a people must be respected. In this case, Taiwan wants nothing but complete independence and peaceful coexistence with its neighbors. For China to allow this would be a good signal and a sign that it can be a rational and compassionate leader in the new era we are about to enter. Can it be entrusted to lead—to lead—not traumatize or conquer?

NOTES

1. "China's Xi Vows 'reunification' with Taiwan but Holds off Threatening Force." CNBC. October 9, 2021. Accessed October 14, 2021. https://www.cnbc.com /2021/10/09/china-president-xi-jinping-on-reunification-with-taiwan.html.

2. Mason, Jeff. "Biden Says He and China's Xi Agree to Abide by Taiwan Agreement." Reuters. October 6, 2021. Accessed October 14, 2021. https:// www.reuters.com/world/asia-pacific/biden-says-he-chinas-xi-have-agreed-abide-by -taiwan-agreement-2021-10-05/.

3. Ibid.

4. "Taiwan Won't Be Forced to Bow to China, President Says." CNBC. October 10, 2021. Accessed October 14, 2021. https://www.cnbc.com/2021/10/10/taiwan -wont-be-forced-to-bow-to-china-president-says.html.

5. Easton, Ian. *The Chinese Invasion Threat: Taiwan's Defence and American Strategy in Asia.* Manchester, UK: Eastbridge Books, 2019; See also Zelikow, Philip and Blackwill Robert D. *United States, China, and Taiwan: A Strategy to Prevent War.* New York: Council on Foreign Relations, 2021.

6. Glaser, Bonnie S., Richard C. Bush, and Michael J. Green. "Toward a Stronger U.S.-Taiwan Relationship." Center for Strategic and International Studies. October 21, 2021. Accessed October 14, 2021. https://www.csis.org/analysis/toward-stronger -us-taiwan-relationship.

7. Stoessinger, John George. *Why Nations Go to War.* Boston, MA: Wadsworth Cengage Learning, 2011.

8. Rein, Shaun. *The War for Chinas Wallet: Profiting from the New World Order.* Boston, MA: Walter de Gruyter, 2018.

9. Please see Accordance with international law of the unilateral declaration of independence in respect of Kosovo (Request for Advisory Opinion) Decided July 22, 2010: https://www.icj-cij.org/en/case/141

10. Rigger, Shelley. *Why Taiwan Matters: Small Island, Global Powerhouse.* Lanham, MD: Rowman & Littlefield, 2014.

BIBLIOGRAPHY

"China's Xi Vows 'Reunification' with Taiwan But Holds Off Threatening Force." *CNBC*, 9 October 2021. https://www.cnbc.com/2021/10/09/china-president-xi -jinping-on-reunification-with-taiwan.html.

Easton, Ian. *The Chinese Invasion Threat: Taiwan's Defense and American Strategy in Asia.* Norwalk, Connecticut: Eastbridge Books, 2019.

Glaser, Bonnie S, Richard C. Bush, and Michael J. Green. "Toward a Stronger U.S.-Taiwan Relationship." Center for Strategic and International Studies (CSIS), 10 October 2021. https://www.csis.org/analysis/toward-stronger-us-taiwan -relationship.

Mason, Jeff. "Biden Says He and China's Xi Agree to Abide by Taiwan Agreement." *Reuters*, 6 October 2021. https://www.reuters.com/world/asia-pacific/biden-says -he-chinas-xi-have-agreed-abide-by-taiwan-agreement-2021-10-05/.

Rein, Shaun. *The War for China's Wallet: Profiting from the New World Order.* Boston/Berlin: Walter de Gruyter Inc., 2018.

Rigger, Shelley. *Why Taiwan Matters: Small Island, Global Powerhouse.* New York: Rowman & Littlefield, 2014.

Stoessinger, John George. *Why Nations Go to War.* Wadsworth: Cengage Learning, 2011.

"Taiwan Won't Be Forced to Bow to China, President Says." *CNBC*, 10 October 2021. https://www.cnbc.com/2021/10/10/taiwan-wont-be-forced-to-bow-to-china -president-says.html.

Zelikow, Philip, and Robert D. Blackwill. *United States, China, and Taiwan: A Strategy to Prevent War.* New York: Council on Foreign Relations (CFR), 2021.

Part III

BEIJING AND TAIPEI

AT HOME AND ABROAD

Chapter 10

China and Taiwan in Africa

Foreign Direct Investment, Institutions, and Regional Development

Guanie Lim and Ding Fei

INTRODUCTION

Much ink has been spilled on Chinese-Taiwanese competition over international recognition, including in Africa. Although China (People's Republic of China, PRC) has seemingly established an unassailable lead in the years after taking over Taiwan's (Republic of China, ROC) seat as a permanent member of the United Nations Security Council in 1971, it has not eliminated Taiwanese influence in Africa.[1] What is certain is the ROC's shifting, malleable engagement in Africa amid an increasingly assertive PRC within the regional and global arena.[2]

To enrich the existing scholarship, this chapter will focus on *one aspect* of PRC and ROC engagement with Africa, that is, foreign direct investment (FDI). Centering the debate on FDI helps to uncover the (different) pathways by which both sides have channeled investment into Africa. In addition, it sheds light on the distribution of PRC and ROC investment in the continent.

The chapter puts forth several interrelated arguments. First, the PRC and ROC governments have built up their respective institutions to channel FDI to Africa. The variation in institutional structure and state-business relations in their home economies means that different sets of actors have been mobilized. Second, there has been a definite increase in PRC FDI to Africa from the early 2000s. The FDI inflow has also evolved—from a heavy emphasis on natural resource-centric activities in the early phases to increasingly more complex ones (e.g., telecommunications and gambling). Third, close to half of PRC investment has gone toward African economies with a large, young population and high endowment of natural resources.

Lastly, based on the limited amount of publicly available data, only a minuscule amount of ROC FDI has been channeled toward Africa. For ROC investors, Africa seems to matter considerably less than the other continents. Their strategy seems to center on three economies, Eswatini, Nigeria, and South Africa (RSA). Notwithstanding Eswatini's limited size, the targeting of Nigeria and RSA means that Taiwanese firms will most likely treat these two economies as the subregional gateways to northwest and southeast Africa. It appears that ROC has stumbled upon a "formula" or "political economic settlement" that does not directly challenge PRC's interest while opening opportunities for ROC firms to operate in specific niches in the continent.

This chapter begins by examining the institutions and mechanisms that PRC and ROC employ to promote economic cooperation (specifically, FDI) with Africa. It then illustrates the flow of PRC FDI entering Africa, utilizing a database from the China Africa Research Initiative at Johns Hopkins University. Although a comparable level of data is not available for ROC investment, certain inferences can still be made by tapping into other literature sources. The chapter concludes by summarizing the key findings, in addition to proposing future research avenues.

INSTITUTIONS AND MECHANISMS

Both PRC and ROC governments have put forward incentives to facilitate the internationalization of their national companies into Africa. In addition to policy incentives, various institutions have been developed over the years to help investors familiarize themselves with the broader contexts of Africa and to develop transnational business relations. For PRC, it has, since 2000, developed much larger-scale and continental-wide multilateral cooperation, drawing in diverse state and non-state actors. The Forum on China-Africa Cooperation (FOCAC) was initiated in 2000 as a high-level official platform for development cooperation. In 2006, the "China's Africa Policy" document was released, which specified China's policy initiatives toward Africa.[3] Chinese president Xi Jinping, upon his inauguration, reinforced the "strategic partnership" between China and Africa, pledged continued support for Africa, and pictured China as an "all-weather friend" of Africa.[4] Chinese-aid or Chinese-led projects, as a result, sprung across the continent. Subsequent FOCAC meetings emphasize close cooperation on a government-to-government, business-to-business, and people-to-people front.[5] Cooperation has expanded over the years from infrastructure construction, mining, agriculture, and manufacturing to clean energy, telecommunications, and financial industries.[6]

In addition to FOCAC, other institutions have been developed to improve business exchange and cooperation among investors, including the China-Africa Business Conference, the China-Africa Business Council, the China-Africa Development Fund, and the Sino-Africa Business and Investment Forum.[7] PRC's activities in Africa are primarily coordinated by the Ministry of Foreign Affairs and the Ministry of Commerce. Other central ministries such as health and education as well as provincial and local governments are also heavily engaged in aid and investment activities across sectors.[8] Chinese companies, ranging from central state-owned enterprises (SOEs) and their regional subsidiaries to provincial-owned enterprises to private multinationals and entrepreneurs, have all engaged in investment and business activities across Africa.[9]

In the case of ROC, two of the multilateral channels utilized are the Africa Taiwan Economic Forum (ATEF) and Taiwan-Africa Business Association (TABA). The ATEF is held jointly by the three African embassies and trade offices in Taiwan—Nigeria, RSA, and Eswatini—and the Ministry of Foreign Affairs of ROC. The forum aims to provide Taiwanese businesses with trade and investment opportunities in these three countries (and their adjacent economies) and facilitate the development of business partnerships. The TABA was established under the sponsorship of the Ministry of Foreign Affairs, the Ministry of Economic Affairs, and the Taiwan External Trade Development Council. It is another platform where government agencies and private actors work together to explore trade and investment opportunities in Africa.

At the bilateral level, ROC's engagement with RSA is most noticeable. Three institutional linkages have been identified: 1) the ROC-RSA Ministerial Conference on Economic and Technical Co-operation (ROC-RSA MCETC) established by the two governments; 2) the RSA/ROC Chamber of Economic Relations (SAROC) in South Africa and its counterpart, ROC/RSA Economic Council (ROCSA) in Taiwan; and 3) contact between the China External Trade Development Council (CETRA) and the South African Foreign Trade Organization (SAFTO) (Tseng 2008).[10] The ROC-RSA MCETC was a bilateral commission established in 1977. It was an annual event that took place alternatively in the respective capitals of ROC and RSA. SAROC and its counterpart ROCSA were established in 1982 to promote bilateral trade and economic cooperation in the private sectors. Members of the two institutions are primarily private and parastatal companies. The CETRA and the SAFTO worked together to enhance private business collaborations between both parties. Overall, it can be said that ROC's engagement with Africa heavily focuses on bilateral relations (targeting a few countries), intending to forge business collaboration in the private sector.

It is generally believed that ROC investment in Africa is driven mostly by the private sector, whereas investment from PRC is led by SOEs and/or directed by the governments. While the overall pattern is true in many African countries, it is crucial to note that in countries where the ROC has greater political and diplomatic influence, the reverse pattern is observed. For example, in Burkina Faso (which had diplomatic relations with ROC until 2018), scholars observe ROC investment has been mostly top-down and politically supported.[11] The ROC Embassy in the country was said to be active in organizing business events; stimulating bilateral cooperation; and delivering assistance in medical care, agricultural development, and human resources training.[12] In contrast, investment from the PRC in Burkina Faso is dominated by private companies, small entrepreneurs, and traders. Their activities primarily concentrate on construction, telecommunication, motorcycle, service, and hospitality sectors.[13]

GEOGRAPHY AND DISTRIBUTION

Figure 10.1 illustrates the flow of PRC FDI entering Africa between 2003 and 2018. From 2003 to 2008, there was an exponential increase as PRC firms, including some SOEs, invested in Africa's natural resources sector. Some of the more prominent investments of that era include Sinopec's and China National Offshore Oil Corporation's projects in the oil and gas industry of Angola[14] and China Nonferrous Metal Mining Corporation's copper mining activities in Zambia.[15]

However, the global banking crisis of 2008 meant that firms had to take on a more cautious stance to prevent getting caught up by slowing business

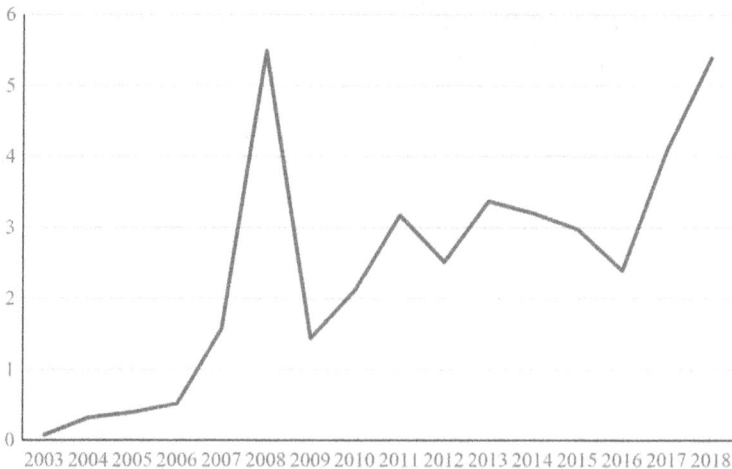

Figure 10.1   Flow of Chinese Foreign Direct Investment into Africa, 2003–2018 (Current USD Billion).

sentiments. This can be seen in the drastic drop of PRC FDI entering Africa in 2009. Although FDI flows did pick up in the ensuing years, figure 10.1 shows that the flow gained decisive momentum only from 2016, attaining a value of USD2.4 billion. In 2018, PRC investors have brought in about USD5.4 billion to the African continent. Preliminary evidence suggests that PRC FDI in the post-2008 era has become more multidimensional. This time around, PRC investors have targeted activities ranging from Ethiopia's telecommunications and construction industries[16] as well as Zambia's gambling industry.[17] Although the natural resource sector remains important, it has certainly been "balanced" by other types of investment.

From 2003 to 2018, RSA has received the largest share of PRC FDI entering the continent (see table 10.1). As much as USD7.0 billion (17.9% market share) worth of PRC FDI had been channeled toward it. Although the chapter does not aim to examine in detail why RSA was the first choice for Chinese investors, they likely saw its relatively stable macroeconomic environment, big domestic market, and trade networks both within and without Africa favorably. Ranked at second is Zambia, garnering a total of USD3.1 billion (7.9% market share) from PRC investors. Despite its landlocked status and small domestic population, Zambia's rich copper reserves have proven an attractive prospect for Chinese firms eager to capture a slice of the market.

Nigeria, the Democratic Republic of the Congo, and Algeria are ranked third, fourth, and fifth, respectively. These countries attracted almost the same amount of PRC FDI; they are worth USD2.5 billion, USD2.4 billion, and USD2.2 billion, respectively. The common variables behind these three economies are their large market (in population size and economic output), relatively young population, and high endowment of natural resources.[18] All of the five countries absorb 44% of PRC FDI during the period observed, with the balance split between the less "popular" African economies.

Table 10.1 Country-by-Country Flow of Foreign Direct Investment from PRC to Africa, 2003–2018

Country	Foreign Direct Investment (USD Billion; Percentage of Total)
South Africa	7.0; 17.9
Zambia	3.1; 7.9
Nigeria	2.5; 6.5
Democratic Republic of the Congo	2.4; 6.2
Algeria	2.2; 5.5
Others	20.5; 56

Source: Created by Guanie Lim and Ding Fei from data derived from the China Africa Research Initiative.

Data on ROC FDI is considerably harder to obtain. According to European Institute for Asian Studies,[19] less than 1% of ROC FDI has gone toward Africa. It is by far the least "popular" among all the continents. The top three destinations of Taiwanese firms are mainland China (64%), the rest of Asia (20%), and Oceania (9%).

Africa's lack of importance to Taiwanese business groups can also be inferred from the low number of Taipei Economic and Cultural Representative Offices (TECRO) in the continent. Currently, the only African nations with TECRO offices are Nigeria and RSA. To put things into context, one can draw inferences from the ten countries that make up Southeast Asia. The ROC government has TECRO in all the countries, except one (Laos). Similarly, the aforementioned ATEF has offices only in Eswatini, Nigeria, and RSA. In particular, RSA's and Nigeria's role as the southeast and northwest regional hubs of ROC businessmen means that they will capture (and hopefully embed) most of the inward FDI, before being channeled to the ultimate host countries.

CONCLUSION

This chapter has unearthed the uneven manners in which PRC and ROC investment has taken shape in Africa. Several interesting findings are worth reiterating. First, PRC and ROC have constructed their respective institutions to facilitate investment into Africa. Although the PRC and ROC governments play a major role in creating these institutions, they have drawn in different sets of actors. For the PRC, a plethora of firms—state owned or otherwise—have been brought into Africa through institutions such as the FOCAC. The ROC relies primarily on the private sector, although it is probably because of the relatively small presence of its SOEs in its economy. The situation might be somewhat different in African countries where the ROC has greater political-economic influence such as Burkina Faso. In these instances, ROC investment has been mostly politically motivated, with Taipei asserting a rather important role. Likewise, PRC FDI is almost entirely driven by the private sector in Burkina Faso.

Second, there is a definite increase in PRC FDI to Africa from the early 2000s. In the early stages, the FDI primarily financed activities related to natural resources. However, as the Chinese and African economies evolved, FDI was channeled to previously unheralded activities (e.g., gambling and telecommunications), although natural resources investment is likely to remain a key component. Third, close to half of PRC investment between 2003 and 2018 has gone toward African economies with a large, young population and high endowment of natural resources. These countries are RSA, Nigeria, the Democratic Republic of the Congo, and Algeria, respectively. Lastly, based on the limited amount of publicly available data, only a very small percentage of ROC FDI has been channeled to Africa. Taiwanese companies prefer to invest in other regions such as Asia and Oceania.

Judging from the preceding information, it can be said that there has been no real economic competition between PRC and ROC in the continent, at least not since the 2000s. While both sides have created institutions to deepen their engagement with the African people, the mechanisms by which the engagement is carried out are vastly different. Moreover, the continent's weightage to PRC and ROC must be taken into consideration. It appears that Africa has become more important to PRC as not only more institutions are built, but also existing ones (e.g., FOCAC) enhanced. For ROC, Africa seems to matter considerably less than other continents. Yet, this should not be interpreted as ROC getting muscled out of Africa definitively. ROC investment will likely continue to target specific countries or niches that do not directly challenge PRC interest.[20] Put another way, the vast size and heterogeneity of the African continent imply that there is ample room for PRC and ROC investors to not only coexist but also establish mutually beneficial cooperation between themselves and with the relevant host economies.

Building on the findings here, there are several avenues by which future research can be directed toward. For one, it will be useful to undertake a more on-the-ground analysis of PRC and ROC investment. A more in-depth analysis can shed light on the local experiences of the communities that *liaise* with Chinese and Taiwanese investors. Ethnographically rich data and analysis, for example, is likely to yield insights into how spillover effects (both positive and negative) have manifested in these locales. Such a bottom-up angle brings out the micro-strategies of the people most intimately involved in fostering PRC- and ROC-African interactions, supplementing state-level perspective that tends to project these dynamics in a static, absolute manner.

Another fruitful research agenda involves the examination of FDI, within the context of South-South cooperation. Following decades of high growth, emerging economies such as China, Taiwan, Brazil, Malaysia, and India are beginning to redefine development cooperation in other Global South countries through capital exports, using a combination of FDI and other measures (e.g., foreign aid and export credit).[21] While there is likely a plurality of approaches between PRC and ROC (and by extension, other emerging economies), there is still much to be examined, as far as their impact on the development landscape of Africa is concerned. The broader hypothesis is that African economies eager to catch up can, in theory, leverage resources from development partners (whether PRC, ROC, or other emerging economies) that can offer them the most appropriate policy tools.

NOTES

1. Rich, Timothy, and Vasabjit Banerjee. 2015. "Running Out of Time? The Evolution of Taiwan's Relations in Africa." *Journal of Current Chinese Affairs* 44(1):141–161; Mishra, Abhishek. 2020. "Taiwan's Africa Outreach Irks China." Observer Research Foundation, Last Modified 29 August 2020, accessed 22 March 2021. https://www.orfonline.org/expert-speak/taiwans-africa-outreach-irks-china/.

2. Hirono, Miwa, and Shogo Suzuki. 2014. "Why Do We Need 'Myth-Busting' in the Study of Sino–African Relations?" *Journal of Contemporary China* 23(87):443–461; Zhao, Suisheng. 2014. "A Neo-Colonialist Predator or Development Partner? China's Engagement and Rebalance in Africa." *Journal of Contemporary China* 23(90):1033–1052; see also Yi-Chong, Xu. 2014. "Chinese State-owned Enterprises in Africa: Ambassadors or Freebooters?" *Journal of Contemporary China* 23(89):822–840.

3. Corkin, Lucy. 2011. "Redefining Foreign Policy Impulses toward Africa: The Roles of the MFA, the MOFCOM and China Exim Bank." *Journal of Current Chinese Affairs* 40(4):61–90.

4. Alden, Chris. 2005. "China in Africa." *Survival* 47(3):147–164; Alden, Chris, and Christopher Hughes. 2009. "Harmony and Discord in China's Africa Strategy: Some Implications for Foreign Policy." *The China Quarterly* (199):563–584.

5. Grimm, Sven. 2012. *The Forum on China-Africa Cooperation (FOCAC) – Political Rationale and Functioning.* Stellenbosch: Centre for Chinese Studies (CCS), Stellenbosch University; Cheng, Joseph, and Huangao Shi. 2009. "China's African Policy in the Post-Cold War Era." *Journal of Contemporary Asia* 39(1):87–115.

6. Fei, Ding. 2020a. "Chinese Telecommunications Companies in Ethiopia: The Influences of Host Government Intervention and Inter-firm Competition." *The China Quarterly*:1–22; Fei, Ding. 2021. "Networked Internationalization: Chinese Companies in Ethiopia's Infrastructure Construction Sector." *The Professional Geographer*:1–11; Shen, Wei, and Marcus Power. 2017. "Africa and the Export of China's Clean Energy Revolution." *Third World Quarterly* 38(3):678–697; see also Shi, Xuefei, and Paul Hoebink. 2020. "From Chengdu to Kampala: The Role of Subnational Actors in China's Foreign Aid." *Journal of Contemporary China* 29(121):125–140.

7. Zhao, Suisheng. 2014. "A Neo-Colonialist Predator or Development Partner? China's Engagement and Rebalance in Africa." *Journal of Contemporary China* 23(90):1033–1052.

8. Yeh, Emily, and Elizabeth Wharton. 2016. "Going West and Going Out: Discourses, Migrants, and Models in Chinese Development." *Eurasian Geography and Economics* 57(3):286–315.

9. Fei, Ding. 2020b. "The Compound Labor Regime of Chinese Construction Projects in Ethiopia." *Geoforum* 117:13–23; Fei, Ding. 2020c. "Variegated Work Regimes of Chinese Investment in Ethiopia." *World Development* 135:105049.

10. Tseng, San-Shiun. 2008. "The Republic of China's Foreign Policy towards Africa: The Case of ROC-RSA Relations." PhD, Faculty of Humanities, University of the Witwatersrand.

11. Cabestan, Jean-Pierre. 2016. "Burkina Faso: Between Taiwan's Active Public Diplomacy and China's Business Attractiveness." *South African Journal of International Affairs* 23(4):495–519.

12. Cabestan, Jean-Pierre. 2016. "Burkina Faso: Between Taiwan's Active Public Diplomacy and China's Business Attractiveness." *South African Journal of International Affairs* 23(4):495–519; Khan Mohammad, Guive. 2014. "The Chinese Presence in Burkina Faso: A Sino-African Cooperation from Below." *Journal of Current Chinese Affairs* 43(1):71–101.

13. Khan Mohammad, Guive. 2014. "The Chinese Presence in Burkina Faso: A Sino-African Cooperation from Below." *Journal of Current Chinese Affairs* 43(1):71–101.

14. Zhao, Shelly. 2011. "The China-Angola Partnership: A Case Study of China's Oil Relations in Africa." China Briefing, Last Modified 25 May 2011, accessed 22 March 2021. https://www.china-briefing.com/news/the-china-angola-partnership-a-case-study-of-chinas-oil-relationships-with-african-nations/.

15. Lee, Ching Kwan. 2018. *The Specter of Global China: Politics, Labor, and Foreign Investment in Africa.* University of Chicago Press.

Li, Pengtao. 2010. *The Myth and Reality of Chinese Investors: A Case Study of Chinese Investment in Zambia's Copper Industry.* Johannesburg: South African Institute of International Affairs.

16. Fei, Ding. 2020a. "Chinese Telecommunications Companies in Ethiopia: The Influences of Host Government Intervention and Inter-firm Competition." *The China Quarterly*:1–22.

Fei, Ding. 2020b. "The Compound Labor Regime of Chinese Construction Projects in Ethiopia." *Geoforum* 117:13–23.

17. Camba, Alvin, and Hangwei Li. 2020."Chinese Workers and Their 'Linguistic Labour': Philippine Online Gambling and Zambian Onsite Casinos." *China Perspectives* 4:39–47.

18. Nigeria and Algeria are both hydrocarbon-rich Organization of the Petroleum Exporting Countries member countries. The Democratic Republic of the Congo is rich in coltan, cobalt, diamond, and copper.

19. European Institute for Asian Studies. 2014. *Taiwan's Outward Foreign Direct Investment (OFDI) into the European Union and Its Member States.* Brussels: European Institute for Asian Studies.

20. Rich, Timothy, and Vasabjit Banerjee. 2015. "Running Out of Time? The Evolution of Taiwan's Relations in Africa." *Journal of Current Chinese Affairs* 44(1):141–161.

21. Quadir, Fahimul. 2013. "Rising Donors and the New Narrative of 'South–South' Cooperation: What Prospects for Changing the Landscape of Development Assistance Programmes?" *Third World Quarterly* 34(2):321–338; Lim, Guanie. 2016. "Firm Entry Modes and Chinese Business Networks: Malaysian Investments in Vietnam." *Singapore Journal of Tropical Geography* 37(2):176–194; and Woods, Ngaire. 2008. "Whose Aid? Whose Influence? China, Emerging Donors and the Silent Revolution in Development Assistance." *International Affairs* 84(6):1205–1221.

BIBLIOGRAPHY

Alden, Chris. 2005. "China in Africa." *Survival* 47 (3):147–164.

Alden, Chris, and Christopher Hughes. 2009. "Harmony and Discord in China's Africa Strategy: Some Implications for Foreign Policy." *The China Quarterly* (199):563–584.

Cabestan, Jean-Pierre. 2016. "Burkina Faso: Between Taiwan's Active Public Diplomacy and China's Business Attractiveness." *South African Journal of International Affairs* 23 (4):495–519.

Camba, Alvin. 2020. "The Sino-Centric Capital Export Regime: State-Backed and Flexible Capital in the Philippines." *Development and Change* 51 (4):970–997.

Camba, Alvin, and Hangwei Li. 2020. "Chinese Workers and Their 'Linguistic Labour': Philippine Online Gambling and Zambian Onsite Casinos." *China Perspectives* 4:39–47.

Cheng, Joseph, and Huangao Shi. 2009. "China's African Policy in the Post-Cold War Era." *Journal of Contemporary Asia* 39 (1):87–115.

Corkin, Lucy. 2011. "Redefining Foreign Policy Impulses toward Africa: The Roles of the MFA, the MOFCOM and China Exim Bank." *Journal of Current Chinese Affairs* 40 (4):61–90.

European Institute for Asian Studies. 2014. *Taiwan's Outward Foreign Direct Investment (OFDI) into the European Union and Its Member States.* Brussels: European Institute for Asian Studies.

Fei, Ding. 2020a. "Chinese Telecommunications Companies in Ethiopia: The Influences of Host Government Intervention and Inter-Firm Competition." *The China Quarterly*:1–22.

Fei, Ding. 2020b. "The Compound Labor Regime of Chinese Construction Projects in Ethiopia." *Geoforum* 117:13–23.

Fei, Ding. 2020c. "Variegated Work Regimes of Chinese Investment in Ethiopia." *World Development* 135:105049.

Fei, Ding. 2021. "Networked Internationalization: Chinese Companies in Ethiopia's Infrastructure Construction Sector." *The Professional Geographer*:1–11.

Grimm, Sven. 2012. *The Forum on China-Africa Cooperation (FOCAC) – Political Rationale and Functioning.* Stellenbosch: Centre for Chinese Studies (CCS), Stellenbosch University.

Hirono, Miwa, and Shogo Suzuki. 2014. "Why Do We Need 'Myth-Busting' in the Study of Sino–African Relations?" *Journal of Contemporary China* 23 (87):443–461.

Kamel, Maha. 2018. "China's Belt and Road Initiative: Implications for the Middle East." *Cambridge Review of International Affairs* 31 (1):76–95.

Khan Mohammad, Guive. 2014. "The Chinese Presence in Burkina Faso: A Sino-African Cooperation From Below." *Journal of Current Chinese Affairs* 43 (1):71–101.

Lee, Ching Kwan. 2018. *The Specter of Global China: Politics, Labor, and Foreign Investment in Africa.* Chicago, IL: University of Chicago Press.

Li, Pengtao. 2010. *The Myth and Reality of Chinese Investors: A Case Study of Chinese Investment in Zambia's Copper Industry.* Johannesburg: South African Institute of International Affairs.

Lim, Guanie. 2016. "Firm Entry Modes and Chinese Business Networks: Malaysian Investments in Vietnam." *Singapore Journal of Tropical Geography* 37 (2):176–194.

Liu, Hong, and Guanie Lim. 2019. "The Political Economy of a Rising China in Southeast Asia: Malaysia's Response to the Belt and Road Initiative." *Journal of Contemporary China* 28 (116):216–231.

Mishra, Abhishek. 2020. "Taiwan's Africa Outreach Irks China." Observer Research Foundation. Last Modified 29 August 2020, Accessed 22 March 2021. https://www.orfonline.org/expert-speak/taiwans-africa-outreach-irks-china/.

Quadir, Fahimul. 2013. "Rising Donors and the New Narrative of 'South–South' Cooperation: What Prospects for Changing the Landscape of Development Assistance Programmes?" *Third World Quarterly* 34 (2):321–338.

Rich, Timothy, and Vasabjit Banerjee. 2015. "Running Out of Time? The Evolution of Taiwan's Relations in Africa." *Journal of Current Chinese Affairs* 44 (1):141–161.

Shen, Wei, and Marcus Power. 2017. "Africa and the Export of China's Clean Energy Revolution." *Third World Quarterly* 38 (3):678–697.

Shi, Xuefei, and Paul Hoebink. 2020. "From Chengdu to Kampala: The Role of Subnational Actors in China's Foreign Aid." *Journal of Contemporary China* 29 (121):125–140.

Tseng, San-Shiun. 2008. "The Republic of China's Foreign Policy towards Africa: The Case of ROC-RSA Relations." PhD, Faculty of Humanities, University of the Witwatersrand.

Woods, Ngaire. 2008. "Whose Aid? Whose Influence? China, Emerging Donors and the Silent Revolution in Development Assistance." *International Affairs* 84 (6):1205–1221.

Yeh, Emily, and Elizabeth Wharton. 2016. "Going West and Going Out: Discourses, Migrants, and Models in Chinese Development." *Eurasian Geography and Economics* 57 (3):286–315.

Yi-Chong, Xu. 2014. "Chinese State-Owned Enterprises in Africa: Ambassadors or Freebooters?" *Journal of Contemporary China* 23 (89):822–840.

Young, Karen. 2019. "The Gulf's Eastward Turn: The Logic of Gulf-China Economic Ties." *Journal of Arabian Studies* 9 (2):236–252.

Zhao, Shelly. 2011. "The China-Angola Partnership: A Case Study of China's Oil Relations in Africa." *China Briefing.* Last Modified 25 May 2011, Accessed 22 March 2021. https://www.china-briefing.com/news/the-china-angola-partnership-a-case-study-of-chinas-oil-relationships-with-african-nations/.

Zhao, Suisheng. 2014. "A Neo-Colonialist Predator or Development Partner? China's Engagement and Rebalance in Africa." *Journal of Contemporary China* 23 (90):1033–1052.

Chapter 11

Communist China's Medical Assistance versus

Nationalist China's Agricultural Aid to Africa and the Politics of Recognition, 1961–1971

Andrea Azizi Kifyasi

INTRODUCTION: THE TWO CHINAS IN AFRICA

The two Chinas (communist and nationalist) penetrated the African continent at the height of Cold War politics. It was the moment when the politics of recognition gained higher momentum. During this period, forging diplomatic relationships was crucial, especially to the disputing power blocs. The People's Republic of China (PRC) declared itself the only legitimate government of China in 1949, and it had since strived to be recognized by the international community and admitted to the United Nations General Assembly (UNGA). At the same time, the government of the Republic of China (ROC), which was recognized by the UN as the primary representative of China, aimed to maintain its status.[1] Votes from African UN member countries were thus of importance to the two Chinas. The ROC did not only want to garner votes to maintain its position but also to enlarge the markets for Taiwanese-made industrial and agricultural products in Africa. Likewise, the PRC sought votes for its admission to the UNGA and a chance to spread communist ideology and win influence over the Soviet Union. Above all, markets for Chinese-made goods and resources from Africa were part of its goals in the continent.[2] Consequently, under the contexts of the Cold War, conflicting power blocs used African states as pawns on a grand chessboard.

Throughout the Cold War period, aid giving was undoubtedly the most natural means of winning allies among low-income countries. Yet the available studies dwell on traditional donors from the North (Euro-American countries) and multilateral donors such as the International Monetary Fund, World Bank, UN, and European Union, criticizing them for manipulating aid to furnish their economic and political ends instead of promoting sustainable development in recipient countries.[3] To date, only a few studies have examined the flow of aid from the South to the South and how such assistance was executed and experienced. As a result, some scholars have ignored how donors from less industrialized countries of the South, such as Cuba, India, and China, manipulated assistance dispensed to Africa for their economic and political benefits.[4] In the present study, I maintain that aid from countries of the South did not perform differently from aid coming from the North. Admittedly, the competition between the ROC and the PRC over international recognition determined Chinese aid policy toward Africa. Both communist China and nationalist China lobbied African states through distinctive forms of assistance to gain their political recognition.

There is consensus among scholars that Taiwan's agricultural aid to Africa played a role in maintaining its position in the UNGA since recipient countries remained loyal to Chiang Kai-shek's government.[5] The present study affirms this claim by outlining contexts where agricultural aid was a necessity to most independent African states. It further shows that the PRC used the same technique to win allies over the ROC. The two Chinas thus provided desperately needed assistance to Africa to furnish their political ends. Nationalist China used its knowledge and experience in agriculture as a bargaining chip, while the communists employed their medical knowledge and experience to dispatch medical assistance to the continent. Agriculture was the backbone of most independent African countries' economies. But inadequacies in the health sectors jeopardized the well-being of their populations. So, both medical and agricultural assistance was of importance to African countries, and the political elites strived to get either or both. As a result, African countries became the focus of Chinas' overall search for global political hegemony.

This chapter begins with an examination of how Cold War politics stirred the struggle for political recognition and of why conflicting power blocs employed different techniques, including aid, to gain allies. This section also unpacks how Afro-Asian movements eased the PRC's recognition. The chapter then considers how the two Chinas executed agricultural and medical aid to Africa and how such assistance functioned as a bargaining chip for political recognition. The subsequent section dwells on a case study of how communist China's medical assistance to the Tanzanian government turned the country's vanguard in favor of the PRC's admission to the UNGA. The final section draws some conclusions. This study relies on archival information, newspapers, and published research literature. Based on these sources, I maintain that the two Chinas used aid as a weapon to win international recognition and political leverage to serve their national interests. The assistance provided by the two Chinas sustained diplomatic relations with recipient countries and won them strategic diplomatic recognition. Yet, their assistance split the continent into pro-Communist, pro-Nationalist, and neutral countries.

THE COLD WAR CONTEXT AND THE STRUGGLE FOR POLITICAL HEGEMONY

In its initial stages, the Cold War was characterized by the politics of recognition. Acquiring diplomatic recognition from many countries was a great political achievement. The struggle for allies was based on how each bloc assumed that it was superior. During this period, each bloc wanted to be recognized by all the countries it signed diplomatic agreements with. But the race for recognition was more severe among countries that were competing with each other to justify their international presence and legitimacy. The disputes between East Germany (the German Democratic Republic) and West Germany (the Federal Republic of Germany) and between communist China and nationalist China are examples. West Germany defined itself as the legitimate government of Germany, and any state that recognized East Germany was no longer a friend of the Bonn government. Its aid was therefore directed to countries that did not sign diplomatic relationships with East Germany. Under the Hallstein Doctrine, West Germany canceled diplomatic relations with countries that recognized what was called the "Soviet-occupied zone."[6]

At the same time, the UN recognized the ROC as the legitimate representative of the whole of China. The Chiang government, which participated in the framing of the UN Charter and was one of the original signatories of such historic documents, was represented in the UNGA from 1945 to October 1971.[7] Although mainland China had been under communist occupation since 1949, the Taipei regime sought to exercise its sovereign rights on Chinese soil. It claimed to represent Chinese people everywhere and articulated their wishes and aspirations in the world community. Such circumstances escalated a fight for diplomatic hegemony between the Beijing and Taipei regimes. The ROC signed diplomatic relations and provided several means of assistance to countries that did not recognize the PRC.[8] On the other hand, the government of the PRC signed diplomatic relations and extended its aid to countries that did not recognize the ROC (see the following text). So, while the PRC and East Germany were struggling to be admitted to the UNGA, the ROC and West Germany were similarly fighting to maintain their political hegemony and recognition in the same international institution.

Throughout the Beijing-Taipei diplomatic battle, the Western bloc led by the United States strongly backed nationalist China. In contrast, the Soviet Union backed communist China up to the mid-1950s. Following the Sino-Soviet dispute, however, African, Asian, Latin American, and other countries became the main allies of the PRC, mostly under the Non-Aligned Movement. Communist China's plans for using African and Asian countries to secure a seat in the UNGA began shortly before the launch of the Bandung Conference. During and after the conference, the Beijing regime strategically advanced its agenda to win recognition over the Taipei regime, which was not invited to the conference. Before attending the conference, the government of the PRC identified the countries that had formal or informal relations with Taipei. Its intelligence information showed that three countries—Japan, the Philippines, and Turkey—had formal diplomatic relations involving the exchange of ambassadors. And nine countries—the Democratic Republic of Vietnam, India, Myanmar, Indonesia, Pakistan, Sri Lanka, Laos, Nepal, and Afghanistan—had diplomatic relations with Taiwan, though not at the level of exchanging ambassadors.[9] Generally, multiple African and Asian countries attending the conference had either formal or informal relations with Taipei. This circumstance informed the PRC of the need and strategies to dilute Taiwan's influence in African and Asian countries.

The Bandung Conference thus functioned as a starting point for communist China's bid for recognition. The conference, which was held in Indonesia on April 18–24, 1955, was attended by delegates from twenty-nine states, six of which were African.[10] It marked the beginning of communist China's serious engagement with Africa. During the conference, Premier Zhou Enlai of the PRC met with delegates from six African countries and established diplomatic relations. Above all, Premier Zhou and his delegates pursued the agenda of gaining admission to the UNGA for the PRC. In his speech at the conference, Zhou emphasized the need for the PRC and the United States to negotiate Taiwan's case and to end tensions between mainland China and Taiwan.[11] The conference gave the PRC a chance to meet not only political elites from Africa but also from Asian countries, which bolstered its influence. For example, the PRC promised to support Indonesia in its demand for sovereignty over West Irian (now Western New Guinea or West Papua) if the Indonesian government would support communist China on the Taiwan case.[12] One can thus say that the Bandung Conference was a successful start for communist China's struggle for admission to the UNGA.

The Bandung Conference was followed in 1957 by the inauguration of the Afro-Asian Peoples' Solidarity Organization (AAPSO), and the PRC shifted its admission agenda to soliciting votes from African and Asian countries at the numerous AAPSO conferences. This was a promising strategy since by 1960, the AAPSO had about sixty member countries, many of which were African and members of the UN. As the founding member and main sponsor of the AAPSO, the PRC had representatives in every committee of the organization, including in the Council, Solidarity Fund, Executive, and in a Permanent Secretariat.[13] No doubt, its representatives played a pivotal role in safeguarding the interests of communist China in the organization. The representatives criticized the UN, claiming that it was an instrument of neocolonialism.[14] Their persuasive voices prompted the AAPSO to demand communist China's admission to the UNGA. For instance, the Executive Committee meeting held in Beirut on November 9–13, 1960, accused the UN of denying mainland China admittance.[15] Needless to say, the AAPSO was a useful vehicle for the PRC to meet and influence Afro-Asian political elites. Since Taiwan was denied membership in the AAPSO, the PRC used its absence to maintain political hegemony over Chiang's regime. As a result, the votes from African members of the UN in favor of seating the Beijing government at the UNGA rose from five in 1959 to twenty-six in 1971 (table 11.1).

But not all Afro-Asian countries supported communist China's bid for admission. As shown in table 11.1, some countries supported the ROC, others the PRC, and a few remained neutral. Some countries from Africa boldly defended Taiwan's legitimacy to represent China. For instance, in the 1967 UNGA, the delegates from Burkina Faso, Rwanda, and Niger dismissed communist China's admission proposal, demanding that Beijing's regime should first end its policy of subversion and war. Having fought against a UN force

Table 11.1   Votes of UN African Members on the Question of Chinese Seating, 1959–1971

Year	ROC	PRC	Abstaining	Total
1959	2	5	3	10
1960	2	9	16	27
1961	9	9	11	29
1962	17	14	2	33
1963	17	12	4	33
1964	–	–	–	–
1965	10	18	9	37
1966	17	17	5	39
1967	19	16	4	39
1968	20	15	6	41
1969	21	18	2	41
1970	17	19	5	41
1971	15	26	0	41

Source: Created by Andrea Azizi Kifyasi from Various Data Points Including: "UNO Yaikataa China kwa Mara Nyingine," *Uhuru*, November 13, 1969, 1; "China Remains Outside U.N," *The Nationalist*, November 21, 1968, 2; Slawecki, "The two China's in Africa," 400; Hsiao-pong, "Planting Rice on the Roof of the UN Building," 383.

in Korea, the PRC objected to the UN Charter's prerequisite of "peace" as the main criterion for admission. At the same time, the delegates from Mali, Mauritania, and Zambia supported the proposal, stating that a small island like Taiwan should not represent the whole of China.[16] It took until 1969— when the African countries of Ghana, Libya, Mauritius, and Nigeria voted for the PRC—for communist China to see the hope of acquiring a sufficient number of votes to become the official representative of mainland China in the UNGA.[17]

In line with Cold War politics, the two Chinas employed several techniques besides medical and agricultural aid (discussed here) to garner more votes. They even sponsored antigovernment groups in Africa to oust lawful leaders who did not recognize their regimes. For instance, the government of the PRC sponsored several attempts aimed to separate Biafra from Nigeria, led by Lieutenant-Colonel Chukwuemeka Odumegwu Ojukwu, the leader of the breakaway Republic of Biafra (1967–1970). Oscar Kambona, a former Tanzanian minister and the secretary-general of Tanzania's ruling party, the Tanganyika African National Union, admitted that communist China transported large quantities of military equipment to Biafra through Tanzania. At the same time, the ROC donated USD 10,000 to Nigeria as relief for refugees in the Nigerian Civil War (Biafran War).[18] Similarly, in the Democratic Republic of the Congo, President Mobutu Sese Seko accused the PRC of training dissidents in the neighboring Congo-Brazzaville to subvert the African governments that recognized Taiwan as the official government of China. Under Patrice Lumumba, the Democratic Republic of the Congo had signed a diplomatic relationship with the PRC. But Mobutu's government severed diplomatic relations with Beijing and recognized Taipei.[19] Because his regime served the interests of the capitalist bloc, communist China's attempt to oust him was opportunistic and aimed at installing a new government that would vote for the PRC's admission to the UNGA.

AGRICULTURAL VERSUS MEDICAL ASSISTANCE AND THE POLITICS OF RECOGNITION

Our assistance to Asian and African countries is keenly important for our competition with the imperialists and revisionists for the middle strip. This is a critical link. It is the material assistance. It will not work without material.[20]

In this statement from 1964, Zhou Enlai underscores the role of aid in winning allies. For Beijing, aid was a useful tool in winning global political and economic influence not only over Taipei but also over Washington, DC, and Moscow. But communist China was not the only one that manipulated aid to serve its ends; all the competing power blocs granted different forms of assistance to win allies. Their assistance included the provision of loans and aid to the newly independent countries of the South as well as moral and military support to countries fighting for political independence.[21] Medical and agricultural assistance were not left out. Not surprisingly, after Algeria requested medical support in 1962, the PRC and the traditional donors of the North responded promptly by dispatching medical teams and other health-related assistance.[22] It is evident that the Eastern and Western blocs used medical aid as a tool for earning international recognition. For instance, while communist China created the Chinese Medical Team (CMT) program to achieve this goal (discussed here), the United States used the Medical International Cooperation Organization, famously known as "medico," for the same purpose.[23] In Africa, Algeria was the first country where a "Cold War of health" manifested before it spread to other countries. Immediately after Algeria's independence, French doctors, nurses, and technicians left the country, which complicated the delivery of healthcare. Faye Marley reports that the United States, the USSR, communist China, and others competed in offering medical assistance to the country. He contended that "MEDICAL and health services are being used all over the world by Communists and democratic peoples [*sic*] alike in a so-called non-political effort to earn international goodwill."[24] Medical teams from the United States were the first to land in Algeria in June 1962. By June 1973, there were 176 US medical personnel in Algiers. The Chinese government countered the United States by dispatching over a hundred medical workers to Algeria in early 1973.[25] The Soviet Union likewise responded by dispatching medical personnel to Algeria in the same year. Such a "chaotic" situation is what Marley calls a "Cold War of Health."[26]

Furthermore, assistance from both blocs was conditional, since it was only extended to countries that forged diplomatic relations with the bloc. Thus, for a country to qualify for continuous assistance, it had first to initiate diplomatic relationships with prospective donors. In this vein, African countries that recognized communist China continued to benefit from medical assistance while governments that recognized nationalist China received agricultural support (discussed here).[27] Medical and agricultural assistance admittedly touched the central needs of independent African countries. While medical aid was vital for building healthy nations, agricultural aid was a necessity for over two-thirds of African countries whose livelihoods depended on agriculture.[28] Securing these two forms of assistance surely belonged to the diplomatic goals of African countries. Forging diplomatic relations with the PRC entailed receiving medical aid but losing agricultural assistance from the ROC, and vice versa. Such circumstances influenced both the PRC and the ROC to begin offering both medical and agricultural assistance to maintain diplomatic relations with their allies.[29]

Starting in the early 1950s, the ROC received economic, military, technological, and political assistance from the United States. Throughout the 1950s, Chiang's government received a grant of up to USD 100 million a year from Washington, DC.[30] Indeed, the United States' support of Taiwan mainly served to dilute the supremacy of communist China. Through US Agency for International Development, the US empowered Taiwan to launch Operation Vanguard, a program that allowed Taiwan to send economic and financial assistance to several low-income countries, most of which were from Africa.[31] The US assistance helped Taiwan reform its land and establish modern industrial infrastructures. Moreover, the Taiwanese acquired simple, low-cost, and advanced knowledge on producing paddy rice, vegetables, and fruits. In addition to the technological advantages, the ROC had a semitropical climate, which meant that it shared similar climatic features with many tropical African countries.[32] Given the limited capital and the demand for food in most independent African countries, Taiwan's agricultural technology and experience were useful in the continent. Above all, through Operation Vanguard, nationalist China vowed to share its agricultural experience with African countries to help them achieve self-sufficiency in food production. Furthermore, it anticipated replacing the African staples of maize, millet, cassava, and sorghum with rice.[33]

Taiwan's agricultural aid included inviting prominent political elites from Africa to Taipei to witness agricultural technology and development. It further sponsored several training seminars for African agricultural experts in Taipei and sent technical agricultural teams to Africa. The government of Taiwan covered nearly all costs related to travel, the salaries of the dispatched teams, and the purchase of tools and equipment. Recipient countries only had to pay for marginal costs related to hosting experts and preparing farms.[34] For instance, in August 1968, about fifty-three African agricultural technicians received training in Taiwan. The technicians came from twenty different African countries, and they attended five months of training.[35] Similar training was held in February 1970, where about sixty-four technicians from twenty-one African countries attended six months of training in Taipei. The training courses encompassed how to select rice seeds, sow seedlings, cultivate rice, harrow it, and transplant it. Such training seminars helped African countries such as Mauritius and Sierra Leone establish large-scale plantations of paddy rice and soybean.[36]

The Taipei government dispatched its first agricultural technical teams to Africa in 1961. Liberia was the first country to benefit from the program, followed by Libya in 1962. While working in Liberia, Taiwanese experts were able to make a site in Gbedin productive after UN and American experts had failed to produce rice in the same area. Such achievements influenced other African countries to request and accept Taiwanese experts.[37] The technical agricultural teams worked for two years or more. After Liberia and Libya, the Taipei regime sent veterinary specialists to Ethiopia, Rwanda, Mauritius, and Botswana to work and train local livestock, farmers, sanitary inspectors, and disease-prevention personnel.[38] By December 1970, there were 913 experts from Taiwan in twenty-two technical agricultural teams working in Liberia, Ivory Coast, Gabon, Cameroon, Burkina Faso, Chad, Togo, Malawi, the Gambia, Congo-Kinshasa, Benin, Madagascar, Botswana, Ghana, the Central African Republic, Lesotho, Eswatini, and Mauritius.[39]

Taiwan's technical assistance strengthened its relations with many African countries to ease its struggle for diplomatic hegemony over the PRC. Some African leaders whose governments received technical assistance pledged to support the Taipei regime. For instance, in his nine-day visit to Taipei, the vice president of Botswana, Quett Masire, said: "China's [the ROC] technical assistance to the developing African countries played an important role in blocking Communist infiltration and expansion in Africa. . . . No people will incline to communism when their country has achieved noticeable economic progress and is heading for a bright future."[40] Similarly, the Liberian secretary of state visited Taipei in August 1968, and Jean-Bédel Bokassa, the president of the Central African Republic, did so as well in October 1970; they pledged to continue supporting the rightful position of the ROC in the UNGA.[41] Moreover, Taiwan's support for Africa gave Taiwanese officials chances to visit the continent regularly. Almost every year, a few months before the opening of the General Assembly, the Taiwanese minister for foreign affairs, Yang Hsin-kun, toured countries that had received aid to solicit votes. For instance, from July to October 1969, Mr. Yang visited about twenty-six African states. As a result, in the 1969 Assembly, the ROC scored twenty-one votes while the PRC received eighteen.[42]

Likewise, communist China's medical aid came at a time when most independent African countries lacked adequate skilled medical personnel. In 1962, the World Health Organization (WHO) reported that twenty-six independent African countries had a total of about 4,700 doctors (Africans and non-Africans). This meant that there was one doctor for every 18,000. Above all, there were very few African doctors. The WHO report shows that in 1965, twenty-six independent African countries had a sum of 1,700 African doctors. With such a figure, the doctor-patient ratio was one doctor for every 50,000 people. Regrettably, some independent African states had no African doctors at all, and others had the ratio of one African doctor for every million people.[43] This indicates that healthcare was scant in independent African countries. These countries needed immediate medical assistance to build up their capacity; they required training for local medical personnel and foreign expatriates who could nurture the few available workers and offer clinical care to patients.

The PRC's medical assistance began in 1963 after dispatching the first medical team to Algeria. Its successful mission marked the beginning of the PRC's medical assistance to Africa, Latin America, Asia, Oceania, and Southern Europe.[44] The CMT program was one of several frontiers of China's medical assistance to Africa. Other frontiers included building hospital infrastructures—this category involved constructing hospitals and donating drugs and medical equipment—building pharmaceutical factories, training health personnel, and helping control endemic diseases such as malaria. The lack of sufficient medical personnel in many African countries made the CMT category a more interventionist form of medical assistance than the rest. For this reason, throughout the 1960s, the largest share of communist China's health aid was spent on the CMTs.[45] The Beijing government recruited medical workers from different provinces, and each province dispatched medical workers to one or more African countries. The local government sent the teams abroad, while the central government, through its Ministry of Public Health, administered the program. A single medical team usually consisted of between fifteen and twenty-five or more people, and each worked for two years. The PRC's government bore most of the costs for maintaining the medical teams, while the recipient countries paid a fraction of it. The PRC paid for language training, food, salaries, medicines, and transport, while recipient countries provided the teams with medical facilities, medical instruments, accommodation, and security. By 1971, about ten African countries had received CMTs.[46] These medical missions in Africa functioned as a soft way of securing allies during the Cold War era and as a vital tool for pursuing political and economic objectives. All ten countries that received CMTs were the vanguard for Beijing's admission to the UNGA.

Both Taipei and Beijing withheld assistance from countries that recognized their opponents. For instance, the PRC suspended medical assistance to Liberia, Burkina Faso, and the Gambia after they had recognized Taiwan.[47] Assistance resumed to countries that withdrew their recognition of Taiwan. Liberia, for instance, received medical aid in 2005 after it had restored diplomatic relations with communist China.[48] In the same vein, the ROC withdrew its agricultural mission from Cameroon and Ethiopia when they recognized the Beijing regime in 1971. And the ROC recommenced its assistance to the Central African Republic following the resumption of diplomatic relations in August 1968.[49] Communist China's withdrawal of medical aid from countries that recognized Taiwan was inconsistent with its Eight Principles for Economic Aid and Technical Assistance to Other Countries endorsed in January 1964. For instance, the second principle states: "In providing aid to other countries, the Chinese government strictly respects the sovereignty of the recipient countries, and never asks for any privileges or attaches any conditions."[50] The withdrawals support Dambisa Moyo's argument that "aid" obviously serves donors' interests.[51] Such deeds are what Kambona perceived as neocolonialism. In his speech to the eighteenth session of the UNGA held on October 7, 1963, he contended: "We want capital for development, but very often the donors of capital say 'I am giving you the loan. You must not only repay the loan, plus the interest on the loan; you must also use the loan to buy my goods.' Sometimes the donors go as far as to say 'I want your vote in the United Nations.' This is neo-colonialism"[52] Kambona did not mention donors with such demands. But considering the prevailing context, he was indirectly referring to the ROC and the PRC, which were fighting for international recognition. The diplomatic race between the two Chinas was thus a primary determinant of aid policy toward Africa.

MEDICAL ASSISTANCE AND TANZANIA'S SUPPORT FOR THE PRC'S ADMISSION TO THE UNGA

Mainland Tanzania began to receive medical assistance from communist China in 1968. The support came at a moment when the country had inadequate medical personnel. For instance, at independence, the government had only seventeen African doctors. Among them, twelve were registered doctors and five were interns.[53] The CMTs dispatched to Tanzania came from the Shandong Province, and they worked in several regions of Tanzania such as Dodoma, Tabora, Mara, Mtwara, Lindi, Kigoma, Shinyanga, Mbeya, Morogoro, Singida, and Dar es Salaam. By April 1971, Shandong Province dispatched about 170 medical personnel to the country.[54] Other health projects funded by the PRC involved establishing the Mabibo Vaccine Institute (1968) and the Keko Pharmaceutical Industry (1968) which became the first government-owned pharmaceutical factories in the country.[55] Undoubtedly, the medical assistance strengthened the Sino-Tanzanian relationship, which, in turn, made the country a leader in communist China's admission campaign. Tanzania's support to the PRC began immediately after its independence in 1961.

But its delegation in the UNGA also cherished the country's neutrality policy. For instance, in 1961, the delegates supported the PRC's admission proposal, but they voted against the expulsion of the ROC. The government's spokesperson underscored that the vote was not against communist China. Instead, it was consistent with the country's neutrality policy.[56] In 1962, the delegates from Tanzania again campaigned for the PRC's admission and insisted on the need for maintaining the ROC's position. In his speech to the assembly, Kambona, the minister for foreign affairs, contended:

There, some would argue that the People's Republic of China is the effective Government of China and succeeds to the rights, privileges and duties of the

Chinese Government. We have no quarrel with this argument, Mr. President. Indeed, we support it. My own Government and delegation here, have consistently held this self-same position whenever this matter was raised. The existence of the People's Republic of China is a fact which neither legalism nor ideologies can dispute. Sooner or later all ostriches must raise their heads from the sands and face the existence of approximately 650 million Chinese inhabitants, occupying an immense portion of the world's land mass, over which they have exercised effective dominion for the past decade or more. The Government of my country has recognized these facts and enjoys trade, diplomatic and cultural relations with the Government and people of the People's Republic. My delegation does not necessarily equate "restoration of the lawful rights of the People's Republic of China" with "admission of the People's Republic of China" as a new member of the United Nations.[57]

The Tanzanian government perceived opposition to the admission of the PRC as illogical. But Kambona did not argue for the expulsion of Formosa's representative to the UNGA in his speech. Instead, he asserted the need for admitting the PRC.

From the mid-1960s, following President Julius Nyerere's first trip to Beijing, the delegates from Tanzania campaigned vigorously for communist China's admission. During his tour, Nyerere met and held intensive conversations with Chinese president Mao Zedong and premier Zhou. The government of the PRC pledged to assist Tanzania's economic and social development projects amid its quarrel with countries from the North, which eventually withheld their support to the country. On a reciprocal basis, the Tanzanian government affirmed its support for the restoration of the legitimate rights of the PRC in the UNGA. Nyerere sympathized with the PRC while opposing imperialist plots to create two Chinas.[58] Commitments from the Tanzanian government enhanced the trust between the two countries, which, in turn, bolstered China's economic, political, social, technological, and military assistance to the country. Communist China's assistance to Tanzania was compensated not only with the country's vote in the UNGA but also with their efforts to persuade other African countries to vote for the PRC.[59] In October 1969, Nyerere argued that the admission of communist China to the assembly would make the assembly stronger. In his view, the exclusion of the PRC was an act of self-amputation that left the assembly lame and weak.[60] In an address to the assembly in October 1970, Nyerere underscored the need for the UN to recognize the government of the PRC and allow it to have a legal seat in the assembly. He argued:

There is one other matter I must mention, and that is the question of member-ship of the United Nations. Mr. President, it is not always easy, at a given point in time, to determine which is the real government of a country that is going through a period of revolutionary upheaval. For that reason, the United Nations—I believe wisely—usually gives the incumbent government the benefit of doubt until the position clarifies itself. But there comes a time when we only make ourselves ridiculous by refusing to face the facts of change—whether we like that change or not. And that point has been reached and passed in relation to China. The territory and people of Mainland China—that is, about 3¾ million square miles, and now about 700 million persons—have been under the effective control of the government of the People's Republic of China in Peking since 1949—for 21 years. Yet they are still represented in our councils by a so-called Government of China, which in fact controls only Formosa—an island of approximately 13,900 square miles in area, and population of about 15 million people. And even this control continues only because of the intervention of an external power.[61]

He then made a request:

How much longer does the General Assembly propose to allow this absurd state of affairs to continue? For it cannot go on indefinitely. I would like to suggest that an appropriate way of celebrating the 25th Anniversary of the Organization would be the admission of the People's Republic of China to its seat here. Only by such an action shall we end the situation whereby we pretend to decide questions of peace or war in the absence of the most populous nation on earth.[62]

Nyerere made such persuasive speeches shortly after he visited the PRC for the first time in February 1965 and mainly after communist China's commitment to sponsor the construction of two pharmaceutical factories, the Tanzania-Zambia Railway Authority, and the dispatch of medical teams to the country.[63] Indeed, this was the period when the Sino-Tanzanian relationship had reached its climax. It is thus plausible to associate Nyerere's campaign for the admission of the PRC with the diplomatic relations between the two countries.

Tireless efforts of the PRC to gain admittance to the UNGA were continually frustrated by the United States and its allies. For more than two decades, the United States and its partners interrupted the motion defending the ROC's status.[64] But starting in 1970, many countries from Africa and a few from Europe and America supported the admission proposal. Some countries that initially recognized Taiwan—such as Canada, Italy, Chile, Ethiopia, and Kuwait—recognized Beijing and severed their diplomatic ties with Taipei. This shocked the ROC and the United States. An editorial in Taiwan's *China News* inquired whether the increasing votes for the PRC suggested that the ROC's assistance to Africa had failed or was inadequate.[65] Above all, the increasing support for the PRC forced Henry

Kissinger, the US national security advisor, to secretly visit the PRC twice in July and October 1971, to discuss the Taiwan case with PRC officials. Kissinger met Premier Zhou and President Mao and affirmed that the US government was not in favor of a solution that ended in two Chinas, one China and one Taiwan, or an independent Taiwan.[66] Although he did not admit to supporting the PRC's demands of one China, his visit suggested that the United States was willing to end the confrontation peacefully. As a result, the United States dropped its outright opposition to communist China's admission at the 1971 General Assembly. Its UN ambassador, Christopher Phillips, switched from uncompromising opposition to Beijing's admission to focusing on retaining a UN seat for Taipei. With such propositions, the United States accepted the admittance of the PRC, but it categorically opposed the expulsion of the ROC. This course, however, was not considered feasible since Beijing and its allies wanted Taipei to be expulsed from the UNGA.[67] As a result, on the evening of October 25, 1971, the twenty-sixth session of the assembly concluded the debate on communist China's admission. It allowed members to vote on the question of "restoration of the lawful rights of the People's Republic of China in the United Nations," a resolution draft brought by the delegates from Albania, Algeria, and twenty other countries. Communist China won by an overwhelming majority of seventy-six votes to thirty-five, with seventeen abstentions.[68] This marked the end of nationalist China's recognition in the UNGA and a victory for communist China and its allies. The victory was celebrated in different ways, and the Tanzanian representative to the UNGA danced in the assembly hall out of happiness.[69]

CONCLUSION

This chapter has discussed how Cold War politics influenced the provision of several kinds of assistance to Southern countries. The assistance played a vital role in maintaining the interests of donor countries. Of course, donors did not overtly spell out their desires, but actions and conditions attached to their assistance spoke louder. The chapter has shown that the PRC and the ROC attached strings to the assistance they dispensed to African countries. For instance, they both severed economic, political, and social aid to countries that recognized their opponents. One is thus justified to claim that the two Chinas assisted independent African countries in return for international recognition and political leverage. Indeed, agricultural and medical assistance played an imperative role in the admission struggle, in which the PRC emerged victorious over the ROC. Yet the struggle for global political hegemony between the PRC and the ROC did not end in October 1971. Communist China continues to erase nationalist China's recognition in different corners of the world. As a result, at the time of writing, only one African country (Eswatini) recognizes Taiwan; Burkina Faso severed its diplomatic relationship on May 26, 2018. This attempt and many others employed by the PRC are intended to push the policy of "one country, two systems" (*yiguo liangzhi*) on Taiwan, which they have been and remain fiercely opposed to.

NOTES

1. George T. Yu and David J. Longenecker, "The Beijing–Taipei Struggle for International Recognition: From the Niger Affair to the UN," *Asian Survey* 34, no. 5 (May 1994): 475.

2. Philip Liu Hsiao-pong, "Planting Rice on the Roof of the UN Building: Analysing Taiwan's 'Chinese' Techniques in Africa, 1961–Present," *The China Quarterly*, no. 198 (June 2009): 382; Leon M. S. Slawecki, "The Two Chinas in Africa," *Foreign Affairs* 41, no. 2 (Jan. 1963): 399–400.

3. See, for instance, Carol Lancaster, *Aid to Africa: So Much to Do, So Little Done* (Chicago: University of Chicago Press, 1999); William Easterly, *The Whiteman's Burden: Why the West's Efforts to Aid the Rest Have Done So Much Ill and So Little Good* (New York: Penguin Press, 2006); Dambisa Moyo, *Dead Aid: Why Aid Is Not Working and How There Is a Better Way for Africa* (New York: Farrar, Straus and Giroux, 2009); Sebastian Edwards, *Toxic Aid: Economic Collapse and Recovery in Tanzania* (Oxford: Oxford University Press, 2014).

4. Li Anshan, "China-Africa Medical Cooperation: Another form of Humanitarian Aid," accessed May 1, 2016, http://www.doctorswithoutborders.org/china-africa-medical-cooperation-another-form-humanitarian-aid, also see Peilong Liu et al., "China's Distinctive Engagement in Global Health," *Lancet* 308 (August 2014); for further details on the contexts that influenced scholars and some political elites in Africa to trust donors from the South more than those from the North, see Paul Tiyambe Zeleza, "Dancing with Dragon: Africa's Courtship with China," *The Global South* 2, no. 2 (Fall 2008): 171–187.

5. Ian Taylor, "Taiwan's Foreign Policy and Africa: The Limitations of Dollar Diplomacy," *Journal of Contemporary China* 11, no. 30 (2002): 138; Hsiao-pong, "Planting Rice on the Roof of the UN Building," 381; Yawsoon Sim, "Taiwan and Africa," *Africa Today* 18, no. 3 (July 1971): 20; Natasha Skidmore, "Taiwanese Development Aid in Africa," *SAIIA Report*, no. 43 (2002): 1.

6. George Roberts, "Politics, Decolonization, and the Cold War in Dar es Salaam c. 1965–72" (PhD thes., University of Warwick, 2016), 87; Priyal Lal, *African Socialism in Postcolonial Tanzania: Between the Village and the World* (New York: Cambridge University Press, 2015), 56–57; Paul Bjerk, *Building a Peaceful Nation: Julius Nyerere and the Establishment of Sovereignty in Tanzania, 1960–1964* (New York: University of Rochester Press, 2015), 214.

7. "A Victory for World's People, Crushing Defeat for U.S. Imperialism," *Peking Review* 14, no. 44, October 29, 1971, 6.

8. "One China," *Free China News*, August 16, 1971, 2. NRC, PMO-RALG, 8/2/03, File Ref. No. LGRD/N2/19, News from Free China (Formosa), 1968–71.

9. "Report from the Chinese Foreign Ministry, "Existence of Diplomatic Relations between Afro-Asian Conference Participant Countries and the Jiang Bandits," February 1, 1955, History and Public Policy Program Digital Archive, PRC, FMA 207-00021-01,1-2, 2.

10. The six African states with delegates at the conference were Egypt, Ethiopia, Ghana, Liberia, Libya, and Sudan. Ministry of Foreign Affairs, Republic of Indonesia, *Final Communique of the Asian-African Conference of Bandung, April 24, 1955*, 2; David H. Shinn, "China-Africa Ties in Historical Context," in *China-Africa and an Economic Transformation*, ed. Arkebe Oqubay and Justin Yifu Lin (London: Oxford University Press, 2019), 63.

11. "Speech by Premier Zhou Enlai at the Closing Session of the Asian-African Conference," April 24, 1955, History and Public Policy Program Digital Archive, 29–31.

12. "Summary of the Views of Afro-Asian Countries on the Taiwan Issue at the Afro-Asian Conference," May 27, 1955, History and Public Policy Program Digital Archive, PRC, FMA 207-00018-01, 1–4, 3.

13. Permanent Secretariat of the Afro-Asian Peoples' Solidarity Organizations, *Afro-Asian Peoples Solidarity Movement* (Cairo), 97–113.

14. See, for instance, the speech by Liu Ning-I, head of the Chinese delegation and vice chairman of the Chinese Committee for Afro-Asian Solidarity at the fourth session of the Afro-Asian People's Solidarity Council held in Bandung on April 10, 1961, in Chinese-African People's Friendship Association, *The Chinese People Resolutely Support the Just Struggle of the African People* (Peking: Foreign Languages Press, 1961), 50.

15. Permanent Secretariat, *Afro-Asian Peoples Solidarity Movement*, 35.

16. "China's Conditions on UN Membership 'Unacceptable,'" *The Standard*, November 23, 1967, 3; "African States Split on Chinese Entry," *The Standard*, November 29, 1967, 3.

17. "UNO Yaikataa China kwa Mara Nyingine," *Uhuru*, November 13, 1969, 1.

18. "Peiping Interferes in Nigerian Civil War," *Free China News*, September 30, 1968, 4; "Help for Nigerian War Victims," *Free China News*, October 7, 1968, 4. NRC, PMO-RALG, 8/2/03, File Ref. No. LGRD/N2/19, News from Free China (Formosa), 1968–71; Bruce D. Larkin, *China and Africa, 1949–1970* (California: University of California Press, 1973), 8.

19. "Red China Trains Subversive Elements," *Free China News*, October 21, 1968, 3. NRC, PMO-RALG, 8/2/03, File Ref. No. LGRD/N2/19, News from Free China (Formosa), 1968–71.

20. Quoted in Olivia J. Killeen et al., "Chinese Global Health Diplomacy in Africa: Opportunities and Challenges," *Global Health Governance* 12, no. 2 (Fall 2018): 6.

21. A. D. Hasan, "China and Non-alignment," *India International Centre Quarterly* 3, no. 3 (July 1976): 66.

22. Faye Marley, "Cold War of Health," *The Science Newsletter* 84, no. 3 (Jul. 20, 1963): 35; Shuang Lin et al., "China's Health Assistance to Africa: Opportunism or Altruism?" *Globalization and Health* (2016): 1. doi: 10.1186/s12992-016-0217-1.

23. Marley, "Cold War of Health," 35.

24. Marley, "Cold War of Health," 35.

25. Li Anshan, *Chinese Medical Cooperation in Africa: With Special Emphasis on the Medical Teams and Anti-Malaria Campaign* (Uppsala: Nordiska Afrikainstitutet, 2011), 7.

26. Marley, "Cold War of Health," 35.

27. See, for instance, Killeen et al., "Chinese Global Health Diplomacy in Africa," 4–6.

28. Skidmore, "Taiwanese Development Aid in Africa," 3.

29. For China's agricultural assistance to Africa, read Debora Brautigam, *Will Africa Feed China?* (New York: Oxford University Press, 2015), and for Taiwan, see "More Help," *Free China News*, December 7, 1970, 1. NRC, PMO-RALG, 8/2/03, File Ref. No. LGRD/N2/19, News from Free China (Formosa), 1968–71.

30. Jonathan Manthorpe, *Forbidden Nation: A History of Taiwan* (New York: Palgrave Macmillan, 2005), 203.

31. Robert A. Madsen, "The Struggle for Sovereignty between China and Taiwan," in *Problematic Sovereignty: Contested Rules and Political Possibilities*, ed. Stephen D. Krasner (New York: Columbia University Press 2001), 152–153.

32. Skidmore, "Taiwanese Development Aid in Africa," 4.

33. Hsiao-pong, "Planting Rice on the Roof of the UN Building," 387; Skidmore, "Taiwanese Development Aid in Africa," 12.

34. Sim, "Taiwan and Africa," 21.

35. "Taiwan-Volta Pact," *Free China News*, August 19, 1968, 4. NRC, PMO-RALG, 8/2/03, File Ref. No. LGRD/N2/19, News from Free China (Formosa), 1968–71.

36. "Seminar Opens," *Free China News*, March 2, 1970, 1; "22 Teams in Africa," *Free China News*, December 15, 1969, 4; "Agricultural Success," *Free China News*, April 6, 1970, 1. NRC, PMO-RALG, 8/2/03, File Ref. No. LGRD/N2/19, News from Free China (Formosa), 1968–71.

37. Hsiao-pong, "Planting Rice on the Roof of the UN Building," 387; Sim, "Taiwan and Africa," 21; Skidmore, "Taiwanese Development Aid in Africa," 12.

38. "Taiwan Vets. in Ethiopia," *Free China News*, 9 September 1968, 3; "Taiwan-Botswana Cooperation," *Free China News*, September 30, 1968, 4; "Taiwan Sugar Plant for Rwanda," *Free China News*, October 7, 1968, 4. NRC, PMO-RALG, 8/2/03, File Ref. No. LGRD/N2/19, News from Free China (Formosa), 1968–71.

39. "More Help," *Free China News*, December 7, 1970, 1. NRC, PMO-RALG, 8/2/03, File Ref. No. LGRD/N2/19, News from Free China (Formosa), 1968–71; also see Shiuh-shen Chien, Tzu-po Yang and Yi-chen Wu, "Taiwan's Foreign Aid and Technical Assistance in the Marshall Islands," *Asian Survey* 50, no. 6 (November/December 2010): 1189.

40. "Taiwan-Botswana Links," *Free China News*, August 5, 1968, 4. NRC, PMO-RALG, 8/2/03, File Ref. No. LGRD/N2/19, News from Free China (Formosa), 1968–71.

41. "Liberia's Gratitude," *Free China News*, August 26, 1968, 3. NRC, PMO-RALG, 8/2/03, File Ref. No. LGRD/N2/19, News from Free China (Formosa), 1968–71; Sim, "Taiwan and Africa," 22.

42. "Sino-African Relations," *Free China News*, November 3, 1969, 2. NRC, PMO-RALG, 8/2/03, File Ref. No. LGRD/N2/19, News from Free China (Formosa), 1968–71; Sim, "Taiwan and Africa," 20. "UNO Yaikataa China kwa Mara Nyingine," *Uhuru*, November 13, 1969, 1.

43. "Paucity of Doctors and Nurses," *Ghanaian Times*, May 14–20, 1967.

44. Li Anshan, "From 'How Could' to 'How Should': The Possibility of a Pilot U.S.-China Project in Africa," in *China's Emerging Global Health and Foreign Aid Engagement in Africa*, ed. Xiaoqing Lu Boyton (Washington, DC: Centre for Strategic and International Studies, CSIS, 2011); 41; Shuang et al., "China's Health Assistance to Africa," 1.

45. Peilong et al., "China's Distinctive Engagement in Global Health," 795.

46. Ten African countries which received the CMTs by 1971 include Algeria, Zanzibar, Somalia, Congo-Brazzaville, Mali, Tanzania, Mauritania, Guinea, Sudan, and Equatorial Guinea. See Global Health Strategies initiatives (GHSi), *Shifting Paradigm: How the BRICS Are Reshaping Global Health and Development* (2012), 64; Li, *Chinese Medical Cooperation in Africa*, 7–11.

47. Li, *Chinese Medical Cooperation in Africa*, 12; Taylor, "Taiwan's Foreign Policy and Africa," 126.

48. Li, *Chinese Medical Cooperation in Africa*, 12.

49. "Interests Impaired," *Free China News*, April 17, 1971, 1; "Rupture Healed," *Free China News*, August 5, 1968, 4. NRC, PMO-RALG, 8/2/03, File Ref. No. LGRD/N2/19, News from Free China (Formosa), 1968–71.

50. Premier Zhou Enlai declared the Eight Principles for Economic and Technical Aid in Ghana on January 15, 1964. See *Afro-Asian Solidarity against Imperialism: A Collection of Documents, Speeches and Press Interviews from the Visits of Chinese Leaders to Thirteen African and Asian Countries* (Peking: Foreign Languages Press, 1964), 149.

51. See, for instance, Moyo, *Dead Aid*, 109.

52. "Speech by the Honourable Oscar S. Kambona, M. P. Minister of External Affairs and Defense, Chairman of the Tanganyika Delegation on Monday October 7, 1963, to the Eighteenth Session of the General Assembly," TNA. Acc. No. 469, Ministry of Commerce and Industries, File No. CIC 70/12 Speeches-Material, 1962–64, 6.

53. "Madaktari Zaidi toka China Watakuja," *Uhuru*, Mei 7, 1968, 1, also see "China Yasaidia Tanzania Dawa na Madaktari," *Ngurumo*, May 7, 1968, 1; John Iliffe, *East African Doctors: A History of the Modern Profession* (UK: Cambridge University Press, 1998), 119.

54. Health Department of the Shandong Province, *The Chinese Medical-Aid Team in the United Republic of Tanzania* (Shandong, 1998), 6 & 117.

55. "Chinese Medical Assistance to Tanzania, May 12, 1972," TNA. Acc. No. 450, Ministry of Health, File No. HEA/90/5 Technical Assistance China; "Dar to have a Vaccine Plant, Government Moves to Combat Smallpox, Tuberculosis," *The Nationalist*, August 22, 1970, 8; Marcelino Komba, "Tanzania Takes a Step towards Self-Reliance in Drugs," *The Nationalist*, May 4, 1971, 3.

56. "Vote at U. N. 'Not against China,'" *Sunday News*, January 7, 1962, 1; "Tanganyika Foreign Policy," TNA. Acc. No. 593, Orodha ya Majalada Idara ya Habari, File No. CA/6/1, Tanganyika Foreign Service, 1961–1964; Slawecki, "The two China's in Africa," 400.

57. "Speech by the Honourable Oscar S. Kambona, M. P. Minister of External Affairs and Defense Chairman, Chairman of the Tanganyika Delegation on Monday October 7, 1963, to the Eighteenth Session of the General Assembly," TNA. Acc. No. 469, Ministry of Commerce and Industries, File No. CIC 70/12 Speeches-Material, 1962–64, 10–11.

58. "Sino-Tanzania Joint Communique," *Peking Review* 18, no. 9 (February 26, 1965): 10.

59. Guido Magome, "Self-Reliance Makes Stronger and Faster Pace," *Daily News*, February 1, 1978, 5–6; Ai Ping, "From Proletarian Internationalism to Mutual Development: China's Cooperation with Tanzania, 1965–95," in *Agencies in Foreign Aid: Comparing China, Sweden and the United States in Tanzania*, ed. Goran Hyden and Rwekaza Mukandala (New York: St. Martin's Press, 1999), 173.

60. "U.N. Weak without China," *The Nationalist*, October 25, 1969, 1, also see "Nyerere Aisalimu U.N.O," *Uhuru*, Oktoba 25, 1969, 1.

61. Julius K. Nyerere, *Freedom and Development/ Uhuru na Maendeleo: A Selection from Writings and Speeches, 1968–1973* (Dar es Salaam: Oxford University Press, 1973), 205.

62. Nyerere, *Freedom and Development*, 205–206.

63. "Chinese Medical Assistance to Tanzania, May 12, 1972," TNA. Acc. No. 450, Ministry of Health, File No. HEA/90/5 Technical Assistance China; Jamie Monson, *Africa's Freedom Railway: How a Chinese Development Project Changed Lives and Livelihoods in Tanzania* (Bloomington, USA: Indiana University Press, 2009), 3.

64. "Another Bid to Admit China," *The Nationalist*, November 9, 1968, 2.

65. Sim, "Taiwan and Africa," 20.

66. Stanton Jue, "Triangular Relations between US, China and Taiwan," *American Journal of Chinese Studies* 23, no. 2 (October 2016): VI; J. Bruce Jacobs, "One China Diplomatic Isolation and a Separate Taiwan," in *China Rise, Taiwan's Dilemmas and International Peace*, ed. Edward Friedman (New York: Routledge, 2006), 89.

67. "US Soft Over Peking's Seat at UN," *The Nationalist*, November 14, 1970, 2.

68. "A Victory for World's People, Crushing Defeat for U.S. Imperialism," *Peking Review*, no. 44, October 29, 1971, 6; David H. Shinn and Joshua Eisenman, "Evolving Principles and Guiding Concepts: How China Gains African Support for Its Core National Interests," *Orbis 64, Issue 2* (Spring 2020): 281; Pasha L. Hsieh, "The Taiwan Question and the One-China Policy: Legal Challenges with Renewed Momentum," *Die Friedens-Warte* 84, no. 3 (2009): 59.

69. Rwekaza Mukandala, "From Proud Defiance to Beggary: A Recipient's Tale," in *Agencies in Foreign Aid: Comparing China, Sweden and the United States in Tanzania*, ed. Goran Hyden and Rwekaza Mukandala (New York: St. Martin's Press, 1999), 47; Martin Bailey, "Tanzania and China," *African Affairs* 74, no. 294 (Jan. 1975): 48.

BIBLIOGRAPHY

"A Victory for World's People, Crushing Defeat for U.S. Imperialism." *Peking Review* 14, no. 44, October 29, 1971.

"African States Split on Chinese Entry." *The Standard*, November 29, 1967.

Afro-Asian Solidarity against Imperialism: A Collection of Documents, Speeches and Press Interviews from the Visits of Chinese Leaders to Thirteen African and Asian Countries. Peking: Foreign Languages Press, 1964.

Ai, Ping. "From Proletarian Internationalism to Mutual Development: China's Cooperation with Tanzania, 1965–95." In *Agencies in Foreign Aid: Comparing China, Sweden and the United States in Tanzania*, edited by Goran Hyden and Rwekaza Mukandala, 156–201. New York: St. Martin's Press, 1999.

"Another Bid to Admit China." *The Nationalist*, November 9, 1968.

Bailey, Martin. "Tanzania and China." *African Affairs* 74, no. 294 (January 1975): 39–50.

Bjerk, Paul. *Building a Peaceful Nation: Julius Nyerere and the Establishment of Sovereignty in Tanzania, 1960–1964.* New York: University of Rochester Press, 2015.

Brautigam, Debora. *Will Africa Feed China?* New York: Oxford University Press, 2015.

Chien, Shiuh-shen, Tzu-po Yang, and Yi-chen Wu. "Taiwan's Foreign Aid and Technical Assistance in the Marshall Islands." *Asian Survey* 50, no. 6 (November/December 2010): 1184–1204.

"China's Conditions on UN Membership 'Unacceptable.'" *The Standard*, November 23, 1967.

"China Yasaidia Tanzania Dawa na Madaktari." *Ngurumo*, May 7, 1968.

Chinese Medical Cooperation in Africa: With Special Emphasis on the Medical Teams and Anti-Malaria Campaign. Uppsala: Nordiska Afrikainstitutet, 2011.

"Dar to Have a Vaccine Plant, Government Moves to Combat Smallpox, Tuberculosis." *The Nationalist*, August 22, 1970.

Easterly, William. *The Whiteman's Burden: Why the West's Efforts to Aid the Rest Have Done So Much Ill and So Little Good.* New York: The Penguin Press, 2006.

Edwards, Sebastian. *Toxic Aid: Economic Collapse and Recovery in Tanzania.* United Kingdom: Oxford University Press, 2014.

"From 'How Could' to 'How Should': The Possibility of a Pilot U.S.-China Project in Africa." In *China's Emerging Global Health and Foreign Aid Engagement in Africa*, edited by Xiaoqing Lu Boyton, 37–46. Washington, DC: Centre for Strategic and International Studies, CSIS, 2011.

Global Health Strategies Initiatives (GHSi). *Shifting Paradigm: How the BRICS Are Reshaping Global Health and Development*, 2012.

Hasan, A. D. "China and Non-Alignment." *India International Centre Quarterly* 3, no. 3 (July 1976): 65–67.

Health Department of the Shandong Province. *The Chinese Medical-Aid Team in the United Republic of Tanzania.* Shandong, 1998.

Hsiao-pong, Philip Liu. "Planting Rice on the Roof of the UN Building: Analyzing Taiwan's 'Chinese' Techniques in Africa, 1961–Present." *The China Quarterly*, no. 198 (June 2009): 381–400.

Hsieh, Pasha L. "The Taiwan Question and the One-China Policy: Legal Challenges with Renewed Momentum." *Die Friedens-Warte* 84, no. 3 (2009): 59–81.

Iliffe, John. *East African Doctors: A History of the Modern Profession*. Cambridge: Cambridge University Press, 1998.

Jacobs, Bruce J. "One China Diplomatic Isolation and a Separate Taiwan." In *China Rise, Taiwan's Dilemmas and International Peace*, edited by Edward Friedman, 85–109. New York: Routledge, 2006.

Jue, Stanton. "Triangular Relations between US, China and Taiwan." *American Journal of Chinese Studies* 23, no. 2 (October 2016): V–IX.

Killeen, Olivia J., Alissa Davis, Joseph D. Tucker, and Benjamin Mason Meir. "Chinese Global Health Diplomacy in Africa: Opportunities and Challenges." *Global Health Governance* 12, no. 2 (Fall 2018): 4–29.

Komba, Marcelino. "Tanzania Takes a Step towards Self-Reliance in Drugs." *The Nationalist*, May 4, 1971.

Lal, Priyal. *African Socialism in Postcolonial Tanzania: Between the Village and the World*. New York: Cambridge University Press, 2015.

Lancaster, Carol. *Aid to Africa: So Much to Do, So Little Done*. London: The University of Chicago Press, 1999.

Larkin, Bruce D. *China and Africa, 1949–1970*. Berkeley, CA: University of California Press, 1973.

Li, Anshan. "China-Africa Medical Cooperation: Another form of Humanitarian Aid." Accessed May 1, 2016. http://www.doctorswithoutborders.org/china-africa -medical-cooperation-another-form-humanitarian-aid.

Lin, Shuang, Liangmin Gao, Melissa Reyes, Feng Cheng, Joan Kaufman, and Wafaa M. El-Sadr. "China's Health Assistance to Africa: Opportunism or Altruism?" *Globalization and Health* (2016): 1–5. https://doi.org/10.1186/s12992 -016-0217-1.

Liu, Peilong, Yan Guo, Xu Qian, Shenglan Tang, Zhihui Li, and Lincoln Chen. "China's Distinctive Engagement in Global Health." *Lancet* 308 (August 2014): 793–804.

"Madaktari Zaidi toka China Watakuja." *Uhuru*, Mei 7, 1968.

Madsen, Robert A. "The Struggle for Sovereignty between China and Taiwan." In *Problematic Sovereignty: Contested Rules and Political Possibilities*, edited by Stephen D. Krasner, 141–193. New York: Columbia University Press, 2001.

Magome, Guido. "Self-Reliance Makes Stronger and Faster Pace." *Daily News*, February 1, 1978.

Manthorpe, Jonathan. *Forbidden Nation: A History of Taiwan*. New York: Palgrave Macmillan, 2005.

Marley, Faye. "Cold War of Health." *The Science News-Letter* 84, no. 3 (July 20, 1963): 35.

Ministry of Foreign Affairs. *The Republic of Indonesia, Final Communique of the Asian-African Conference of Bandung*, April 24, 1955.

Monson, Jamie. *Africa's Freedom Railway: How a Chinese Development Project Changed Lives and Livelihoods in Tanzania.* Bloomington: Indiana University Press, 2009.

Moyo, Dambisa. *Dead Aid: Why Aid Is Not Working and How There Is a Better Way for Africa.* United States: Farrar, Straus and Giroux, 2009.

Mukandala, Rwekaza. "From Proud Defiance to Beggary: A Recipient's Tale." In *Agencies in Foreign Aid: Comparing China, Sweden and the United States in Tanzania,* edited by Goran Hyden and Rwekaza Mukandala, 31–67. New York: St. Martin's Press, 1999.

NRC. PMO-RALG, 8/2/03. File Ref. No. LGRD/N2/19. News from Free China (Formosa), 1968–71.

"Nyerere Aisalimu U.N.O." *Uhuru,* Oktoba 25, 1969.

Nyerere, Julius K. *Freedom and Development/Uhuru na Maendeleo: A Selection from Writings and Speeches, 1968–1973.* Dar es Salaam: Oxford University Press, 1973.

"Paucity of Doctors and Nurses." *Ghanaian Times,* May 14–20, 1967.

Permanent Secretariat of the Afro-Asian Peoples' Solidarity Organizations. *Afro-Asian Peoples Solidarity Movement.* Cairo.

PRC. FMA 207-00021-01, 1-2.

PRC. FMA 207-00018-01, 1-4.

Roberts, George. "Politics, Decolonization, and the Cold War in Dar es Salaam c. 1965–72." PhD Thesis, University of Warwick, 2016.

Shinn, David H. "China-Africa Ties in Historical Context." In *China-Africa and an Economic Transformation,* edited by Arkebe Oqubay and Justin Yifu Lin, 61–83. London: Oxford University Press, 2019.

Shinn, David H., and Joshua Eisenman. "Evolving Principles and Guiding Concepts: How China Gains African Support for Its Core National Interests." *Orbis* 64, no. 2 (Spring 2020): 271–288.

Sim, Yawsoon. "Taiwan and Africa." *Africa Today* 18, no. 3 (July 1971): 20–24.

"Sino-Tanzania Joint Communique." *Peking Review* 18, no. 9, February 26, 1965.

Skidmore, Natasha. "Taiwanese Development Aid in Africa." *SAIIA Report,* no. 43 (2002): 1–22.

Slawecki, Leon M. S. "The Two Chinas in Africa." *Foreign Affairs* 41, no. 2 (January 1963): 398–409.

Taylor, Ian. "Taiwan's Foreign Policy and Africa: The Limitations of Dollar Diplomacy." *Journal of Contemporary China* 11, no. 30 (2002): 125–140.

The Chinese-African People's Friendship Association. *The Chinese People Resolutely Support the Just Struggle of the African People.* Peking: Foreign Languages Press, 1961.

TNA. Acc. No. 450. Ministry of Health. File No. HEA/90/5. Technical Assistance China.

TNA. Acc. No. 469. Ministry of Commerce and Industries. File No. CIC 70/12 Speeches-Material, 1962–64.

TNA. Acc. No. 593. Orodha ya Majalada Idara ya Habari. File No. CA/6/1. Tanganyika Foreign Service, 1961–1964.

"U.N. Weak without China." *The Nationalist*, Saturday, October 25, 1969.

"UNO Yaikataa China kwa Mara Nyingine." *Uhuru*, November 13, 1969.

"US Soft Over Peking's Seat at UN." *The Nationalist*, November 14, 1970.

"Vote at U. N. 'Not against China.'" *Sunday News*, January 7, 1962.

Yu, George T., and David J. Longenecker. "The Beijing-Taipei Struggle for International Recognition: From the Niger Affair to the UN." *Asian Survey* 34, no. 5 (May 1994): 475–488.

Zeleza, Tiyambe. "Dancing with Dragon: Africa's Courtship With China." *The Global South* 2, no. 2 (Fall 2008): 171–187.

Chapter 12

Rereading Nigeria-Taiwan Affairs

Alternatives to Sino-Centric Narratives

Abdul-Gafar Tobi Oshodi, Jeremiah Chigozie Anakor, and Oluwasola Obisesan

INTRODUCTION

On January 12, 2017, a *Reuters* report opened with this intro: "Taiwan objected on Thursday to an 'unreasonable' Nigerian request to move its representative office out of the capital Abuja, a day after China announced plans to invest a further $40 billion in the African country."[1] The report was accompanied by a picture taken a day earlier, where the Nigerian president, Muhammadu Buhari, was seen shaking hands with Zhou Pingjian, Chinese ambassador to Nigeria, while China's foreign minister Wang Yi looked on. The *Reuters* report added that the "protest highlighted Taiwan's frustration with Beijing's use of diplomatic and economic power to isolate it internationally."[2] While the report echoes a dominant view, such Sino-centric narratives are not only popular in news media but also in academic literature—a fixation that is not unique to Nigeria-China-Taiwan discourse. Over the past fifty years, the deepening Africa-China relations have coincided with a decline in Africa-Taiwan relations. Academic literature and popular media have often located this complex dialectical shift within a troubling but simplistic binary. The binary: that China's growing economic importance in Africa has led to the gradual decline in the recognition of Taiwan on the continent. This dominant (Sino-centric) narrative suggests that Africa's shift in favor of China (and against Taiwan) can only be solely propelled by the latter's relative weakness vis-à-vis what we discuss here as "China's development diplomacy" marked by large projects, loans, and investments on the continent. But while economic considerations are crucial for understanding the shift, they are nonetheless not the only considerations.

The aforementioned Sino-centric fixation and the neglect of other equally important explanations nonetheless raise salient interconnected questions. First, it challenges the (extent of) agency of African states—or at least reduces it to mere *economic*—in their responses to China's national question (i.e., whether there are one or two Chinas). Second, the dominance of the aforementioned Sino-centric narrative underlies the deep-seated nature and assumptions of broader Africa-China scholarship. Using the example of Nigeria, we discuss some alternative arguments for the shift from Taiwan to China. Building on an earlier op-ed entitled "Nigeria-Taiwan Row: Understanding China's Influence in Africa," written in the University of Nottingham's *Taiwan Insight*,[3] our intervention draws attention to the often-neglected alternative narratives to explain an African country's shift to China. In our chapter, we argue that there are alternative explanations for a shift in Nigeria's response to the Chinese national question. We adopt a critical theoretical approach to tease out some latent explanations for the shifts in Nigeria-Taiwan affairs. For us, critical theory essentially is about emancipation in our understanding and interpretation of global affairs,[4] in this case, Nigeria's shift from Taiwan to recognizing China. But our operationalization of emancipation is not only in the arena of empowering the weak but also challenging dominant histories and knowledge systems. By drawing attention to alternative explanations in Nigeria, we aim to contribute to an emerging discourse about Africa's agency and dormant Afro-centric views in broader Africa-China relations.

Structurally, the rest of our chapter is divided into four sections. The next section provides a general sketch of Africa's shift(s) in recognition from Taiwan to China as the representative of the Chinese people. This is followed by a focus on the Nigerian case, a section that precedes the main section that discusses five alternative arguments for why Nigeria shifted from Taiwan to China. This is followed by a conclusion.

BRIEF COMMENTARY ON AFRICA'S SHIFTS FROM TAIWAN TO CHINA

China's presence in Africa, though can be traced to the precolonial era, has generated significant interest in the last twenty years. While some have challenged the long-term benefits of Africa-China relations to the African continent, others have warned about China's colonization of the continent.[5] For the

West (i.e., the United States and Western Europe), China is viewed as a rising power that can impact their strategic interest and relevance, that is, a strategic threat.[6] China's importance in Africa is linked to the former's continuing visibility in development finance on the continent: a reality we will discuss as "China's development diplomacy." This diplomacy, in turn, is at the center of the Sino-centric narrative of Taiwan's decline in Africa.

Prior to 1971, Taiwan was considered by many African countries as the representative of the Chinese people. But China's economic development support for Africa began in the heat of the Cold War. Blending a nationalistic economy with ideological solidarity, China began to be perceived as a formidable partner among the new African leaders. Although it has been observed that Chinese diplomacy in the 1960s shifted from indirect to direct support for liberation movements and frontline states in Africa,[7] its contemporary manifestation has taken a strong economic dimension often tied to the One-China Policy. Given the increasing visibility of Chinese-built roads, airports, railways, and other projects in many African countries amid Taiwan's decline, it is somewhat assumed that China's economic trade and collaborative developmental arrangement is the single bullet that sets in motion the receding Africa-Taiwan relations. It is thus popularly argued that African countries that accept Beijing's One-China Policy have access to Beijing-backed large construction projects, loans, and other development assistance.

If Chinese development diplomacy—or what some describe as "checkbook diplomacy"[8]—is the sole driver for Africa's shift to recognizing China, then it appears that this has worked, given the number of countries that have switched from Taiwan. Taiwan's recognition has reduced to one country: Eswatini, a tiny kingdom in South Africa, formerly referred to as Swaziland. Yet, while this may be construed to be the case, in reality, the history of the switch from Taiwan to China is not always one way. There have been shifts, switches, and re-recognitions. For instance, while some African countries have retained their shift to either Taiwan or China over a long period, others have flip-flopped. Burkina Faso switched its allegiance to China in 1973, switched back to Taiwan in 1994, and back to China in 2018,[9] and "nine African countries have recognized Taiwan more than once, two of which—the Central African Republic (CAR) and Liberia—have switched between Beijing and Taipei three times."[10] Despite these instabilities, China's rise and growing presence in Africa has coincided with the switch away from Taiwan on the continent.

Mono-causal economic Sino-centric narrative of Taiwan's decline in Africa has been challenged. For instance, some submit that such a narrative is fixated on economic development and represents an incomplete account of Africa-Taiwan's downsized relations in that other intersectional variables explain the dwindling foreign relations of Taiwan and incremental recognition of China in Africa.[11] Ndzendze highlighted the role of African democratization (liberal elections and its politicking), China's solid economic aid, developmental soft power, and Taiwan's stagnated economic ability as some of the core reasons for the decline in Taiwan recognitions on the continent.[12] In this context, he explains how seven countries, namely Liberia, the Gambia, Chad, Burkina Faso, Malawi, São Tomé and Príncipe, and Senegal, were expediently confronted by electoral waves in their decisions toward resigning their recognition from Taiwan. Besides, the inability of Taiwan to meet the developmental aid aspirations of these countries did count. Further, the need for political backing at the UN, especially for countries such as Liberia, Burkina Faso, and the Gambia which faced electoral pressure-related cases, influenced their switch of interests. Such political moves become more tangible than the materialistic consideration in the survival game and politics of acceptance at the international level.

Others have noted that "peer pressure"—and not just "checkbook diplomacy"—influenced Burkina Faso, a country that has switched away from both Taiwan and China, latest decision to switch from Taiwan to China in 2018.[13] As Burcu and Bertrand put it, Burkina Faso was motivated by "growing peer pressure"—a year after the government rejected a $50 billion incentive to do so.[14] The pressure came from neighboring Sahelian countries (i.e., Chad, Mali, Mauritania, and Niger) who had set up, in conjunction with Burkina Faso, the G5 Sahel Joint Force in July 2017. China was willing to support the force, but in a roundtable in Brussels in February 2018, Beijing's delegate reportedly made it clear that China "cannot fund the G5 Sahel because of Burkina's presence."[15] A few months after the Brussels event, Burkina Faso switched from Taiwan to China again. Our intervention is therefore not the first to draw attention to noneconomic alternative arguments for the switch by African countries to China.

NIGERIA-TAIWAN RELATIONSHIP AND CHINA

In the case of Nigeria and many African countries, the first major shift from Taiwan to China followed a 1971 decision in the UN, where countries in Africa and others supported a resolution to accept China as the representative of the Chinese people. With this recognition, China became a member of the UN's Security Council, displacing Taiwan on many other UN-backed sub-organizations. Prior to that period, Nigeria recognized Taiwan as influenced by its pro-West foreign policy. Nigeria-Taiwan trade relations can be traced to the activities of Taiwanese traders in the 1960s in the southeastern region of Nigeria, especially Nnewi.[16] Some have argued that China had backed the Biafran forces against the federal government's forces during the Nigerian Civil War (1967–1970).[17]

But that Taiwan was dumped in favor of China must not be construed to mean that all contacts and relations with Taiwan were jettisoned. Nigeria-Taiwan trade continued years after the recognition of China. For example, trade volume between Nigeria and Taiwan reached "788 million USD in 2014, 195 million USD in 2015, 363 million USD in 2016, and 460 million USD in 2017, 290 million USD in 2018."[18] As presented in table 12.1, there were occasions when the destination for Nigeria's crude oil was more to Taiwan than China. For instance, Nigeria's crude oil export to Taiwan surpassed those to China in some years between 2000 and 2011.[19] The news report in 2017, about the row between Nigeria and Taiwan,[20] further demonstrates the enduring Nigeria-Taiwan trade. The row was caused by the decision of Muhammadu Buhari's administration in Nigeria to direct the Taiwan Trade Office in Abuja to leave the country's capital—but not closing it to business in the country as a whole. The aforementioned 2017 row strongly illustrates the enduring Nigeria-Taiwan exchanges despite the recognition of China as the representative of the Chinese people.

Given that the One-China Policy is accepted by successive Nigerian governments since 1971, the 2017 Nigeria-Taiwan row and how it was quietly resolved raise two important points. First, Nigeria, in reality, pursues a policy of accommodation—but not recognition—of Taiwan. It is this accommodation that has made Nigeria the third trading country of Taiwan in Africa after "Angola and South Africa."[21] The Trade Office was established in Lagos in April 1991, moved to Abuja in 2001, and relocated in 2017 following the row. Second, the context within which the 2017 row took place seems to buttress the Sino-centric narrative of Nigeria's shift from Taiwan to China. The dominant justification and discourse in the media focused on China's development diplomacy. This is usually hinged on China's visibility in Nigeria's development: ranging from the large infrastructure projects that include roads, railways, rehabilitation of airports to loans.[22] This is particularly hinged on the fact that Nigeria's decision to expel the Taiwan Trade Office in Abuja came against the background of a widely reported high-level Chinese visit. The 2017 relocation order coincided with the visit of Wang Yi, Chinese foreign minister, who had reportedly promised Nigeria a $40 billion investment.[23] It is also important to mention that Nigeria's decision happened within a broader context where Beijing considered the emergence of Tsai Ing-wen's pro-independence Democratic Progressive Party government in 2016 in Taipei as a threat to its One-China Policy. Nonetheless, the 2017 row was an episodic experience that must be located within the broader epochal considerations that explain Nigeria's shift from Taiwan to China. This is the focus of the next section.

Table 12.1   Nigeria Crude Oil Exports by Destination (in Million Barrels)[a]

Year	1999	2000	2001	2002	2003	2004	2005	2006	2007	2008	2009	2010	2011	2012	2013	2014
China	6	5	7	2	3	8	9	1	5	0.9	8	12	4	7	7	11
Taiwan	5	12	10	7	8	7	–	0.9	3	–	0.9	9		0.9	0.9	0.9

Source: Dele Seteolu and Abdul-Gafar Tobi Oshodi, 2017. Reprinted by permission from Springer Nature: *Journal of Chinese Political Science.*
[a]Reprinted by permission from Springer Nature: [Springer Nature] [*Journal of Chinese Political Science*] [(Oscillation of Two Giants: Sino-Nigeria Relations and the Global South, Seteolu, D., Oshodi, AG.T.) J OF CHIN POLIT SCI 23, 257–285 (2018). https://doi.org/10.1007/s11366-016-9453-8], Copyright © Spring Nature (2017).

ALTERNATIVE ARGUMENTS FOR
NIGERIA'S SHIFT TO CHINA

The fixation on Sino-centric analysis of China in Africa is strong but it remains limited. Inadvertently, it limits the space for unpacking and reimagining the agency of African actors, thereby eliminating alternative arguments. In the case of Nigeria's shift from Taiwan to China, at least five alternative reasons are offered. The five alternative arguments include: (i) those linked to the Biafran Civil War and Nigeria's first shift, (ii) legacies of military rule, (iii) persistence and dictates of Nigeria's national question, (iv) Pan-African ideals, and (v) extended pragmatism. The five are not necessarily mutually exclusive in that some can reinforce the other. Most importantly, they are offered not as replacements for the Sino-centric economic narrative discussed in the second section but to complement the economic perspective on Nigeria's switch with China and Taiwan.

First, Nigeria experienced a bloody civil war which was fought over the continued unity of the country. Given this background, recognizing Taiwan over China would have meant that Africa's most populous country supports an outcome (i.e., secession) that it fought against back home. How will a country that just survived its own civil war support the outcome of another civil war elsewhere within a short end to its own? Simply put, it is difficult for a country that fought for the unity of its territory to support a supposedly "breakaway" region in China. To further underscore the difficult circumstances within which Nigeria made its shift from Taiwan to China, the UN resolution happened in 1971, one year after the official end of the Biafran Civil War. Besides, the question of secession or separatism in Nigeria is still active with the pressures of the Indigenous Peoples of Biafra (IPOB), led by Nnamdi Kanu, whose group the government declared illegal and branded as a terrorist group.

A second argument for Nigeria's shift to Taiwan is linked to the country's military past. Between October 1960 when it had its independence from British rule and February 2021, Nigeria has had fifteen governments, eight of which were military regimes. Between 1971 when Nigeria joined other African countries in recognizing China and May 1999, which marked the beginning of the country's Fourth Republic, there were seven different military regimes. Taiwan is a democratic country with a close relationship with the United States, while China operated a Communist Party dominant system with a noninterference foreign policy that suited the military. Indeed, when the United States and its allies pressurized Nigeria to democratize in the 1990s, General Sani Abacha's military regime responded by approaching China for development assistance and international support.[24] In addition to sticking to the One-China Policy, it was under General Abacha that the Nigerian-Chinese Chamber of Commerce was formed to improve bilateral relations. In 1995, the Abacha regime signed an agreement with the China Civil Engineering Construction Corporation (CCECC), a company that will become a major player in the Nigerian construction sector, for the rehabilitation of the Nigerian Railways and the supply of coaches at a cost of 529 million USD. In May 1997, Abacha also played host to the highest-ranking Chinese official to visit in recent times, Li Peng, a former Premier of the State Council.[25]

If the democratic peace theory suggests that democratic countries tend to have a friendly relation and do not often go to war against each other,[26] then the argument could be made that China's foreign policy offers noninterference in the domestic affairs of Nigeria during military regimes that were compatible to both parties. There appears to be no added incentive for a military regime like Abacha's to discard China for a democratic Taiwan. Aside from representing an alternative source of development support to the West, switching to China offers Nigeria under the Abacha military regime the support of a Permanent Member of the UN's Security Council.

The third argument for Nigeria's switch to—and continued recognition of—China is not mutually excluded from the first point that stems from the civil war: that is, the persistence of Nigeria's national question, a question that is marked by "contestations over statehood and citizenship"[27] and represented

Table 12.2   Heads of State and Their Tenure in Nigeria[a]

Head of State	Regime Type	Duration of Tenure
Tafawa Balewa	Civilian	October 1960–January 1966
Johnson Aguiyi-Ironsi	Military	January 1966–July 1966
Yakubu Gowon	Military	July 1966–July 1975
Murtala Muhammed	Military	July 1975–February 1976
Olusegun Obasanjo Military	Military	February 1976–October 1979
Shehu Shagari	Civilian	October 1979–December 1983
Muhammadu Buhari	Military	December 1983–August 1985
Ibrahim Babangida	Military	August 1985–August 1993
Ernest Shonekan	Civilian	August 1993–November 1993
Sani Abacha	Military	November 1993–June 1998
Abdulsalami Abubakar	Military	June 1998–May 1999
Olusegun Obasanjo	Civilian	May 1999–May 2007
Umaru Yar Adua	Civilian	May 2007–May 2010
Goodluck Jonathan	Civilian	May 2010–May 2015
Muhammadu Buhari	Civilian	May 2015 till date

Source: Dele Seteolu and Abdul-Gafar Tobi Oshodi, 2017. Reprinted by permission from Springer Nature: *Journal of Chinese Political Science*.
[a]Reprinted by permission from Springer Nature: [Springer Nature] [*Journal of Chinese Political Science*] [(Oscillation of Two Giants: Sino-Nigeria Relations and the Global South, Seteolu, D., Oshodi, AG.T.) J OF CHIN POLIT SCI 23, 257–285 (2018). https://doi.org/10.1007/s11366-016-9453-8], Copyright © Spring Nature (2017).

by "challenge of nation-building."[28] Like China, Nigeria is faced with centrifugal forces that seek to secede from the federation. In China, Taiwan is considered a breakaway region, and the Tibet question persists.[29] In Nigeria, although the country survived a civil war and still exists as a single multiethnic country, the challenge of nation-building has been an ongoing and stubborn one. The Biafran question that led to the 1967–1970 war has not yet been resolved and new groups such as IPOB still struggle for the creation of the Biafran State.[30] To address its nation-building challenges, Nigeria has implemented several policies and programs such as the introduction of national service programs, unity schools for multiethnic mixing, a federal character in appoints to public offices, among others.[31] A country grappling with its own nation-building challenges and centrifugal agitations will arguably not be in the best position to support a breakaway region in other countries. Managers of the Nigerian state will thus arguably find supporting Taiwan difficult at least because China could respond by doing the same to secessionist group(s) within Nigeria, as was suspected during the Biafran Civil War.[32]

The fourth reason for Nigeria's shift to China is based on the country's Pan-African ideals. For many years, Africa had been the centerpiece of Nigeria's foreign policy. It would have been contradictory for the country's foreign policy to have taken a position different from other African countries on the question of the recognition of China. The majority of African countries voted to recognize China as the representative of the Chinese people in the UN. To have taken a different position would have meant that Nigeria went against the position of many of the African countries. Although the Sino-centric argument is based on the strength of China's development diplomacy in Africa (and in this case Nigeria), it must be recalled that Nigeria's shift to China happened in a period when Nigeria-China trade was relatively minimal compared to what it has become post-2000. In any case, the example of Burkina Faso, a relatively smaller economy than Nigeria, exemplifies how checkbook diplomacy can be entangled with consideration for neighbors in the switch from Taiwan to China. China is recognized by all countries in the Economic Community of West African States that Nigeria belongs to, and almost all countries in Africa except Eswatini.

A fifth argument—and an extension of the country's Pan-African decision to recognize China and not Taiwan—is extended pragmatism. Nigeria is a pivotal country in Africa, but it is located in a West African subregion with neighboring countries with a significant Chinese presence. To stick with Taiwan against other neighboring countries would not have been strategic as the country will be excluded from platform—an important African countries platform, the Forum on China-Africa Cooperation (FOCAC). Needless to reiterate the important position of FOCAC in China's Africa relations.[33]

CONCLUSION

In this chapter, we drew attention to important but neglected dimensions of China's rise and Taiwan's decline in Nigeria, Africa's most populous country. We highlighted five alternative arguments: that is, relating to (i) the Biafran Civil War, (ii) legacies of military rule, (iii) persistence of Nigeria's national question, (iv) Pan-Africanism, and (v) extended pragmatism. Having discussed the five alternative narratives, our conclusion is twofold. First, the five narratives must be understood as an attempt to provide other justification for why Nigeria has continued to recognize China and not Taiwan. They are not exhaustive in that other narratives could still be investigated further and added. For instance, China's soft power bureaucratization successes in Nigeria as one of the justifications of Nigeria's continuous recognition of the country as the representative of the Chinese people are often uncaptured in the discourse, as is the case with the broader Africa-China relations. Yet, China's growing power and influence in Africa has garnered success in the perception of competence at the bureaucratic level. China is not only seen as a partner but also one which delivers on its words in the bureaucratic corridor. The extent to which this bureaucratic support for China in Nigeria persists over time is a worthwhile subject of future research. In the case of Nigeria, the role of specialized government institutions and the broader foreign policy bureaucracy—like the Ministry of Foreign Affairs and the Nigerian Institute of International Affairs (NIIA) established in 1961 to provide "a nursery of ideas on what direction Nigeria should take on international affairs"[34]—need to be captured in our analysis of why Nigeria recognizes China and not Taiwan. Interestingly, to deepen Nigeria-China relations, in 1978 the NIIA initiated a Dialogue Series with Chinese officials.[35] Thus, the unexploited agency of the personnel heads of government offices has not gone without its critics.[36]

Second, we are aware that the alternative arguments we highlight are not universal because African countries are confronted by differing local realities that might have impacted or continue to shape their recognition of China and not Taiwan. Although it is impossible to situate all five in all African countries, this consideration must not foreclose future investigations that go beyond the dominant economistic explanations in popular media. Regardless of the difficulty in generalizing the Nigerian example to other African countries, the alternative arguments discussed in this chapter nonetheless underscore the complexities of Africa-China relations. It serves as a reminder for scholars of the subject to further explore other possible considerations— beyond the economic—for why Africa has ditched Taiwan for China in virtually all countries in Africa. Our intervention contributes to challenging the fixation on economic matters as the sole driver of Nigeria-China relations. The main implication of our contribution to broader Africa-China scholarship is therefore to instigate a more complex explanation of why African states and actors have shifted from Taiwan to China.

NOTES

1. Reuters (2017). "Nigeria Trims Ties with Taiwan as It Courts China," 12 January, https://www.reuters.com/article/us-taiwan-nigeria-idUSKBN14W1BI

2. Ibid.

3. Oshodi, A.T. (2018). "Nigeria-Taiwan Row: Understanding China's Influence in Africa," *Taiwan Insight*, University of Nottingham, UK, 22 January, https://taiwaninsight.org/2018/01/22/nigeria-taiwan-row-understanding-chinas-influence-in-africa/

4. Ferreira, M.F. (2017). "Critical Theory." In: B. Mcglinchey, R. Walters, & C. Scheinpflug (eds.), *International Relations Theory*. Bristol: E-International Relations Publishing, pp. 49–55.

5. Oshodi, A.T. (2012a). "Colonialism or Post-colonial Recolonisation: A Comparative Analysis of British Colonialism and China's Presence in Post-colonial Africa." In: Joseph Mangut & Terhemba Wuam (eds.), *Colonialism and the Transition to Modernity in Africa*. Lapai: Ibrahim Badamasi Babangida University, pp. 767–790. See also Oshodi, A. T. (2012b). "Does China's Activities in Africa Mean Colonisation?" *The Constitution* 12(3), 1–54.

6. Sun, Yun & Olin-Ammentorp, Jane. (2014). "The US and China in Africa: Competition or Cooperation?" Bookings Institute, https://www.brookings.edu/blog/africa-in-focus/2014/04/28/the-us-and-china-in-africa-competition-or-cooperation/

7. Utomi, P. (2008). "China and Nigeria," Center for Strategic and International Studies, pp. 39–48, https://www.csis.org/analysis/china-nigeria

8. Burcu, O. & Bertrand, E. (2019). "Explaining China's Latest Catch in Africa," *The Diplomat*, 16 January, https://thediplomat.com/2019/01/explaining-chinas-latest-catch-in-africa/

9. Ibid.

10. Luedi, J. (2018). "Saying No to China in 2018: Taiwan's Last African Allies," Asia by Africa, 22 April, https://www.asiabyafrica.com/point-a-to-a/taiwan-allies-africa-burkina-faso

11. Ndzendze, B. (2020). "African Democratisation and the One China Policy," *E-International Relations*, 1–6.

12. Ibid.

13. Burcu and Bertrand, "Explaining China's Latest Catch in Africa."

14. Ibid.

15. Ibid.

16. Bräutigam, D. (2003). "Close Encounters: Chinese Business Networks as Industrial Catalysts in Sub-Saharan Africa," *African Affairs* 102(408), 447–467.

17. Ogunbadejo, O. (1976). "Nigeria and the Great Powers: The Impact of the Civil War on Nigerian Foreign Relations." *African Affairs* 75(298), 14–32; see also Diamond, S. (2007). "Who killed Biafra?" *Dialectical Anthropology* 31, 339–362.

18. See https://www.roc-taiwan.org/ng_en/post/5.html

19. Seteolu & Oshodi (2018). "Oscillation of two Giants: Sino-Nigeria Relations and the Global South."

20. Oshodi (2018). "Nigeria-Taiwan Row: Understanding China's Influence in Africa."

21. See https://www.roc-taiwan.org/ng_en/post/5.html

22. Seteolu & Oshodi (2018). "Oscillation of Two Giants: Sino-Nigeria Relations and the Global South."

23. Oshodi (2018). "Nigeria-Taiwan Row: Understanding China's Influence in Africa."

24. Udeala, S.O. (2010). "Nigeria-China Economic Relations under the South-South Cooperation." *African Journal of International Affairs* 13(1&2), 61–88. See also NIIA (2003). *Nigeria-China: Bilateral Ties in a New World Order – Proceedings of the Fourth Nigeria-China Dialogue on Foreign Policy.* Lagos: Nigerian Institute of International Affairs (NIIA).

25. Seteolu & Oshodi (2018). "Oscillation of Two Giants: Sino-Nigeria Relations and the Global South," 267.

26. Rousseau, D. L., Gelpi, C., Reiter, D., & Huth, P.K. (1996). "Assessing the Dyadic Nature of the Democratic Peace, 1918–1988."*American Political Science Review* 90(3), 512–533.

27. Osaghae, E. E. (2010). "Revisiting the Concept of State Fragility and State Building in Africa." In. S. Akinboye & M. M. Fadakinte (eds.), *Fifty Years of Nationhood? State, Society and Politics in Nigeria (1960–2010).* Lagos: Concept Publications, p. 113.

28. Obi, C. (2004). "Nigeria: Democracy on Trial." *Occasional Electronic Paper* 1. Uppsala, Sweden: Nordiska Afrikainstitutet, p. 9.

29. Crowe, D. (2013). "The 'Tibet Question': Tibetan, Chinese and Western Perspectives," *Nationalities Papers* 41(6), 1100–1135.

30. BBC (2021). "Nigerian Separatist Nnamdi Kanu's Facebook Account Removed for Hate Speech," 4 February, https://www.bbc.com/news/world-africa-55934277

31. Ukiwo, U. (2007). "Education, Horizontal Inequalities and Ethnic Relations in Nigeria." *International Journal of Educational Development* 27(3), 266–281. See also Ojo, E. (2009). *Mechanisms of National Integration in a Multi-ethnic Federal State: The Nigerian Experience.* Ibadan: John Archers.

32. Ogunbadejo, "Nigeria and the Great Powers," 14–32; see also Diamond, S. (2007). "Who Killed Biafra?" *Dialectical Anthropology* 31, 339–362.

33. Taylor, I. (2011). *Forum on China-Africa Cooperation (FOCAC).* London: Routledge. See also Grimm, S. (2012). "The Forum on China-Africa Cooperation (FOCAC) – Political Rationale and Functioning," *Policy Brief*, Centre for Chinese Studies (CCS), Stellenbosch University.

34. See https://niia.gov.ng/about-us/

35. Omoweh, D., O. Oche, & O. Agbu. (2005). *Nigeria and China: Bilateral Ties in a New World Order – The Fourth Nigeria-China Dialogue on Foreign Policy.* Lagos: NIIA.

36. Sun, Y. (2016). *African China's Foreign Policy*. Brookings: John L. Thomas China Centre and Africa Growth Initiative. See also Hanaeur, L & Morris, L. J. (2014). *Chinese Engagements in Africa*. RAND Corporations; and Utomi, P. (2008), "China and Nigeria," Center for Strategic and International Studies, pp. 39–48, https://www.csis.org/analysis/china-nigeria

BIBLIOGRAPHY

BBC. (2021). "Nigerian Separatist Nnamdi Kanu's Facebook Account Removed for Hate Speech." 4 February. https://www.bbc.com/news/world-africa-55934277.

Bräutigam, D. (2003). "Close Encounters: Chinese Business Networks as Industrial Catalysts in Sub-Saharan Africa." *African Affairs* 102(408): 447–467.

Burcu, O., and Bertrand, E. (2019). "Explaining China's Latest Catch in Africa." *The Diplomat*, 16 January. https://thediplomat.com/2019/01/explaining-chinas-latest-catch-in-africa/.

Carmody, P. (2011). *The New Scramble for Africa*. Cambridge: Polity Press.

Crowe, D. (2013). "The 'Tibet Question': Tibetan, Chinese and Western Perspectives." *Nationalities Papers* 41(6): 1100–1135.

Diamond, S. (2007). "Who Killed Biafra?" *Dialectical Anthropology* 31: 339–362.

Ferreira, M. F. (2017). "Critical Theory." In: Mcglinchey, B., Walters, R., and Scheinpflug, C. (Eds) *International Relations Theory*. Bristol: E-International Relations Publishing, pp. 49–55.

Grimm, S. (2012). "The Forum on China-Africa Cooperation (FOCAC)—Political Rationale and Functioning." *Policy Brief*. Centre for Chinese Studies (CCS), Stellenbosch University.

Hanaeur, L., and Morris, L. J. (2014). *Chinese Engagements in Africa*. RAND Corporations.

Ikebberry, G. (2010). "The Liberal International Order and Its Discontents." *Millennium: Journal of International Studies* 38(3): 509–521.

Luedi, J. (2018). "Saying no to China in 2018: Taiwan's Last African Allies." *Asia by Africa*, 22 April. https://www.asiabyafrica.com/point-a-to-a/taiwan-allies-africa-burkina-faso.

Ndzendze, B. (2020). "African Democratisation and the One China Policy." *E-International Relations*, pp. 1–6.

NIIA. (2003). *Nigeria-China: Bilateral Ties in a New World Order – Proceedings of the Fourth Nigeria-China Dialogue on Foreign Policy*. Lagos: NIIA.

Obi, C. (2004). "Nigeria: Democracy on Trial." *Occasional Electronic Paper 1*. Uppsala, Sweden: Nordiska Afrikainstitutet.

Ogunbadejo, O. (1976). "Nigeria and the Great Powers: The Impact of the Civil War on Nigerian Foreign Relations." *African Affairs* 75(298): 14–32.

Ogunbadejo, O. (1980). "Nigeria's Foreign Policy under Military Rule 1966–1979." *International Journal* 35(4): 748–765.

Ojo, E. (2009). *Mechanisms of National Integration in a Multi-Ethnic Federal State: The Nigerian Experience*. Ibadan: John Archers.

Omoweh, D., Oche, O., and Agbu, O. (2005). *Nigeria and China: Bilateral Ties in a New World Order – The Fourth Nigeria-China Dialogue on Foreign Policy.* Lagos: NIIA.

Osaghae, E. E. (2010). "Revisiting the Concept of State Fragility and State Building in Africa." In Akinboye, S., and Fadakinte, M. M. (Eds) *Fifty Years of Nationhood? State, Society and Politics in Nigeria (1960–2010).* Lagos: Concept Publications, pp. 75–131.

Oshodi, A. T. (2012a). "Colonialism or Post-Colonial Recolonisation: A Comparative Analysis of British Colonialism and China's Presence in Post-Colonial Africa." In Mangut, J., and Wuam, T. (Eds) *Colonialism and the Transition to Modernity in Africa.* Lapai: Ibrahim Badamasi Babangida University, pp. 767–790.

Oshodi, A. T. (2012b). "Does China's Activities in Africa Mean Colonisation?" *The Constitution* 12(3): 1–54.

Oshodi, A. T. (2018). "Nigeria-Taiwan Row: Understanding China's Influence in Africa." *Taiwan Insight,* University of Nottingham, UK, 22 January. https://taiwaninsight.org/2018/01/22/nigeria-taiwan-row-understanding-chinas-influence-in-africa/.

Reuters. (2017). "Nigeria Trims Ties with Taiwan as It Courts China." 12 January. https://www.reuters.com/article/us-taiwan-nigeria-idUSKBN14W1BI.

Rousseau, D. L., Gelpi, C., Reiter, D., and Huth, P. K. (1996). "Assessing the Dyadic Nature of the Democratic Peace, 1918–1988." *American Political Science Review* 90(3): 512–533.

Seteolu, F., and Oshodi, A. T. (2018). "Oscillation of Two Giants: Sino-Nigeria Relations and the Global South." *Journal of Chinese Political Science* 23(2): 257–285.

Sun, Y. (2016). *African China's Foreign Policy.* Brookings: John L. Thomas China Centre and Africa Growth Initiative.

Sun, Y., and Olin-Ammentorp, J. (2014). "The US and China in Africa: Competition or Cooperation?" *Bookings Institute.* https://www.brookings.edu/blog/africa-in-focus/2014/04/28/the-us-and-china-in-africa-competition-or-cooperation/.

Taylor, I. (2011). *Forum on China-Africa Cooperation (FOCAC).* London: Routledge.

Udeala, S. O. (2010). "Nigeria-China Economic Relations under the South-South Cooperation." *African Journal of International Affairs* 13(1&2): 61–88.

Ukiwo, U. (2007). "Education, Horizontal Inequalities and Ethnic Relations in Nigeria." *International Journal of Educational Development* 27(3): 266–281.

Utomi, P. (2008). "China and Nigeria." In *Center for Strategic and International Studies,* pp. 39–48. https://www.csis.org/analysis/china-nigeria.

Chapter 13

Eswatini-Taiwan Relations

Absolute Monarchy, Domestic Audience Absence, and China's Irrelevance

Bhaso Ndzendze and Nomzamo Gondwe

INTRODUCTION

"I'm healthy and happy to say that my sins were left in Taipei"—so said Barnabas Sibusiso Dlamini in his thanksgiving message to his fellow congregants at the Bhekinkhosi Church of the Nazarene in July 2017.[1] The septuagenarian Mr. Dlamini, at the time the prime minister of Eswatini (a position he had held earlier, between 1996 and 2003), made these remarks following a return from successful medical treatment in Taiwan. The ailment he suffered from was an undisclosed illness. But by his telling, his condition was so dire as to presage death—prompting the traditional confession of one's sins required by his religious affiliation. When not more than a year later (in April 2018) his health was again in a tenuous state, it was Taiwanese physicians who flew to his country to provide him treatment at the Mbabane Government Hospital Intensive Care Unit. While African leaders commonly, and notoriously,[2] seek treatment from experts outside their own countries, the usual destinations include South Africa, Europe, the United Arab Emirates, and Singapore.[3] Taiwan, though distinguished in the medical field (a fact reinforced by its world-leading and efficient response to the COVID-19 pandemic despite World Health Organization machinations[4]), is not a common choice. The choice, we must presume, must have been determined by politics. We thus have in this single instance a demonstration of the peculiar but strong Taiwan-Swati relations (as they would have been called before 2018 when the latter changed its official name into Eswatini in 2018). This relationship, increasingly Taiwan's most special in the world, is shaped by elite relations, conditioned by Taiwanese assistance to its African counterpart, and characterized by a resilience that is always given a short prognosis by observers. This short prognosis is no doubt inspired by China's apparent steamroll over Taiwan in the 2000s. To wit, the landlocked Kingdom of Eswatini is the only country on the African continent, and one of less than twenty countries worldwide, which has relations with the island Republic of China (ROC; also referred to as Taiwan hereinafter) and not the mainland People's Republic of China (PRC). This has not always been the case. Indeed, at the onset of Africa's independence decade, the 1960s, the country could once boast of having more diplomatic relations on the continent than the PRC. And yet Eswatini is pragmatic in its relations with the two Chinas and has even found common cause with the PRC in multilateral organizations without turning its back on its ROC ally.

In light of recent literature that highlights democratization or electoral pressures on African governments in their decisions to switch to mainland China over Taiwan in the twenty-first century, this chapter examines the role of authoritarian survival within the Kingdom of Eswatini's foreign and economic policy and argues that relations with Taipei are likely to continue insofar as its system continues to be headed by an authoritarian, absolute monarchy that has an asymmetrical social contract with its population and thus has no pressure to switch to potentially more lucrative economic relations with Beijing. In this sense, relations with Taiwan are likely to be relinquished only if there is a change in governance or meaningful reforms that render the monarchy more responsive to domestic audience costs. A key indicator of this possibility has been the Swazi Democratic Party (SWADEPA)—the country's only party to have participated in elections and sent a member to Parliament—expressing support for the One-China Policy. Independent-minded legislators have also undertaken visits to the PRC as recently as 2019, albeit in their personal capacity. Increasingly, there appears to be a cleavage between the monarchical/executive branch of government, which is not democratically accountable, and the legislative, which is marginally more accountable to the populace.

The chapter begins with an overview of democratization as a factor in the switches affected by other African countries in the post-2000 period. Second, it reviews the nature of the Eswatini monarchy and state-society relations in the country intending to assess the lack of state responsiveness to economic considerations of the country based on reports and key indices. Third, it reviews the country's relations with Taiwan and highlights the impact of its governance system in shaping and perpetuating its pro-Taiwan stance. Finally, the chapter lays out future policy options that may avail themselves for the United States, China, and Taiwan.

The first section of the chapter provides an overview of the hypothesized role of democratization as a mechanism for African states' switch toward

China. The second section consists of an analysis of the Swati government and government-society relations. The third section assesses the sources of resilience in Eswatini's relationship with Taiwan and shines a light on China's irrelevance so far. We also discuss the prospects of Eswatini switching to China, arguing that it would take considerable reforms in Eswatini for there to be any hope of a relationship between the two.

OVERVIEW OF DEMOCRACY AS A FACTOR IN THE FORMATION OF DIPLOMATIC RELATIONS WITH CHINA OVER TAIWAN

The history of the diplomatic tussle between China and Taiwan may be roughly detailed in four to five phases: (1) the post-Civil War and late colonial era in the late 1940s and early 1950s; (2) the independence era in which the contest was at its most competitive and saw PRC sought to lever-age alliances in the Third World (1950s to 1960s); (3) the period following China's entry into the United Nations at Taiwan's expense (1971) followed by a slowdown in China's diplomatic zeal under Deng (1978 to late 1990s) in the Third World and Taiwan made modest gains; and (4) the "post-FOCAC era" (since 2000) which is ongoing, but which has undergone a resurgence in the period following the end of the "diplomatic truce" seen between 2008 and 2015.

In the first phase, numerous states globally maintained no official relations with neither the ROC nor the PRC after the end of the Chinese Civil War in 1949, because many "were presumably waiting for a final settlement" on the One China problem.[5] The second phase of the 1950s and 1960s saw the independence of many former colonies in Asia and sub-Saharan Africa. At this time, Chinese leader chairman Mao Zedong perceived the new states in Africa as potential partners "in the struggle against imperialism."[6] Nevertheless, the ROC did well in Africa at this time, gaining the recognition of some thirteen out of twenty-three independent African countries from 1960 to 1963. The PRC only eked out five—the Central African Republic (CAR), the Ivory Coast, Ethiopia, Niger, and Sierra Leone.[7] But the attainment of further independence by numerous African states in the 1960s meant that by the time of the third phase, some twenty-seven of the seventy-six votes which led to China's entry came from African states. Noticeably, Eswatini was one of fifteen African states who voted against China's entry. The others were CAR, Chad, the DRC, Dahomey (present-day Benin), Gabon, the Gambia, Ivory Coast, Lesotho, Liberia, Madagascar, Malawi, Niger, South Africa, and the Upper Volta (present-day Burkina Faso). By the year 1979, when the United States came to recognize the PRC and downgraded its relations with the ROC, the latter was left with only five allies out of a total of fifty African states in the UN.[8]

During the Deng Era (1978–1990s) we see a reemergence by the ROC. By 1997, the ROC was recognized by ten African states; soon CAR and Guinea-Bissau switched in 1998 bringing the number to twelve. What we may term the "FOCAC era" (post-2000 to 2008, then 2015 to the present) has seen further gains for the PRC; Liberia and Senegal in 2003 and 2005, respectively, then Chad in 2006 and Malawi in 2008. It is at this point that we partition the Forum on China-Africa Cooperation (FOCAC) era into two phases, one before and another after the diplomatic truce of 2008–2015. During this period, the countries formed relations with none of each other's allies. The major cause behind this was the election of the Kuomintang's Ma Ying-jeou. The Kuomintang has a policy of rapprochement with the PRC and is opposed to independence. Under President Ma, the two Chinas established a framework for increased trade, and after the Gambia dropped its relations with Taiwan and appealed to China for recognition in 2013 it was not given recognition by the mainland. However, Tsai Ing-wen's ascendance to the presidency of Taiwan in 2016 led to the immediate recognition of the Gambia by China in 2016. A free trade agreement followed in 2018. Thus, the end of the diplomatic truce may be regarded as the beginning of a new phase. New relations formed in this Contemporary Period (2015–present) have included those with the island of São Tomé and Príncipe in 2016 and Burkina Faso in 2018.

Ndzendze[9] proposes that a combination of two factors could be at play in determining African countries' decisions to switch to and maintain relations with either China. Namely, regime change and multiparty competition in newly democratized states. These may have ushered in competitive democratic politics and free media which may have led to the African states being more likely to respond to the domestically rooted and socially distributed opportunity costs of not recognizing the demographically larger PRC over the smaller and economically stagnating ROC. This is especially plausible considering the developmental/poverty-reduction imperatives that permeate most African states. In "Domestic Audiences and Economic Opportunity Cost: African Democratisation as a Determinant in the Recognition of China over Taiwan, 2001–2018,"[10] case study analyses found that leaders in the new democracies switched to China for economic and developmental rationales. Indeed, all new democracies on the continent in the twenty-first century—Liberia, the Gambia, and Burkina Faso—have gone on to switch to China within one to three years of democratization. Of the three states that were not new democracies but still switched (i.e., Senegal, Chad, and Malawi), two (Chad and Malawi) did so within a year of an upcoming election following a declining performance in the preceding presidential election by the incumbents. Senegal, on the other hand, switched to the PRC not in the context of an election but during a growing economy. This would appear to make the country an outlier. However, it is to be noted that its switch in 2005 took place a year prior to the FOCAC summit of 2006, where it had been invited despite its Taiwan alignment. The country subsequently had its China-bound exports grow, from 78 million USD in 2005, the year of the switch, to 161 million USD by 2016; additionally, the country also gained interest-free loans from China[11] and has subsequently been appointed cochair of FOCAC (2018–2021).

It is evident, however, that some literature has noted that despite democratizing many African states have remained characterized by corrupt governments and less than transparent governance systems. Coined by Bueno de Mesquita and colleagues, the term "selectorate" is the concept that every government—whether dictatorial or democratic—rests on a winning coalition whom it needs to maintain power. These are the interests a ruler must constantly appease to retain its power. (This "selectorate" in the case of Eswatini is captured in the following section.) Even in such a landscape, there, the chapter proposes that the process of democratization was accompanied by an *expansion* of the elite and thus the necessity of the recognition of China if there are to be consummately increased rents. The Gambian case is interesting in this regard because although under an autocratic government when the country initially unsuccessfully reached out to China in 2015, the country was also anticipating what proved to be the freest election in its history, set to take place in late 2016.[12] The decision to relent relations with the ROC within a year of the election also perhaps indicates a desire to gain economically from the PRC by the troubled regime and therefore resuscitate the economy, which had reached a technical recession in 2014, at −0.94%. This was the second such recession in three years, as 2011 had also seen a nominal GDP decline of −4.295%, along with a GDP per capita decline of −7.141% in the same year (World Bank, 2019). This occurred in a context in which the Gambia could not rely on aid from Taiwan due to the 2008–2015 diplomatic truce.

Given the findings in the seven case studies, we could deduce that the process of democratization or regime change (or a weakened autocracy, as in the case of pre-2017 Gambia) in a given African state, in either case, is a critical determinant of recognition of China in the twenty-first century, with those in power expecting that the new relations with mainland China will lead to increased trade and in turn translate these into domestic electoral dividends. Importantly, the thesis is not that China increases democracy on the continent. Rather, it is the other way around: democratization and electoral competitiveness in African states in the twenty-first century have led to the recognition of China (which was, in turn, ascribed the role of the dependent variable). In this work, we seek to understand the inverse of this pattern. We seek, in other words, to conduct a within-case analysis that interrogates the theory under conditions that approximate a falsification.

THE STRUCTURE OF THE ESWATINI GOVERNMENT

The Kingdom of Eswatini is historically known for its nationalistic tribal society, unified in its narrative on culture and various traditions. After decades of colonial rule (first by the South African Republic and then the British) beginning in 1894 and concluding in 1968, the kingdom adopted components of the Western form of government, particularly a written constitution, and merged these with the system of chiefdom known as Tinkhundla. Per the most recent constitution (promulgated in 2005),[13] the king, or Ngwenyama, is the absolute ruler and co-governs with a female counterpart known as Ndlovukati, which the mother of the king usually holds. Eswatini's King Mswati III is the main and absolute ruler. He took over as king in 1986 following a brief regency after the death of his father King Sobhuza II in 1982. Following independence, the country has a bicameral parliament that is partially elected, which takes place every five years. Crucially, however, these do not take place under the auspices of political parties and are not entirely by direct election.

The thirty-member Senate is composed of twenty appointed members and ten members elected by the Lower House of Assembly. In turn, the House consists of seventy-six members who are nominated by the Tinkhundla in their capacity as councils of the various districts in the country. The existence of political parties has been illegal since 1973, and political groupings are categorized as a division of terrorist entities that seek to overthrow the already existing system of government. As a result, no officially recognized political formations remain, and civil society organizations require explicit approval (Amnesty International, 2019). The only major political party to have ever operated legally in the country, the Imbokodvo National Movement, was pro-royalist by inclination (being led by members of the king's advisory National Council) and acted in concert with the monarchy between independence and 1973 when political parties became illegal by royal decree. Because of these challenges, most political issues only gain significance and political prominence in the form of worker unions. But these have been noted to be mainly complicit with the government in upholding labor laws. Political and democratic sentiments are frequently limited within these unions as well as a result. Moreover, the king heads the judicial system and appoints the prime minister, who leads the cabinet and shapes domestic and foreign policy.

Observing King Mswati's system of governance sheds light on the sources of his legitimacy to rule. This is grounded on the features rather than just his political and economic capabilities. Max Weber's theory of power relations serves as a useful framework for explaining the quest for legitimacy and domination in any polity, including Eswatini. Notably, the three archetypes of legitimacy—tradition, charisma, and legal domination—remain the main elements in understanding the role and power of the king. In doing so, it is lucrative in understanding the government's responsibility to the domestic society and its approach to foreign dealings, or lack thereof, with other states such as Taiwan and China. Notably, legitimacy based on tradition has undoubtedly been a key factor behind the monarchy in Eswatini holding power. While the world around them changes, the monarchy and its supporters rely heavily on tradition, nationalism, and the history and national identity of the Swazis. Traditional power structures, ceremonies, rites, and even clothing are important factors in the nation-building process.[14] It is in favor of the monarchy that the national identity continues to be built on traditions just as it is, if not more, on the processes aligned with Westernization. Although it is interesting to note that the system in its current version is no more than a few generations old, it is formed around a romanticized historical narrative from "precolonial times." Linked to this is the idea of charisma, which is another of Weber's explanations for existing power structures. A strong superhuman and heroic narrative supports the charismatic legitimacy of the king. Overwhelmingly, however, most of this narrative is shaped by his illustrious forebears and not by the present monarch.

State-Society Relations in Eswatini

State-society relations may be defined as the interplay linking both the societal groups and state institutions. Scholarship in this area provides direction on how negotiations of public authority are exercised and how it can impact the people. It focuses on matters regarding mutual rights and the various duties of the state and society, and it provides a platform to negotiate how public resources can be distributed and formulate various modes of representation and liability.[15] According to Benequista, the focus is not centered around particular institutional forms but rather around the *relation* and relational functions of the state and society institutions.[16] Moreover, the state nor the civil society can be observed as acting in isolation, meaning that citizens should be viewed as people with virtues, responsibilities, and aspirations, which can collectively count in the process of governance.

The notion of state-society relations informs the efforts to foster positive and mutually constructive relations. This function of state-society relations focuses on its role in encouraging or generating trust in the government and public institutions. This provides that there be mutual responsibility for government toward respecting citizenship and sociopolitical cohesion. According to Joubert, Masilela, and Langwenya,[17] the current state of government and society relations in Eswatini can be summarized by taking note of the following: it is a state that encompasses a fragile and fragmented civil society, which is mostly unable to influence a governmental decision, unable to access governmental decision-making procedures both at local and national levels. Notably, the main civil society participants are the churches, nongovernmental organizations (NGOs), as well as trade unions. Trade unions had played a vital role since before independence in Eswatini but have been substantially disempowered since independence. Similar to other states, the government of Eswatini provides for several trade unions and under their umbrella bodies (the Swaziland Federation of Trade Unions and the Swaziland Federation of Labour). But observers have noted that they play a role in preventing general strikes. Nonetheless, most efforts have not warranted governmental intervention, and they, just like the efforts of the opposition, have continuously remained the subject of harsh and brutal state repression. As previously discussed, political parties have also suffered greatly at the hands of such repression, and they have been increasingly radicalized by the intransigence of the state.

Although the Constitution of the Kingdom of Swaziland 2005, in Section 20 (1) enshrines equality before the law, and Section 59 (1) commits the government to ensuring that citizens economic needs are met. Section 63(e) also outlines the duties bestowed on citizens in the process of participating in democracy; it outlines that citizens have a collective responsibility to promote the rule of law and democracy. However, the Institute for Security Studies stresses the need for democratic and economic reforms in the kingdom, more specifically with regard to the formation of the Tinkhundla government. Community centers (Tinkhundla) should be established and rally support for the king's endeavors to bring about proportional development of the country as well as its various democratic limitations. The institute further urges the government to acknowledge and uphold human rights.[18] To be sure, Eswatini encompasses seventy NGOs and informs the Coordinating Assembly of Non-Governmental Organisations, the governing behind the existing NGOs proves to be weakening at an alarming rate—since 2005. Moreover, the fact that these NGOs are under the administrative control of the Ministry of Home Affairs and register with the Ministry of Justice and Constitutional affairs means that the efforts to uphold the role of NGOs have proven to be equally challenging.[19] The interest of the ministry and those of the state matter more than the interest of the civil society.

Churches also account for a huge portion of society as they provide for religious views and shape beliefs system, which encourages the need for public state intervention, which can potentially make state-society processes more lucrative and accommodating.[20] However, churches tend to be hesitant when dealing with any political matters or political interventions methods. While 88% of the population in Eswatini are affiliated with churches and thus theoretically have the potential to intercede in state affairs, they hardly have the liberty to do so.[21] Indeed, in a July 22, 2005, address, the king "cautioned religious observers not to enter the arena of politics."[22]

State Responsiveness to Economic Pressures from the Population

Section 59(5) of the country's constitution provides that all citizens should receive equal economic opportunities and that social and cultural rights should be of paramount importance according to individual civic aspirations. Observing the role of NGOs, churches, and various trade unions provides a glimpse into the Swazi society's limited ability to intercede and communicate their concerns to their government. Notably, the Constitution of Eswatini describes the Swazi government as a democratic, participatory, and Tinkhundla-based system that frequently emphasizes the decentralization of state power from the core government in the various Tinkhundla regions. As noted, the system of government is approached on a nonpartisan (perhaps better understood as anti-partisan) basis as the establishment of political parties is banned. This system provides for very little in the way of state responsiveness and societal participation as it does not lead to the institutionalization of political and policy positions.[23] According to Mansfield and Snyder, democratization has historically created a broader spectrum of a diverse number of political organizations with conflicting interests. Amid this, Eswatini has a history of large-scale socioeconomic declines.[24] It is estimated that 60% of the Swazi societies live below the poverty line (with the twelfth-lowest life expectancy in the world, at fifty-eight years), while the royal family flourishes in a wealthy and extravagant lifestyle. Evidently, then, the imbalances and economic pressures continue to strain the livelihoods of the people, with increasing unemployment rates (the unemployment rate is estimated at around 40%), poor infrastructure, and poor economic development at the grassroots levels.

Additionally, the need for income generation is of dire need in the country, as a lower middle-income country in southern Africa. Some 75% of the 1.1 million people living in the country live off subsistence agriculture (higher than the continental average of 60%). Together with these challenges, the country is compounded by having the world's highest HIV/AIDS-related deaths. The already existing challenges continue to put a strain on communities. The country has faced protests, with calls for service delivery, political and labor reform, among others. However, the government appears to remain impervious to the needs of the population, with the system apparently primed for elite domination and minimal state responsiveness. In this regard, relations with South Africa may act as a valve, and strong economic ties, bucked by no conditions such as governance reform, with the United States, South Africa, and European countries perhaps acting as guarantors of the regime.

Tellingly, the country ranked 141 out of 180 countries in 2020 in terms of press freedom (see figure 13.1). The country's media openness has been declining steadily since 2016 (figure 13.1). This indicates the lack of avenues for the peaceful and effective communication of grievances, which would, in turn, inform the decision processes when it comes to foreign policy. This is analyzed in the section which follows.

Table 13.1   List of Diplomatic Missions of the Eswatini, 2021

High Commission	Country Representation	Formation Date
Brussels, Belgium	Belgium	1968
Copenhagen, Denmark	Denmark	1968
Nairobi, Kenya	Kenya	1968
Kuala Lumpur, Malaysia	Malaysia (host), Brunei Darussalam, Japan, Thailand, Indonesia, Philippines, South Korea, Bangladesh, India, Sri Lanka, Pakistan, Australia, Tonga Kingdom, and New Zealand	1968
Maputo, Mozambique	Mozambique[a]	1975
Rabat, Morocco	Morocco	2020
New Delhi, India	India	2019
Pretoria, South Africa	South Africa (host),[b] Botswana, Kingdom of Lesotho, Namibia, Zambia, and Zimbabwe	1993
Taipei, Republic of China (Taiwan)	Republic of China (Taiwan)	1968
London, United Kingdom	United Kingdom (host), Greece, Cyprus	1968
New York City, the United States	United Nations (host), Mexico	1968
Washington, DC, the United States	United States (host), Canada, Brazil, Chile, Argentina, and Venezuela	1968

Source: Compiled with data from the government of Eswatini's website.
[a]According to the website of the Eswatini High Commission in Maputo, Mozambique, these are missions with which the commission works closely with (and to which Eswatini is accredited): Algeria, Angola, Brazil, Egypt, France, India, Italy, Spain, Malawi, Norway, Portugal, Sweden, Tanzania, and Zimbabwe. However, the High Commission in Maputo is solely accredited to Mozambique.
[b]Additional representation to subregional organizations such as the Southern African Customs Union and the Southern African Development Cooperation.
Government of Eswatini. 2020. Missions Abroad. Ministry of Foreign Affairs and International Cooperation. https://www.gov.sz/index.php/departments-sp-336728999

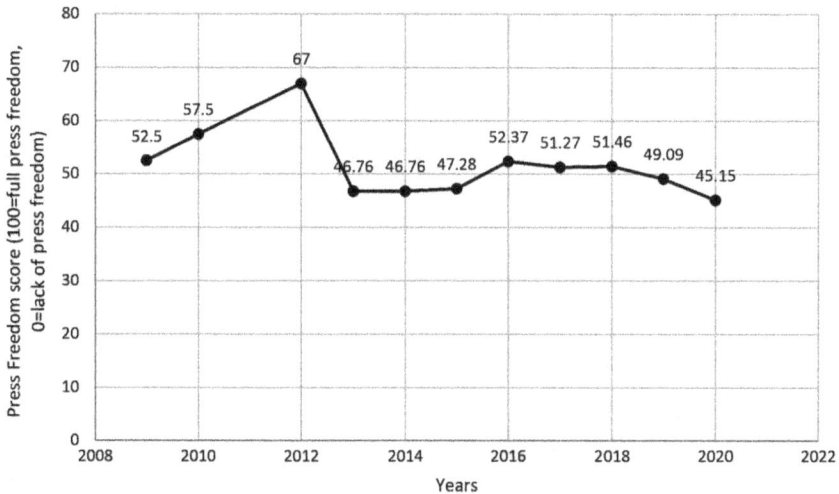

Figure 13.1 Eswatini's Press Freedom Score, 2009–2020

ESWATINI-TAIWAN DIPLOMATIC
RELATIONS AND ECONOMIC TRENDS

Eswatini is the only country to have never reversed its relations with the ROC. Upon obtaining independence from Britain under whom it had been a protectorate since 1906, the kingdom formed diplomatic relations with the ROC on September 6, 1968, the very day it became an independent state, under King Sobhuza II and Prime Minister Prince Makhosini Jaheso Dlamini. According to Potholm,[25] the kingdom's Taiwan recognition route was "conditioned by its relationship with Pretoria prior to independence,"[26] wherein Eswatini, economically dependent as it was on the Apartheid regime, followed South Africa's route of recognizing the ROC.

By the 1980s, only South Africa, Malawi, and Swaziland still maintained diplomatic ties with the ROC. In the 1990s, the ROC achieved some positive gains with ten African countries having ambassadors in Taiwan by 1997. Also, official delegations from the ROC were established in Kinshasa, Antananarivo, and Luanda.[27] Nevertheless, its relationship with Taipei has seemingly "been mutually satisfactory and ROC aid has been generous."[28]

Another example suffices: in terms of square kilometers, "judging by the size of the ROC's embassy in Mbabane, Taipei greatly values Swaziland as a strategic diplomatic ally in the region."[29] Furthermore, at any given point, Eswatini's leaders had visited Taiwan more regularly than their fellow African counterparts even when they too had relations with Taipei.[30] Yet, as shall be seen, contemporary economic relations are strong between Eswatini and the PRC; indeed, they even exceed those with Taipei.

Trade between Beijing and Mbabane has existed, though at a relatively low level. As the table 13.2 below demonstrates, though higher than those to the ROC, Eswatini exports, even at their peak, are nominally lower than those of now PRC-recognizing African states apart from São Tomé and Príncipe. While multiple factors, including supply-side factors, could be at play, the role of the lack of diplomatic relations cannot be discounted.

Politically, Mbabane has historically also appeared to be nurturing some relations with Beijing, but these excursions have consistently proved inconsequential. For example, "there was in 1992, a slight indication of a possible thaw in relations between the PRC and Mbabane upon a meeting between Beijing's mayor and a Swaziland representative serving as an International Olympic Committee member but the incident came to nothing. In 1995, the Swazi king paid a visit to Taipei.[31] A further example is the fact that in April 2004, Swaziland was one of the states supporting PRC's prevention of Beijing's having its human rights record "censured" in the UN Commission on Human Rights, "making it China's eleventh success at the Commission since 1990 in discussing China's human rights thrown out."[32] But this can also be attributed to Eswatini's own desire to not set a precedent due to its human rights record,[33] and perhaps to also not jeopardize its trade relations with the PRC.[34] A further symptom of Beijing's alienation from Eswatini was displayed by the fact that it was one of the initial sixteen states (which then became twenty-eight) which were promoting the admission to the United Nations of "the free people of the Republic of China" in October 1996.[35] At present, Taiwanese-Swazi ties seem secure, and China remains excluded from the country.[36]

An important aspect of the Taiwan-Swati relationship is the extent to which Eswatini has benefitted from the continual elimination of allies for the ROC. In other words, the reduction of the aid burden has been correlated with more aid toward the kingdom. For instance, funding for students from São Tomé studying in Taiwan through the Taiwan Scholarship program was suspended after diplomatic links between the two countries were severed.[37] In turn, the ROC increased the provision of medical experts and university scholarships to the monarchical state.[38]

Most interestingly, during the early diplomatic truce, "aid was often *increased* to Taiwan's loyal diplomatic allies after the latter 'lost' a country to China."[39] More specifically, aid which was meant for Malawi was re-rerouted and "given to Swaziland in 2008 after Malawi switched recognition months before the diplomatic truce."[40] This touches on what may be called a special relationship between the two countries: from the larger-than-average embassy to the above-average visitation frequencies to the fact that, unlike other African countries, Eswatini has never once switched to the PRC.

This also highlights the role of a lack of democratic/electoral pressure which renders the government impervious to the need to switch to China regardless of how "rational" it may look from the outside. Internally, it is sustained by its logic—the Taiwanese government has only an audience of one. Thus, as long as the monarch is gaining from the relationship, the effects of an opportunity cost are not felt. Additionally, we may hypothesize through the prism of opportunity cost that Eswatini has the best of both worlds through its close relationship with South Africa (itself a close ally to Beijing) from whom it obtains large sums of aid and has major trade ties (representing 66.58% of its foreign markets), it can indirectly gain from ties to Beijing economically benefits though South Africa and at the same time obtain special attention from Taiwan. Given this reality, therefore, the country has calculable rationales for maintaining relations with the ROC. Table 13.2 may reinforce this, as it demonstrates the declining importation of Eswatini goods by Taiwan—on their own and compared to PRC.

Examining Eswatini-China trade over the past ten years also reveals some interesting patterns that should be subject to closer examination. Noticeably in 2014, there was a sudden dip in Eswatini exports to China from 46.11 million USD to only US$289,000 in 2015. This may indicate political pressure, as the latter was a FOCAC year. But this may be an incongruent hypothesis, as in the subsequent pre-FOCAC and FOCAC years, 2017 and 2018, Chinese

Table 13.2   Eswatini's Trade Relations with the ROC and PRC, 2001–2018

Year	Total ROC Imports from Eswatini, in thousands of USD	Total PRC Imports from Eswatini, in thousands of USD
2001	0	78,375
2002	2,400	67,746
2003	582,407	0
2004	4	106,334
2005	17	45
2006	0	0
2007	0	4
2008	298	13,650
2009	17	39,578
2010	439	4,005
2011	101	32
2012	44	11,329
2013	227	58,358
2014	39	36,168
2015	91	39
2016	62	8
2017	227	618
2018	291	25,211

Source: Calculated by authors with data from UN TradeMap. 2020. Swaziland. https://www.trademap.org /Bilateral_TS.aspx?nvpm=1%7c748%7c%7c156%7c%7cTOTAL%7c%7c%7c2%7c1%7c1%7c1%7c2 %7c1%7c1%7c1%7c1%7c1 and https://www.trademap.org/Bilateral_TS.aspx?nvpm=1%7c748%7c %7c490%7c%7cTOTAL%7c%7c%7c2%7c1%7c1%7c1%7c2%7c1%7c1%7c1%7c1%7c1.

Table 13.3   PRC versus ROC Trade with Eswatini Averaged, 2019

	ROC	PRC
Total imports from Eswatini in 2019 (in US$-millions)	664	260
Total exports to Eswatini in 2019 (in US$-millions)	15,310	131,198
Total share of Eswatini exports (%)	0.02	1.48
Total share of Eswatini imports (%)	0.8	6.2

Source: Calculated by authors with data from UN TradeMap. 2020. Swaziland. https://www.trademap.org/Bilateral_TS.aspx?nvpm=1%7c748%7c%7c156%7c%7cTOTAL%7c%7c%7c2%7c1%7c1%7c1%7c2%7c1%7c1%7c1%7c1%7c1   and   https://www.trademap.org/Bilateral_TS.aspx?nvpm=1%7c748%7c%7c490%7c%7cTOTAL%7c%7c%7c2%7c1%7c1%7c1%7c2%7c1%7c1%7c1%7c1%7c1.

imports from Eswatini *increased* from US$3.25 million to US$27.46 million. But this subsequently dropped to US$766,000 the next year (2019). Could this indicate a change of tact—whereby China attempts to lure the kingdom through increased imports of its goods? We can only speculate, but recent calls by the mainland for the country to drop Taiwan indicate that Eswatini is not completely off China's radar. In a February 2020 open letter (titled "No Diplomatic Relations, No Business Benefits") by Lin Songtian, then the ambassador of the PRC to South Africa, China effectively threatened to cut off trade with Eswatini if the country did not change its recognition of Taiwan. In this regard, commercial ties have been used as a threat—with China seemingly nonchalant about its exports to the kingdom.[41] But nothing came of this.

To be sure, there have been glimpses of what appears to change. For example, "since at least 2017 public sector workers and unions have regularly clashed with Eswatini police during protests demanding higher wages, reforms to the state pension fund, and calls for great political freedoms," reported *Reuters* in November 2019.[42] Following media reports of a team of parliamentarians that visited the PRC on a familiarization tour in July 2019, the government of Eswatini made clear that this was not an official visit:

> Government did not sanction the familiarisation tour of some Parliamentarians to the People's Republic of China and, as such, their conclusions from the excursion are purely personal and have no bearing on the relationship between the Kingdom of Eswatini and Taiwan.[43]

The government also reiterated its "commitment to strong diplomatic ties with Taiwan remains unshaken and enduring," adding that "any cynical campaign of coercion threatening the relationship shared by the two countries shall not succeed." This action would appear to have taken place despite the king and the executive and was conducted by independent-minded legislators. Given recent trends, we should expect that any reforms which make the country's leaders more capable of organizing along popular-minded lines will lead to a reconsideration of relations with Taiwan. When it comes to the One China issue, there increasingly appears to be a cleavage between the monarchical branch of government, which also happens to be the executive and in charge of policy, and the legislative, which is marginally more accountable to the populace. In 2013, Jan Sithole—widely seen as a pro-democracy activist and leader of the illegal SWADEPA—was elected to the lower branch of the Eswatini parliament. With funding received from the Danish Social Democratic Party for SWADEPA (Danish Institute for Parties and Democracy, 2020), his pledge was changing the government from the inside.[44] Nothing came of these efforts by the time Sithole passed away in September 2020. But he had pledged that his aim—"[to] achieve a multi-party Swaziland but through a strategy of participating, as opposed to non-participation"—was shared by others, and that he was not the only member of his party elected, he was just the only one embracing its badge.[45] At the time, however, this makes the prospect of multiparty democracy that much more complicated.

CONCLUSION

This chapter has discussed the nature of Eswatini's political system and its implications for foreign relations as they pertain to its stance on the One China issue. It has noted the restricted civil society space as well as the unresponsive nature of the executive branch to the economic concerns of the populace which result from it. At the same time, the country would appear to be experiencing the first signs of a division between Parliament and crown when it comes to the One China issue, with the more (though not completely) directly accountable parliamentarians (who must be voted in at frequent intervals) becoming increasingly in favor of relations with the mainland. In this regard, the Eswatini case study showcases the crucial difference played by political parties in affecting the change in policy as seen in the other countries which recognized China after becoming democracies.[46] The only political party to participate and win in elections, SWADEPA, was pro-China and voiced support for the formulation of relations with the mainland. These are evident areas for future research and require engagement with actors and archives in Eswatini and elsewhere in Africa where there has been a recent switch in recognitions.

NOTES

1. Quoted in Sithembile Hlatshwayo, "PM Sick, Admitted to ICU," *Times of Swaziland*, 2018 http://www.times.co.sz/news/118112-pm-sick-admitted-to-icu.html.

2. For example, it is estimated that the total funds spent in the overseas treatment of Uganda's top officials is the monetary equivalent of ten hospitals that could be built every year. See Nyasha K. Mutizwa, "Africa's 'health tourism' Presidents," *Africa News*, October 3, 2019, https://www.africanews.com/2019/10/03/africa-s-health-tourism-presidents-travel/.

3. Tahiru Azaaviele Liedong, "African Politicians Seeking Medical Help Abroad Is Shameful, and Harms Health Care," *The Conversation*, August 24, 2017, https://theconversation.com/african-politicians-seeking-medical-help-abroad-is-shameful-and-harms-health-care-82771.

4. Javier C. Hernández, and Horton, Chris, "Taiwan's Weapon against Coronavirus: An Epidemiologist as Vice President," *New York Times*, May 9, 2020, https://www.nytimes.com/2020/05/09/world/asia/taiwan-vice-president-coronavirus.html.

5. James C. Hsiung, "China's Recognition Practice and Its Implications in International Law," in Jerome Allen Cohen (ed.), *China's Practice in International Law* (Cambridge, MA: Harvard University Press, 1972), 54–55.

6. Mao Zedong, "Africa's Talk Is to Struggle against Imperialism," 21 February 1959, in Mao Zedong *On Diplomacy* (Beijing: Foreign Languages Press, 1998), 286–287.

7. Hsiung, "China's Recognition Practice," 55.

8. Sarah Raine, *China's African Challenges* (London: International Institute for Strategic Studies and Routledge, 2009), 10.

9. Bhaso Ndzendze, "Domestic Audiences and Economic Opportunity Cost: African Democratisation as a Determinant in the Recognition of China over Taiwan, 2001–2018," *Journal of Asian and African Studies* (2020). doi: 10.1177/0021909620926531. Rich and Banerjee (2015) initially observed that Taiwan tended to do better with countries with whose regime types it differed (i.e., it did relatively best with democracies when it itself was an autocracy and vice versa after its democratic transition in the 1980s). Ndzendze focuses on the 2000 era and introduces a role for upward pressure via elections. See Rich, T.S. and Banerjee, V., "Running Out of Time? The Evolution of Taiwan's Relations in Africa," *Journal of Current Chinese Affairs* 44(2015): 141–161.

10. Ndzendze, "Domestic Audiences."

11. David S. Menjor, "Liberia-China Relationship Not for Political Gains," *Liberian Observer*, May 21, 2017, https://www.liberianobserver.com/news/liberia chinarelationshipnotforpoliticalgains/.

12. The regime was to longer enjoy the acquiescence of the ECOWAS regional bloc.

13. Constitution of Swaziland, Act No. 001/2005 which came into force on July 26, 2005.

14. Signe Cecius Larsen Pejstrup, "Swaziland in Transition," *The Interdisciplinary Journal of International Studies* 7(2011): 22.

15. Danish Institute for Parties and Democracy, "The Danish Social Democrats and Swaziland's Swazi Democratic Party | Danish Institute for Parties and Democracy," 2011, http://dipd.dk/partnerships/swaziland/the-danish-social-democrats-and-swazilands-swazi-democratic-party/.

16. N. Benequista, "Putting Citizens at the Centre: Linking States and Societies for Responsive Governance," in the Conference Paper, *The Politics of Poverty, Elites, Citizens and States*, 21–23 June 2010, London, 10.

17. P. Joubert, Z. Masilela, and M. Langwenya, *Consolidating Democratic Governance in the SADC Region: Swaziland* (EISA: Johannesburg, 2008), 2.

18. Institute for Security Studies, "Will Swaziland Become a Bhutan or a Nepal? Let the Debate Begin," ISS, 2013, https://issafrica.org/iss-today/will-swaziland -become-a-bhutan-or-a-nepal-let-the-debate-begin.

19. Joubert, Masilela, and Langwenya, "Consolidating," 5.

20. Christa Rautenbach, "Comments on the Constitutional Protection of Religion in Swaziland," *African Human Rights Law Journal* 8 (2008): 440.

21. Family Search, "Kingdom of eSwatini Church Records," *Family Search*, 2021, https://www.familysearch.org/wiki/en/Kingdom_of_eSwatini_Church_Records#cite _note-1.

22. Rautenbach, "Comments," 440.

23. Benard Onyinkwa, "The Nature of Political Parties in Africa: What Is the Role of Political Parties in a Democratic Process?," *SSRN* (2017). doi: 10.2139/ ssrn.3086575.

24. Edward D. Mansfield and Jack Snyder, "Democratization and the Danger of War," *International Security* 20 (1995): 5.

25. C. Potholm, "Swaziland in Transition to Independence," *Africa Report* 12(1967): 49–54.

26. Potholm, "Swaziland in Transition," 54.

27. San-shiun Tseng, *The Republic of China's Foreign Policy towards Africa: The Case of ROC-RSA Relations*. PhD Thesis (University of the Witwatersrand, 2008).

28. Mduduzi Ginindza, "Let's Leave Taiwan," *Times of Swaziland*, November 21, 2013.

29. Taylor, Ian, *China and Africa: Engagement and Compromise* (London and New York: Routledge, 2006), 194.

30. Ibid.

31. Ibid, 201.

32. *Xinhua News*, "Goodwill Visit," January 24, 1994, *Xinhua News*; Taylor, Ian, *China and Africa: Engagement and Compromise* (London and New York: Routledge, 2006), 200.

33. Raine, *China's African Challenges*,

34. Ibid.

35. Ginindza, "Let's Leave Taiwan."

36. Taylor, *China and Africa*, 201.

37. Chen Chih-chung, and Elizabeth Hsu, "Taiwan Scholarship Suspended after São Tomé-Taiwan Ties Cut," *Focus Taiwan*, 21 December 2016.

38. P.G. Bax, S. Gongo, and L. Dlamini, "Chinese Billions Fail to Sway Taiwan's Last Two Allies in Africa," Bloomberg, January 24, 2017, https://www.bloomberg .com/news/articles/2017-01-24/chinese-billions-failto-sway-taiwan-s-last-two-allies -in-africa.

39. Theodora C Thindwa, "China-Malawi Relations: An Analysis of Trade Patterns and Development Implications," *African East-Asian Affairs* 4 (2014): 42–77.

40. Theodora C. Thindwa, "China-Malawi Relations," 42.

41. Songtian Lin, "No Diplomatic Relations, No Business Benefits," open letter published in *Swaziland News*, February 1, 2020, http://www.swazilandnews.co.za/fundza.php?nguyiphi=168.

42. Reuters Staff, "eSwatini's Economic Growth to Sink to 1% without Urgent Reforms – IMF," *Reuters*, November 4, 2019, https://www.reuters.com/article/eswatini-economy-idAFL8N27K5Q6.

43. Government of eSwatini, "Government Press Statement No. 18/2019," Government of eSwatini website, July 28, 2019, http://www.gov.sz/index.php/latest-news/2291-eswatini-taiwan-relations.

44. Danish Institute for Parties and Democracy, "The Danish Social Democrats and Swaziland's Swazi Democratic Party | Danish Institute for Parties and Democracy."

45. BBC News, "Jan Sithole: Swaziland Activist Elected MP," *BBC News*, 2013. https://www.bbc.com/news/world-africa-24232007.

46. Ndzendze, "Domestic Audiences."

BIBLIOGRAPHY

Amnesty International. "Eswatini 2019." 2019. https://www.amnesty.org/en/countries/africa/eswatini/report-eswatini/#_ftnref2.

Bax, P. G., S. Gongo, and L. Dlamini. "Chinese Billions Fail to Sway Taiwan's Last Two Allies in Africa." *Bloomberg*, January 24, 2017. https://www.bloomberg.com/news/articles/2017-01-24/chinese-billions-failto-sway-taiwan-s-last-two-allies-in-africa.

BBC News. "Jan Sithole: Swaziland Activist Elected MP." *BBC News*, 2013. https://www.bbc.com/news/world-africa-24232007.

Benequista, N. "Putting Citizens at the Centre: Linking States and Societies for Responsive Governance." In the Conference Paper, *The Politics of Poverty, Elites, Citizens and States*, 21–23 June 2010. London.

Chih-chung, Chen, and Elizabeth Hsu. "Taiwan Scholarship Suspended after São Tomé Taiwan Ties Cut." *Focus Taiwan*, December 21, 2016.

Danish Institute for Parties and Democracy. "The Danish Social Democrats and Swaziland's Swazi Democratic Party | Danish Institute for Parties and Democracy." 2011. http://dipd.dk/partnerships/swaziland/the-danish-social-democrats-and-swazilands-swazi-democratic-party/.

Ginindza, Mduduzi. "Let's Leave Taiwan." *Times of Swaziland*, November 21, 2013.

Government of Eswatini. "Government Press Statement No. 18/2019." Government of eSwatini website, July 28, 2019. http://www.gov.sz/index.php/latest-news/2291-eswatini-taiwan-relations.

Hernández, Javier C., and Chris Horton. "Taiwan's Weapon against Coronavirus: An Epidemiologist as Vice President." *New York Times*, May 9, 2020. https://www .nytimes.com/2020/05/09/world/asia/taiwan-vice-president-coronavirus.html.

Hlatshwayo, Sithembile. "PM Sick, Admitted to ICU." *Times of Swaziland*, 2018. http://www.times.co.sz/news/118112-pm-sick-admitted-to-icu.html.

Hsiung, James C. "China's Recognition Practice and Its Implications in International Law." In *China's Practice in International Law*, edited by Jerome Allen Cohen, 54–55. Cambridge, MA: Harvard University Press, 1972.

Institute for Security Studies. "Will Swaziland Become a Bhutan or a Nepal? Let the Debate Begin." *ISS*, 2013. https://issafrica.org/iss-today/will-swaziland-become-a -bhutan-or-a-nepal-let-the-debate-begin.

Joubert, P., Z. Masilela, and M. Langwenya. *Consolidating Democratic Governance in the SADC Region: Swaziland*, 2. Johannesburg: EISA, 2008.

Liedong, Tahiru Azaaviele. "African Politicians Seeking Medical Help Abroad Is Shameful, and Harms Health Care." *The Conversation*, August 24, 2017. https:// theconversation.com/african-politicians-seeking-medical-help-abroad-is-shameful -and-harms-health-care-82771.

Lin, Songtian. "No Diplomatic Relations, No Business Benefits." Open Letter Published in *Swaziland News*, February 1, 2020. http://www.swazilandnews.co.za /fundza.php?nguyiphi=168.

Mansfield, Edward D., and Jack Snyder. "Democratization and the Danger of War." *International Security* 20 (1995): 5.

Mao, Zedong. "Africa's Talk Is to Struggle against Imperialism." 21 February 1959. In *On Diplomacy*, edited by Mao Zedong, 286–287. Beijing: Foreign Languages Press, 1998.

Menjor, David S. "Liberia-China Relationship Not for Political Gains." *Liberian Observer*, May 21, 2017. https://www.liberianobserver.com/news/liberiachinarel ationshipnotforpoliticalgains/.

Mutizwa, Nyasha K. "Africa's 'Health Tourism' Presidents." *Africa News*, October 3, 2019. https://www.africanews.com/2019/10/03/africa-s-health-tourism-presidents -travel/.

Ndzendze, Bhaso. "Domestic Audiences and Economic Opportunity Cost: African Democratisation as a Determinant in the Recognition of China Over Taiwan, 2001–2018." *Journal of Asian and African Studies* (2020). DOI: 10.1177/0021909620926531.

Onyinkwa, Benard. "The Nature of Political Parties in Africa: What Is the Role of Political Parties in a Democratic Process?" *SSRN* (2017). DOI: 10.2139/ ssrn.3086575.

Pejstrup, Signe Cecius Larsen. "Swaziland in Transition." *The Interdisciplinary Journal of International Studies* 7, no. 1 (2011): 15–26.

Potholm C. "Swaziland in Transition to Independence." *Africa Report* 12 (1967): 49–54.

Raine, Sarah. *China's African Challenges*, p. 10. London: International Institute for Strategic Studies and Routledge, 2009.

Rautenbach, Christa. "Comments on the Constitutional Protection of Religion in Swaziland." *African Human Rights Law Journal* 8 (2008): 440.

Reporters Without Borders. "2020 World Press Freedom Index." *Reporters Without Borders*. 2020. https://rsf.org/en/ranking#.

Reuters Staff. "eSwatini's Economic Growth to Sink to 1% without Urgent Reforms – IMF." *Reuters*, November 4, 2019. https://www.reuters.com/article/eswatini -economy-idAFL8N27K5Q6.

Rich, T. S., and V. Banerjee. "Running Out of Time? The Evolution of Taiwan's Relations in Africa." *Journal of Current Chinese Affairs* 44 (2015): 141–161.

Taylor, Ian. *China and Africa: Engagement and Compromise*, p. 194. London and New York: Routledge, 2006.

Thindwa Theodora C. "China-Malawi Relations: An Analysis of Trade Patterns and Development Implications." *African East-Asian Affairs* 4 (2014): 42–77.

Tseng, San-shiun. *The Republic of China's Foreign Policy towards Africa: The Case of ROC RSA Relations*. PhD Thesis, University of the Witwatersrand, 2008.

UN TradeMap. "Swaziland." 2020. https://www.trademap.org/Bilateral_TS.aspx ?nvpm=1%7c748%7c%7c156%7c%7cTOTAL%7c%7c%7c2%7c1%7c1%7c1 %7c2%7c1%7c1%7c1%7c1%7c1 and https://www.trademap.org/Bilateral_TS .aspx?nvpm=1%7c748%7c%7c490%7c%7cTOTAL%7c%7c%7c2%7c1%7c1 %7c1%7c2%7c1%7c1%7c1%7c1%7c1.

Xinhua News. "Goodwill Visit." *Xinhua News*, January 24, 1994.

Appendix

Appendix Tables from Chapter 8

Kristina Kironska and Thiombiano Dramane

APPENDIX TABLE A.1 TAIWAN-AFRICA AND CHINA-AFRICA OFFICIAL DIPLOMATIC RELATIONS

Country	Independence Date	Period of ROC Recognition	Period of PRC Recognition	No. of Switches	ROC Diplomatic Missions in Africa
Algeria	1962	Never	1962–2020	0	No
Angola	1975	Never	1983–2020	0	No
Benin	1960	1966–1972	1964–1966, 1972–2020	2	No
Botswana	1966	1966–1975	1975–2020	1	No
Burkina Faso	1960	1961–1973 1994–2018	1973–1994 2018–2020	3	No
Burundi	1962	Never	1960–2020	0	No
Cameroon	1960 / 1961	1960–1971	1971–2020	1	No
Cape Verde	1975	Never	1976–2020	0	No
Central African Republic	1960	1962–1964 1968–1976 1991–1998	1964–1968 1976–1991 1998–2020	5	No
Chad	1960	1962–1972 1997–2006	1972–1997 2006–2020	3	No
Comoros	1975	Never	1975–2020	0	No
Democratic Republic of the Congo	1960	1960–Feb 1961 Sep 1961–1972	Feb 1961–Sep 1961 1972–2020	3	No
Republic of the Congo	1960	1960–1964	1964–2020	1	No
Djibouti	1977	Never	1979–2020	0	No
Egypt	1922 / 1953	1942–1956	1956–2020	1	In the process of setting up
Equatorial Guinea	1968	Never	1970–2020	1	No
Eritrea	1993	Never	1993–2020	0	No
Ethiopia	1941	Never	1970–2020	0	No
Gabon	1960	1960–1974	1974–2020	1	No

Country					
The Gambia	1965	1968–1974	1974–1995	3	No
		1995–2013	2013–2020		
Ghana	1957	Never	1960–2020	0	No
Guinea	1958	Never	1959–2020	1	No.
Guinea-Bissau	1973 / 1974	1990–1998	1998–ongoing	1	No
Ivory Coast	1960	1963–1983	1983–ongoing	1	No
Kenya	1963	Never	1963–ongoing	0	No
Lesotho	1966	1966–1983	1983–1990	3	No
		1990–1994	1994–ongoing		
Liberia	1847	1957–1977	1977–1989	5	No
		1989–1993	1993–1997		
		1997–2003	2003–ongoing		
Libya	1951	1959–1978	1978–ongoing	1	Only in the past
Madagascar	1960	1960–1972	1972–ongoing	1	No
Malawi	1964	1966–2008	2008–ongoing	1	No
Mali	1960	Never	1960–ongoing	0	No
Mauritania	1960	Never	1965–ongoing	0	No
Mauritius	1968	Never	1972–ongoing	0	No
Morocco	1956	1956–1958	1958–ongoing	1	No
Mozambique	1975	Never	1975–ongoing	0	No
Namibia	1990	Never	1990–ongoing	0	No
Niger	1960	1963–1974	1974–1992	3	No.
		1992–1996	1996–ongoing		
Nigeria	1960	1960–1971	1971–ongoing	1	Taipei Trade Office in the Federal Republic of Nigeria: Lagos 1991–2001, then Abuja 2001–2017, then again Lagos, in 2021 moving again to Abuja

Country	Independence Date	Period of ROC Recognition	Period of PRC Recognition	No. of Switches	ROC Diplomatic Missions in Africa
Rwanda	1962	Never	1971–ongoing		No
São Tomé and Príncipe	1975	1997–2016	2016–ongoing	1	No
Senegal	1960	1960–1964 1969–1973 1996–2005	1964–1969 1973–1996 2005–ongoing	5	No
Seychelles	1976	Never	1976–ongoing	0	No
Sierra Leone	1961	1964–1971	1971–ongoing	1	No
Somalia	1960	Never	1960–ongoing	0	No
Somaliland	1991 (self-declared, internationally considered part of Somalia)	X	X	X	Taiwan Representative Office in Somaliland: Hargeisa
South Africa	1910	1976–1998	1998–ongoing	1	Taipei Liaison Office in the Republic of South Africa: Pretoria and Cape Town
South Sudan	2011	Never	2011–ongoing	0	No
Sudan	1956	1956–1959	1959–ongoing	1	No
Eswatini (Swaziland)	1968	1968–2020	Never	0	Embassy of the Republic of China in the Kingdom of Eswatini: Mbabane
Tanzania	1961	Never	1964–ongoing	0	No
Togo	1960	1960–1972	1972–ongoing	1	No
Tunisia	1956	Never	1964–ongoing	0	No
Uganda	1962	Never	1962–ongoing	0	No
Zambia	1964	Never	1964–ongoing	0	No
Zimbabwe	1980	Never	1980–ongoing	0	No

Source: Compiled by the authors from various sources.
'X' represents data not available.

APPENDIX TABLE A.2 VOTING FOR A CHANGE IN THE REPRESENTATION OF CHINA IN THE UN

Year	YES *African Countries/All Countries*	NO *African Countries/All Countries*	ABSTENTION *African Countries/All Countries*
1955	0/12	3/42	0/6
1956	2/24	4/47	2/8
1957	4/27	3/47	1/7
1958	3/28	3/44	2/9
1959	4/29	2/44	3/9
1960	8/34	2/42	13/22
1961	8/36	9/48	9/20
1962	13/42	17/56	2/12
1963	11/41	17/57	3/12
1965	17/47	9/47	7/20
1966	16/46	17/57	5/17
1967	15/45	19/58	4/17
1968	14/44	20/58	7/23
1969	18/48	21/56	2/21
1970	18/51	18/49	5/25
1971	25/76	15/35	1/17

Source: Compiled by authors from various sources.
Note: 1964—no voting due to financial crisis.

Index

Note: *Italicized* pages refer to tables.

About the Editor

Sabella Ogbobode Abidde is a tenured/full professor of political science and member of the graduate faculty at Alabama State University. He is the series editor for Lexington Books' *African Governance, Development, and Leadership Series*. Dr. Abidde is an interdisciplinary scholar with a BA in international relations; an MSc in educational administration from Saint Cloud State University Minnesota; an MA in political science from Minnesota State University Mankato, Minnesota; and a PhD in African Studies, World Affairs, Public Policy, and Development Studies from Howard University. His scholarship includes published volumes on Africa, Latin America, and the Caribbean. His forthcoming books are on the contest and contestations between China and Taiwan in Africa. Sabella Abidde is a member of the Association of Global South Studies, the African Studies and Research Forum, the Latin American Studies Association, the Caribbean Studies Association, and a lifetime member of the American Association for Chinese Studies. He was a weekly columnist for Nigeria's newspaper of record, *The Punch*.

About the Contributors

YEN-HSIN CHEN is a visiting assistant professor in the Department of Political Science at Trinity University. He is from Taiwan, and he earned his PhD (2017) in political science from the University of North Texas. His primary research interests are in the fields of Chinese politics and government, Asian politics and governments, and protest participation in China. At the moment, he teaches International Politics, Chinese Foreign Policy, East Asian Security, and War and Alliance.

SAIDAT ILO is an assistant professor of political science at the University of Houston-Victoria. She received her PhD in political science from Howard University and MPA and BA in political science from Texas State University—San Marcos. Her research interests include international relations, American government, African Politics, and international political economy.

ANDREW MICHAEL MASHINGAIDZE is a PhD candidate at the University of Western Australia. Andrew holds a MA in international relations (University of Witwatersrand); BA (Hons) politics and international relations (University of Johannesburg); and BA in politics, philosophy, and economics (University of Johannesburg). His research interests are in Chinese foreign policy, particularly China's diplomatic relations with African political organizations and states. Andrew's PhD research broadly explores China's foreign policy toward Africa and the impact it has on governance in Africa. He argues that China uses party-to-party exchanges as a strategy to export the Chinese way of doing things (China model) to Africa, with the ultimate goal of influencing African politics.

EMMANUEL EZI OBUAH is a professor of international relations in the Department of History and Diplomatic Studies, University of Port Harcourt where he teaches history and international relations. He was a former associate professor of Political Science and History Department at Alabama A&M University, USA (2004–2012) and Alabama State University, Montgomery, USA (2012–2014). He holds a doctorate degree in International Relations. He has published books and many articles in learned referred international journals including *Understanding the Dynamics of Sino-Africa Relations: Building Communities of Practice* (2013), *Glossary of Key Terms in International Relations* (2016), and Outsourcing prosecution of the Somali pirates to Kenya, *African Security Review* volume 21(13), 2012.

CHARLES SIKIBO IJUYE-DAGOGO is a PhD candidate of Diplomacy and International Studies in the Department of History and Diplomatic Studies, University of Port Harcourt. He is currently working on a comparative study of American and Chinese aid to Nigeria from 1960 to 2015. Charles holds a Master's degree in Diplomacy and International Studies which he attained with a distinction. He obtained a bachelor's degree with honors from Benson Idahosa University in Benin City, where he studied Political Science and Public Administration. Charles's research interests focus on foreign aid, diplomacy, international development, international political economy, and foreign policy. His previous research works include Democracy and Socio-Economic Development West Africa: The Ghana Experience from 1957 to 2012 (Master's dissertation submitted in 2017) and Terrorism as a Consequence of the Nigerian Political Economy: The Movement for the Emancipation of the Niger Delta as Case Study (Bachelor's project submitted in 2012).

PRIYE S. TORULAGHA is an associate professor of political science and public administration in the Department of Social Sciences, Florida Memorial University, Miami Gardens, Florida. He holds a MA in comparative politics and public administration from the Oklahoma State University, Stillwater, Oklahoma; MHR in counseling and human resource management from the University of Oklahoma, Norman; and a PhD in political science from the same university. Dr. Torulagha writes regularly on Nigerian and African affairs, Third World politics, international terrorism, and democratic governance. He is the author of "Fidel Castro: His Impact on African Liberation and Governance" in *Fidel Castro and Africa's Liberation Struggle*, edited by Sabella Abidde and Charity Manyeruke (2020). He is also the author of "China and Africa: The Beginning of a New World Order or a New Form of Colonialism" in *China in Africa: Between Imperialism and Partnership in Humanitarian Development*, edited by Sabella Abidde and Tokunbo A. Ayoola (2021).

ABDUL-GAFAR TOBI OSHODI holds a PhD in social sciences and lectures in the Department of Political Science, Lagos State University. A former journalist in Vanguard newspapers, Abdul-Gafar was awarded the Social Science Research Council's "Next Generation of Social Science in Africa" Fellowship (2013–2014), a Doctoral Fellowship at the Centre for Research on Peace and Development in KU Leuven (2013–2017), and the University of Edinburgh Centre for African Studies' Catalyst Fellowship (in 2019 and 2020). He is currently a postdoctoral fellow of the American Council of Learned Societies' African Humanities Program (2020–2021), working on a book entitled *Imageries of Mao Zedong's China in Ghanaian Newspapers, 1957–1976*. His research interests broadly revolve around the "development question" in Africa with a strong bias for China in Africa, youth service, nation-building, research ethics, and knowledge (re)production. He has published several articles on these subjects and presented them at major conferences in Africa, Europe, and North America.

ABDUL-WASI BABATUNDE MOSHOOD holds a PhD from the University of KwaZulu-Natal. A senior lecturer, he currently lectures at the Department of Political Science, Lagos State University. His research interest spans peace and conflict studies, international relations, and comparative studies. He has published work on: "The Role of Civil Society Groups in Conflict Resolution in Nigeria," "The Political Economy of the Amnesty Program in the Niger Delta Region of Nigeria and Implications for Durable Peace," "Insurgency and Development in Nigeria: Assessing Reintegration Efforts in the Northeast," and "South Africa's Inclusion in the BRICS." His latest published work on the university is "Breaking the Ice: The Nigerian University System and Its Funding Challenges," in Olanrewaju Fagbohun and Adewale Aderemi (eds.). *Global Aids and Tertiary Education in Nigeria*. Lagos: Profemative Concepts Int'l, 61–93. With Dr. Oshodi, he recently completed research on "Revisiting *The Talented Tenth*: Pan-Africanism and the Nigerian University."

MARY CHINELO UBABUDU bagged a Bachelor of Arts Degree in History Education (BA. Ed.) graduating with Second Class Upper Division from the University of Nigeria, Nsukka, in 1993. She earned her master's degree in educational management (MEd Educational Management with specialization in Human Resources) from the University of Ibadan in 1997. She obtained a Doctor of Philosophy Degree (PhD) in Educational Management with specialization in Human Resources Management from Olabisi Onabanjo University in 2005. After completing her PhD, she obtained another master's in public and international affairs from the University of Lagos in 2010. She was formerly an employee of the Nigerian Army School of Finance and Administration in Lagos where she served as a senior lecturer, researcher, and head of Research and Development Department before joining a sister military institution—The Air force Institute of Technology, Kaduna. Her research has been published in journals and edited books and has been presented at local and international conferences. Her research focuses on human resources management, educational management and administration, and international relations and diplomacy.

ISAAC OWUSU FRIMPONG is a PhD candidate at the University of Western Australia, Political Science and International Relations Department. His research interests cover China-Africa relations broadly, peace and security in Africa, and migration. His PhD research focuses on China's increasing security engagement in Africa. He is also a postgraduate fellow at the UWA Africa Research & Engagement Centre. He holds a bachelor's degree in political science from the University of Ghana, Legon, and a master's degree in international relations from Jilin University, China.

KRISTINA KIRONSKA is a socially engaged interdisciplinary academic with experience in Myanmar affairs, Taiwan studies, China-CEE relations, human rights, activism, and election observation in African countries. She studied International Relations in Slovakia, Portugal, and Taiwan, and conducted doctoral research in Myanmar. In the past, she worked as a campaigner for Amnesty International in Slovakia and as a lecturer at the University of Taipei in Taiwan. She also organized monthly human rights lectures for the public in Taiwan. Currently, she is researching within the Sinophone Borderlands project at the Palacký University Olomouc in Czechia, and she is also a research fellow at the Central European Institute of Asian Studies. During her research career, she has spent some time in Taiwan conducting research—in 2019 with the Taiwan Fellowship, and 2020 with the TFD Human Rights Fellowship.

THIOMBIANO DRAMANE is from Burkina Faso, West Africa. He is an assistant professor at the International Master Program in Asia-Pacific Affairs at National Sun Yat-sen University in Taiwan, where he earned his master's (2010) and PhD (2016). His research and interests deal with China and Africa relations, Taiwan political economy, cross-strait relations, Taiwan-Africa relations, and so on. He is the author/coauthor of publications that include "The impact of China on the agency and bargaining power of African countries on the international system" (*International Journal of Political Science and International Relations* (*AJPSIR*, 2019); "Impacts of Colonial Era Policies and Institutions on the Post-Independence Development of Former Colonies: Case Study of Japanese Colonization of Taiwan and French Colonization of Burkina Faso" (2014); "The Beijing Consensus versus the

Washington Consensus in Africa: Why is the Chinese Model Gaining Ground in Africa?" (*Sun Yat-sen Journal of Humanities*, 2016).

GUANIE LIM is assistant professor at the National Graduate Institute for Policy Studies (GRIPS), Japan. His main research interests are comparative political economy, value chain analysis, and the Belt and Road Initiative in Southeast Asia. Lim is also interested in broader development issues within Asia, especially those of China, Vietnam, and Malaysia. In the coming years, he will be conducting comparative research on how and why China's capital exports are reshaping development in two key developing regions— Southeast Asia and the Middle East and North Africa.

DING FEI is a postdoctoral research associate at the School of Geographical Sciences and Urban Planning, Arizona State University. Her research focuses on the relationship among state, capital, and human agency in the uneven process of China's globalization, and its implications for industrial transformation and local capacity building in Africa.

ANDREA AZIZI KIFYASI earned his PhD from the Department of History of the University of Basel, Switzerland. His ongoing project surveys the history of several medical projects funded by the Chinese government in Tanzania from the 1960s to the present. He has presented research papers at several international conferences. Among them includes: "From the Periphery to the Periphery: China's Influence on Tanzania's Health Policies, 1960s–1990," July 2019 in Beijing; "Cold War Politics and Medical Aid to Africa: A Case of Communist China's Medical Aid to Post-colonial Tanzania," June 2018 in Brussels; "An Assessment of Achievements and Challenges of China-Africa Medical Cooperation: A Case Study of Tanzania, 1960s–2010," August 2016 in Beijing; copublished an article with Maxmillian J. Chuhila titled "A Development Narrative of a Rural Economy: The Politics of Forest Plantations and Land Use in Mufindi and Kilimanjaro, Tanzania; 1920s to 2000s." *International Journal of Social Science and Humanities Research* Vol. 4, Issue 3, (July–September 2016) pp. 528–538.

JEREMIAH CHIGOZIE ANAKOR is a graduate of History and International Studies at Lagos State University. His latest article (with Odunayo Posun and Cecilia Anakor) is entitled "Perception of Secondary School Students on Quota System in Accessing Federal Government Tertiary Institutions in Nigeria," published in the *LASU Social Sciences Journal*, 14(1) in 2020. Jeremiah is an independent researcher finalizing plans for his postgraduate studies in African and Diaspora Studies. He was involved in the Centre for Democracy and Development's 2020 project on "Electoral

Corruption in Nigeria's 2019 Election" (with Professor Adele Jinadu, Dr. Adewale Aderemi, and Professor Shola Omotola among others).

OLUWASOLA OBISESAN completed his BA and MA in international relations at the Obafemi Awolowo University in Ile-Ife. He was a 2019 laureate of the prestigious *Democratic Governance Institute* hosted by the Council for the Development of Social Science Research in Africa in Dakar where he presented a paper entitled "The #Hash Tag Generation: Social Media and Youth Participation in the 2019 General Election in Nigeria." He worked with Dr. Akin Iwilade and Professor Charles Ukeje to produce the 2018/2019 Tana Forum Peace and Security Report. A former speaker of the International Relations Students' Association at OAU, Obisesan completed his MSc at OAU with distinction. He is currently finalizing a PhD proposal that aims to shed light on Chinese energy and securitization policy in Africa.

BHASO NDZENDZE, PhD (University of the Witwatersrand), is head of department and senior lecturer, Department of Politics and International Relations at the University of Johannesburg. He is the former research director at the Centre for Africa-China Studies at the University of Johannesburg. He has conducted field research on Africa-China relations in several East and Southern African countries. His publications have appeared on numerous platforms including in his books as well as international journals such as the *European Foreign Affairs Review*, *International Affairs*, and the *Tamkang Journal of International Affairs* among others.

NOMZAMO GONDWE holds a bachelor's and honors degree in international relations and politics from the University of Johannesburg. She has three years of experience in higher education teaching. A member of the Southern African Association of Political Studies, Ms. Gondwe has recently completed her master's at the University of Johannesburg and runs an independent initiative with NISAA Institute for Women's Development in the South of Johannesburg.